Data Governance in AI, FinTech and LegalTech

Data Governance in AI, FinTech and LegalTech

Law and Regulation in the Financial Sector

Edited by

Joseph Lee

Reader in Corporate and Financial Law, University of Manchester, UK

Aline Darbellay

Assistant Professor, Faculty of Law, University of Geneva, Switzerland

EE Edward Elgar PUBLISHING

Cheltenham, UK • Northampton, MA, USA

Published by
Edward Elgar Publishing Limited
The Lypiatts
15 Lansdown Road
Cheltenham
Glos GL50 2JA
UK

Edward Elgar Publishing, Inc.
William Pratt House
9 Dewey Court
Northampton
Massachusetts 01060
USA

A catalogue record for this book
is available from the British Library

Library of Congress Control Number: 2022932887

This book is available electronically in the **Elgar**online
Law subject collection
http://dx.doi.org/10.4337/9781800379954

Printed on elemental chlorine free (ECF)
recycled paper containing 30% Post-Consumer Waste

ISBN 978 1 80037 994 7 (cased)
ISBN 978 1 80037 995 4 (eBook)

Printed and bound in the USA

Contents

Figures

Contributors

Christopher Chao-hung Chen received his PhD from University of London (UCL). He was a law faculty in Singapore Management University for over ten years. His research interests focus on corporate law, financial law and regulations, insurance law and legal empirical studies. He has had publications in the US, UK, Europe, Singapore and Taiwan. Christopher Chen is currently an Adjunct Associate Professor of Law at National Chengchi University.

Aline Darbellay is an Assistant Professor of Law at the Center for Banking and Finance Law at the University of Geneva. In 2010, she was a research associate at the University of San Diego School of Law. In 2014–15, she was a research fellow at the Chair in Law and Finance at the University of Zurich. She has taught corporate law as a visiting lecturer at the University of Zurich. She is admitted to practise law in New York. She is the author of a monograph, *Regulating Credit Rating Agencies*, published in 2013. She has written publications on matters of international financial regulation, sovereign debt, digital capital markets and sustainable finance. She is Director of the Certificate in Advanced Studies (CAS) in Digital Finance Law at the University of Geneva.

David C. Donald is Emeritus Professor in the Law Faculty of The Chinese University of Hong Kong. David's publications focus on corporate law and securities market infrastructure, with an emphasis on comparative law issues, economic development, and the application of new technology to finance and law. In addition to Hong Kong, David has taught law in Beijing, Frankfurt, Taipei and Vienna, and practiced commercial law with leading international firms in the US, Italy and Germany.

Manuela Geranio is Associate Professor of Finance at the University of Bergamo (Italy) and Adjunct Professor at Bocconi University (Milan). Her recent research focuses on the evolution of the exchange industry and related strategies, both at the domestic and international level. She is a member of the Group of Economic Advisers at ESMA and cooperated with industry players and regulators for the development of the Italian Stock Exchange.

Antonios Karaiskos (LLM, Athens University (Greece); LLD, Waseda University (Japan)) is an Associate Professor in the Faculty of Law/Graduate School of Law, Kyoto University (Japan). His areas of expertise are Japanese and European civil and consumer law. Antonios Karaiskos has taught in various universities in Japan and abroad. He was a lawyer in Greece and is currently a member of the board of directors of the Japan Association of Consumer Law and the Kansai Consumers Support Organization (a Specified Qualified Consumer Organization certified by the Prime Minister of Japan). He is also a member of scientific and editorial boards and committees as well as law associations in Japan and overseas.

Joseph Lee is a reader in corporate and financial law in the school of law at the University of Manchester UK. He was a senior lecturer in corporate and commercial law at the University of Exeter UK and Assistant Professor of Law at the University of Nottingham UK, which he joined immediately after the completion of his PhD at the University of London. Joseph Lee has also been visiting Professor at the University of Liège, Belgium, the National Taiwan University, and the Judicial Training Institute of Thailand. He is a member of the LawTech Advisory Council of the Astana International Financial Centre (AIFC) and an attorney-at-law of New York State.

Jan Lieder LLM. (Harvard), born in 1979, is Director Department Business Law of the Institute for Business, Labor and Social Law at Albert Ludwigs University of Freiburg, Germany, Full Professor for Civil Law, Commercial Law and Business Law, as well as Judge at the Court of Appeals for the federal state of Schleswig-Holstein, Schleswig, Germany. He has studied law at Friedrich-Schiller-University of Jena School of Law, Germany (First State Examination 2003, Second State Examination 2008) and at Harvard Law School, Cambridge, USA (Master of Laws 2009). He received his degree as Doctor of Laws in 2006 and his Habilitation in 2013. From 2014 to 2016, he served as the Managing Director of the Institute for Business and Tax Law at Christian Albrechts University of Kiel, Germany. From 2018 to 2020, he has been Dean for Student Affairs, Faculty of Law, Albert Ludwigs University of Freiburg.

Marc Van de Looverbosch is preparing a doctoral thesis on good faith acquisition of financial assets at KU Leuven. He started his legal career as an associate at Baker McKenzie and is currently a Lead Lawyer at DLA Piper. He received a Master of Laws degree from the University of Antwerp, a Bachelor of Laws degree from KU Leuven and a Master of Music degree from LUCA School of Arts. He lives in Leuven, Belgium with his wife and children.

Georgios Pavlidis is Associate Professor of International and EU Law at the School of Law of Neapolis University Pafos (NUP) in Cyprus and holder of a Jean Monnet Chair (2020–2023). He is attorney-at-law in Greece, with post-graduate studies in the US and the UK (LLM. in International and Comparative Law, SMU Dallas, LLM in International Economic Law, University of

Warwick) and he has obtained his PhD in Law from the University of Geneva. Before joining NUP, he has worked as academic assistant at the University of Geneva, the University of Piraeus and the International Hellenic University. His research interests include the regulation of financial markets, digital finance, virtual assets and the fight against money laundering.

Radim Polčák is the vice-rector of Masaryk University (MU) and the head of the Institute of Law and Technology at the Law Faculty at MU (Czech Republic). He is the general chair of the Cyberspace conference and the founder of the *Masaryk University Journal of Law and Technology* and the *Review of Law and Technology* (Revue pro právo a technologie). He is a founding fellow of the European Law Institute and the European Academy of Law and ICT, a panellist at the .eu ADR arbitration court and a member of various governmental and scientific expert and advisory bodies and project consortia around the EU. He also served as a Special Adviser for Robotics and Data Protection Policy to the European Commission. Radim authored or co-authored over 150 scientific papers, books and articles, namely on topics related to cyberlaw and legal philosophy.

Philipp Pordzik, born in 1992, studied law at the Albert-Ludwigs-University of Freiburg. In 2017 he passed the first state examination in law. He subsequently became a research assistant at the Institute for Commercial and Business Law at the Albert-Ludwigs-University of Freiburg, where he also worked on his dissertation. He was appointed as a lecturer in 2020 and was awarded the Faculty teaching prize in the same year. After completing his dissertation and receiving his degree as Doctor of Laws in 2021, he is now a law clerk at the Higher Regional Court of Frankfurt am Main and continues his teaching assignment at the Albert-Ludwigs-University of Freiburg.

Julia Schmidt is a Lecturer in Law at the University of Exeter. Julia holds an LLM in European Legal Studies from the University of Glasgow and a PhD from the University of Edinburgh. She is a qualified but non-practising lawyer in Germany. Julia is the author of *The European Union and the Use of Force* (Brill, Nijhoff, 2020). Her research focuses on Public International Law and European Union Law, with a particular emphasis on EU External Relations Law and Policy.

Yueh-Ping (Alex) Yang is an Associate Professor at National Taiwan University Law School. He received his LLB and LLM at National Taiwan University in 2005 and 2010 respectively, and he also practiced law at Jones Day International Law Firm during that period. In 2011, sponsored by Taiwan's Ministry of Education, he commenced his LLM and SJD studies at Harvard University Law School and received the SJD degree in 2017. Currently, his research interest focuses mainly on financial regulation and corporate governance, including FinTech, financial institution governance, financial consumer protection, capital markets, international finance, etc.

Preface

Data governance has been one of the most discussed issues in the digital economy. As digital finance is beginning to play a big role in the digital economy and global trade, data governance in the finance services sector will become a critical infrastructure in supporting the development of the global digital economy. This book is the result of a research project titled 'Digital Financial Services: Law, Regulation, and Governance' convened by Dr Joseph Lee of the University of Manchester (and when he was at the University of Exeter), Professor Aline Darbellay of the University of Geneva, and Professor Joeri Vananroye of KU Leuven. This book is valuable for a wide audience. It offers insights relevant to both research and practice. National particularities are depicted through examples chosen from selected key jurisdictions, including the European Union, Japan, Singapore, the United Kingdom and the United States.

The project benefited from the support of the GenEx Joint Seed Funding stemming from a strategic partnership between the University of Exeter and the University of Geneva. The project is also supported by the European Network Fund, a University of Exeter Global Partnerships Award, to collaborate with KU Leuven. All chapters were peer-reviewed. We would like to thank the following persons for providing institutional and personal support to this research project: Professor Luc Thévenoz, Director of the Centre of Banking and Financial Law, University of Geneva; Professor Christian Bovet, University of Geneva; Professor Richard Moorhead, University of Exeter; Professor Philippe Cullet, Director of the Law, Environment and Development Centre at the University of London, School of Oriental & African Studies; Dr Jochen Dürr and Ms Nadine Ehrler of SIX Switzerland; Ms Tina Maria Hilgarth, CEO of New Way Consulting Zurich; Dr Migual Vaz of Börse Stuttgart; Professor Thomas Lambert of the Erasmus University Rotterdam; Mr Arnaud Van Caenegem of KU Leuven; Dr Stefano Alderighi of the UK Endorsement Board; Mr Marcus Tsai of the Taiwan Financial Supervisory Commission; Mr Philip Tremble, Dr Giles Spungin, Mr Ted Sheils of HSBC; and Mr Nick Chavasse, Assistant Head of Global Partnerships (Europe) at the University of Exeter. Last but not least, we are grateful to Dr Yonghui Bao, Mr

Yannick Caballero Cuevas, and Ms Nastassia Merlino for their diligence and excellent research assistance.

21 September 2021
Dr Joseph Lee, London
Professor Aline Darbellay, Geneva

Abbreviations

ABA	American Bar Association
ADR	Alternative Dispute Resolution
AI	Artificial Intelligence
AIDA	Artificial Intelligence and Data Analytics
AktG	Aktiengesetz - German Stock Corporation Act
AML	Anti-Money Laundering
APEC	Asia-Pacific Economic Cooperation
APIs	Application Programming Interfaces
APPI	The Japanese Act on the Protection of Personal Information
B2B	Business-to-Business
B2C	Business-to-Consumer
B-A-T	Baidu, Alibaba and Tencent
BATS	Better Alternative Trading System
BBO	The Best Bid and Offer prices
BBVA Group	Banco Bilbao Vizcaya Argentaria Group
BBX	BondbloX Bond Exchange
BCRs	Binding Corporate Rules
BIA Trinity	Blockchain, Internet of Things and Artificial Intelligence
CAB	Conformity Assessment Bodies
CBDC	Central Bank Digital Currency
CDA	Communications Decency Act of 1996
CDBF	Centre for banking and finance law of the University of Geneva
CE	'Conformité Européenne' or European Conformity
CJEU	Court of Justice of the European Union
CRAs	Credit Rating Agencies
CSD	Central Securities Depository

CSIRT	Computer Security Incident Response Team
CUHK	Chinese University of Hong Kong
DAO	Decentralised Autonomous Organisation
DBMSs	Database Management Systems
DCEP	Chinese Digital Currency Electronic Payment
DLT	Distributed Ledger Technology
DRS	Direct Registration System
ECA	Early Case Assessment
ECCG	European Cybersecurity Certification Group
ECJ	European Court of Justice (now known as the Court of Justice of the European Union (CJEU))
EFAMA	European Funds and Asset Management Association
EIB	European Investment Bank
EMEA	Europe, Middle East, and Africa
ENISA	European Network and Information Security Agency
EPA	The EU-Japan Economic Partnership Agreement
ESG	Environmental, Social and Governance
ESMA	European Securities and Markets Authority
ETL	Extraction, Transformation and Load
EU	European Union
EU MiCA	European Commission's Regulation of Markets in Crypto-Assets
F-A-A-N-G	Facebook, Apple, Amazon, Netflix and Google
FEAT Principles	Fairness, Ethics, Accountability and Transparency Principles
FINMAC	Financial Instruments Mediation Assistance Center
FinTech	Financial Technology
FMA	Financial Market Authority
FSA	Financial Services Agency
FTSE	Financial Times Stock Exchange
GDPR	General Data Protection Regulation
GFRI	Geneva Finance Research Institute
GIIN	Global Impact Investing Network
GIS	Geographic Information Systems

HR	Human Resources
ICMA	International Capital Market Association
ICSA	International Council of Securities Associations
InsurTech	Insurance Technology
IoT	Internet of Things
IPO	Initial Public Offering
ISO	International Organization for Standardization
IT	Information Technology
JSDA	The Japan Securities Dealers' Association
KII	Key Information Infrastructure Operators
KPI	Key Performance Indicators
KWG	Gesetz über das Kreditwesen - German Banking Act
KYC	Know-Your-Customer
LegalTech	Legal Technologies
LSE Group	London Stock Exchange Group
MAS	Monetary Authority of Singapore
MiFID	Markets in Financial Instruments Directive
MiFID II	Markets in Financial Instruments Directive II
MiFIR	Markets in Financial Instruments Regulation
ML	Machine Learning
NASDAQ	National Association of Securities Dealers Automated Quotations
NCAC	National Consumer Affairs Center
NEM Token	New Economic Movement Token
NIS Directive	Directive (EU) 2016/1148 of the European Parliament and of the Council of 6 July 2016 Concerning Measures for a High Common Level of Security of Network and Information Systems across the Union [2016] OJ L194/1
NMS	The National Market System
NOBOS	Non-Objecting Beneficial Owners
NYSE	New York Stock Exchange
ODR	Online Dispute Resolution
OECD	Organisation for Economic Co-operation and Development

PDPA	Singapore's Personal Data Protection Act 2012
PDPC	Singapore's Personal Data Protection Commission
PFOF	Payment For Order Flow
PSD2	Payment Services Directive 2
PSR	UK Payment Systems Regulator
R&D	Research & Development
RPA	Robotic Processing Automation
SCCG	Stakeholder Cybersecurity Certification Group
SDG	Sustainable Development Goals
SEC	U.S. Securities and Exchanges Commission
SIFMA	Securities Industry and Financial Markets Association
SME	Small- and Medium-sized enterprises
SPA	Strategic Partnership Agreement
SRLC	The Swedish Revenue Law Commission
SRO	Self-Regulatory Organisation
SSA	Sovereigns, Supranationals and Agencies
STO	Securities Token Offering
TAD	Transfer Agent Depository
TEU	Treaty on European Union
TFEU	Treaty on the Functioning of the European Union
TPP	Trans-Pacific Partnership
TPSP	Third-Party Service Provider
TRM	Technology Risk Management
TRM Guidelines	MAS's Technology Risk Management Guidelines
TVRA	Threat and Vulnerability Risk Assessment
UK	United Kingdom
UN	United Nations
UNDP	United Nations Development Programme
USA or US	United States of America
USD	US Dollar
VAT	Value-Added Tax

1. Introduction: Data and its governance in the financial services sector

Joseph Lee

I. DATA IN FINANCIAL SERVICES

Data fuel the development of artificial intelligence and are one of the most contested resources in the digital economy. But data have always been a fundamental source in the development of business in the financial services sector, whether in securities trading or consumer insurance. Over many years, the financial services industry has invested in data acquisition, storage, transfer and monetisation. The industry's data strategy was developed as a core part of business development and internal governance long before the modern information systems of blockchain and data analytics were introduced. Data have also long been an asset that the financial sector has paid to possess and monetise, and the huge mass of data that has been built up over the years is something that competitors within or outside the sector are keen to have access to, as we have seen in Open Banking. Financial firms are well aware of data as a competitive asset class and have created strategic defences to protect their interests.

As well as the competition between the financial industry and the technology sector, a new issue concerning individual rights to data and data protection has created a battleground where individuals are keen to exercise power over their own data and to protect it from others who would like to use it for their own gain or to provide services to data subjects. How this battle over data rights and data protection law will be resolved depends on the value attached to individual autonomy, business models, industry policy, international trade dynamics and politics. These factors will set the standards for data governance in the future.

II. AIMS AND CONTRIBUTIONS OF THE BOOK

This book seeks to understand and identify what the rationale for data governance is, what legal bases and tools for its governance are available, and what models of governance are envisaged for the sector. To examine these issues, various financial services are investigated, including the cryptocurrency market (Lee), crypto-asset providers (Lee and Van de Looverbosch), legal services for mergers and acquisitions (Donald), consumer insurance (Chen), consumer finance (Karaiskos), digital platform services (Darbellay), securities exchanges (Geranio), and the green bond market (Pavlidis). In the future, data governance is likely to be multi-layered, based on corporate law (Lieder and Pordzik), private law (Karaiskos), insurance market regulation (Chen), cybersecurity law (Polčák), and international trade norms (Schmidt).

The book also offers three contributions to the field of data governance in the digital economy. We use the financial services sector, one of the most advanced sectors, first, to show the relationship between data and law by identifying different kinds of data ownership and the policy and legal tools used for owners' or users' protection, and secondly, to identify the tools available for constructing a multi-layered public-private partnership for data governance. In addition, the book provides assistance for academics, practitioners and policy makers as they construct matrix systems for data governance in the financial services sectors with a view to creating a more standardised data governance and promoting a digital economy.

In bringing together the contents of this book, a number of principal questions have been borne in mind. What is the relationship between an individual's data and data protection? What policy concerns are there for enterprise data? Why are states keen to claim ownership and assert control over data and impose restrictions on data use?

III. INDIVIDUAL DATA, PROTECTION OF AUTONOMY, AND PRIVATE LAW MODEL

Individual data have long been collected by financial institutions either to provide services to their customers or to improve their competitiveness without necessarily benefiting clients. Often such collection has been done for regulatory purposes and data are forwarded to the state. Individuals are protected through confidentiality law, privacy law, and human rights law but more recently, they are also protected by data protection laws. But whether data are personal property is not clear cut and the proprietary nature of data remains a legal debate. The Open Banking initiative in the UK has to some extent shown the proprietary nature of data thus enabling individuals not only to restrict the use of their personal data by financial institutions, but also to allow them to 'bring' them to another financial institution, under so-called data portability. *Lee* discusses how individual autonomy may be at risk when using cryptocurrency as a means of payment in three different types of systems: unstable, stable and state-backed cryptocurrency systems. *Chen* shows how individual data, personal background and behaviour is vital for the insurance industry to calculate risk premiums and the impact on the financial consumer. *Darbellay* identifies conflicts of interest when digital platform providers act as information gatekeeper, a potential fiduciary, whilst providing services to users (principal). *Donald* investigates how law firms together with third-party technology firms use data belonging to clients to develop lawtech, to improve their services without the knowledge of their clients, and without payment to them. *Lee* and *Van de Looverbosch* discuss the uncertain relationship between property and data, and identify the confusion this creates in the crypto-market. *Karaiskos* and *Chen* examine the use of private law, specifically consumer protection law, to ensure the autonomy of individual users. *Yang* questions the effectiveness of consent-based protection, currently used in both data and consumer protection law, and argues for the need to see the bigger picture of what big data can deliver to individuals. *Schmidt* discusses the use of public law-based norms in trade negotiation to protect individual autonomy in the digital economy.

IV. ENTERPRISE DATA, INDUSTRIAL POLICY, AND REGULATORY FRAMEWORK

Enterprise data is data controlled by an enterprise and on which it has a strong proprietary claim. For example, exchanges collect data using sophisticated super-power equipment which then, by combination and analysis, enhances their value. This value-added proprietary data is used to provide a service to clients, in particular institutional users such as traders, to whom the data can be provided under a licencing agreement. Data service companies of this kind, such as Refinitiv and Bloomberg, claim ownership in the data, often to the extent that they create an effect of market foreclosure and are able to charge whatever price they wish as there are no other providers. Individual sets of data may well be of limited value until they are combined into larger sets of data. For example, climate data may need to be combined with finance data in order to make them of practical use in green financing. *Geranio* discusses how data becomes an important source for the securities trading market and how the way prices are set can affect innovation and competitiveness in the exchanges industry. *Lee* shows how enterprise data in the cryptocurrency market can have a foreclosure effect on the development of other tools for data analysis. *Pavlidis* demonstrates the relationship between data and green finance. *Chen* argues that flexible approaches to data governance can enhance financial innovation in the insurance sector. *Donald* indicates how law firms treat their clients' data as their own and suggests that professional rules should be created to regulate such lawtech development. Sectoral development and industry policy will determine the outlook for data governance.

V. STATE DATA, TRADE POLICY, AND TREATY NORMS

States control large data pools, either through direct collection as they provide public or private services such as health and telecommunications, through law enforcement proceedings to protect public safety, or through regulatory reporting from the private sector. These data sets can be utilised by the state to provide further services, or it can share data with private sector service providers, either free or for a fee, when conditions may be imposed. A state may claim ownership of data its subjects (or residents) are required to provide when they are situated in the country (data localisation) or it may impose rules on the use of the data by third parties. *Lee* discusses how data collected in the crypto-market may be treated as state data for development purposes. The state claims ownership of the data under the principle of public ownership and imposes restrictions on the benefits of domestic economic development. *Pavlidis* discusses how data can be utilised to develop a green bond market for combating climate change. Climate data may be considered to be a matter of national security and states may impose rules on the collection, control and processing of the datasets.

Data are an increasingly important issue in international trade negotiations. *Schmidt* discusses this and emphasises how values should be adhered to in digital trade. The protection of personal data is related to privacy, which is deeply rooted in human rights law. Some jurisdictions have used the value of personal data in trade negotiations, seeing poverty alleviation as a more urgent consideration than the protection of human rights. Others, such as China and Vietnam, consider certain data to be critical for national security and insist on data localisation. In the Trans-Pacific Partnership Agreement negotiation, the US insisted that financial data were a matter of national security and should not be part of the free trade agreement. Discussion of data trade is starting to take place at international forums such as the WTO, and there is a need to hear the voices of smaller jurisdictions, particularly those of developing economies.

VI. PUBLIC-PRIVATE PARTNERSHIPS

There is no question that the future model for data governance will be public-private partnership, based either on private law such as civil law (Karaiskos), fiduciary law (Darbellay and Donald), company law (Lieder and Pordzik), property law (Lee and Van de Looverbosch) and consumer protection laws (Karaiskos), or else on public law relating to cybersecurity (Polčák), privacy, human rights and data protection (Schmidt), codes of practices, industry guidelines (Chen), and professional rules (Donald). This is because some data belong to the state through the way the state acquired them. States may consider some datasets as of national security importance and therefore require data to be under state control (public ownership) and with heightened state supervision. However, a state may not have the capacity to safeguard all the data and may need to rely on private entities to keep safe the data on its behalf.

Some data belong to private entities. States may impose restrictions on how private entities can transfer data as a matter of industry policy, to improve the competitiveness, innovation or competition of the sector or to protect an under-developed sector. States may also impose rules defining data governance so that for some of the datasets derived from personal data, data dividends can be shared with the individual who provided the data. *Yang* proposes a public-private partnership for data governance on the basis that there is a broken link between consent and data protection. *Lieder* and *Pordzik* also discuss how company directors need to put in place rules for data governance as one of their duties. *Polčák* further proposes a certification regime that is incorporated in the data governance requirement for financial institutions.

The book offers an overview of the available tools for constructing multi-layered data governance. Yet, what any regime of domestic data governance will look like will depend on how the jurisdiction approaches individual data and its protection, how it allows enterprises to claim ownership in data collected and created according to industry policy, and how it negotiates data in trade deals.

2. Data utility and data governance in cryptocurrencies

Joseph Lee

I. INTRODUCTION: ACCESS TO FINANCE AND EQUAL ECONOMIC OPPORTUNITY

The rise of cryptocurrency is a response to dissatisfaction with the current financial markets which are dominated by a few powerful currencies, financial institutions, and advanced economies.[1] There is also a growing frustration that investors are looking for returns on assets that are not correlated to stock markets due to the low interest rates.[2] As a consequence, the creation and distribution of wealth have favoured individuals holding these international currencies and the shareholders of financial institutions. The rise of cryptocurrency carries some clear messages: financial inclusion, wider access to finance, and disruption of the current global financial system.[3] This potentially attracts a lot of attention from both private and public entities as they decide how to respond to the demands of a new global financial system that can close gaps between advanced and underdeveloped economies and societies.[4] How can cryptocurrency empower people who have been deprived of their eco-

---

1 Marek Dabrowski and Lukasz Janikowski, Virtual Currencies and Central Banks Monetary Policy: Challenges Ahead, (Monetary Dialogue, Policy Department for Economic, Scientific and Quality of Life Policies of European Parliament, July 2018).

2 Brian Edmondson, 'Popular Cryptocurrency Hedge Funds' (2021) https://www.thebalance.com/best-cryptocurrency-hedge-funds-4582184 accessed 27 June 2021.

3 Peter Gomber and others, 'On the FinTech Revolution: Interpreting the Forces of Innovation, Disruption and Transformation in Financial Services' (2018) 35(1) Journal of Management Information Systems 220, 265, https://www.tandfonline.com/doi/full/10.1080/07421222.2018.1440766 accessed 24 July 2021.

4 Lieve Fransen, Gino Del Bufalo and Edoardo Reviglio, Boosting Investment in Social Infrastructure in Europe: Report of the High-Level Task Force on Investing in Social Infrastructure in Europe (European Commission and European Association ELTI Long-Term Investors, 2018); UNCTAD, 'Harnessing the Promise of Blockchain to Change Lives' (2021) https://unctad.org/news/harnessing-promise-blockchain-change-lives accessed 27 June 2021.

nomic rights by not being able to participate in a centralised and intermediated global financial system?

Many virtual, mobile, digital currencies can empower users,[5] particularly those who are unable to create wealth due to lack of access to finance for project funding or to receive wealth due to them because of financial instability, corruption or high cost of currency exchange.[6] In today's increasingly IT-based world, by providing access to finance, welfare, public services, and justice through technology such as blockchain, cryptocurrency can provide not only better access to finance but also to other public services such as justice,[7] thus enabling developmental 'leapfrog' for the poorer regions and nations.[8] Private entities,[9] government agencies[10] and other consortia have launched programmes that create cryptocurrencies that are virtual, cross-border, peer-to-peer, global, algorithmic and data-based.

---

5 Dante Disparte, 'Could Digital Currencies Make Being Poor Less Costly' (2020) https://hbr.org/2020/08/could-digital-currencies-make-being-poor-less-costly accessed 27 June 2021.

6 Vrajlal Sapovadia, 'Financial Inclusion, Digital Currency, and Mobile Technology' in David Lee Kuo Chuen and Robert Deng (eds), Handbook of Blockchain, Digital Finance and Inclusion, Volume 2: ChinaTech, Mobile Security, and Distributed Ledger (Academic Press 2018), 361, 385.

7 Robby Houben and Alexander Snyers, Cryptocurrencies and Blockchain: Legal Context and Implications for Financial Crime, Money Laundering and Tax Evasion (Policy Department for Economic, Scientific and Quality of Life Policies of the European Parliament, July 2018); Darshan Bhora and Aisiri Raj, 'Blockchain Arbitration – The Future of Dispute Resolution Mechanisms?' (2020) http://cilj.co.uk/2020/12/16/blockchain-arbitration-the-future-of-dispute-resolution-mechanisms/ accessed 27 June 2021.

8 Douglas Arner, Janos Nathan Barberis and Ross Buckley, 'The Evolution of FinTech: A New Post-Crisis Paradigm?' (2019) University of Hong Kong Faculty of Law Research Paper No.2015/0467, https://core.ac.uk/download/pdf/38088713.pdf accessed 20 July 2021.

9 Tom Wilson and Peter Schroeder, 'Facebook-Backed Crypto Project Diem to Launch US Stablecoin in Major Shift' (Reuters, 12 May 2021) https://www.reuters.com/technology/facebook-backed-crypto-project-diem-launch-us-stablecoin-major-shift-2021-05-12/ accessed 27 June 2021.

10 Grégory Claeys, Maria Demertzis, Konstantinos Efstathiou (Bruegel), Cryptocurrencies and Monetary Policy (Monetary Dialogue, Policy Department for Economic, Scientific and Quality of Life Policies of the European Parliament, July 2018); David Lee and Ernie Teo, 'The New Money: The Utility of Cryptocurrencies and the Need for a New Monetary Policy' (2020), https://papers.ssrn.com/sol3/papers.cfm?abstract_id=3608752 accessed 26 June 2021; Agustín Carstens, 'Digital Currencies and the Future of the Monetary System' (27 January 2021) BIS Working Paper, https://www.bis.org/speeches/sp210127.pdf accessed 20 July 2021.

As in many smart technology-based spaces, data protection and violations of privacy rights are major risks to users,[11] particularly to vulnerable and marginalised people who lack effective access to finance, services, and justice. Cryptocurrency is no exception, despite any reassurance that cryptography and encryption technologies can be embedded in the system to provide adequate safeguards. In this chapter, I intend to show how issues of personal data and privacy are major risks to the users of cryptocurrency, which despite potential benefits, can exacerbate exclusion through discriminatory user profiling, state surveillance,[12] and data rendition practices (so-called surveillance capitalism).[13]

I will use three policy goals – personal autonomy, the development of digital economy, and crime prevention – to measure the effectiveness of data protection law and privacy rights under different types of cryptocurrency: unstable coins on the public chain (Bitcoin);[14] stable coins on the private chain created by private entities such as DIEM;[15] and state-backed cryptocurrency created by a central bank, e.g., the Chinese Digital Currency Electronic Payment (DCEP).[16] I will then discuss the extent to which information generated by cryptocurrency will enhance economic rights, such as access, or whether in addition it is likely to diminish or transform political rights. In particular, how the development of cryptocurrencies will affect and be affected by international relations will be examined.

---

[11] Gilad Rosner and Erin Kenneally, Privacy and the Internet of Things: Emerging Frameworks for Policy and Design (White Paper, Center for Long-Term Cybersecurity, 2018).

[12] Jules Polonetsky and Omer Tene, 'Privacy and Big Data: Making Ends Meet' (2013) 66(25) Stanford Law Review Online https://cyberlaw.stanford.edu/files/publication/files/PolonetskyTene.pdf accessed 18 October 2020.

[13] Shoshana Zuboff, The Age of Surveillance Capitalism: The Future at the New Frontier of Power (Profile Books, Main Edition, January 2019).

[14] Joseph Lee and Florian L'heureux, 'A Regulatory Framework for Cryptocurrency' (2020) 31(3) European Business Law Review 423, 446.

[15] Brühl Volker, 'LIBRA – A Differentiated View on Facebook's Virtual Currency Project' (2019) CFS Working Paper Series No. 633, https://papers.ssrn.com/sol3/papers.cfm?abstract_id=3477599 accessed 20 July 2021.

[16] Jemma Xu and Dan Prud'homme, 'China's Central Bank has Taken the Lead in Digital Currencies. What does it Mean for Businesses?' (LSE Business Review, 3 August 2020) https://blogs.lse.ac.uk/businessreview/2020/08/03/chinas-central-bank-has-taken-the-lead-in-digital-currencies-what-does-it-mean-for-businesses/ accessed 24 July 2021.

II. RISK OF DATA VIOLATION AND PRIVACY RIGHT VIOLATION THROUGH CRYPTOCURRENCY

A. Does Privacy Benefit the Public?

The rise of unstable coins on the public chain is both a political movement and an economic response to dissatisfaction with the current global financial system. It is also a preferred method of transaction by users who need privacy (or secrecy) in their transactions. Anonymity[17] is essential for those who require or prefer their identity to be unknown to the world or even to the counter party in a transaction. Detailed information about the transactions remains confidential to third parties, secret to the world and, more significantly, untraceable by anyone, including the parties themselves. Criminals have been exploring anonymity to engage in illicit and illegal activities,[18] thereby tainting the reputation of cryptocurrency as a legitimate way of disrupting the established economic and political order. Anonymity is now seen as a 'public bad'. These criminal activities are often associated with market manipulation, fraud, money laundering, tax evasion, and the drug trade.

One of the public goods of fiat currency (cash) is to protect the privacy of users through anonymity in transactions. Users do not need to reveal their identity when using fiat currency to make a transaction, unless required by law or mutual agreement. Once the transaction is concluded, it cannot be traced unless the parties keep a record e.g., a contract or a receipt. With the invention of the credit card (third-party payment systems) and digital money (PayPal and the like), both anonymity and privacy have been greatly eroded. An array of information such as name, age, gender, nationality and address can be revealed. In addition, third-party intermediaries – such as the credit card companies and merchant acquirers – can also access information related to transactions,[19] including the price, the subject matter, the location of the transactions, and the financial intermediaries (banks or third-party payment systems) used. Whether or not the transaction information is of public good must be assessed

---

[17] The Financial Action Task Force (FATF), FATF Report to the G20 Finance Ministers and Central Bank Governors on So-Called Stablecoins (2020).

[18] Joseph Lee, 'Law and Regulation for a Crypto-Market: Perpetuation or Innovation?' in Chiu Iris and Deipenbrock Gudula (eds), Routledge Handbook on FinTech and Law – Regulatory, Supervisory, Policy and other Legal Challenges (1st edn, Routledge, 2021).

[19] Susan Herbst-Murphy, Clearing and Settlement of Interbank Card Transactions: A MasterCard Tutorial for Federal Reserve Payments Analysts (Discussion Paper of Payment Cards Center, Federal Reserve Bank, 2013).

against different policy goals: personal autonomy,[20] the development of digital economy, and crime prevention.[21] These policy goals will affect users' understanding of what public goods are. These policy goals will also determine how to establish trust in the cryptocurrency system.

Over the course of history, fiat currency has replaced the barter system[22] in trade and replaced the use of treasury stone such as gold and silver as means of payment.[23] In the same way, central banks have replaced private institutions or associations as trusted third parties in issuing currency and have performed the economic and political functions of monetary control that had not previously been taken on.[24] Unstable coins on the public chain, such as Bitcoin, now resemble another form of financial system and governance that facilitates the exchange of goods and services. They allow users to transact goods and services in the virtual world more cheaply, while protecting the privacy of the users who exercise their autonomy in the virtual economic and social spaces. The unanswered question is what form of democratised governance[25] should be adopted in this new virtual space and how users should be able to exercise

---

20 Arjen Mulder, 'Government Dilemmas in the Private Provision of Public Goods' (2004) Erasmus Research Institute of Management Research Paper, https://repub.eur.nl/pub/1790/EPS2004045ORG_9058920712_MULDER.pdf accessed 20 July 2021.

21 United Nations Secretary-General's High-Level Panel on Digital Cooperation , The Age of Digital Interdependence, (Report, 2019).

22 In his book, Debt, David Graber gives a powerful argument that credits on informal accounts were the main form of transacting, and barter never really was used as the goods were available at different times and in different quantities to be bartered. But to this day, no one has been able to locate a part of the world where the ordinary mode of economic transaction between neighbors takes the form of 'I'll give you twenty chickens for that cow.' The definitive anthropological work on barter, by Caroline Humphrey, of Cambridge, could not be more definitive in its conclusions: 'No example of a barter economy, pure and simple, has ever been described, let alone the emergence from it of money; all available ethnography suggests that there never has been such a thing.'

See David Graeber, Debt, Updated and Expanded: The First 5,000 Years (Melville House, 2011) 29.

23 Ross Starr, 'Money: In Transactions and Finance' (2003) University of California Working Paper, https://econweb.ucsd.edu/~rstarr/Money%20in%20Transactions%20and%20Finance.pdf accessed 18 October 2020.

24 Stefano Ugolini, 'The Historical Evolution of Central Banking' in Stefano Battilossi, Youssef Cassis and Kazuhiko Yago (eds), Handbook of the History of Money and Currency (Springer Nature, 2018).

25 Yan Chen, 'Blockchain Tokens and the Potential Democratisation of Entrepreneurship and Innovation' (2018) 61(4) Business Horizons 567, 575 https://www.sciencedirect.com/science/article/pii/S0007681318300375 accessed 24 July 2021.

their political rights in terms of monetary control for market stability, currency manipulation for market integrity, and fiscal transparency.[26]

B. Information as a Public Good?

Information is the foundation of the modern financial system,[27] and the modern financial infrastructure needs to perform a monetary function, to supervise the market, and to allow innovation of products and services. Information infrastructure controls the way information can be gathered, stored, processed, utilised, and shared.[28] The information infrastructure of unstable coins on the public chain, such as Bitcoin using an open-source technology, is a consensus system, in which a consortium or a group of people or entities can take collective decisions to deliver transparency and immutability of any transactions that are recorded.[29] However, many aspects of this consensus-based information infrastructure remain opaque.[30] It is difficult to know if the information collected through this consensus-based infrastructure is beneficial or detrimental to the public. It is difficult to assess how privacy is guaranteed, how information will be used to increase the system's digital capability, or how the risk of crime will be mitigated.[31] On the one hand, unstable coin on the public blockchain promises total anonymity and privacy protection; but on the other, it also promotes transparency and immutability as a unique selling point.[32] This

---

[26] Huw Van Steenis, 'Future of Finance - Review on the Outlook for the UK Financial System: What It Means for The Bank of England' (June 2019) https://www.bankofengland.co.uk/-/media/boe/files/report/2019/future-of-finance-report accessed 20 October 2020.

[27] Mario Strassberger, 'Thoughts on Foundations of the Modern Theory of Finance' (2015) https://papers.ssrn.com/sol3/papers.cfm?abstract_id=2648520 accessed 18 October 2020.

[28] World Economic Forum, 'The Future of Financial Infrastructure: An Ambitious Look at how Blockchain can Reshape Financial Services' (An Industry Project of the Financial Services Community, 2016).

[29] Ibid.

[30] Marcella Atzori, 'Blockchain Technology and Decentralised Governance: Is the State Still Necessary?' (2017) 6(1) Journal of Governance and Regulation 45, 62 https://virtusinterpress.org/IMG/pdf/10.22495_jgr_v6_i1_p5.pdf accessed 24 July 2021.

[31] Jeroen Van Den Hoven and others, 'Privacy and Information Technology', Stanford Encyclopedia of Philosophy (Summer 2020) https://plato.stanford.edu/entries/it-privacy/ accessed 18 October 2020.

[32] Andrej Zwitter and Mathilde Boisse-Despiaux, 'Blockchain for Humanitarian Action and Development Aid' (2018) 3(16) Journal of International Humanitarian Action 1, 7 https://jhumanitarianaction.springeropen.com/articles/10.1186/s41018-018-0044-5 accessed 20 July 2021.

contradiction has caused not only developers, but also regulators to take a 'wait and see' approach. Developers want to see what information can be legally collected and processed on the chain in order to develop the technology, and regulators want to see what the industry develops and to construct laws to mitigate any risks. However, the 'regulatory sandbox' provided by regulators[33] as a safe space to test the functionality of cryptocurrency does not contribute to the discussion of how privacy and data can be for or against the public good. The answer lies in the policy goals of cryptocurrency. If cryptocurrency is going to be developed as a digital payment system which is able to collect transaction information, the existing legal and regulatory treatment for information management by digital payment operators can easily be applied to it.[34] Digital payment operators such as debit and credit card operators or third-party payment operators are already able to obtain personal information and are required to protect data subjects under the data protection law and privacy law. These operators are able to monetise information, through creating ownership in the information, and are able to share information with third parties under legal obligations such as law enforcement agencies.[35] Large amounts of personal information are in the hands of the operators of the digital payment services. As more digital transactions are carried out, more information can be generated through the systems. However, each operator has its own system to manage the information and, by default, cannot share information without the data subject's consent. 'Big Data' can be created through the information collected and processed without the possibility of revealing personal data.[36] The operator may not even share such a valuable 'Big Data' asset (a private good) with others, including government agencies, unless required by the law for regulatory reporting or law enforcement purposes (public good). But crypto-

---

[33] Jayoung James Goo and Joo-Yeun Heo, 'The Impact of the Regulatory Sandbox on the FinTech Industry, with a Discussion on the Relation between Regulatory Sandboxes and Open Innovation' (2020) 6(43) Journal of Open Innovation: Technology, Market, and Complexity 1, 18 https://www.mdpi.com/2199-8531/6/2/43 accessed 20 July 2021.

[34] The International Telecommunication Union (ITU), Rory Macmillan, 'Digital Financial Services: Regulating for Financial Inclusion – An ICT Perspective', (2016) https://www.itu.int/dms_pub/itu-d/opb/pref/D-PREF-BB.REG_OUT02-2016-PDF-E.pdf accessed 18 October 2020.

[35] Heiko Richter and Peter Slowinski, 'The Data Sharing Economy: On the Emergence of New Intermediaries' (2019) 50 International Review of Intellectual Property and Competition Law 4, 29 https://link.springer.com/article/10.1007/s40319-018-00777-7 accessed 20 July 2021.

[36] Priyank Jain, Manasi Gyanchandani and Nilay Khare, 'Big Data Privacy: A Technological Perspective and Review' (2016) 3(25) Journal of Big Data 1, 25 https://journalofbigdata.springeropen.com/articles/10.1186/s40537-016-0059-y accessed 20 July 2021.

currency is more than just a digital payment system like a credit card company, third-party payment system (PayPal), or a merchant acquirer.

C. Unstable Coins' Public Chain Operations – Opaque Information Infrastructure and Space for Criminality

Advocates of unstable coins on the public chain such as Bitcoin claim that users or participants are able to view all the transactions on the blockchain network (information as public good), however, personal identity (private good) is encrypted to safeguard personal autonomy. In this way, access to information can be achieved whilst protecting individual data and privacy. Whether it is technologically or legally possible is yet to be seen. There is a risk that the encryption technology is not secure. With time, computing power will be able to decrypt the information.[37] Hence, personal data and privacy are only temporarily safe, and cannot be protected in the long term.

On the other hand, even if the encryption is secure, the government would lose its ability to supervise the system, to prevent criminality, to act as a trusted party to adjudicate disputes and enforce promises. Nor would it be able to understand the social and economic exchanges in order to devise the monetary and fiscal policies that are important for providing access to finance, public services, and justice. Cryptocurrency developers and regulators need to resolve this informational dilemma. They need to have clear policy goals for cryptocurrency development and policy goals are needed to guide how information will be managed: who has access to what information between operators, developers, and regulators; what information is of private good and of public good; what measures should be in place to mitigate the risks. Whilst international standards are being formed for cryptocurrency,[38] what the technology is capable of doing is linked to what it is legally able to do. Policy goals must be the basis for such international standards but there can be conflicting and competing goals amongst the various international actors.

---

[37] Christopher Mims, 'The Day When Computers Can Break All Encryption Is Coming' (2019) The Wall Street Journal https://www.wsj.com/articles/the-race-to-save-encryption-11559646737 accessed 18 October 2020.

[38] Sandra Maguire, 'International Crypto Standards: Who will Define Them?' (2019) Irish Tech News https://irishtechnews.ie/international-crypto-standards-who-defines-them/ accessed 18 October 2020.

D. Information as a Market Power for Stable Coin Operators and Surveillance Capitalism

The risks associated with unstable coins, such as value fluctuation and complete anonymity, are said able to be mitigated by stable coins issued by a private consortium such as DIEM, a known network operator registered in Switzerland.[39] DIEM differs from Bitcoin's opaque system in that the identity of the operators and the design of the information infrastructure are known.[40] Private consortium issuers of stable coins aim to act as a trusted third party, an intermediary, that issues stable coins based on known methodology, as opposed to the opaque 'mining' process[41] used by unstable coins on the public chain such as Bitcoin. A private issuer acts not only as a digital payment operator, like credit card issuers or PayPal, and as a bank custodian, but also as a central bank that can issue money as a means of payment and investment. On the network, the operator will be able to collect, store, process, use and monetise information, including personal and transaction information so it will be able to obtain a broad view of transaction information recorded across the private blockchain network.[42] In addition, it will be able to gain access to personal information if it is on a private blockchain network. In the current digital payment systems, such as credit cards or PayPal, operators usually know only part of the transaction data but not the whole chain of information related to transactions. For instance, credit card companies only know about transactions made through their system, but not the amount of money that users have in their bank accounts. Banks know the amount of money in clients' accounts but may not know the details of each transaction made, such as the object of the transaction or even the counter party. In a private chain network of stable coins, detailed information such as the specific goods and services purchased, the price paid or 'coins' exchanged, the details of the counter party and their respective locations, can all be collected and stored on the network.

---

[39] Salomon Fiedler and others, Public or Private? The Future of Money, (Monetary Dialogue, Policy Department for Economic, Scientific and Quality of Life Policies of the European Parliament, December 2019).

[40] Peter Van Valkenburgh, 'The Differences between Bitcoin and Libra Should Matter to Policymakers' (Coin Center, 8 July 2019) https://www.coincenter.org/the-differences-between-bitcoin-and-libra-should-matter-to-policymakers/ accessed 18 October 2020.

[41] G7 Working Group on Stablecoins, Investigating the Impact of Global Stablecoins, (October 2019).

[42] United Nations Economic Commission for Europe (UNECE), United Nations Centre for Trade Facilitation and Electronic Business (UN/CEFACT), Blockchain in Trade Facilitation, (White Paper, 2019) http://www.unece.org/fileadmin/DAM/cefact/GuidanceMaterials/WhitePaperBlockchain.pdf accessed 18 October 2020.

This raises three issues: (1) security; (2) consumer protection; and (3) market competition.[43] There is a higher risk of security breaches as information is more centralised, hence prone to cyber-attacks.[44] Secondly, the network operators control the behavioural data of the users (particular individuals), and there is a risk that this information can be used to herd or manipulate users' behaviour,[45] for instance the consumers. Thirdly, as operators can claim ownership of the data, there is a risk of foreclosing the market at the expense of other payment operators,[46] especially if data portability or Big Data sharing becomes more difficult. There is a risk that individuals do not obtain a fair exchange for the data rendered to the operators.[47]

E. Information by State-backed Currency Used for a 'Paternal' Economy and Social Surveillance

Some argue that state-backed cryptocurrency can represent a major risk to democratic values, such as surveillance.[48] Currently, central banks do not have automatic access to individual data or individual transaction data which are distributed amongst different layers of the financial markets: banks, payment operators, trusts, and custodian banks. If individual users use cash and keep their money in their own possession, only they have the transaction information. This coincides with the liberal view of a modern state in which the role of a central bank is to act as lender of last resort and monetary policy is used to maintain financial and monetary stability. In a state-backed currency, central banks can exercise greater monetary control and provide more targeted access to finance for individuals or entities perceived as being in need.[49] Central banks are not usually designated as law enforcement agencies against tax evasion,

---

43 The Commonwealth Working Group on Virtual Currencies, Regulatory Guidance on Virtual Currencies (October 2019).

44 Julian Jang-Jaccard and Surya Nepal, 'A Survey of Emerging Threats in Cybersecurity' (2014) 80(5) Journal of Computer and System Science 973, 993 https://www.sciencedirect.com/science/article/pii/S0022000014000178 accessed 20 July 2021.

45 Ryan Calo, 'Digital Market Manipulation' (2014) 82(4) The George Washington Law Review 995, 1051 http://www.gwlr.org/wp-content/uploads/2014/10/Calo_82_4.pdf accessed 20 July 2021.

46 Organisation for Economic Co-operation and Development (OECD), Digital Disruption in Banking and Its Impact on Competition (2020).

47 Ben Williamson, 'Learning from Surveillance Capitalism' (Code acts in education, 30 April 2019) https://codeactsineducation.wordpress.com/2019/04/30/learning-from-surveillance-capitalism/ accessed 18 October 2020.

48 Atzori (n 30).

49 The Financial Action Task Force (FATF), Guidance for a Risk-Based Approach: Virtual Currencies (Working Paper, 2015).

fraud, money laundering, terrorist financing, or market manipulation. They can set rules and guidelines for the internal or organisational risk management of the financial institutions under their supervision but do not target individuals or entities that are not under their supervision. However, state-backed cryptocurrency on the blockchain network creates the potential for state surveillance[50] under which personal data and privacy will be at risk. Because of the centralised character of the private chain, there is also a greater security risk through hacking and other types of cyber-attack. As state-backed cryptocurrency aims at reaching beyond national borders, the risks associated with it, in terms of individual autonomy and safety, are raised to a transnational level. It becomes easier for the state to collect, store, process, and share information for the legitimate purpose of managing the cryptocurrency system and to prevent crime. The capacity for state surveillance is even greater than in cryptocurrency networks operated by private institutions. It is also easier for the state to exercise extra-territorial jurisdiction over transactions on the network and it can more easily obtain information belonging to foreign parties.[51] Because of this, national authorities may begin to impose a data location requirement in order to block links with the state issuing the cryptocurrency, or to use other laws to stop foreign issuing states exercising jurisdiction over its citizens or entities.[52]

III. POLICY GOALS FOR INFORMATION MANAGEMENT ON CRYPTOCURRENCY SPACE

A. Personal Autonomy

Data protection rights and privacy rights are to protect personal autonomy but these two aspects overlap and differ in many respects.[53] Both can be based on

[50] Per Aarvik, 'Blockchain as an Anti-Corruption Tool: Case Examples and Introduction to the Technology', (2020) U4 2020:7 https://www.u4.no/publications/are-blockchain-technologies-efficient-in-combatting-corruption accessed 18 October 2020.

[51] Matthew Kohen and Justin Walse, 'State Regulations on Virtual Currency and Blockchain Technologies' (Carlton Fields, 17 October 2017) https://www.carltonfields.com/insights/publications/2018/state-regulations-on-virtual-currency-and-blockchain-technologies accessed 18 October 2020.

[52] Tom Tobin, 'GDPR and EU Data Location Requirements' (Twilio, 4 May 2018) https://www.twilio.com/blog/2018/05/gdpr-and-eu-data-location-requirements.html accessed 18 October 2020.

[53] European Commission, Directorate General for Research and Innovation, Ethics and Data Protection, (2018) https://ec.europa.eu/info/sites/info/files/5._h2020_ethics_and_data_protection_0.pdf accessed 18 October 2020.

fundamental human rights[54] although some jurisdictions have a different legal basis for privacy and data protection. For instance, in English common law, privacy is based on the duty of confidentiality in the law of tort[55] whereas data protection law gives a stronger proprietary claim to the data subject, as well as a personal claim to the data subjects against discrimination, market manipulation, and market and state surveillance. [56] Data protection law is particularly aimed at abuse by tech companies, whereas privacy rights, as a social contract between the state and the individual, focus on abuses by the state.[57] This distinction is becoming blurred, as tech companies increasingly provide public services on behalf of the state through which they obtain personal information about individuals.

The anonymity of unstable coins on the public chain, if it is effective, gives the best level of privacy and data protection. However, personal autonomy also involves the way individuals can control their data, and exercise proprietary ownership in it. Unstable coins on the public chain do not provide individuals with the power to negotiate with operators about how their data should be used, or at what price, or to decide when data can be withdrawn and erased from the system.[58] This personal autonomy is both economic and social. Since the information infrastructure of unstable coins is opaque, it is difficult for an individual who wishes to exercise personal autonomy to identify the data controllers and processors. Personal autonomy also needs legal guarantee and although unstable coins use the argument of 'code as law' to minimise the requirement of a conventional legal institution to protect personal autonomy, there is a strong risk that systems can be hacked and individual information obtained illegally.[59]

---

[54] Juliane Kokott and Christoph Sobotta, 'The Distinction between Privacy and Data Protection in the Jurisprudence of the CJEU and the ECtHR' (2013) 3(4) International Data Privacy Law 222, 228 https://academic.oup.com/idpl/article/3/4/222/727206 accessed 20 July 2021.

[55] Robert Walker, 'The English Law of Privacy – An Evolving Human Right' (The Supreme Court, UK) https://www.supremecourt.uk/docs/speech_100825.pdf accessed 18 October 2020.

[56] Information Commissioner's Office, Guide to the General Data Protection Regulation (GDPR) (2018) https://ico.org.uk/media/for-organisations/guide-to-the-general-data-protection-regulation-gdpr-1-0.pdf accessed 18 October 2020.

[57] William R M Long and others, "EU Overview" in Alan Charles Raul (eds), The Privacy, Data Protection and Cybersecurity Law Review (6th edn, The LawReviews 2019) 5, 40.

[58] Orna Rabinovich-Einy and Ethan Katsch, 'Blockchain and the Inevitability of Disputes: The Role for Online Dispute Resolution', (2019) 2019(2) Journal of Dispute Resolution 47, 75 https://scholarship.law.missouri.edu/cgi/viewcontent.cgi?article=1837&context=jdr accessed 20 July 2021.

[59] Gabrielle Patrick and Anurag Bana, Rule of Law Versus Rule of Code: A Blockchain-Driven Legal World (IBA Legal Policy & Research Unit Legal Paper, International Bar Association (IBA), 2017).

Furthermore, without a system of identification, this personal autonomy is at risk due to the lack of a trusted third-party dispute resolution mechanism to provide redress to harmed individuals. An automated online dispute resolution mechanism[60] will not be able to guarantee such protection without a credible digital identification system. Privacy, once breached, is difficult to restore and data obtained by others cannot be 'forgotten' by returning it to the owners. In an economy, individuals are free to exchange goods and services, and a legal institution is required to safeguard this market space so that individuals can enforce their legal rights (i.e., contractual right) when goods or services are not of good quality. Without the identification system,[61] there will be higher transaction costs and personal autonomy to transact will be compromised. Stable coins can potentially address enforcement issues by installing a legal institution to resolve disputes. Its private network system would be able to identify users and the transactions.

The use of data by operators can lead to discrimination, behavioural manipulation, surveillance capitalism, and surveillance for the state. When this takes place, personal autonomy will be taken away. It is, therefore, important to know what data the operators will collect and process, and what and how they will share with third parties. In a private consortium such as DIEM, there are social media companies, retail companies, payment system operators such as credit or card companies, and banks. Personal information can easily be shared amongst these organisations whose common objective is to increase revenues.[62] Even though users may find using stable coins convenient and cheaper due to lower currency exchange costs, their personal autonomy to select products and services can be distorted by algorithms that give customised treatment according to users' profiles. Transaction data generated biased algorithms can affect credit ratings and affect how individuals might be treated by financial institutions.[63] Users with more spending power will find that the

[60] Orna Rabinovich-Einy and Ethan Katsch (n 58).

[61] Department for Digital, Culture, Media & Sports, Matt Warman MP, Next Steps Outlined for UK's Use of Digital Identity (2020) https://www.gov.uk/government/news/next-steps-outlined-for-uks-use-of-digital-identity accessed 18 October 2020.

[62] Luke Irwin, 'The GDPR: What Exactly is Personal Data'(IT Governance, 12 November 2020) https://www.itgovernance.eu/blog/en/the-gdpr-what-exactly-is-personal-data accessed 18 October 2020.

[63] Nicol Turner Lee, Paul Resnick and Genie Barton, 'Algorithmic Bias Detection and Mitigation: Best Practices and Policies to Reduce Consumer Harms' (Brookings, 22 May 2019) https://www.brookings.edu/research/algorithmic-bias-detection-and-mitigation-best-practices-and-policies-to-reduce-consumer-harms/ accessed 18 Oct 2020.

product ranges offered to them are limited to the higher price bracket.[64] At a macro-market level, Big Data can be created through gathering personal and transaction data allowing network operators to gain a market advantage and to develop more effective algorithms. When Big Data are not shared with other networks, participants in the network, particularly operators and their business associates, are able to foreclose the market, leading the users to have fewer market choices. If users wish to leave the network, they would need to convert their currency into another fiat currency, thus incurring extra costs which, if too high, become a disincentive to switching.

A state-backed cryptocurrency can potentially enhance access to finance.[65] With personal information and Big Data, the state can target disadvantaged regions, businesses, households, and individuals.[66] It can inject money into the regions and businesses that need finance through giving aid or zero-interest credit to households and individuals for living expenses and personal development. However, this will also allow the state to monitor more closely how users manage their finances. The state is then able to set spending parameters, limiting the amount that can be spent and what it can be spent on. The state can also decide whether an individual should spend or save by using stricter monetary control. For instance, it can impose a negative interest rate on cryptocurrency saved in the digital wallet,[67] encouraging the users to spend. Furthermore, the state will have access to personal finance information and can exercise fiscal enforcement on entities and individuals. The state will be able to collect tax more easily. However, some may argue that entities and individuals would lose their tax-planning autonomy. Whilst the state can also participate in the market by offering goods and services, state-run businesses would have an information advantage over private businesses. This asymmetric information will concentrate social and market powers amongst state entities at the expense of personal autonomy.

---

64 Oxera, When Algorithms Set Prices: Winners and Losers (Discussion Paper, 2017).

65 G7 Working Group on Stablecoins (n 41).

66 Ibid; 'Financial Inclusion Overview', (The World Bank, 2018) https://www.worldbank.org/en/topic/financialinclusion/overview accessed 18 October 2020.

67 Amber Wadsworth, 'The Pros and Cons of Issuing a Central Bank Digital Currency' (2018) 81(7) Reserve Bank of New Zealand Bulletin https://www.rbnz.govt.nz/-/media/reservebank/files/publications/bulletins/2018/2018jun81-07.pdf accessed 20 July 2021.

B. Development of Digital Economy

Digital economy is a common vision of many governments and private entities.[68] But for the relevant hardware to be developed, companies need to be convinced of a promising future before making the necessary investment. Software companies play an important part here in driving market demand for intensive hardware R&D.[69] A smart economy and a smart society encourage this market demand and it is unlikely that law in the advanced economies and some emerging powers will reverse this trend. Intensive investment in data centre technology will need to find a market for these products to provide yields, and cryptocurrency will need just such data centres,[70] with super computing power, to maintain its ecosystem sustainably.

The transactional data recorded will also provide unprecedented social and market information in a more efficient way. Currently, transactional data is fragmented and it is difficult for smaller entities and private individuals to benefit from data intensive economy. Data companies have the infrastructure to aggregate data along with greater market power to provide data streams to users who can afford them. This data space is currently not available to ordinary individuals because they lack sufficient computing power to process the data and lack finance to purchase the data streaming services.[71] Cryptocurrency can potentially remedy these problems and provide a data facility to the users. As data protection only covers personal data, corporate transaction data, both current and historical, can be made available. This can allow individuals or other smaller entities to design their own algorithms with the available data sets thus opening up the data streaming markets that have been dominated by major players.[72] Whilst data protection law does not protect corporate data, companies are able to claim privacy rights.[73] It is, therefore, important to

---

[68] United Nations Conference on Trade and Development, Digital Economy Report 2019 - Value Creation and Capture: Implications for Developing Countries (2019).

[69] Fumio Kodama, 'Technology Fusion and the New R&D' (Harvard Business Review, July/August 1992) https://hbr.org/1992/07/technology-fusion-and-the-new-rd accessed 26 June 2021.

[70] Organisation for Economic Co-operation and Development (OECD), The Tokenisation of Assets and Potential Implications for Financial Markets (2020).

[71] Information Commissioner's Office (n 56).

[72] Jens Prufer and Patricia Prufer, 'Data Science for Entrepreneurship Research: Studying Demand Dynamics for Entrepreneurial Skills in the Netherlands' (2020) 55 Small Business Economics 651, 672 https://link.springer.com/article/10.1007/s11187-019-00208-y accessed 20 July 2021.

[73] European Commission, 'Data Protection Under GDPR' (2020) https://europa.eu/youreurope/business/dealing-with-customers/data-protection/data-protection-gdpr/index_en.htm accessed 18 October 2020.

continue to protect corporate entities' privacy rights and the ability of users to benefit from the data streaming services. In order to enable this to happen, data sharing is the key. Legal issues pertinent to this include (1) how personal data can be exchanged; (2) how personal data can be portable to increase competition within networks or between the different networks; and (3) how Big Data can be transferred to different countries.

C. Unstable Coin

In an unstable coin space, there is limited opportunity to manage personal data as it is an anonymous system on the public chain. However, it is claimed that an overall view can be obtained. For instance, it is possible to know how many users are transacting Bitcoins,[74] when, and at what amount. However, without specific information, this is not useful data for the users, even for the algorithm developers. With regards to illicit transactions using Bitcoins as payment, the trading data are of little use to law enforcement agencies in developing anti-money laundering algorithms to detect such activities.

D. Stable Coin

In a stable coin space on the private chain, transactional data are available to the operators. It is not clear how individuals, as data subjects, could monetise personal data as a commodity, but a plug-and-play mechanism could allow data subjects to provide and withdraw data from the system. In such a system, they would be able to exercise consent, withdraw data, and erase their personal data. The problem is whether such a plug-and-play mechanism can also deliver the function of Big Data. Even if personal data are erased from the system, data subjects can continue to claim part ownership of the Big Data and claim entitlements to benefits through the monetisation of Big Data by the operators. This is an area that data protection law has yet to address. In addition to this, data portability gives data subjects the right to choose another service that requires personal data.[75] How such a private consortium can enable data portability is questionable; it would require the operators to provide interop-

---

[74] Satoshi Nakamoto, 'Bitcoin: A Peer-to-Peer Electronic Cash System' (2008) https://bitcoin.org/bitcoin.pdf accessed 21 July 2021; 'Protect your privacy: Understanding Bitcoin traceability' (Bitcoin) https://bitcoin.org/en/protect-your-privacy accessed 21 July 2021; Rainer Böhme and others, 'Bitcoin: Economics, Technology, and Governance' (2015) 29(2) The Journal of Economic Perspectives 213, 238 https://www.jstor.org/stable/24292130 accessed 21 July 2021.

[75] Lachlan Urquhar, Neelima Sailaja and Derek McAuley, 'Realising the Right to Data Portability for the Domestic Internet of Things' (2018) 22 Personal and

erable systems. In other words, the data, such as on the DIEM blockchain, would need to be made interoperable to another private blockchain network so that the data are 'readable'.[76] Otherwise, the data would only be readable on DIEM's own machine and would defeat the aim of data portability to achieve more competition and provide more choices to users.

This also raises the question of transfer of mass data. If data are to be transferred to another entity to increase digital capability, both transferor and transferee entities would need to comply with rules to safeguard data subject's rights and privacy right. The participants in the network may not be able to share data freely unless they are within the same entity. They will need to comply with additional data protection safeguards such as binding corporate rules (BCRs).[77] BCRs are an effective mechanism for assuring appropriate safeguards for third-country data transfers, which has been recognised by the GDPR.[78] As there are restrictions on the transfer of personal data outside the European Union by GDPR, BCRs are an approach that data controllers and data processors can use to comply with the requirements of GDPR on third-party data transfers.[79]

This will make the original transferor of data and the transferees both liable if there are data breaches. In the case of DIEM, they will need to make sure that participants in the network, who have access to the data, also comply with the additional safeguards. This can make it difficult to share data with parties outside the network. The difficulties of data portability and transferability may, however, be an advantage to networks which do not share data with outsiders.

E. State-backed Currency

In a state-backed currency network, the state has all the data. The mass data allows the state to provide better and targeted public services through more

---

Ubiquitous Computing 317, 332 https://link.springer.com/article/10.1007/s00779-017-1069-2 accessed 20 July 2021.

76 Carlo R.W. De Meijer, 'Blockchain and Interoperability: Key to Mass Adoption' (Finextra, 6 July 2020) https://www.finextra.com/blogposting/18972/blockchain-and-interoperability-key-to-mass-adoption accessed 18 October 2020.

77 'International Personal Data Transfers: Binding Corporate Rules (BCRs) under the GDPR' (i-Scoop, 2017) https://www.i-scoop.eu/gdpr/binding-corporate-rules-bcrs-gdpr/ accessed 18 October 2020.

78 Articles 26 (2) (b) and 47, Regulation (EU) 2016/679 (General Data Protection Regulation, GDPR).

79 PwC, Binding Corporate Rules: The General Data Protection Regulation (2019) https://www.pwc.com/m1/en/publications/documents/pwc-binding-corporate-rules-gdpr.pdf accessed 26 June 2021.

sophisticated algorithms.[80] As mentioned, since the state has access to all the data, it can also come up with better monetary tools, better fiscal control, and can provide aid to those in need. There is, however, a risk that the state may be less efficient in providing public services through the lack of incentives, lack of expertise, bureaucratic processes, and corruption. The question then is who owns the data, whether the state should share the data, and what governance is required. The exceptions granted to the state to control and process data are based on the legitimate functions it carries out, the public interest it seeks to serve and its public policy.[81] The state could claim ownership of the data and sell it to create revenue. The state could share data amongst its various departments under these exceptions without additional safeguards such as the corporate binding rules. They can refuse to share data with non-state entities or charge them fees for sharing them. The state can decide how they want to control and process the data, and their right to do so would not be subject to data subject's right to data portability and right to erasure. The state has the power to require other network entities to disclose data and can then integrate the datasets. These powers and exceptions can lead to the state holding a data monopoly[82] in which private entities cannot compete.

In the conventional banking sphere with several layers in the market, the state does not have full access to transaction data and would, according to law, need to request such data.[83] But the data sets generated by state-backed cryptocurrency could lead to the foreclosure of data market and the formation of a monopoly in the development of technology for data centres. Since the state can claim ownership in the data, it is difficult to request the state to share it as a 'public good'. Even if the data is treated as a public good, the state would be able to impose conditions on its use and increase the state's power over private entities.

---

80 Organisation for Economic Co-operation and Development (OECD), Data Driven Innovation for Growth and Well-Being, (Interim Synthesis Report, 2014).

81 Gabriela Zanfir-Fortuna and Teresa Troester-Falk, Processing Personal Data on the Basis of Legitimate Interests under the GDPR: Practical Cases (Research Paper of the Future of Privacy Forum, The Future of Privacy Forum and Nymity) http://www.ejtn.eu/PageFiles/17861/Deciphering_Legitimate_Interests_Under_the_GDPR%20(1).pdf accessed 18 Oct 2020.

82 Joe Kennedy, 'The Myth of Data Monopoly: Why Antitrust Concerns about Data are Overblown' (Information Technology & Innovation Foundation (ITIF), March 2017) http://www2.itif.org/2017-data-competition.pdf accessed 18 October 2020.

83 Organisation for Economic Co-operation and Development (OECD) (n 46).

F. Crime Prevention

Many technologies can generate both positive and negative results but it is up to both policy and law to make them fulfil our objectives. Smart technology is multifaceted when it comes to crime and crime prevention. It can facilitate crime through complete anonymity whilst at the same time making crime easy to detect and prosecute. Unstable coins on the public chain with their complete anonymity have shown how the public chain network can become a hotbed for criminal activities. State-backed cryptocurrency significantly reduces the opportunity for theft, welfare fraud, money laundering, tax evasion, and terrorist financing. This is not only because transactions can be linked with identified users, but also because the surrounding data of the transactions can contextualise them, i.e., where they took place and why the goods were purchased. The data can also create user profiles, showing the pattern of behaviour of individuals and their associates.[84] This helps the state to develop algorithms to detect the behavioural pattern of fraud, tax evasion, and money laundering.[85] What is more, since the state is watching the users of the network, users would be less inclined to commit crime. With the sophisticated algorithms, users may not even need to file a tax return since every transaction is recorded on the network and tax can be collected by the tax authorities at the click of a button. This begs the question of how many people would use a state-backed cryptocurrency when there are effective alternatives. How many of us would use emails if the state had easy access to our email inbox? The state may rely on its legitimate public function, public interest, and public policy around crime prevention to justify its surveillance capability but it is unlikely that any democratic state would allow these principles to be used to stretch the state powers without accountability. The doctrines of proportionality and the principle of reasonableness are the safeguards against such omnipotent state power.[86] There are cases in the EU showing a clear stance on human rights against state

---

[84] Brad Brown and others, 'Capturing Value from Your Customer Data' (McKinsey & Company: McKinsey Analytics, 2017) https://www.mckinsey.com/business-functions/mckinsey-analytics/our-insights/capturing-value-from-your-customer-data# accessed 18 October 2020.

[85] Suhaib Alzou'bi, Haitham Alshibly and Mohammad Al-Ma'aitah, 'Artificial Intelligence in Law Enforcement, A Review' (2014) 4(4) International Journal of Advanced Information Technology 1, 9 https://airccse.org/journal/IJAIT/papers/4414ijait01.pdf accessed 24 July 2021.

[86] Alice Ristroph, 'Proportionality as A Principle of Limited Government' (2005) 55 Duke Law Journal 263, 265 https://scholarship.law.duke.edu/dlj/vol55/iss2/2/ accessed 15 December 2021.

surveillance.[87] There may be exceptional circumstances where state surveillance is required to protect public health but it is unlikely that a liberal and democratic state would be given the power to hack into a data system for the purpose of law enforcement without concern about human rights violations. The current financial market multilayer infrastructure is designed to safeguard financial privacy even though it may also facilitate (or not be able to prevent) tax fraud and criminal activity.[88]

The more problematic area is the stable coins issued by private consortia and private entities such as DIEM. The questions are: what are their obligations in crime prevention? should they provide access to their data to the state? and should they allow others to have access to the data for the purpose of developing anti-crime tools? For anti-money laundering purposes, financial institutions such as banks, brokers, and payment companies are under a legal duty to prevent money laundering through detecting and reporting suspicious transactions. However, financial institutions have no legal duty to do so if they do not have sufficient data and information to identify suspicious transactions. For instance, central banks, trading venues, clearing houses, and some custodian banks only process information about large institutional members[89] and do not have the details of individual users' transactions revealing money laundering activities. This means that it is entities that have a client-facing entry point that should act as gatekeeper as they collect detailed information under the 'Know-your-customer' (KYC) requirement.[90] The KYC requirement in private chains will be made easier through digital identification. If, however, a consortium such as DIEM that issues stable coins does have access to detailed individual information – fund transfers, trade financing, and retail purchasing – and has the capability to identify suspicious transactions through its algorithms, it then has an obligation to report its suspicions to the authori-

87 Such as Big Brother Watch and Others v. The United Kingdom App nos 58170/13, 62322/14 and 24960/15 (ECtHR, 25 May 2021).

88 Depository Trust & Clearing Corporation (DTCC), Moving Financial Market Infrastructure to the Cloud: Realising the Risk Reduction and Cost Effective Vision While Achieving Public Policy Goals (2017) https://www.dtcc.com/~/media/Files/downloads/Thought-leadership/moving-financial-markets-infrastructure-to-the-cloud.pdf?utm_source=perspective&utm_medium=forms&utm_campaign=thought_leadership accessed 27 June 2021.

89 Ben Norman, Rachel Shaw and George Speight, The History of Interbank Settlement Arrangements: Exploring Central Banks' Role in the Payment System (Working Paper No. 412, 2011, Bank of England).

90 Emily Lee, 'Financial Inclusion: A Challenge to the New Paradigm of Financial Technology, Regulatory Technology and Anti-Money Laundering Law' (2017) 6 Journal of Business Law 473, 498 http://researchblog.law.hku.hk/2017/08/emily-lee-on-financial-inclusion.html accessed 20 July 2021.

ties. This obliges DIEM and similar network operators to act as a surveillance mechanism for the state, rather than the state directly monitoring its citizens. States need to follow the legal procedure to obtain data, either for reasons of monetary policy or for law enforcement purposes and this provides an additional layer of safeguard to civil liberty. To provide further safeguards, the law should be able to specify only certain participants, such as wallet providers and cryptocurrency exchangers, that can access detailed information. This would prohibit network operators from providing a back-door facility[91] to the state authorities. Even if the network operators have the data, the obligation to provide information to the state, through reporting or at the state's legal request, rests with the wallet providers[92] and trade financiers.

The data that network operators have access to can be used for the purpose of research, such as understanding the pattern of criminal activities. This would require operators to have a robust data governance mechanism to ensure data security, accuracy and quality, along with other internal cyber security measures. Algorithms that are developed from datasets generated by the network for the purpose of crime prevention would need to be tested in a safe environment and should be free of discrimination. In this way, data generated for the public good can be used for the public interest of crime prevention while safeguarding personal liberty.

IV. POLITICS OF INFORMATION IN CRYPTOCURRENCY

A. From Economic to Political

The fourth industrial revolution will disrupt the financial system and will result in socio-economic impacts on job security, democratic values, and humanity.[93] Cryptocurrency's disintermediation is intended to reduce transaction costs for users and its de-centralisation aims to create more distributive justice by giving back powers of wealth creation and sharing to them. The data aspect of cryptocurrency is at the centre of the debate about how one should own data, who has the right to manage it in the collective interest, and who has the right to use data in the public interest. Transparency and accountability have been key

[91] Cynthia Dion-Schwarz, David Manheim and Patrick Johnston, Terrorist Use of Cryptocurrencies: Technical and Organizational Barriers and Future Threats (RAND Corporation, 2019) https://www.rand.org/content/dam/rand/pubs/research_reports/RR3000/RR3026/RAND_RR3026.pdf accessed 18 October 2020.

[92] Robby Houben, Alexander Snyers (n 7).

[93] Department for Business, Energy & Industrial Strategy, Regulation for the Fourth Industrial Revolution, (Policy Paper, 2019).

in the democratic politics. In a representative democracy, we put the emphasis on transparency and accountability of the politicians and government agencies (intermediaries) to make the political system function.[94] In a direct democracy, such as by referendum, more emphasis is placed on the individual's right to information and the power of vote to show the centralised, collective sovereignty.[95] It is still difficult to ascertain what disintermediation and decentralisation cryptocurrency are intended to achieve in the political space. These intentions will affect the design of a disintermediated and decentralised cryptocurrency operating system. Who operates the system and for whose benefit are questions still to be answered. There should be different requirements, in terms of privacy and data protection, for private and public entities who, in turn, have different political powers. For whose benefit is even harder to answer, as users are not monolithic individuals (high net-wealth or low income) or corporations (consortium or state). These differences would affect the understanding and applications of legitimate interest and public interest under privacy law and data protection law. Just as technology has shown its power of increasing inequality, disintermediation can cause job losses in the payment services sector.[96] Furthermore, there are potential discriminatory effects of the use of smart technology. In a decentralised system, there is a risk of reduced transparency due to data and privacy protection; and reduced accountability due to the lack of a centralised power to respond to instability. *To make cryptocurrency legal and technologically interoperable, we will need to define the purpose of such mobile currency.* When the Euro was introduced, its purpose was to bring unity to the single market; there are reasons why one currency is pegged to another,[97] for preventing market manipulation of the weaker currency. To make such cryptocurrency fundamental rights and innovation compliant, one would need to enquire again about the fundamental rights that are to be achieved and what priority is to be given to each fundamental right. Decisions are needed about

---

94 John Gaventa and Rosemary McGee, 'The Impact of Transparency and Accountability Initiatives' (2020) https://assets.publishing.service.gov.uk/media/57a08aabed915d622c00084b/60827_DPRGaventaMcGee_Preprint.pdf accessed 27 June 2021.

95 Sherman Clark, 'A Populist Critique of Direct Democracy' (1998) 112 Harvard Law Review 434, 482 https://www.jstor.org/stable/1342426?seq=1#metadata_info_tab_contents accessed 24 July 2021.

96 Carla Hobbs, Europe's Digital Sovereignty: From Rulemaker to Superpower in the Age of US-China Rivalry (Essay Collection of the European Council on Foreign Relations, 2020).

97 Virginie Coudert, Cécile Couharde and Valerie Mignon, 'Pegging Emerging Currencies in the Face of Dollar Swings' (2013) 45(36) Applied Economics 1, 28 https://www.tandfonline.com/doi/full/10.1080/00036846.2013.818215 accessed 24 July 2021.

the kind of governance that cryptocurrency should be linked to and, in addition to the expectation of privacy, the need for cybersecurity, and the agreeable level of surveillance, who controls the computing power i.e., the nodes on the cryptocurrency network. The nodes can have the power to decide what to register on the blockchain, how to revise the protocol, how to manage the split of the system i.e., hard fork problem,[98] and how to manage the data obtained from users. In other words, the nodes are the intermediaries for processing transactions for users and for possessing distributive decision-making powers in cryptocurrency operations, such as controlling the level of liquidity. No country currently allows its citizens to decide monetary policy through direct democracy such as the referendum. Many central banks are independent of the government so that their policies are not made on the basis of short-term political appeal to win votes. However, in practice, central bankers also face political pressure from governments when making their decisions, and in some countries central banks are subject to parliamentary scrutiny. At a more local level, we have also witnessed how interest rates are being made by private consortia in a market-based manner, such as LIBOR, rather than by a centralised mechanism. The issue is whether we are ready to trust the nodes, assuming each node makes an independent decision, to make monetary decisions on behalf of the community. This would resemble a representative democracy where politicians and agencies make decisions for its people. However, the emphasis in this representative democratic system is transparency and accountability. How can the users hold the nodes in the distributed power system accountable? The users do not elect nodes, unless they can and there are agreements between the nodes and the users on how decision-making power is to be exercised on the network. Yet, how should voting secrecy be preserved? The function of the nodes is to process the transactions for users and, at the same time, to make monetary decisions for them. Will nodes act on the instructions given by the users who elect or choose them? It may also be the case that the nodes refuse to follow users' instructions and refuse users' participation in the network through its node. Rather than empowering the users, the system could operate to exclude. There is a need to ensure that the nodes act as good steward of the users.[99]

---

[98] Tae Wan Kim and Ariel Zetlin-Jones, 'The Ethics of Contentious Hard Forks in Blockchain Networks with Fixed Features' (2019) Frontiers https://www.frontiersin.org/articles/10.3389/fbloc.2019.00009/full accessed 18 October 2020.

[99] A. Keay, 'Stewardship Theory: Is Board Accountability Necessary?' (2017) 59 International Journal of Law and Management 1292, 1314 https://eprints.whiterose.ac.uk/109675/3/BOARD%20ACCOUNTABILITY%20AND%20THE%20STEWARDSHIP%20THEORY%20J%20Law%20and%20manrevised.pdf accessed 20 July 2021.

B. Data Location Requirement

The data location requirement demands that data of a particular type are situated in a jurisdiction or a region. For instance, EU law requires its citizens' data to be situated in the EU.[100] Data location gives rise to jurisdiction competition.[101] A country or region's legal requirement of data location can affect data transferability and data portability. The restriction on data transferability through the location requirement can affect regulatory capability, law enforcement, competition in the tech sector, and transnational cooperation. In other words, this requirement affects how personal autonomy is guaranteed, how the digital economy can be developed further to compete, and how the risk of crime can be effectively managed. In some countries, data location law requires data generated from that country to be situated in its jurisdiction with or without data transferability.[102] Even with data transferability, the law may demand a copy or replica to be kept within the jurisdiction. In some countries, such a data location requirement has different applications according to the type of data. For instance, in the Trans-Pacific Partnership, the US demands that US financial data are located in the US and are not subject to the principle of free data flow. This is because in the opinion of the US government, there is a strong policy reason to keep financial data in the region. The recent Court of Justice of the European Union (CJEU) decision invalidating the EU-US Privacy Shield[103] has shown that data transfers may not be easily carried out even for the purpose of law enforcement of the requesting state. This case shows how human rights law and other constitutional and fundamental safeguards require European data controllers and processors to protect its data subjects from a third country's state power. Even though individual consent could be the basis, it is unlikely that a blanket consent of an individual would allow such cross-border data transfers. The problem is that when data need to

---

100 Lokke Moerel, 'The Long Arm of EU Data Protection Law: Does the Data Protection Directive Apply to Processing of Personal Data of EU Citizens by Websites Worldwide?' (2011) 1(1) International Data Privacy Law 28, 46 https://academic.oup.com/idpl/article/1/1/28/759646 accessed 20 July 2021.

101 Jacques Crémer, Yves-Alexandre de Montjoye and Heike Schweitzer, Competition Policy for the Digital Era (Research Report, European Commission, Directorate-General for Competition, 2019).

102 The GDPR restricts the transfer of personal data to countries outside the EEA. For more details, see Information Commissioner's Office, 'International transfers after the UK exit from the EU Implementation Period' https://ico.org.uk/for-organisations/guide-to-data-protection/guide-to-the-general-data-protection-regulation-gdpr/international-transfers/ accessed 18 October 2020.

103 Data Protection Commissioner v. Facebook Ireland Ltd, Maximillian Schrems [2018] High Court (Ireland), [2018] Case C311/1.

be transferred for legitimate purposes,[104] once the transfer to the third country for processing has taken place, it would be difficult for the data controllers in the EU and the data subjects in the EU to prevent data being seized by the third-country authorities. The challenge for cryptocurrency is how to protect individual data against state power as conferred by criminal law or by national security law. This case shows how the EU can use the equivalence regime[105] to control the flow of data to third countries. In some countries, such as China, data transferability is subject to cyber security law. The China's Cyber Security Law came into force from 1 June 2017 with an array of supporting regulations to facilitate the interpretation and implementation of this law. The Cyber Security Law emphasised the issues in relation to the data localisation and cross-border data transfers. For instance, in accordance with the Cyber Security Law, 'personal information[106] and important data[107] collected and generated by entities designated as Key Information Infrastructure Operators (KII) must be stored domestically within China'.[108]

Data on the cryptocurrency network will show specific local dynamics, geographical, demographical, and temporal. This will reveal the sentiment in a particular location – train tickets showing if workers are returning to work, mask sales showing the rise of a pandemic, energy sales showing population behaviour in a particular time. Such data can be of strategic importance both economically and politically. Smart contracts on the network with detailed terms and conditions can further contextualise the data. This no longer just provides the broad picture of what Big Data can show, but very specific dynamics in a sector (e.g., pharmacy), in a region (e.g., around government buildings), and a particular retail establishment such as bars and pubs showing the level of risk to Covid-19 infection. Hence, data are not just financial, but can be about medical well-being, educational capabilities, entertainment provisions, social media activities, and small and medium enterprises' moves. In terms of personal autonomy, the citizens of a state would be less willing to engage in

[104] Tess Blair and Vincent M. Catanzaro, 'Transfer of Data in the GDPR: The Definition of Legitimate Interest' (Morgan, Lewis & Bockius LLP, 2020) https://www.lexology.com/library/detail.aspx?g=bbd12b14-79c8-4141-a585-7b7eb0ca59e2 accessed 18 October 2020.

[105] Data Protection Commission, 'Transfers of Personal Data to Third Countries or International Organisations' (2020) https://www.dataprotection.ie/en/organisations/international-transfers/transfers-personal-data-third-countries-or-international-organisations accessed 18 October 2020.

[106] Article 76(5), Cybersecurity Law of the People's Republic of China (Cyber Security Law of China).

[107] The Cyber Security Law of China does not provide the definition of important data.

[108] Article 37, Cyber Security Law of China.

the network if they knew that they were being watched by their state, let alone a foreign state. Such restricted personal autonomy will not only affect political freedom but also the economic activities in the space. Citizens may feel inhibited from spending, fearing that it would attract tax authorities' attentions. The unwillingness to engage in the crypto-space will affect the level of data generated to feed into the development of digital economy and society. This will substantially reduce the competitiveness of the tech industry in the jurisdiction and the region. This will have a long-term digital capability issue and can directly affect regional security. In terms of crime prevention, prosecuting crime is a national sovereign power.[109] This power can be exercised on an extra-territorial basis.[110] We have witnessed how long-arm jurisdiction[111] has been exercised against entities and individuals for fraud, money laundering, tax evasion, terrorism, and security breaches. In *R (KBR Inc) v. Director of the Serious Fraud Office* [2018] EWHC 2368 (Admin) the High Court concluded that section 2 of the Criminal Justice Act 1987 permits the Serious Fraud Office to compel the production of documents held by a foreign person, even where those documents are outside the jurisdiction, provided that the foreign person has a 'sufficient connection' to the jurisdiction and that the section 2 notice is validly served on the foreign person. The court also concluded that the implied intention behind the SFO's section 2 regime created sufficient justification to permit extraterritorial application.

Giving away data will mean giving away a jurisdiction's legal power and technological capability to understand crime, detect, and prosecute crime. Cryptocurrency space i.e., on the private chain also allows national law enforcement agencies to impose sanctions more easily, both in law and in technology. This is the reason why certain states, including the USA in the Trans-Pacific Partnership,[112] require data to be located in their jurisdiction so that they retain law enforcement powers. Any request for these data by a state

---

[109] Mireille Caruana, 'The Reform of the EU Data Protection Framework in the context of the Police and Criminal Justice Sector: Harmonisation, Scope, Oversight and Enforcement' (2017) 33(3) International Review of Law, Computers & Technology 249, 270 https://www.tandfonline.com/doi/abs/10.1080/13600869.2017.1370224 accessed 20 July 2021.

[110] Danielle Ireland-Piper, 'Extraterritorial Criminal Jurisdiction: Does the Long Arm of the Law Undermine the Rule of Law?' (2012) 13 Melbourne Journal of International Law 2, 35 https://law.unimelb.edu.au/__data/assets/pdf_file/0007/1687246/Ireland-Piper.pdf accessed 20 July 2021.

[111] Financial Action Task Force (FATF), Global Money Laundering & Terrorist Financing Threat Assessment (FATF Report, July 2010).

[112] Michael Geist, 'Data Rules in Modern Trade Agreements: Toward Reconciling an Open Internet with Privacy and Security Safeguards' (2018) Center for International Governance Innovation https://www.cigionline.org/articles/data-rules-modern-trade

power would need to be done at inter- or intra-governmental level,[113] reaffirming national sovereignty. This is the rationale behind the CJEU's ruling on the EU-US Privacy Shield; any request of personal data for the purpose of law enforcement would need to be done at inter-governmental level.

The data location requirement has the potential to create regional data barriers, data nationalism and data protectionism.[114] The possible effect is the creation of a data silo.[115] Data flows would be subject to a number of legal safeguards, such as the third-country equivalence regime. In a virtual space, smaller jurisdictions would need to form alliances with each other or with larger regimes to operate in the digital space. In terms of cryptocurrency, the countries using them would need to form a silo in order to achieve the said benefits of cryptocurrency at the cross-border level. There will need to be inter-governmental agreement to decide on data governance.[116] A cryptocurrency network without such a data silo would substantially reduce the effectiveness of it. An EU citizen using a Chinese state-backed cryptocurrency can request its data in the EU to be erased. This will affect the operations of the Chinese DCEP. Equally, a UK citizen can request the same action to be carried out to DIEM based in Switzerland. It is likely that such a data silo will be formed based on the locations of the users i.e., EU and EU-Japan.[117] It will be cross-border but the alliances would be formed. The defunct US-led TPP[118] was aimed to form such an alliance. Data fortress might be an inevitable outcome, albeit different from data nationalism and data protectionism.

-agreements-toward-reconciling-open-internet-privacy-and-security accessed 18 October 2020.

[113] OECD, International Co-operation against Tax Crimes and Other Financial Crimes: A Catalogue of the Main Instruments (2nd Annual Forum on Tax and Crime, June 2012).

[114] Nigel Cory, 'Cross-Border Data Flows: Where Are the Barriers, and What Do They Cost' (Information Technology & Innovation Foundation (ITIF), May 2017) http://www2.itif.org/2017-cross-border-data-flows.pdf accessed 18 October 2020.

[115] Edd Wilder-James, 'Breaking Down Data Silos' (2016) Harvard Business Review https://hbr.org/2016/12/breaking-down-data-silos accessed 18 October 2020.

[116] European Commission, Secretariat-General, Data Governance and Data Policies, (2020) https://ec.europa.eu/info/sites/info/files/summary-data-governance-data-policies_en.pdf accessed 18 October 2020.

[117] European Commission, 'European Commission Adopts Adequacy Decision on Japan, Creating the World's Largest Area of Safe Data Flows' (2019) https://ec.europa.eu/commission/presscorner/detail/en/IP_19_421 accessed 18 October 2020.

[118] Xianbai Ji and Pradumna Rana, 'A Deal that Does Not Die: The United States and the Rise, Fall and Future of the (Comprehensive and Progressive Agreement for) Trans-Pacific Partnership' (SWP Working Paper No. 5, October 2018) 34 (2) Pacific Focus https://onlinelibrary.wiley.com/doi/full/10.1111/pafo.12143#accessDenialLayout accessed 20 July 2021.

V. CONCLUSION

In this chapter, I have discussed how the policy goals of personal autonomy, development of digital economy, and crime prevention can be enhanced or damaged in three different types of cryptocurrencies. Current data protection law and privacy law can only address some of these issues, and the discussion of their propriety and effectiveness need to be made against the policy goals. I have shown that cryptocurrency is not just a financial tool, but also a political space. It is for governments to implement effective monetary and fiscal policy, for the tech companies of the region to obtain future technological capability, and for sovereign states to exercise sovereign powers individually or collectively. There is scope for users and citizens to exercise their political power in the crypto-space. The question is how desirable is direct participation in cryptocurrency? and how such direct democracy of users can be written into the new social contract with the state or the network provider? How data artefacts are generated on the crypto-space and are to be used will depend on the political ideology of the day in the country.

3. The client data windfall nourishing the birth of legal technologies

David C. Donald[1]

I. INTRODUCTION

Suppose two average people, call them Buya and Targat, are in a romantic relationship. They both use Facebook, and their many posts show the history and growth of their relationship from meeting to engagement. Posts also show how Buya started to act in a way that Targat perceived as an 'undervaluation' of Targat's worth and these posts documented the road to their eventual and unfortunate breakup. Now suppose that Facebook has a data analytics function called 'Fantastic Friendship', which applies a machine learning model worked out by psychologists on the basis of the thousands of posts that people like Buya and Targat entrust to Facebook. Another user, Offrr, subscribes to Fantastic Friendship – which has further improved itself by learning from the (anonymised) data history of Buya and Targat, among others. Thanks to advice received from Facebook's Fantastic Friendship function, Offrr successfully hooks up with Sella in a long and mutually satisfactory relationship. Did Buya and Targat approve of this use of their data? Should they condone it because personal data was de-identified? Should they condone it because, after all, they too can subscribe to Fantastic Friendship and benefit from services enriched in expertise from every successful and unsuccessful relationship documented on Facebook?

These are the questions that every law firm client should be asking. Clients understand at some level that lawyers learn from the problems brought to them by a client they represent. Such learning is the stuff of 'experience' and 'expertise'. However, most clients probably do not fully understand that the exact legal research and work product they pay for in connection with representation

[1] I am extremely grateful to Shuo Chen, Robert Chu, Christian Fischer, Adrian Fong, Scott Johnson, Joseph Lee, Jyh-An Lee, Padraig Walsh, Wolfgang Zankl and Terry Wong for their comments and suggestions on the original concept and an earlier draft of this chapter. All shortcomings in this work remain my own.

will find its way into the services provided to other clients represented by the firm, even if this client is potentially a competitor. With increasing use of legal technologies,[2] a law firm's repeated use of client research, work product, and even case facts, will become much more visible and precisely measurable. Beyond industrial scale exploitation of the data within a law firm is the sharing or transfer of this data with or to unregulated data analytics services developing or improving their legal technology applications. The legal profession is subject to licensing requirements and strict regulation of its behaviour, but such automated services training on client data currently undergo no such supervision. At some point these services will perform basic legal tasks more effectively than do lawyers. Yet they would not have been able to reach such levels of competence without the data and work product that lawyers feed into them. Serious thought should thus be given to the use of client data to grow legal technologies, and to the possible conflict between a lawyer's duty to safeguard the data of individual clients and the incentive to pool information of *all* clients for better analytical exploitation.

A system built to review contracts or analyse pretrial discovery improves with training – the more data the better.[3] Yet this pool of data originates from separate clients, each of whom – prior to releasing their information to the firm – have entered into an attorney-client relationship, which is one of the world's most protected legally. Both the information attorneys obtain from clients and the work product they generate in each such relationship are highly confidential and even protected against use in court by the doctrine of 'privilege'.[4] Running contrary to this emphasis on protecting client data in a law firm is the fact that the 'key ingredient in any data science process is data, so it is not surprising that … effort goes into finding, aggregating, and cleaning the data'.[5]

---

[2] 'Legal technology' as used in this chapter is essentially the use of automated computation models to:

> break down a complex human intellectual task, such as estimating the settlement value of a product liability suit or analyzing an offer and acceptance problem… into a set of computational steps or algorithm. The models specify how a problem is input and the type of legal result to output. In between, the model builders have constructed a computational mechanism to apply domain knowledge to perform the steps and transform the inputs to outputs.

Kevin Ashley, *Artificial Intelligence and Legal Analytics: New Tools for Law Practice in the Digital Age* (CUP 2017) 4.

[3] John Armour and Mari Sako, 'AI-enabled business models in legal services: from traditional law firms to next-generation law companies?' (2020) 7 *Journal of Professions and Organization* 27, 30, 36–7.

[4] See e.g., American Bar Association Model Rules on Professional Conduct, r 1.6 and New York Rules of Professional Conduct, r 1.6.

[5] John Kelleher and Brendan Tierney, *Data Science* (MIT Press, 2018) 73.

Finding data means locating actual data containing the informational configurations sought in the analytic process, and for legal technology services, such data is found in law firms' work product or the cases of their clients – from successful contractual or financing arrangements to facts that trigger problems in corporate transactions or litigation. *Aggregating* data likely means storing data collected from different firm clients together in a single data warehouse. As one provider of data analytics for law firms puts it, their service seeks to 'unlock the information that's hidden in data already housed by law firms'.[6]

Such unlocking through *pooling* the legally isolated data of individual clients is thus understood by some as the 'creative destruction' of legacy data storage to achieve innovation. With reference to financial institutions, McKinsey & Company advises firms to 'break through data-architecture gridlock' to replace legacy treatment of data.[7] However, the breaking down of walls to create a 'data warehouse' or 'data lake' within a law firm by aggregating data from individual firm clients for general use could mean knowing violation of professional conduct rules applicable to lawyers in places like New York.[8] Moreover, an aspiring legal technologies firm would also seek to aggregate some content of this data across law firms, creating a vast data lake unavailable to any given firm. Google at one point attempted to patent a 'system and method for policy-based confidentiality management' of data in law firms,[9] but this system does not currently appear to be offered. Such a system would allow an automated use of 'scrubbed' yet legally relevant facts and work product spanning the legal profession.

The mingling of client data has at some level always been part of legal practice. It is an assumed, albeit often undeclared, custom of law practise that lawyers use legal knowledge, skills and information learned or created in representing one client to better serve another – and render the service with less effort and cost. Such data accumulates over time and constitutes a lawyer's or a firm's experience, know-how and expertise. As Susskind observes, 'one of

---

6 Matthew Terrell, 'The tip of the iceberg for legal technology' (*vLex Blog*, 29 July 2020) https://blog.vlex.com/the-tip-of-the-iceberg-with-legal-technology-29bd8c74bd35 accessed 28 June 2021.

7 Sven Blumberg, Jorge Machado, Henning Soller and Asin Tavakoli, 'Breaking through data-architecture gridlock to scale AI' (*McKinsey Digital,* (26 January 2021) https://www.mckinsey.com/business-functions/mckinsey-digital/our-insights/breaking-through-data-architecture-gridlock-to-scale-ai accessed 28 June 2021.

8 The New York Rules of Professional Conduct, Rule 1.6, adds 'use' to the prohibited activities: 'A lawyer shall make reasonable efforts to prevent the inadvertent or unauthorized disclosure *or use of*, or unauthorized access to, information protected' by the Rule 1.6(c), emphasis added.

9 Google Inc, 'System and method for policy-based confidentiality management,' US 2015/0026760 A1 (22 January 2015).

the reasons clients select one lawyer over another, or one firm over another, is precisely that they believe that the lawyer or firm has undertaken similar work previously'.[10] Indeed, this 'idea is at the heart of how law firms market themselves – long lists of transactions and cases, suggesting seasoning and wisdom derived from prior work (without, of course, revealing any confidences)'.[11]

It is thus clear that the adoption of legal technologies should force the legal profession consciously to face its use of client data to create a generally profitable product. This awakens the basic conflict between principles of loyalty to the individual client, including strict fiduciary and confidentiality duties to that client, and a business model based on data sharing within the firm. It should also awaken careful consideration of the future of law firms which currently benefit from cost-saving legal technologies but may be training their own replacements. As law firms use and facilitate machinery and arrangements having the express purpose to monetise client data through automated services, they are building a new industry they may not control. Data analytics firms that parse or construct legal documents without providing traditional legal advice will in all likelihood replace the 'non-advisory' tasks of the law firm.[12] These developments force the clear question: what access and use of client data are permitted?

If very liberal use were to be allowed, this could stimulate the growth of data analytics services eclipsing traditional law firms in the analysis of documents (whether contracts, pre-trail evidence or pre-merger due diligence), the filing of forms (in areas like immigration, tax, customs, trademark registration and corporate compliance) and the creation of documents (from contracts to prospectuses for initial public offerings). Such data analytics providers could easily build up their data to surpass knowledge available to even the largest law firms, giving consumers legal answers and solutions based on a vast pool of data almost as easily as a web search. If, on the other hand, a very strict rule were to be adopted so that the data of one client could not be mingled with that of another for processing, legal data analytics would be restricted primarily to the law offices of individual firms – giving inhouse counsel significant advantages over external representation. Companies generating large amounts of data about their own legal problems could create highly automated, in-house 'legal operations'[13] divisions to process legal matters with the same

---

[10] Richard Susskind, *Tomorrow's Lawyers: An Introduction to Your Future* (OUP, 2017) 28.

[11] Observation made by a partner of major international law firm interviewed for this chapter.

[12] Armour and Sako (n 3) 32–3.

[13] 'Legal expertise is only one component of the human capital input in the legal operations model, itself only one part of the overall asset mix for value capture. Profit

focus on efficiency applied by their other divisions processing information about design, manufacturing or marketing problems. In the author's opinion, however, the most likely scenario is one that respects both the tradition of law practice and the real power of the law lobby. In this scenario, a single law firm would be permitted to share all client data on the basis of a standard consent given in its contracts with clients. Firm-wide data sharing would accelerate the consolidation of the legal profession into platforms feeding on network effects.[14] The largest firms today already have extensive global networks of data,[15] and would have first-starter advantage to potentially become Amazons or Facebooks of legal services. However, many firms now feed their client data into legal technology companies that they do not own or control, and these now nascent companies could well – on the basis of capacity developed from processing such data – come to surpass those law firms in providing certain scalable services. A point could be reached where such legal technology firms will seek independence on the basis of providing better, cheaper services to the public, and how legal regulators should deal with that moment should be carefully considered.

This chapter examines the questions raised, the incentives at hand, and the possible practical results arising from the opposing forces of client data sanctity and data exploitation in a law firm. Following this introduction, section II will present an overview of legal technologies, highlighting the need of data science to access pooled data for processing through machine learning or other forms of artificial intelligence. Section III will then review the type of rules generally applicable to lawyers when handling client data while also offering an informal survey of what appears to be tacitly accepted industry practice. To provide an example of how the value of controlling client data can completely reshape an industry, section IV examines the creation of the 'indirect holding system' for securities, a watershed moment in which a change of technology caused transfer of data and ownership from the issuers of securities and their investors to the financial industry. Section V will model the potential outcomes for the legal profession of three hypothetical rules for the use of client data (strict, medium, and liberal) and their potential impact on the shape of legal services. Section VI concludes.

---

in the legal operations model is captured by enhancing efficiency with key assets in project and process management capabilities.' Ibid., 33.

[14] *See* A McAfee and E Brynjolfsson, *Machine, Platform, Crowd: Harnessing Our Digital Future* (W. W. Norton & Company, 2017) 140.

[15] Susskind (n 10) 48.

II. DATA MANAGEMENT FOR LEGAL TECHNOLOGIES

This section will lay out the data management goals of a firm whose business depends on exploiting that data. It will then outline the most popular legal technology services currently offered, the organisational arrangements through which they tend to be offered and the general problems their data accumulation appears to present. Lastly, this section will present what have been seen as the main risks of exploitation that data analytic services present for persons whose data is being collected and processed.

While there is some disagreement about exactly how many 'Vs' data management should achieve for successful analysis of information, it is clear that they include at least 'volume', 'variety' and 'velocity'.[16] For a profitable, analytical undertaking, data is 'a raw material for business, a vital economic input and source of value'.[17] Because the economic power of a data-based business derives from network effects amongst the providers, processor and users of data, such business will seek to pull in an increasing volume of data to improve its products,[18] which should attract still more users carrying even more data, creating a virtuous growth cycle. This drive to increase the amount of information under management and build on network effects is already inherent in the practice of law, and is referred to with terms like experience, depth and expertise, but the exploitation of client data is becoming much more explicit as an increasing number of law firms use machine data analytics to provide services.[19]

While most firms hitherto have stored client data in files partitioned by client (which were then merged informally by the assimilated knowledge of lawyers, or teams of lawyers, working those files), such compartmentalisation does not allow full exploitation through data processing and thus stymies the network logic of law firm as platform. Efficiency requires that the client data and work product in possession of a firm be stored, structured and managed

---

16 Samuel Wamba, et al., 'How 'big data" can make big impact: findings from a systematic review and a longitudinal case study' (2015) 165 *International Journal of Production Economics* 234–46; Francesco Ciampi, et al., 'The big data-business strategy interconnection: a grand challenge for knowledge management. A review and future perspectives' (2020) 24 *Journal of Knowledge Management* 1157–76; David Gewirtz, 'Volume, velocity, and variety: Understanding the three V's of big data' ZDNet (March 21, 2018).

17 David Olsen, *Data Mining Models* (Business Expert Press, 2nd edn, 2018) 2.

18 McAfee and Brynjolfsson (n 14) 193.

19 See e.g., J O McGinnis and R G Pearce, 'The great disruption: How machine intelligence will transform the role of lawyers in the delivery of legal services, (2014) 82 *Fordham L. Rev.* 3041, 3052.

in a way that its full *volume* and *variety* are accessible at high *velocity*. As Kelleher and Tierney explain:

> The key ingredient in any data science process is data, so it is not surprising that in many data science projects the majority of time and effort goes into finding, aggregating, and cleaning the data prior to their analysis. If a data warehouse is available in a company, then the effort and time that go into data preparation on individual data science projects is often significantly reduced.... Constructing a centralized repository of data involves more than simply dumping the data from multiple operational databases into a single database.... Extraction, transformation, and load (ETL) is the term used to describe the typical processes and tools used to support the mapping, merging, and movement of data between databases.[20]

If a firm's legacy data storage is not already designed to be accessed through ETL, business sense advises that this be replaced with 'data architecture that provides the agility to meet today's need for speed, flexibility, and innovation', including 'a data lake and data pipeline', to facilitate data processing and consumption.[21] Such amalgamation of data is necessary whether the data is to be consumed in an unstructured or structured condition.[22]

Depending on the organisation of their operations and the services they provide, legal technology suppliers and users may either accumulate data on their own, encourage law firms to manage client data in a way that maximises the volume and variety available for rapid processing, or arrange for maximum data access in-house. If a legal technology application is developed within a corporation, it may be accompanied with a complete reorganisation of how information with legal relevance is stored and accessible. Beyond accumulating all data generated by a firm into a generally available data warehouse, in a firm with many offices, the 'need for low cost scalable DBMSs [database management systems]' requires a data management system to 'replicate data across geographically remote data centres, and ensure high availability'.[23] This triggers the application of the data-handling rules discussed in section III, as applicable in each jurisdiction.

Most of the legal technology products offered today can be divided into Susskind's categories of document automation, document analysis and machine prediction.[24] Each of these depends on underlying access to data

---

20 Kelleher and Tierney (n 5) 73–4.

21 Blumberg et al. (n 7) 3–6.

22 On the distinction between unstructured and structured data and the costs involved in creating a structured database, see Kelleher and Tierney (n 5) 48–9.

23 Divyakant Agrawal, Sudipto Das and Amr El Abbadi, *Data Management in the Cloud Challenges and Opportunities* (Morgan & Claypool, 2013) 25.

24 Susskind (n 10) 45 also see McGinnis and Pearce (n 19) 3046.

in order to guide or enable algorithmic processing. Some products assemble documents, such as contracts, on the basis of information regarding the relevant contract types and components. Others analyse documents ranging from working drafts of contracts and documentary evidence reviewed pretrial, to records examined in connection with corporate transactions. Another group of products generate predictions about the potential behaviour of important actors like judges, based on past records and the current decision at hand. The operational structures through which these services are offered range from completely external – such as firms to which one submits a contract remotely for review – to those completely embedded within a law firm's or corporation's archiving, library and billing processes. A number of service providers operate from outside, straddling the data walls of many firms and apparently increasing the quality of their own technology with the improvement of their own processing systems on the basis of client data.

Examining one example of each of these arrangements, we find different ways and places in which data will be aggregated and merged. If many small firms submit draft contracts for review to the portal of an internationally available document analysis platform like LawGeex,[25] the programming applied by this firm to the documents can be expected to 'learn' from the strengths and weakness found in the contents and organisation of each contract, which means the service exploits the data submitted from each client in order to improve their service. The service explains handling of personal data that is generally in line with the GDPR,[26] but such personal data will be of little or no use to a firm seeking to develop a machine learning algorithm that conducts sophisticated reviews of contracts. To that end, data regarding configurations of contractual problems and solutions chosen for those problems will constitute the core focus and the key to the review service's attraction to potential customers. No reference is made to this data, which is the data actually valuable to the service provider, in such firm's guarantees on handling client data.[27]

---

[25] At www.lawgeex.com.

[26] For example, the European General Data Privacy Regulation defines 'personal data' to mean 'any information relating to an identified or identifiable natural person ('data subject').' Regulation (EU) 2016/679 of the European Parliament and of the Council of 27 April 2016 on the protection of natural persons with regard to the processing of personal data and on the free movement of such data, and repealing Directive 95/46/EC, L 119/1 (GDPR).

[27] 'We may receive personal data when Users use our Services by submitting legal documents (such as contracts and drafts for review).... Such data may include contact details such as business e-mail and phone number.... Specifically, we use Personal Data ... [t]o further develop, customize and improve the Services.', https://www.lawgeex.com/privacy-policy/ accessed 28 June 2021.

Similarly, if 'due diligence' information in the context of a corporate transaction is given to an external service provider for processing within its own system, such as Luminance,[28] information on contextualised problems and risks would be key to providing and improving the document analysis service. As Luminance notes, its service has been trained on the basis of concrete, labelled data and is thus in part supervised: 'By blending both supervised and unsupervised machine learning, Luminance provides lawyers with the most rigorous analysis and understanding of their documents, instantly highlighting anomalous areas.'[29] Client data known to evidence legal and economic risk in the real contexts of corporate activity can guide the data labelling that makes the supervised component of the analysis valuable. It is of little importance whether the analytical service provider takes possession of data or is given access to a warehouse controlled by the law firm. Moreover, 'personal data' is of little interest in this process; rather, the legal problems and solutions contextualised within such case data are what feeds the service, improving it not only for the client at hand but for all future clients. Although it cannot be excluded that further protections are offered in the service contract, the firm's privacy policy merely states that 'personal data' could be used for purposes including '[d]eveloping and enhancing products, services, and our infrastructure'.[30]

Total data management in connection with the provision of legal technologies may be the logical goal of legal technology's evolution, and such a service is found in the business model of Exterro, which recommends that it manage client data with Early Case Assessment (ECA) in order to pre-structure the information that will be processed in legal analytics.[31] Platform coverage of the kind provided by Exterro (Figure 3.1) is designed to facilitate the low-cost, high velocity exploitation of data, facilitating the functions indicated in the graphic reproduced from their advertising graphic.

With a platform that anticipates the delivery of legal technology services from the moment a firm captures client data, the components of that data relevant to the contemplated service – whether pre-trial discovery, due-diligence for a future sale or acquisition, or the assembly of contracts – will be identified, preserved and labelled for analysis. Because the provision of services also trains the service provider, a law firm could seek out some business activity merely to collect data that would improve its overall supply of data to train legal services applications, as do major data analytics platform like Google.

---

28 At https://www.luminance.com/ accessed 14 December 2021.

29 At https://www.luminance.com/product/diligence.html accessed 28 June 2021.

30 At https://www.luminance.com/legal.html accessed 28 June 2021.

31 This is described in its service presentation as the Exterro Platform. See https://www.exterro.com/e-discovery-software/platform accessed 14 December 2021.

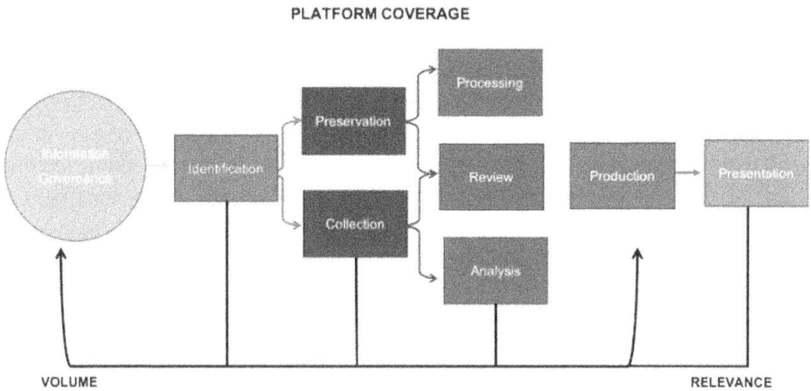

Source: Graphic reproduced from Exterro, 'E-Discovery Technology at a Glance: E-Discovery Platform Technology' (2021) https://www.exterro.com/resources/ediscovery-technology-technology-platform-white-paper accessed 28 June 2021.

Figure 3.1 *Platform coverage*

If the data management and processing is indeed performed by an external service, that service would have significant influence over what client data a law firm captures, and this could be determined by the type of future processing expected rather than the immediate needs of the client in a given representation. Such a platform would seem to entail both a merging of client data and access for the data processor (whether external or an internal IT division). At least during the first decade of legal technology's growth, such data management maneuvers would be unusual and unexpected by a law firm client, but not necessarily a violation of confidentiality as discussed in section III.

Because a firm providing legal technology services will improve the quality of its data analytics services as the volume and variety of data increase, client data will become a very valuable commodity. As remarked previously, this has also been true for centuries about human lawyers practicing law – accumulation of know-how and experience from working on a client's affairs creates experience, skill and reputation. The question for the legal profession and its clients to decide is whether this informal and tacit practice may now pass smoothly and without regulation into an industrial-scale collection and processing of that same data by machines.

Huq offers three examples of how one might understand data processing platforms to exploit data subjects (persons whose data is processed by a platform), and each of them could be understood to apply to a law firm exploiting client data with legal technologies. First, data subjects are often ignorant that their data is being collected and exploited, so that they provide an uncompensated subsidy to the data-exploiting firm.[32] While clients generally seek out lawyers because of their experience, they rarely understand at any conscious level that the details of their own case file will be used to generate better representation for other, future clients of their lawyer. The structure of a contractual arrangement like a 'credit default swap' painstakingly worked out for one client can be quickly offered to another. Second, the data processor exploits a relationship that is basically trusting, so that 'the ordinary work of human contact and interaction is seized and transformed into an information asset'.[33] For lawyers, in particular, this is true. A candid relationship between lawyer and client is necessary and robustly protected by the rules of privilege discussed in section III. A law firm might learn from and train its junior associates on interactions with clients – so that while a client is seeking only representation the firm is testing out ways to provide more services with less man hours, increasing revenue. Third, a data subject's own information can be used by the data processor to offer services that are either not in the subject's best interest or are offered at unfavourable rates.[34] This is true in two ways for law firms: commercial or legal solutions devised in connection with one client can make their way into the market generally via a law firm and benefit competitors, and a lawyer with hourly billing could potentially charge the first client for which such solution is created a far higher total fee than is asked from later clients who are supplied the solution once it has become more or less a standard form.

III. GENERAL RULES ON CLIENT DATA FOR THE LEGAL PROFESSION

With the aggregation and use of client data becoming ever more pronounced and explicit through the introduction of data analytics into law firms, the ethical limits on such practice – if any – should be explored. The matter can be divided into two, interrelated issues: first, it is clear that client data must be kept confidential and its security protected against unauthorised access, but

---

[32] Aziz Huq, 'The Public Trust in Data' (forthcoming, 2022) *Georgetown Law Journal* 18, available at https://ssrn.com/abstract=3794780. Huq cites on this point, Paul M. Schwartz, 'Property, privacy, and personal data' [2003] 117 *Harvard Law Review* 2056, 2079.

[33] Huq (n 32), citing Kim Doyle, 'Facebook, Whatsapp and the commodification of affective labour' (2015) 48 *Communications, Politics and Culture* 51, 61–2.

[34] Huq (n 32) 19, citing Leanne Roderick, 'Discipline and Power in the Digital Age: The Case of the U.S. Consumer Data Broker Industry' (2014) 40 *Critical Sociology* 729, 732.

second, the law takes no position on a lawyer exploiting the 'transactional' information found in client data or related work product without compensating the client. It is wholly possible to extend requirements on the sanctity of client data and work product to cover all such exploitation, and this is arguably done by the European General Data Privacy Regulation,[35] but this step does not appear to have been taken by any legislature or professional body – in the United States or the European Union – regulating the legal profession, through either law specifically applicable to lawyers or their professional ethics.

Confidentiality requirements for lawyers' handling of client information date back to Roman and early Common Law,[36] and stand at the very heart of the legal profession. The confidentiality of client data is protected both by law establishing privilege and by very specific rules of practice for the legal profession. As discussed below, these latter rules have been expressly interpreted in the US to address an increasing cyberthreat. The rule of attorney-client privilege protects against both voluntary and compelled disclosure of client data, although the protection against compulsion is more well-known. As Gergacz points out: 'First, the attorney has an ethical duty to refrain from disclosing confidences. The client is reassured that personal problems or business plans will not become "backyard barbecue talk." Additionally, the privilege creates a legal barrier to compelled disclosure.'[37] Privilege prevents the attorney from being 'perceived as a potential threat to the client's interests'.[38]

While the general thrust of privilege is understood by many to focus on *compelled* disclosure of client data, a lawyer's duty of confidentiality is more straightforward. For example, the American Bar Association's Model Rules of Professional Conduct provide: 'A lawyer shall not reveal information relating to the representation of a client unless the client gives informed consent.'[39] As law firms have increasingly come into the crosshairs of hackers,[40] the ABA has interpreted its general professional conduct rule on lawyer competence to include a requirement that, 'a lawyer should keep abreast of changes in the law and its practice, including the benefits and risks associated with relevant

---

[35] The GDPR applies to 'processing of data' (art 1) and defines 'processing' to include 'any operation or set of operations which is performed on personal data or on sets of personal data … such as … structuring … adaptation … retrieval, consultation [or] use (art 4(2)).'

[36] John Gergacz, *Attorney-Corporate Client Privilege* (Thomson Reuters, 2021) s 1:4.

[37] Ibid s 1:7.

[38] Ibid s 1:8.

[39] American Bar Association, Model Rules of Professional Conduct, r 1.6(a).

[40] See e.g., Mary Ellen Egan, 'Cyberthreats 101' *ABA Journal* (1 March 2018).

technology',[41] and this is understood to create a specific duty to protect client data against cyberthreat.[42]

Hard law has also joined such rules in the shape of the California Consumer Privacy Act of 2018, which provides: 'A business that collects a consumer's personal information shall implement reasonable security procedures and practices appropriate to the nature of the personal information to protect the personal information from unauthorised or illegal access, destruction, use, modification, or disclosure.'[43] This parallels the GDPR 'integrity and confidentiality' provisions requiring that a data controller store data with 'appropriate security',[44] and 'implement appropriate technical and organisational measures ... in order to ... protect the rights of data subjects.'[45]

While the GDPR also protects against *exploitation* of a client's data (see reference to 'processing' above), neither US law nor ABA rules include specific provisions on the topic. Indeed, practice seems to condone such exploitation. Clients understand that lawyers learn from representing them and others before them, gaining 'experience' and 'expertise'. Nevertheless, Armour and Sako, perhaps with more reference to UK law, assume that client consent to the merging and use of data will be necessary.[46] While most clients may not consciously grasp that the exact work product they pay a law firm to create on their behalf will feed into work for another client of the same firm, some clients do specifically protect against it in the contract of representation with the firm.[47] Other firms anticipate such reservations, by including the following type of provision in their standard contract with clients:

> We shall retain ownership of the copyright and all other intellectual property rights in the product of the Services, whether oral or tangible, and ownership of our working papers. You shall acquire ownership of any product of the Services in its tangible form on payment of our Charges for any such product. For the purposes of delivering services to you or other clients, we shall be entitled to use, develop

---

41 ABA Rule of Professional Conduct, 1.1, comment.

42 John G. Loughnane, *ABA Techreport 2020, 2020 Cybersecurity* (19 October 2020).

43 California Consumer Privacy Act of 2018, s 1798.100(e).

44 GDPR, art. 5(1)(f).

45 GDPR, art. 25(1).

46 '[L]egal services providers might have the potential to scale analysis of data provided by many clients, provided of course that clients are amenable to sharing data.' Armour and Sako (n 3) 37.

47 One lawyer working in a leading financial services law firm responded in interview to the author that, 'Certain clients don't want their documents to be available to all attorneys at the firm and if negotiated as part of the engagement, that wish will be respected.'

> or share with each other knowledge, experience and skills of general application gained through performing the Services.[48]

For the GDPR, the above provision would likely constitute 'consent'[49] to processing of the client's data through a legal technologies application that combines contracts written for all clients, problems found in pre-trial or pre-acquisition document analysis of the firms' clients, positions and outcomes of settlement negotiations on the basis of the cases of the firms' clients. It is unclear, however, whether a provision of this kind offered on a take-it-or-leave-it basis would be consistent with the kind of fiduciary duty in the holding of data that Balkin has ascribed to lawyers.[50]

In offering a model of data use that would control exploitation by the Facebooks of the world, Balkin refers to the fiduciary duty that he attributes to professionals like lawyers. Because of this duty, a lawyer 'must keep their clients' interests in mind and act in their clients' interests,' and they may not 'harm or undermine the … client, or create conflicts of interest with the … client.'[51] Such standard fiduciary duty would also force a fiduciary to account to the beneficiary for any (side) profit made on the basis of the relationship. Unfortunately, on the topic of exploiting data against a client's interest, Balkin restricts himself to the painfully clear hypothetical of a physician who posts his patient's medical records and photos in an art gallery, calling it free expression ('Crazy Stuff My Patients Say').[52] He of course concludes that the fiduciary duty would not allow this disclosure of client data to be seen as constitutionally protected speech. However, a much more realistic hypothetical would be the same physician merging all client data into a data lake used to train the machine learning algorithm of a diagnosis application.[53] Such applications are valuable both to the physician concerned and to society. May the physician exploit client data in this way? It seems that Balkin does not see this as problematic, and he observes with regard to the big data intermediaries:

> Because personal data is a key source of wealth in the digital economy, information fiduciaries should be able to monetise some uses of personal data … What informa-

---

48 Contractual provision for retention of services for a law firm interviewed by the author.

49 See GDPR art 6(1)(a).

50 Jack Balkin, 'Information fiduciaries and the First Amendment', (2016) 49 *U.C. Davis L. Rev.* 1183; and Jack Balkin, 'The fiduciary model of privacy' (2020) 134 *Harvard Law Review Forum* 11.

51 Balkin, ibid., 1208.

52 Ibid., 1210–11.

53 David Townend, 'EU laws on privacy in genomic databases and biobanking' (2016) 44 *Journal of Law, Medicine & Ethics* 128, 132.

> tion fiduciaries may not do is use the data in unexpected ways to the disadvantage of people who use their services or in ways that violate some other important social norm.[54]

Although there is no question taking 'a key source of wealth' from one's client would 'violate an important social norm' in most societies, as well as fiduciary duties, it is understandable that Balkin overlooks this point as his argument focuses on privacy and the responsible use of information by the major information intermediaries, seen primarily from the point of view of constitutional law.

If we follow Balkin's assumption that 'personal data is a key source of wealth', a position with which the GDPR and most commentators agree,[55] we can reformulate the question: Should a lawyer either account to a client for profits or obtain express approval from that client for extracting the value of work product and case details acquired from that client to develop or improve a legal technology application? If data is an asset, the rule is quite clear. Legal ethics are in uniform agreement that a lawyer should not use or even mix a client's assets with her own absent instruction or other very good reason: 'A lawyer shall hold property of clients or third persons that is in a lawyer's possession in connection with a representation separate from the lawyer's own property.'[56] Further, if we take seriously the argument that a lawyer owes a client fiduciary duties, then the general rule is that the fiduciary may not profit from its relationship with the beneficiary beyond the properly disclosed fee earned.[57]

From the above, we can conclude the following. Lawyers must keep client information confidential, but this can be waived with client consent. Lawyers must not use client property or mix it with their own unless otherwise instructed. While most commentators agree that data is valuable, and even arguably property, the general consensus is that lawyers may learn from accumulated information acquired from each client, and there is no evidence of a client seeking judicial remedy against a lawyer for generally exploiting know-how gained in representation to improve her practice. There is evidence, however, that some sophisticated clients prohibit such use of work product deriving from their case. Thus, silence on the issue cannot be said to constitute express approval for law firms to use client data as a basis for generating further revenue. As noted above, some firms do expressly provide in their contract with a client for representation that the firm shall acquire a right in all

---

54 Balkin [2016] (n 50) 1227.

55 Huq (n 32) with further references.

56 ABA Rules of Professional Conduct, r 1.5(a).

57 See e.g., *Regal (Hastings) Ltd. v. Gulliver and Others* [1967] 2 A.C. 134.

work product created in connection with the client. Thus, if such a contractual provision exists, the only hurdle remaining would be to ensure that the consent is sufficient (voluntary on the basis of complete information), particularly in that it must overcome the restrictions of a fiduciary duty.

To some lawyers looking happily toward a monetisation of their client data, this discussion may appear relatively unnecessary. After all, if clients now assume that lawyers gain experience and knowhow through representation, it would be against accepted custom to change this, even if the processing of client data and work product takes place on an industrial scale. The transition from intuitive and informal aggregation and exploitation of client data to systematic pooling and algorithmic combing is in many ways comparable to the transition we have seen from human to machine facial recognition, the permissibility of which is also debated. For lawyers who see no problem in connection with the machine exploitation of client data, the real concern will arise when law firms have transferred enough client information to data analytics companies so that such companies no longer need law firms as a data source to train their applications. As in other instances of automation, particularly in the digital platform economy, such companies will easily outstrip lawyers for certain tasks, and they will have been trained at low cost and under very little supervision.

If clients now object to use of their data and the attorney work product derived from it in this new context, or if law firms without controlling stakes in legal technology firms do not wish freely to train their potential replacements, it would be a relatively simple matter to negotiate compensation in the form of a fee discount or license for use of the same in legal technology. Google provides us with a search engine, email, a digital assistant, and cloud storage free of cost in order to analyse our behaviour for the purpose of selling advertising and designing better artificial intelligence products.[58] Why should lawyers or their service providers not do the same?

Nevertheless, the history of the securities market shows that once a detour of data ownership is in place, it can be extremely difficult to restore control of information to its owners. Struggles over the control of data can change the shape of an industry, and much is at stake in the attorney-client relationship and the role of lawyers in society. Section IV offers as example a description of how the creation of the 'indirect holding system' for trading securities led to a transfer of information about shareholders from listed companies to financial institutions and a transfer of ownership in the relevant securities from investors to these same financial institutions. Despite close regulatory

---

[58] J L M de la Iglesia and J E Gayo, 'Doing business by selling free services', in Miltiadis Lytras et al. (eds) *Web 2.0: The Business Model* (Springer, 2009).

scrutiny and promises to the contrary, neither the data nor the full ownership has been restored to corporations even after the problem necessitating the shift was solved.

IV. BREAKING LEGACY DATA MANAGEMENT FOR INVESTORS IN LISTED COMPANIES

A predicable moment in the development of legal technology is that at which non-lawyer service providers, fed on client data received from law firms happy to outsource cheaply, surpass those law firms in competence on some basic services. At that pivotal moment, a transition could take place. This transition could be comparable to that which has taken place in the corporate world as financial technology exceeded the information processing capacity of traditional methods.

Corporate law provides a good arrangement of data for transparency and communication between investors and issuers. Ownership of data is shared between shareholders and the issuer of the securities held. US corporations always use registered (rather than bearer) shares,[59] so shareholder names and contact details are registered with the corporation. This registration is what legally constitutes the status of shareholder in corporate law.[60] Notices for annual meetings or rights offerings are given and dividends are paid to these persons at the contact addresses provided.[61] If one counts from incorporation of the Dutch *Vereenigde Oostindische Compagnie*,[62] this method of data management has served issuers and investors well for over 400 years.

In the late 1960s, when volumes of trading on US stock exchanges started to exceed the capacity to transfer shares in the traditional way,[63] many found it was time for a change. The ordinary transfer of a registered share under commercial law requires (i) endorsement of the share certificate, (ii) delivery of endorsed certificate to the buyer, (iii) the cancellation of that certificate and

---

59 A search in the library 'All States' on WestLaw for the words 'bearer share' only yields cases referring to foreign companies. A similar finding also results from an examination of the corporate law statutes of the states of Delaware, New York, California, Illinois and Texas, as well as the Model Business Corporation Act.

60 See e.g., Delaware General Corporation Law s 219(c); *Williams v. Sterling Oil of Oklahoma, Inc.* 267 A.2d 630, 634 (Del. Ch. 1970).

61 See e.g., Delaware General Corporation Law s 219.

62 See G L Balk et al, *The Archives of the Dutch East India Company (VOC) and the Local Institutions in Batavia (Jakarta)* (Brill, 2007).

63 US Securities and Exchange Commission, *Study of Unsafe and Unsound Practices of Brokers and Dealers* (December 1971) 28. Also *see* Chris Welles, *The Last Days of the Club* (Dutton, 1975) 172 and Donald T. Regan, *A View from the Street* (New American Library, 1972) 104.

creation of a new one for the buyer by the issuer's transfer agent, and (iv) entry of the buyer as shareholder in the register of shareholders. Because this transfer process was too time-consuming and legally cumbersome for increasing trading volumes, market participants sought a shortcut. The choice made by leading banks and endorsed by regulators and legislators was to *omit transferring the shares altogether*, by putting them all in the vaults and in the registered name of a central securities depository (CSD) and just transferring claims against custody accounts held with that CSD.[64] The process is referred to as 'immobilisation', and the transactions on accounts containing immobilised shares are called 'book-entry' transfers.[65] Immobilisation meant, however, that all data about shareholders was taken away from issuers and legal property in shares of stock was taken away from investors. Immobilisation became the dominant model for securities settlement globally.[66]

This epochal transfer of data and property was ordered by the US Congress in the name of efficiency and at the recommendation of the largest banks.[67] However, it was not the least disruptive model discussed at the time. The least disruptive model was a distributed network of electronic ledgers controlled by issuers, the 'Transfer Agent Depository,' or TAD,[68] which would keep data and ownership in the hands of issuers and investors. The SEC promised to correct the matter as soon as technology permitted.

Twenty years later, with the internet now available for general use, issuers' transfer agents proposed a descendent of the TAD system, the 'direct registration system' (DRS), to restore data to its previous, transparent distribution.[69] Although the SEC did allow a pilot DRS to become operational in 1996,[70] the brokers and banks who had fallen into possession of share ownership and data

---

64 Securities Acts Amendments of 1975, Pub. L. 94-29, June 4, 1975, 89 Stat. 97 (1975).

65 Committee on Payment and Settlement Systems [CPSS] & Technical Committee of the International Organization of Securities Commissions [IOSCO], *Recommendations for Securities Settlement Systems* (2001) 45–7.

66 Ibid.

67 Backers of this model were the Banking and Securities Industry Committee (BASIC), which was chaired by Morgan Guaranty Chairman John M. Meyer (one of the creators of Euroclear, a successful depository-based settlement entity located in Brussels). Peter Norman, *Plumbers and Visionaries: Securities Settlement and Europe's Financial Market* (Wiley, 2007) 141.

68 US Securities and Exchange Commission, *Final Report of SEC on the Practice of Recording the Ownership of Securities in the Records of the Issuers in Other Than the Name of the Beneficial Owner of Such Securities* (1976) 41.

69 See Concept Release, Transfer Agents Operating Direct Registration System, Exchange Act Release No. 34-35038, 59 Fed. Reg. 63652, 63653 (8 December 1994).

70 Self-Regulatory Organizations; The Depository Trust Company; Order Granting Accelerated Approval of a Proposed Rule Change Relating to the Procedure to

in the 1970s argued that the DRS could be stable only if integrated into the CSD[71] (which they owned and managed). The SEC concluded that retaining CSD control of transfers created a 'more efficient mechanism',[72] and the data was kept in the hands of the financial industry. This was despite the fact that paper certificates – the cause of the original problem in the 1960s – were being phased out and are no longer used on US securities exchanges. To this day, nearly all shareholder data is controlled by CSDs in major markets, and those CSDs or their nominees are the legal owners of shares traded.

A lesson the rise of the indirect holding system offers for other industries is that a 'temporary' transfer of even the most fundamental data can become permanent. In the 1960s, when technology triggered a major disruption in securities trading, leading banks were well-placed to recommend that data be transferred to them. The systematic ramifications for those affected were argued to be merely technical in nature and the value of the data in question was not clearly understood. Once the transfer was complete, powerful interests cemented this substantial reorganisation of data and ownership into the globally dominant model. It then became all but impossible to return the data back to its owners after the import of the data transfer became clear.

The goal of any participant in such a battle for data would be to make the necessary data endogenous to their own processing operations by bringing it under their control. For the case of law firm client data, the current interested parties are the clients themselves, their lawyers, and the service providers which are expert in data management. Each of parties will have or create a stake for treating client data or work product as their own, with clients seeking separation, firms merging data within their partnerships, and the processors having an incentive to treat all data in a given area as a fungible mass. The logic of efficiency and network effects supports the growth and increasing importance of external legal technologies firms, as the more data they absorb (whether from lawyers or retail users), the better their products become. For the financial industry, the rearrangement required a pressing need and a change in status and nomenclature as shareholders who wanted to receive information

---

Establish a Direct Registration System, Exchange Act Release No. 34-37931, 61 *Fed. Reg.* 58600, 58601 (15 November 1996).

[71] Self-Regulatory Organizations; The Depository Trust Company; Notice of Filing of Amendment and Order Granting Accelerated Approval of a Proposed Rule Change Relating to Implementation of the Profile Modification System Feature of the Direct Registration System, Exchange Act Release No. 34-41862, 64 *Fed. Reg.* 51162, 51163 (21 September 1999).

[72] Ibid., 51165.

from issuers were turned into 'non-objecting beneficial owners' ('NOBOS'),[73] and issuers became clients of 'corporate action services' in order to communicate with these NOBOS.[74] Possible futures for the legal industry are considered in section V.

V. LEGAL TECHNOLOGIES AND POSSIBLE LAW FIRM FUTURES

Like the financial industry, where 'indirect holding' became the norm and the 'quants' began to replace traditional brokers over 30 years ago,[75] the legal profession is largely a data management industry in which success depends on finding the right data, discerning its meaning, and applying rules to data or grasping the shape of future trends through its analysis. Also like the financial industry, the legal services industry is tightly regulated, so that future development propelled by technological change can be strongly channelled by rules. Currently, rules allow complete and unrestricted access to important data like statutes, judicial decisions, regulations and publicly filed documents. The personal data of clients and much of the work attorneys produce for them, by contrast, must be kept confidential absent client consent to release it, and disclosure may be successfully resisted even when sought in judicial proceedings. In the middle sit contracts and other solutions designed by lawyers for one client and commonly used in advising another. Exploiting this pool of information creates some of the most valuable data for legal technologies. At times, its use is contractually permitted and at other times it is contractually prohibited. However, no conscious public decision has been made on who may lay claim to its collection, processing and monetisation. No clear regulation prohibits its use by legal technology companies to create systems of labelling data or otherwise train their machine learning. For the sake of discussion, this chapter divides the possible future rules on such use into three, stylised scenarios.

---

[73] Originally adopted by Exchange Act Release No. 34-20021, now codified at 17 CFR § 240.14b-1(b)(3)(i) in connection with § 240.14a-13(b)-(c).

[74] See Michael Simmons and Elaine Dalgleish, *Corporate Actions: A Guide to Securities Event Management* (Wiley, 2006).

[75] In 1986

> Shaw moved to Morgan Stanley as vice-president for automated proprietary trading technology, or as he describes his role in APT, 'the guy who did the technology there.' What interested him most, though, was the idea that quantitative and computational methods could be used to beat the market ... he saw how a different sort of research project could search more systematically for undetected anomalies in the financial markets—an academic model, brought to Wall Street.

Andrew Lo, *Adaptive Markets: Financial Evolution at the Speed of Thought* (Princeton University Press, 2016) 237.

The first scenario is the least problematic as the pooling and use of own data is already clearly possible today: a data subject is free to collect, process and use *its own* data. That is, a corporation or other organisation can collect the data generated in its dealings with the world, including any contracts and court filings, identify and label items understood to have value, and review, analyse or apply solutions derived from such data to address future legal problems or relationships. A large corporation would be able to generate and organise sufficient volume of data in-house. Armour and Sako also seem to find in-house activity of a corporation less problematic by stressing that the corporation is more amenable to technology-heavy 'legal operations', while traditional law partnerships are organisationally oriented toward the 'advisory' business model,[76] although they do not address the question of data ownership at any length.

From the point of view of legal technologies, a large corporation would have little or no interest in retaining and using either the personal data or the legal solutions of its customers or business partners. It would be party to any contract, legal proceeding or corporate transaction, and as such would have an independent claim on the related data's use. If the volume of data generated by the corporation alone permitted useful labelling to guide supervised machine learning for future processing, it need only build or license processing technology. Once a system of this type is in place, the corporation's legal operations may be much more efficient than with previous staffing. This could lead the firm to downsize its general counsel office and depend on outside representation for uniquely occurring complex matters or, on the contrary, increase its in-house capacity to reduce its general reliance on external representation. If a corporation licenses a legal technology service rather than the technology itself, the use question would then arise with regard to its data applied to improve the service's processing capabilities, a question addressed in scenario three, below.

The second scenario is perhaps the least likely in the near future, given the political role and standing of the legacy legal services industry. If legal technology applications like DoNotPay[77] were to become so popular that the monopoly of the legal profession came to be challenged as an untenable cartel, then governments could approve a regulatory climate in which legal data is treated like any other data, under laws like the California Consumer Privacy Act of 2018. With the legal profession's monopoly on representation removed,

---

[76] Armour and Sako (n 3) 36.

[77] This is a phone and web application that contains the basic steps for simple administrative proceedings like traffic fines or contract problems like the cancellation of services. See https://donotpay.com/ accessed 14 December 2021.

data analytics services like LawGeex, Luminance and Exterro could directly collect client data and grow to a size that far eclipses any traditional law firm in activities like the analysis of documents (whether contracts, pre-trial evidence or pre-merger due diligence), the filing of forms (in areas like immigration, tax, customs, trademark registration and corporate compliance) and the assembly of documents (from contracts to prospectuses for initial public offerings). The open flow of data could rival that now available in the financial markets, leading to even better analytical services and a paradigm shift for law within the economy. It is realistic to compare a potential growth of algorithmic legal representation to the development of algorithmic trading in the financial industry.[78] As data volume and network effects create positive growth reinforcement, legal services could well take on a whole new meaning for society. Consumers would have solutions to their legal problems almost as easily as undertaking a web search, and the solutions they receive could be based on experience exceeding even the best lawyer by a quantum of magnitude.

While such a world could potentially arise smoothly in China – given its strong central government, weak legal profession, and comparatively young legacy legal services industry[79] – it is a very unlikely future for the US or Europe. Rather, one should expect a third scenario in which a conservative regulatory environment largely tracking current client expectations allows law firms to slowly build powerful legal technology services that piggyback on existing licensing. If a single partnership or other sanctioned association of lawyers is permitted to share all client data on the basis of one standard consent – or perhaps absence of objection – embedded in its contract for representation, a firm-internal data lake could be formed. If current, albeit nascent, practice continues, firms will allow external service providers to train their own applications on such data lakes. If regulators wake up to this activity, they might make a conscious decision to prohibit such exploitation of client data by external service providers not under the control of licensed lawyers. If that is done, larger firms with greater resources would be the initial home of legal technology firms.

These firms would have sufficient internal data to create a critical mass for modelling and training legal technology applications, as well as the funds necessary to support the creation of such applications. An example in recent years

---

[78] Both activities involve processing data with professional skill on the basis of knowledge gained through experience. The more data about a type of situation available, the easier it is to generalize behavior in that situation to algorithmic patterns that can be run in computers. Irene Aldridge, *High-Frequency Trading: A Practical Guide to Algorithmic Strategies and Trading Systems* (Wiley, 2nd edn, 2013) 9–10.

[79] See e.g., Lu Wang, 'Legal Tech in China' in Markus Hartung et al (eds) *Legal Tech: How Technology is Changing the Legal World* (Beck, 2018).

is the backing of Luminance by the firm of Slaughter and May.[80] Large firms acting as first-starters would be able to leverage their size to build superior data warehouses and better legal technology applications, attracting more clients and data. If regulation were to restrict data use to a group of law partners, legal technology applications would not – as is now done – straddle law firms, but rather be contained within those firms which could afford to develop or license the technology.

In a world with such regulation, the problem then becomes the external providers which are not operated within a firm, but process data for a number of law firms. They are neither licensed to practice law nor subject to the confidentiality regime that binds lawyers. However, lawyers do now feed them the client data and work product they need to develop and train their applications. Law firms do this because the services are cheap and useful. As already noted, if lawyers are permitted to continue sharing client data with such service providers, increasing the quality of their service while only extracting a promise to protect personal data, these lawyers would not only arguably fail to meet their duties to clients, but also train their eventual replacement.

As outlined in the history of the financial system takeover of corporate data, a moment could arrive in which society would choose a cheap analytics solution based on vast amounts of information over a traditional lawyer constrained by human limitations. However, this prospect was discussed under scenario two, above, and it is highly unlikely that any developed jurisdiction would consciously choose such a result in the near future. Rather, they would likely fall into it by accident, with law firms gradually building the legal technology companies until some event triggers a shift, as with the creation of the indirect holding system, which was caused by the strong increase of trading volumes during the 1960s.

If legal technology continues on its current course under the radar of any careful regulatory oversight, the transition from legacy law to legal technology could certainly resemble the watershed presented in section III. It should be noted that once the financial industry took over the data and proprietary position that had been in position for nearly 400 years between stock corporations and their investors, things did not return to the *status quo*. It would be preferable that such threshold be crossed with eyes open, rather than in a blind rush to maximize partner returns, waiting to repair any breakdown or surge in unlicensed practice after-the-fact.

Data analytics and traditional rules on the professions protecting client information are creating a major point of 'systemic stress' for lawyers. The coevolution of the professions and new data services now often occurs when

---

80 Law Society, *Lawtech Adoption Research* (February 2019) 30.

a technologically savvy external service dips into law firm data, perhaps even taking control of a law firm's data management in the name of more efficient warehousing. Such external services are probably improving the quality of legal practice, and are in most cases providing analytical capability that lawyers cannot. However, legal technology is building a future empire with bricks bought and paid for by law firm clients, and working toward a moment when those clients may be better served to transfer their business to the legal analytics company rather than stay with the lawyers who designed the solutions on which the legal technology algorithms were trained.

VI. CONCLUSIONS

This chapter begins discussion of an issue which has received little attention but lies at the core of legal technologies. We are all familiar with the need for data privacy. We are also familiar with the need for data security, and this increasingly means cybersecurity. Legal technology raises the question of *data exploitation*, as it is built on data containing solutions, like contract clauses or corporate control arrangements, and case data containing the kinds of problems found in pre-trial discovery or due diligence. Real data of this kind allows labelling for supervised machine learning and offers the best training ground for unsupervised machine learning. The valuable configurations of facts offered by real client case files would be almost impossible to build in the laboratory. Clients provide these facts and pay for the work product that contains solutions addressing their real-world contexts. Should lawyers be free to build new and highly profitable legal technology services on this data? What level of control and compensation should clients be given? Is it good for the future of the legal profession that lawyers intentionally or accidentally build non-lawyer legal technologies companies by allowing them to train on client data and related work product?

It appears likely that consensual use, along the lines of what some firms currently practice and what is required by the GDPR, will be the position taken by legislatures and bar associations – if the matter is addressed at all. A further point for consideration is to compensate clients for use of their data and work product through fee discounts and licenses. Once arrangements have been made for fair treatment of clients, law firms and their regulatory bodies should reflect on the current trajectory of legal technologies. Law firms are increasingly using external, non-lawyer legal technology services and feeding them the client data they need to grow and stabilise. This may generate short-term cost savings, but the likely end point of this process will be for such services to replace lawyers, at least for non-advisory, document- or rule-oriented activities. As many types of technology services could not develop without training on real client data, this development should not be pursued blindly. Rather well-informed choices should be made about use of the data to train legal technologies and whether such technologies should be kept within law firms or permitted to eventually outgrow and surpass them.

4. Data protection in the big data era: The broken informed consent regime and the way forward

Yueh-Ping (Alex) Yang[1]

I. INTRODUCTION

The world has evolved into a data-driven world thanks to the development of big data technologies. BigTech companies, such as the F-A-A-N-G (Facebook, Apple, Amazon, Netflix, and Google) in the United States or the B-A-T (Baidu, Alibaba, and Tencent) in China, operate digital platforms to collect data of their platform consumers and employ big data technologies to improve their capacity in targeted promotion or advertisement. Financial institutions, such as banks or insurance companies, collect their customers' data and use big data technologies to improve their analysis of their customers' credit ratings or financial preferences. Even the government, such as law enforcement and financial regulators, collects citizens' data and employs big data technologies to strengthen their regulatory and supervisory capacity. Data processing[2] has become unavoidable in this modern world.

---

[1] Part of this chapter was published in the Conference on FinTech, Governance, and Sustainability: Legal Obstacles and Regulatory Challenges hosted by the University of Exeter School of Law on May 29, 2020. The author would like to thank Dr. Joseph Lee for hosting this conference. The author would also like to thank the assistance provided by Yi-Hsiang Huang and Jhen-Teng Hung to the author's study.

[2] In this chapter, the term 'data processing' follows the definition under General Data Protection Regulation – Regulation (EU) 2016/679 of the European Parliament and of the Council of 27 April 2016 on the protection of natural persons with regard to the processing of personal data and on the free movement of such data, and repealing Directive 95/46/EC (General Data Protection Regulation) [2016] OJ L119/32 (GDPR) art 4(2), which refers to:

> any operation or set of operations which are performed on personal data or sets of personal data, whether or not by automated means, such as collection, recording, organization, structuring, storage, adaptation or alteration, retrieval,

Big data technologies, however, have an inherent conflict with data protection laws. As a principle, modern data protection laws require data controllers[3] to obtain the 'consent' of the data subject before processing the data that involves personal data.[4] Moreover, such consent must be adequately informed, meaning that data controllers must inform data subjects of the information related to the data processing, such as the controller's identity and the processing purposes.[5] Whilst this 'informed consent' principle confirms the data subject's autonomy in her data, it necessarily imposes additional time, labour, and cost on data processing. For big data technologies, which feature the processing of a massive volume of data, the incurred cost is even higher.

The informed consent regime, however, is on the verge of collapse. The majority of data subjects simply accept the terms and conditions for processing their data without carefully reading them. Even if on rare occasions they do read them, they rarely take them into serious account when making their consumption decision. Accordingly, in the real world, the informed consent regime serves little, if any, data protection function.[6] In contrast, data controllers are using informed consent to cover their abusive data processing. BigTech companies, for instance, legitimise their large-scale processing of consumers' data based on unfavourable data processing clauses to which their consumers blindly consent.[7] Eventually, the informed consent regime imposes an unneglectable cost on big data technologies in the name of data protection, but its protective effect is minimal.

In this chapter, I attempt to rebalance the development of big data technologies and data protection by proposing an alternative model to the informed consent regime. In section II, I review the development of big data technologies and analyse how the informed consent requirement under modern data protection laws restricts the development. In section III, I discuss how the informed consent regime fails to accomplish its objective to protect personal data based on the observation of neoclassical economics and behavioural economics. In section IV, I review the proposals on the table that attempt to improve

---

consultation, use, disclosure by transmission, dissemination or otherwise making available, alignment or combination, restriction, erasure or destruction.

3 In this chapter, the term 'controller' follows the definition under GDPR art 4(7), which refers to: 'the natural or legal person, public authority, agency or other body which, alone or jointly with others, determines the purposes and means of the processing of personal data'.

4 *See* GDPR, art 6.1(a).

5 *See* GDPR, Recital 42.4.

6 For a similar observation, *see generally* John A Rothchild, 'Against Notice and Choice: The Manifest Failure of the Proceduralist Paradigm to Protect Privacy Online (or Anywhere Else)' (2018) 66 *Cleveland St L Rev* 559.

7 For a comprehensive survey, ibid., 621–6.

the informed consent regime and put forward my public-private-partnership model that contains a public template proposal and an enhanced internal control proposal. I finally conclude this chapter in section V. I anticipate that the proposed alternative model may enhance data protection and facilitate the adoption of big data technologies, creating a win-win outcome for both consumers and the data economy.

II. BIG DATA TECHNOLOGIES AND DATA PROTECTION ISSUES

A. Informational Asymmetry and Big Data Technologies

Informational asymmetry is a typical cause of market failure.[8] Taking financial markets, for instance, the inherent informational asymmetry in financial markets leads to at least two significant problems: adverse selection and moral hazard. Adverse selection refers to the problem created by asymmetric information before the transaction occurs. That is, potential financial consumers who are the most likely to produce undesirable outcomes are often the ones that most actively seek out a transaction, which may reduce the incentive of financial institutions to engage in transactions.[9] Moral hazard, in contrast, refers to the problem created by asymmetric information after the transaction occurs. That is, the risk that financial consumers might engage in activities undesirable from the viewpoint of financial institutions.[10] These informational asymmetry problems prevent transaction parties from making informed transactional decisions, which plagues the market economy's functioning.

Recent development in big data technologies has the potential to mitigate the informational asymmetry in the market. Big data technologies refer to technologies that significantly increase the '4 Vs' of data management, i.e., volume, variety, velocity, and validity.[11] In terms of volume, big data technologies can process data sets whose orders of magnitude are larger than those accommodated by a common spreadsheet application. In terms of variety, big data technologies can process more data varieties, ranging from structured tabular data to unstructured web content such as social media posts. In terms of velocity, big data technologies significantly reduce the time between data

---

8 Robert Cooter and Thomas Ulen, *Law and Economics* (6th edn, Berkeley Law Books 2016) 41–42.

9 Frederic S Mishkin, *The Economics of Money, Banking, and Financial Markets* (10th edn, Pearson 2013) 39–40.

10 Ibid., 40–41.

11 *See* Simone de Castri and others, 'The SupTech Generations' (2019) 19 *FSI Insights* 1, 4.

collection and data generation and the time needed for turning data into reports or actions. In terms of validity, big data technologies also enhance the quality of data by establishing consistent metadata standards.[12] In general, big data technologies encompass numerous technologies, including data lake, web portal, chatbot, application programming interfaces ('APIs'), data cubes, web scraper, cloud computing, distributed ledger technology ('DLT'), robotic processing automation ('RPA'), dashboards, text mining, machine learning, geographic information systems ('GIS'), etc., to enable and govern the collection, processing, storage, analysis, and visualisation of data.[13]

Big data technologies have the potential to make the market more transparent. Businesses may employ them to assess their consumers' product preferences and make the promotion efforts more targeted. Financial institutions may use them to evaluate customers' credit risk and thus enhance the risk management capacity. Even the regulator may employ them to assess the market's specific risk and improve supervisory capacity.[14] In sum, by enhancing the data analysis capacity, big data technologies help reduce the market's information barriers and improve market function.

B. Informed Consent: The Core of Modern Data Protection Laws

The functioning of big data technologies requires a key ingredient, that is, the data. However, data processing, including data collection and use, is not without limit. Modern data protection laws confirm individuals' data rights and set out rules for governing data processing. These rules, in turn, pose high costs on the application of big data technologies.

Modern data protection laws focus more on the protection of personal data. Whilst the exact definition of personal data differs in different jurisdictions, it, in general, refers to any information relating to an identified or identifiable natural person.[15] Under this definition, a crucial element of personal data is 'an identified or identifiable natural person'. Any data that refers to an identifier of a natural person, such as a name, an identification number, location data, an online identifier, or any factors specific to the physical, physiological, genetic, mental, economic, cultural, or social identity of that natural person, is subject to data protection laws.[16]

---

[12] Ibid.

[13] Ibid. (n 11) 4–5.

[14] This is understood as the supervisory technology or SupTech. For a comprehensive review of how big data technologies facilitate SupTech, see generally Castri and others, ibid.

[15] GDPR, art 4(1).

[16] Ibid.

Modern data protection laws protect the data right of data subjects by, amongst others, acknowledging their right to consent to the processing of their data. Taking the General Data Protection Regulation ('GDPR') for instance. In principle, processing of personal data is lawful only when 'the data subject has given consent to the processing of his or her personal data for one or more specific purposes'[17] or the processing satisfies the enumerated necessity tests.[18] Under this regime, the processing of personal data is not forbidden, but it is, in principle, subject to the consent of the data subject. In some sense, modern data protection laws treat personal data as private property; accordingly, they assign the property right to data subjects and acknowledge the right of data subjects to trade or transfer their data. This is essentially a market approach to balance data protection and data processing.

Modern data protection laws also borrow heavily from consumer protection laws to introduce discipline into the data market. Specifically, to ensure that data subjects trade or transfer their data according to their free will, modern data protection laws set out a series of rules regulating the manner for data controllers to obtain consent from data subjects. For instance, the consent must be specific, informed, and unambiguous,[19] in the sense that data controllers must inform data subjects of at least the information related to the data processing, such as the controller's identity and the processing purposes.[20] In essence, these rules require data controllers to disclose to data subjects sufficient information regarding the prospective data uses before obtaining consent. This formulates an 'informed consent' regime for protecting the data right of data subjects.

C. When Big Data Technologies Meet Modern Data Protection Laws

Like other markets, the data market built on the above informed consent regime inevitably comes with some transaction costs and prevents the market from developing to its optimal scale. Specifically, obtaining informed consent from data subjects is costly. When the data market proceeds into the big data era, this transaction cost gradually grows into an enormous or even prohibited size.

The inherent large-volume feature of big data technologies inevitably increases big data companies' cost to obtain the required informed consent. As the volume of personal data to be processed increases, big data companies have

17 GDPR, art 6.1(a).
18 *See* GDPR, art 6.1(b)–(f).
19 *See* GDPR, Recital 32.1.
20 *See* GDPR, Recital 42.4.

to spend considerable costs to inform data subjects and obtain their consent. Besides, data subjects might refuse to consent to the proposed data processing, resulting in big data companies' data loss. These are all the costs that big data companies undertake under the informed consent regime.

Moreover, obtaining qualified consent from data subjects might be legally challenging on some occasions. For instance, modern data protection laws require data controllers to specify data processing's purpose before obtaining consent from data subjects.[21] This could be challenging for big data companies because they might not have a concrete plan for processing the data when collecting data from data subjects. To elaborate, big data companies often gather data before they act. They often identify a specific purpose for analysing their data after they have accumulated a sufficient amount of data. Therefore, when collecting data from data subjects and seeking consent, big data companies might not know for what specific purposes the data will be processed. In this context, they can hardly identify a specific purpose when collecting data from data subjects. To comply with modern data protection laws, they will have to return to data subjects for separate consent when they have identified data processing's specific purpose afterward.

To avoid applying modern data protection laws, the anonymisation of data might be a possible way out. If big data companies can anonymise the data to the degree that the data subject is no longer identifiable, directly and indirectly, the data is no longer personal data, and data protection laws no longer apply.[22] However, to adopt this idea, big data companies have to anonymise the data to the full extent. The data subject must be no longer identifiable by any reasonable means that are likely to be used to identify the data subject, taking into account the costs and amount of time required for identification and available technology.[23] Mere data pseudonymisation, under which data can be attributed to a natural person using additional information, is not enough.[24] That said, the complete anonymisation of data might risk diminishing the analytical value of such data. Whilst the fully anonymised data still bears some statistical value, big data companies might not be able to use it to infer the behavioural patterns, such as purchasing preference or creditworthiness, of specific individuals. Therefore, data anonymisation might not be a panacea for big data companies.

---

21 Ibid.

22 *See* GDPR, Recital 26.5.

23 *See* GDPR, Recital 26.3 and 26.4.

24 *See* GDPR, Recital 26.2.

D. Summary

Big data technologies have the potential to reduce the informational asymmetry in the market and facilitate desirable transactions. To the extent that the data necessary for big data technologies' functioning often involves personal data, big data companies face modern data protection laws built upon the informed consent regime. However, obtaining informed consent consistent with modern data protection laws is costly and even prohibited. Modern data protection laws, thus, pose a significant legal risk on big data companies.

III. THE BROKEN INFORMED CONSENT REGIME

Whilst informed consent requirements limit the development of big data technologies, it safeguards data subjects' right to their data. This is of merit, especially in balancing between data protection and data processing. As the practice develops, however, it is found that the informed consent regime fails to offer the safeguard function as expected. In most cases, big data companies manage to obtain blanket consent to the data clauses that are favourable to them. This casts doubt on the continued application of the informed consent regime in the big data era.

A. The Unsuccessful Functioning of Informed Consent

To obtain the data necessary for big data technologies whilst complying with modern data protection laws, big data companies, in practice, primarily seek to obtain blanket consent from data subjects. For example, a survey of the privacy policies of the 25 most-visited commercial websites found that these policies permitted websites to use cookies and web bugs to collect information from website visitors, to collect a unique identifier to the user's computing device, to allow advertising networks to collect the users' information, and to share user data with third parties, etc.[25] A survey of the privacy policies of the top ten mobile apps also found similar results.[26] These privacy policies failed to inform data subjects of the specific type of data to be collected, how the collected data will be processed, and the purpose of data processing, etc. Instead, what these policies sought was blanket consent that data controllers may collect whatever type of data, make whatever processing, and for whatever purpose.

---

25 Rothchild, (n 6) 621–4.
26 Ibid., 625–6.

This blanket consent practice works in the current data market because data subjects consent to these data clauses blindly.[27] Admittedly, in recent years, an increasing number of consumers have become more data-conscious, who do read and even express their disagreement with the data clauses. That said, the majority of consumers remain to click on the 'I agree' button blindly without reading the data clauses. They do not know how big data companies will process their data. They choose to automatically consent to whatever data clauses are designed for them by big data companies even if they have the option not to authorise the processing of their data. This gives big data companies the room to design extremely favourable data clauses.

Whether the data clauses so derived are consistent with modern data protection laws is doubtful.[28] It might be difficult to argue that these clauses have delivered sufficient information to data subjects and that the consent so obtained is adequately informed. For instance, these clauses might fail to specify the type of data to be collected and processed. They might also fail to identify the purpose of collecting and processing the data.[29] In the absence of these pieces of information, data subjects' consent is not an informed one. Thus, the data processing based on these unqualified consents should be inconsistent with modern data protection laws.

That said, data subjects rarely challenge the validity of these data clauses. They tend to accept the clauses without raising disagreement. Thus, big data companies find the justification in processing the data so obtained because they may claim that their processing is based on data subjects' consent. The informed consent regime, in the end, becomes a tool for big data companies to mask their blatant and large-scale data processing. Based on data subjects' informed consent, data protection laws offer limited personal data protection, if any.[30]

---

27 For a similar observation, see ibid., 628. *See also* Daniel J Solove, 'Introduction: Privacy Self-Management and the Consent Dilemma' (2013) 126 *Harvard L Rev* 1880, 1884.

28 For a discussion of this blanket consent practice, *see* Rothchild, ibid., 633–4.

29 For a similar observation, *see* Moira Paterson and Maeve McDonagh, 'Data Protection in an Era of Big Data: The Challenges Posed by Big Personal Data' (2018) *44 Monash U L Rev* 1, 13-15; Kritika Bhardwaj, 'Preserving Consent within Data Protection in the Age of Big Data' (2018) 5 *Nat'l LU Delhi Stud LJ* 100, 104–7.

30 For a similar discussion, see, e.g., Christopher C French, 'The Big Data Revolution and Its Impact on the Law: Introduction' (2019) 123 *Penn St L Rev* 585, 587–8.

B. The Neoclassical Economics Explanation

Neoclassical economics offers us several perspectives for explaining why, in practice, informed consent ends up functioning in the above manner. According to neoclassical economics, market functions can fail due to monopoly, externalities, public goods, and informational asymmetry.[31] Based on these market failure theories, we may explain why data subjects consent to unfavourable data clauses offered by big data companies.

To be sure, we cannot exclude the possibility that the above practices reflect the rational choice of data subjects. For instance, many services provided by big data companies inherently rely on the personal data of consumers. Google Map services is an example. In these cases, data subjects may value the services provided by big data companies so much that they are willing to exchange their data for these services after calculation. For another instance, data subjects may find it time-consuming to study the data clauses and negotiate for different terms; thus, they may prefer to give blanket consent to the data clauses and save time for other purposes.[32] In sum, there can be good reasons for data subjects to consent to unfavourable data clauses.

That said, the market failure caused by monopoly or market powers could be a sound explanation. Many big data companies, such as the search engine giants like Google or Baidu or the digital platform giants like Amazon or Alibaba, possess dominant market powers in their markets. This monopoly, or dominant oligopoly, leaves consumers with limited choices if they want to receive the services. Even in cases where big data companies are in a competitive relationship, these competitors' data clauses might resemble each other, resulting in less meaningful competition in the data market. To that extent, data subjects accept the data clauses out of reluctance instead of rational choice.[33]

The market failure caused by public goods could also be an explanation. Data clauses designed by big data companies pose a typical free-rider problem to data subjects. Challenging the data clauses comes with a tremendous amount of time, effort, and litigation costs, but all data subjects reap the benefit once a data subject successfully invalidates the data clauses. In light of this, any single data subject may have less incentive in initiating a challenge against the data clause, which sustains the data clause designed by big data companies.

The market failure caused by informational asymmetry could be another explanation. Data subjects often have limited information on how big data

---

[31] Cooter & Ulen (n 8) 38–42.

[32] For a detailed description of how many hurdles a data subject needs to go through to secure his/her data rights, *see* Rothchild, (n 6) 615–18.

[33] For a similar observation, see, ibid., 621–7.

companies process their data and how much value the big data companies derive from their data, which prevents data subjects from assessing their data's value. Data subjects also have limited information on how big data companies protect their data from being leaked to or hacked by third parties, which prevents data subjects from assessing the level of data risks they are exposed to. This lack of information disadvantages the bargaining power of data subjects, resulting in the blanket consent practice.[34]

C. The Behavioural Economics Explanation

In addition to the above explanations based on market failure theories under neoclassical economics, behavioural economics also offer us several perspectives explaining why the informed consent regime does not work as expected.

Behavioural economics supplement neoclassical economics by adjusting the fundamental assumption. Neoclassical economics assumes that people are rational and thus make choices based on rationality. This assumption contains the following features: first, people have well-defined preferences and unbiased beliefs and expectations; second, they make optimal choices based on these beliefs and preferences, implying that they have infinite cognitive abilities and infinite willpower; and third, their primary motivation, subject to some occasional exceptions, is self-interest.[35] Behavioural economics, however, rebut these assumptions and advocate that actual behaviours of real people exhibit bounded rationality, bounded willpower, and bounded self-interest.[36] Real people are bounded in rationality because they are psychologically subject to several behavioural limitations, such as available heuristic, loss aversion, anchoring effect, overconfidence, etc.[37] Real people are bounded in willpower because, psychologically, they face self-control difficulty.[38] Real people are also bounded in self-interest because sometimes they do care about other values such as fairness.[39]

Several behavioural limitations of real people observed by behavioural economics might explain why the majority of data subjects tend to accept unfavourable data clauses. The limited focus of real people, for instance, might

---

[34] For a detailed discussion of data subjects' information barriers, see, ibid., 614–15.

[35] Richard H Thaler, 'Behavioral Economics: Past, Present, and Future' (2016) 106(7) *American Economic Rev* 1577, 1578.

[36] Christine Jolls, Cass R Sunstein and Richard Thaler, 'A Behavioral Approach to Law and Economics', (1998) 50 *Stanford L Rev* 1471, 1476.

[37] Ibid., 1477–8.

[38] Ibid., 1479.

[39] Ibid.

play some role here. Big data companies draft data clauses in complicated and lengthy wordings, and they often incorporate data clauses in an even more complex and lengthy user agreement. Therefore, data subjects, who are ordinary people, can hardly study these clauses and bargain for more favourable terms.[40] The limited calculation of real people might serve as another explanation. Even if data subjects are conscious that their consent to data clauses may result in potential monetary loss or risk, their capacity to calculate these possible losses or risks and monetise them into a specific value is limited.[41] Other behavioural theories, such as heuristics, may also offer some explanation.[42]

D. Summary

To be sure, the informed consent regime is not entirely in vain. As data security awareness increases, an increasing number of consumers now pay attention to data clauses and refuse to accept them. That said, still, an unneglectable number of consumers are less concerned with their data rights and give blind consent to big data companies. Whilst some of them make this decision out of rational choices, a lot of them do not. Both neoclassical and behavioural economics offer accounts of why the informed consent regime fails to function as expected. The market failures in the data market and the behavioural limitation of real people are both sound explanations.

With these observations in mind, one may wonder whether data protection laws should continue centring on the informed consent regime in the big data era. After all, if the informed consent regime frustrates big data technologies whilst bringing limited benefits in protecting data subjects, it can hardly pass the cost and benefit analysis. This warrants a second thought of the necessity of the informed consent regime.

IV. PROPOSING A PUBLIC-PRIVATE-PARTNERSHIP MODEL OF DATA PROTECTION

Recognizing that the current data protection laws are incapable of striking a delicate balance between data processing and data protection in the big data era, I review the possibility of introducing an alternative model to the informed consent regime in this section. Specifically, I highlight the government's critical role in the *ex-ante* design of data clauses and the *ex-post* internal control

---

[40] For similar observation, *see* Rothchild, (n 6) 615–18.

[41] For a similar discussion, see David M Parker, Steven G Pine and Zachary W Ernst, 'Privacy and Informed Consent for Research in the Age of Big Data' (2019) 123 *Penn St L Rev* 703, 723–8.

[42] Rothchild, (n 6) 619.

of data processing. In the end, I propose a public-private partnership model of data protection to supplement the current informed consent regime.

A. A Review of the Available Proposals

Many studies on data protection laws have noticed the inadequacy of the informed consent regime in protecting data subjects.[43] They have further proposed various alternatives, depending on the root problems they identified.

1. Proposals to improve the manner of disclosure

Some studies attribute the failure of the informed consent regime to the limited focus of ordinary consumers. They find that data subjects blindly consent to unfavourable data clauses because big data companies hide these terms in the lengthy and complicated privacy policies, which prevents data subjects from understanding their data rights.[44] In their view, the root problem is that data subjects have limited information on how big data companies take advantage of their data rights.[45]

Accordingly, some studies invoke the salience theory of behavioural economics and advocate that what matters is not merely the disclosure but the *manner of* disclosure.[46] In this light, big data companies shall disclose data clauses more simply and clearly. For instance, the notification of privacy policies shall address not only what information is collected but also *the significance* of such information. The notification can, for example, add some examples about how the data collected can be used to learn about the data subject. The notification shall further disclose how the collected information will be used in combination with the *next* collected data package.[47] These changes to data clauses can contribute to more informed consent from data subjects.[48]

---

[43] See, e.g., ibid.; Parker, Pine and Ernst, (n 41) 723–8; French, (n 30). *See also* Christoph Busch, 'Implementing Personalized Law: Personalized Disclosures in Consumer Law and Data Privacy Law' (2019) 86 *U Chi L Rev* 309; Ignacio N Cofone and Adriana Z Robertson, 'Consumer Privacy in a Behavioral World' (2018) 69 *Hastings LJ* 1471.

[44] Empirical evidence found that consumers did not react to different kinds of disclosure language. *See* Lior Jacob Strahilevitz and Matthew B Kugler, 'Is Privacy Policy Language Irrelevant to Consumers' (2016) 45 *J Legal Stud* S69, S92–93.

[45] See, e.g., Solove, (n 27) 1883–8.

[46] For discussing the difference between these two prescriptions from a behavioural perspective, *see* Jolls, Sunstein and Thaler, (n 36) 1533–7.

[47] Cofone and Robertson (n 43), 1503–7. *See also* Leslie E Wolf, 'Risks and Legal Protections in the World of Big-Data' (2018) 11 *Asia Pacific J Health L & Ethics* 1.

[48] Others further proposed to strengthen consumer education as a supplement to improve the awareness of data subjects. *See* Parker, Pine and Ernst, (n 41) 730–32.

This proposal makes sense to the extent that the root problem of informed consent rests in the limited focus of ordinary consumers. The root problem, however, is perhaps more than that. For instance, data subjects are subject to not only limited focus problems but also limited calculation problems as mentioned above. After all, related rights and obligations contained in data clauses are inherently complicated. It might be difficult for big data companies to simplify the data clauses to the acceptable level to behavioural economists in the first place.[49] Even if they do, which allows data subjects to be fully aware of their rights and obligations, data subjects might have difficulty in calculating their overall costs and benefits to make rational choices. Therefore, whilst improving the disclosure manner is desirable, simply improving it might not be sufficient for curing all the informed consent regime's problems.

2. Proposals to improve the default mechanism for protecting personal data

Some studies attribute the failure of the informed consent regime to the inertia of ordinary consumers. They observe that data subjects blindly consent to unfavourable data clauses because they refrain from undertaking the cost and efforts in studying these clauses and are used to simply consenting to whatever terms and conditions presented to them. In the view of these studies, the inertia of data subjects towards accepting the status quo prevents them from safeguarding their data rights against big data companies.[50]

Accordingly, some studies invoke the endowment effect observed by behavioural economics[51] and advocate the importance of designing an appropriate default rule of data protection. For instance, they may prefer to design the consent requirement on an opt-in instead of an opt-out basis because an opt-out consent might be the product of mere inertia or lack of awareness of the option to opt-out.[52] Instead, an opt-in regime might force data subjects to pay more attention to notifications about how their data will be used.[53]

This proposal makes sense to the extent that the root problem of informed consent rests in the inertia of ordinary consumers. Many studies, however,

---

[49] Empirical evidence suggests that complexity in the language of data clauses might not be the primary driver. See Omri Ben-Shahar and Adam Chilton, 'Simplification of Privacy Disclosures: An Experimental Test' (2016) 45 *J Legal Stud* S41, S65–66.

[50] Rothchild (n 6) 619. *See also* Omer Tene and Jules Polonetsky, 'Privacy in the Age of Big Data: A Time for Big Decisions' (2011-2012) 64 *Stan L Rev Online* 63, 67–8.

[51] For a discussion of the endowment effect, *see* Jolls, Sunstein and Thaler, (n 36) 1497–501.

[52] Solove, (n 27) 1899.

[53] Ibid.

have questioned whether requiring opt-in consent can make a significant difference. They pointed out that big data companies have strong incentives to play on consumer biases to confuse consumers into opting in the data clauses.[54] The dominant market power of big data companies further leaves ordinary consumers with little room not to opt-in the data clauses.[55] In that case, with the opt-in consent of consumers, big data companies might feel even more legitimate to process the personal data of data subjects, resulting in little change in the long run.[56]

3. Public intervention in the data clauses

In contrast to the previous studies, which have faith in consumers' rationality, some studies find that the market failure in the data market and the behavioural limitation of data subjects mentioned above are too severe for consumers to make rational choices. They thus advocate that some form of public intervention is necessary.[57] Some studies advocate that courts consider invoking the unconscionability doctrine, find unfavourable data clauses as unconscionable, and invalidate these clauses.[58] Some studies also note the possible role of competition authorities in invoking the fairness principle and finding unfavourable data clauses as unfair practices under competition laws.[59] Others also advocate the direct regulation of permissible and prohibited use of personal data to replace the informed consent regime when the latter fails to function.[60]

Introducing public intervention is a reasonable way to enhance data protection in the data market. The problem, however, lies in the specific form of public intervention. Court intervention based on the unconscionability doctrine might be a reasonable option. That said, data clauses involve complicated rights and obligations, and they are even intertwined with other terms and conditions of the user agreement. Courts can, at most, invalidate specific unfavourable terms, but they can hardly calculate the give and take of data subjects in this legal relationship and come up with a complete set of data

---

[54] *See generally* Lauren E Willis, 'Why Not Privacy by Default' (2014) 29 *Berkeley Tech LJ* 61.

[55] Solove, (n 27) 1898–9.

[56] Ibid., 1899.

[57] *See, e.g.,* Rothchild, (n 6) 613–35; Solove, (n 27) 1898–9; Joseph Jerome, 'Big Data: Catalyst for a Privacy Conversation' (2014) 48 *Ind L Rev* 213, 228–30.

[58] Philipp Hacker and Bilyana Petkova, 'Reining in the Big Promise of Big Data: Transparency, Inequality, and New Regulatory Frontiers' (2017) 15 *Nw J Tech & Intell Prop* 1, 28-30; Rothchild, (n 6) 645–6.

[59] Rothchild, ibid., 637–45.

[60] Viktor Mayer-Schonberger and Yann Padova, 'Regime Change: Enabling Big Data through Europe's New Data Protection Regulation' (2016) 17 *Colum Sci & Tech L Rev* 315, 331–3.

clauses for data subjects. The intervention of competent authorities based on unfair practices has a similar concern. Therefore, establishing a form of public intervention that comprehensively assesses the overall desirability of data clauses remains a challenge.

B. An Opt-in Public-Private-Partnership Proposal

The above proposals are all reasonable ways to strengthen the protection of data subjects. In this section, I propose an opt-in model parallel to the current informed consent regime to incorporate the above proposals' essence. The proposal involves some public intervention elements but preserves the party autonomy element, formulating a collaborative relationship between public entities and private parties. Specifically, it contains two tiers of proposals, a public template proposal, and an enhanced internal control proposal.

1. Proposing a public template for data clauses

The first fundamental problem of the informed consent regime is that it relies too much on data subjects' self-motivation. Experience shows that ordinary consumers largely fail to study data clauses and bargain for more favourable ones to secure their data rights. Both neoclassical economics and behavioural economics have explained such failure, including monopoly, informational asymmetry, collective action problem, limited focus, limited calculation, inertia, etc. It seems difficult to expect that, without the help of public intervention, ordinary consumers can stand up against big data companies and safeguard their interests.

Proposals made by far might have their limits. Requiring big data companies to present their data clauses in a more salient manner helps, but ordinary consumers might still consent to unfavourable data clauses because they have inherent limits in reading these clauses and thus have the inertia in simply ignoring the data clauses. Enacting a set of default rules that are more favourable to data subjects helps, but ordinary consumers might still consent to opt-out of the default rules because of the same inertia. Court or government intervention in invalidating the unfavourable clauses help, but only a relatively limited number of consumers would file cases against big data companies. Besides, courts and relevant authorities can only invalidate unfavourable clauses *ex-post* but cannot rewrite the whole agreement to balance big data companies' interests with that of data subjects *ex-ante*.

I propose that the executive branch should intervene and draft template data clauses for future use by big data companies in the name of consumer protection. Under this proposal, the responsible authority should design a multiple set of templates on an industry-by-industry basis covering the major industries involving big data technologies, considering that different industries may need a different design of data clauses. To adopt this proposal, the consumer protection authority or the competition authority should be primarily responsible for drafting this template, supplemented by the competent authorities of individual regulated industries.

This public template can contain both mandatory and non-mandatory provisions. For those terms and conditions involving crucial rights of data subjects, the responsible authority may designate them as mandatory (or prohibitive) provisions and require big data companies to (in the case of mandatory provisions) or not to (in the case of prohibitive provisions) incorporate them into the user agreement. Any data clauses in the user agreement inconsistent with these mandatory or prohibitive provisions are automatically null and void. This approach is similar to a mandatory law approach, which seeks to ensure that data subjects do not relinquish their fundamental data rights under the current informed consent regime.

In addition to mandatory provisions, the responsible authority may further draft other non-mandatory provisions that stipulate the terms and conditions regarding data subjects' data. Big data companies may choose to opt-out these templates when designing their data clauses. In that case, however, they have to disclose the specific departure and obtain the consumers' specific consent to these departures. This approach is an application of the salience theory and the endowment theory. For one thing, under this novel 'comply-or-disclose' regime, the deviation from the government's template becomes more salient to consumers. Consumers can thus make more informed choices when determining whether to consent to these opt-outs. Even if consumers agree to opt-out due to their inertia, responsible authorities can more easily notice the potential predatory practices of big data companies under this novel regime. Similarly, the public media can also more easily notice it and impose reputational sanctions on big data companies. This novel 'comply-or-disclose' regime implements and upgrades the disclosure proposal and default rule proposal as mentioned above.

Responsible authorities should update these template data clauses on a rolling basis. In the beginning, they may adopt a principle-based approach and design the template in a relatively general manner. As more cases accumulate, and as their communication with big data companies and consumer representatives increases, they may understand more about the industry and develop more specific terms and conditions. Incrementally, the template provided by responsible authorities would turn from a relatively incomplete contract to a complete one.

Whilst the above proposal sounds innovative, some jurisdictions have implemented it, at least partially. Taiwan, for instance, is a good example. In Taiwan, the Consumer Protection Act mandates central competent authorities to stipulate mandatory or prohibitive provisions for specific businesses to follow when designing standard contracts.[61] If a standard contract contains prohibitive provisions, such provisions are null and void.[62] If, in contrast, a standard contract fails to contain mandatory provisions, these mandatory provisions automatically become part of the contract.[63] The competent authority even possesses the power to examine the standard contracts of the regulated businesses.[64] Based on this mandate, competent authorities in Taiwan have promulgated mandatory or prohibitive provisions for a wide variety of standard contracts.[65] In addition to these mandatory or prohibitive provisions, relevant competent authorities also promulgate many non-binding standard contract templates for the industry's reference.[66] Whilst Taiwan has not introduced the 'comply-or-disclose' regime as proposed above, these non-binding templates serve as the industry's best practice and function as an implicit benchmark.

2. The enhanced internal control proposal

Despite its merits, the public template proposal alone is not enough. The second fundamental problem of the informed consent regime, which is more related to big data technologies, is that no one can exhaustively foresee the potential future uses of the data and incorporate all these uses in the data clauses in advance. Responsible authorities cannot overcome this problem as well. Accordingly, this requires an adjustment to modern data protection laws.

Modern data protection laws require big data companies to enumerate the specific purpose and specific manner of data processing in the data clauses for the data subjects' consent. This puts big data companies in a dilemma. In most cases, they simply act inconsistently with the above requirement by mentioning the purpose and manner of their future processing in abstract terms to accommodate their future needs. In other cases, they undertake a significant amount of cost in repeatedly returning to consumers for their consent after the purpose and manner of data processing become specific at a later time. However, relying on this approach to protect the data rights of data subjects could be in vain and turn out to be simply imposing costs on big data companies.

To address this fundamental problem more efficiently, the incomplete contract theory offers us some insights. According to the incomplete contract

---

61 Consumer Protection Act (Taiwan) art 17(1).

62 Ibid., art 17(4).

63 Ibid., art 17(5).

64 Ibid., art. 17(6).

65 According to the LawBank database, the most comprehensive law database in Taiwan, relevant authorities have promulgated mandatory or prohibitive provisions for 102 standard contracts as of the end of March 2021.

66 As of the end of March 2021, 147 standard contract templates are in effect in Taiwan, according to the LawBank database.

theory, attempting to design a complete contract to address all the contractual issues between the parties in advance is impracticable and inefficient. Contract designers should seek a balance between *ex-ante* contracting and *ex-post* dispute settlement to make contracting more efficient. For instance, for matters that are unpredictable at contracting and are thus difficult to be stipulated in specific contract terms, contract designers may consider adopting abstract or general contract wordings to regulate them, leaving them to be resolved on a case-by-case basis when actual disputes arise later on.[67] Following this incomplete contract theory, requiring big data companies to specify all the prospective purposes and manners of processing data *ex-ante* is unnecessary. Responsible authorities, when designing the template clauses, should also consider this *ex-post* aspect of data protection.

Specifically, modern data protection laws should not be merely about the *ex-ante* 'contracting' aspect of data protection, which focuses on data subjects' informed consent. They should also concern the *ex-post* 'performance' aspect of data protection, focusing on how data processors protect the collected data after contracting for it.[68] Many consumers might not mind permitting big data companies to process their data for providing better services, but they do care whether big data companies misuse their data, such as leaking it to third parties. From this perspective, perhaps policymakers should shift the focus away from designing a complete data clause to developing a robust internal control mechanism for preventing data misuse. Specifically, this internal control mechanism should ensure that big data companies process the collected data for a purpose and in a manner that is aligned with the interests of the data subject. If such an internal control mechanism is in place, it could be more effective in protecting data rights than requiring separate informed consent by data subjects.

To substantiate this proposal, I propose that big data companies consider establishing an enhanced internal control mechanism. This mechanism should contain at least the following elements. First, big data companies should have a clear policy stipulating the guidelines and procedures for processing the collected personal data. The guidelines and procedures can be principle-based and general as long as they are consistent with related data protection laws and

---

[67] For a recent summary of the incomplete contract theory, see generally Oliver Hart, 'Incomplete Contracts and Control' (2017) 107(7) *American Economic Rev* 1731.

[68] To be sure, modern data protection laws do address this *ex-post* aspect. GDPR, for instance, requires data processors to implement appropriate technical and organisational measures, including appropriate data protection policies, to ensure and to be able to demonstrate that processing is performed in accordance with GDPR. GDPR, art 24(1) and (2).

do not constitute data misuse. That said, a data committee shall administer the guidelines and procedures for using the data. This leads to the second element.

Second, big data companies should establish an independent data committee. Specifically, this committee should include an adequate number of outside experts to represent consumers' interests in their data. Committee members, together, determine whether to modify the data policies of the company. Most importantly, when big data companies attempt to process the data in a manner or for a purpose to which data subjects have not specifically consented, this committee should step in. It should determine whether the proposed processing meets its guidelines and whether the proposed processing misuses the data. If the committee approves the proposal, the big data company can process it without data subjects' consent. If, however, the committee declines it, the big data company should turn to data subjects for separate informed consent before processing the data. In some way, this committee functions as an interim arbitrator who arbitrates the proposed data processing.[69]

Third, big data companies should further introduce some external audits of their internal control mechanism. The power of this independent data committee is not without limitation, and its exercise of discretion should be subject to some level of external scrutiny. Traditional gatekeepers, such as attorneys, may play this scrutiny role. Some international standard-setting bodies dedicated to setting data protection standards, such as the International Organization for Standardization ('ISO'), are also suitable candidates.

I propose that responsible authorities should contain this enhanced internal control proposal in their template data clauses. That said, the provisions related to this enhanced internal control proposal should be non-mandatory and on an opt-in basis. Big data companies may choose not to adopt this internal control proposal and follow the current data protection laws. In that case, their processing of the personal data shall be based on the data subject's specific consent, meaning that they have to inform consumers of the specific purpose and manner of data processing in their data clauses.[70]

---

[69] This proposal differs from the data protection officer requirement under the GDPR. While GDPR requires some data controllers to establish data protection officers to conduct specific tasks, including monitoring data controllers' compliance with the GDPR, they do not possess the arbitrator character as mentioned above. Besides, GDPR does not require the independence of data protection officers, while my proposal requires a minimum level of independence of the data committee to ensure that it has the legitimacy in representing consumers.

[70] Overall, this enhanced internal control proposal echoes the observation that modern data protection laws should shift their focus to forcing internal changes within a company that raises their self-awareness about data collection and use. Solove, (n 27) 1900.

C. Rethinking the Foundation of Data Protection Laws

I propose the above two-tier proposals with an attempt to rethink the foundation of data protection laws. I argue that data protection laws in the big data era should be founded on the optimality of the contract terms instead of data subjects' consent. This is because consumers are too vulnerable and behaviourally limited to safeguard their data rights. Moreover, obtaining qualified consent from consumers is becoming increasingly costly as the application of big data technologies expands. In light of the limited merits and increasing costs of the informed consent regime, data protection laws in the big data era need an alternative way out.

Public intervention in the contractual design of data clauses and private governance of the internal control of the data misuse can be a more efficient way. *Ex-ante*, responsible authorities intervene by designing public templates for big data companies, which awards consumers a minimum data protection level and sets an anchor in the data market. *Ex-post*, the independent data committee and external auditors supplement the unavoidable incompleteness in data clauses and prevent potential data misuse more efficiently. Instead of leaving the allocation of data interests to data subjects' informed choices, my proposal introduces independent data committees, external auditors, and responsible authorities to form a public-private partnership to coordinate the allocation.

To be sure, my proposal is an opt-in complement instead of a substitute for the current data protection laws. Except for those mandatory template clauses, big data companies may choose not to opt-in with my proposals and follow the current data protection laws. After all, it is imaginable that some big data companies may find my proposal too costly and prefer the existing laws. My proposal can work parallel to the current data protection regime.

V. CONCLUSION

Big data technologies have posed a challenge to the existing data protection laws. Modern data protection laws adopt an informed consent regime to balance data protection and data processing. However, such a regime does not appear to be an efficient way to accommodate big data technologies from both a neoclassical economic perspective and a behavioural economic perspective. In this chapter, based on the salience theory and endowment theory of behavioural economics and the incomplete contract theory, I propose a public-private partnership model that contains a private template proposal and an enhanced internal control proposal to supplement the informed consent regime. I anticipate that as big data technologies develop, big data technology laws may also keep up their pace, at least incrementally!

5. Algorithm-driven information gatekeepers: Conflicts of interest in the digital platform business models

Aline Darbellay[1]

I. INTRODUCTION

The tech-driven economy has led to shifting business models in multiple industries. This transformation has been ongoing for several decades. What is relevant for this chapter is the increasing adoption of platform business models in the banking and financial sector. This study does not focus on traditional actors but on competition stemming from the entry of tech firms into the banking and finance segment, thereby potentially leading to a disruption of banking and finance activities. New business models have generated new forms of conflicts of interest. Digital platforms operate in two-sided markets where they deal with both users of content and commercial customers that have diverging interests. This study explores the specific forms of conflicts of interest that are generated by digital platform business models.

The question arises as to how legal and regulatory frameworks deal with these shifting business models. First, there are certain areas where law and regulation have encouraged the evolution of business models. Most notably, in the EU, policymakers and regulators have paved the way towards open banking.

[1] The author thanks Kern Alexander, Deborah DeMott and Michel José Reymond for precious comments. She is deeply grateful for constructive feedback from the organisers and attendees of the Research colloquium of the Centre for banking and finance law (CDBF) of the University of Geneva, the Research Seminar of the Geneva Finance Research Institute (GFRI) of the University of Geneva, the 'IAPP Global Privacy Summit 2019' in Washington DC, the Research Conference on 'Unpacking the Complexity of Regulatory Governance in a Globalized World' at the Chinese University of Hong Kong (CUHK), the Research Conference on 'FinTech, Governance and Sustainability: Legal Obstacles and Regulatory Challenges' organised in partnership between the University of Exeter, the University of Geneva and KU Leuven, and the 'Second Digital Economy and the Future Rule of Law Summit' of the Law School of Renmin University of China.

Second, it is important to examine how the law and regulation shall apprehend related issues such as conflicts of interest. The focus is laid on US law as a key jurisdiction that the leading digital platforms have to comply with. At any rate, most of the issues addressed in this chapter are relevant across jurisdictions.

In the market for information, policymakers and regulators have traditionally mandated disclosure requirements. Disclosure has been part of the regulatory response to conflicts of interest. It is argued that corporate governance mechanisms shall be redesigned with a view to mitigating new forms of conflicts of interest. As for digital platforms, corporate governance mechanisms have to be revisited, thereby leading to the concept of platform governance. Governance structures shall enable users to gain control over decisions that affect them. This is partly treated by self-regulatory frameworks that promise to put the human at the centre of the concerns. Nevertheless, amending the legal and regulatory framework is necessary to the extent that existing mechanisms fail to protect important stakeholders that are beneficiaries of information. In addition, it is argued that judicial oversight plays a role where digital platforms breach fiduciary duties they owe to users. This analysis falls within the debate over regulation as an *ex-ante* instrument *versus* liability as an *ex-post* response.[2]

Academics have already explored the concept of surveillance capitalism.[3] Users give up autonomy and rely on digital platforms who know their preferences and habits. Accordingly, user choice and autonomy are at stake. This chapter sheds light on the entry of this growing business model into the financial sphere. This trend is illustrated throughout the chapter by referring to the case of digital payments.

The leading digital platforms have been transforming the traditional banking and financial industry in a way that may jeopardise the position of incumbent banks. Access to state-of-the-art technologies enables them to compete in retail banking markets. In addition, digital platforms benefit from asymmetric regulation as regulatory thresholds often fail to subject them to the relevant financial regulation and they may enter retail banking markets without being restricted by risk and compliance considerations in the build-up phase of their business models.[4] The question arises as to what extent this disruption will serve the interest of the consumers. Since there are both opportunities and risks, it is worth examining the role of law and regulation at preserving con-

---

[2] Frank Partnoy, 'The Timing and Source of Regulation' (2014) 37 *Seattle University Law Review* 423, 425.

[3] Shoshana Zuboff, *The Age of Surveillance Capitalism, The Fight for the Future at the New Frontier of Power* (Profile Books 2019).

[4] Miguel de la Mano and Jorge Padilla, 'Big Tech Banking' (2018) 14(4) *Journal of Competition Law & Economics* 494, 504.

sumer welfare. Even though digital platforms do not face the same regulatory constraints as banking actors, it is argued that they are still subject to rules, for instance relating to conflicts of interest. This chapter assesses to what extent existing theories apply to evolving business models. Accordingly, there is no need to create a completely new governance framework for the interests of stakeholders such as users. The analysis conducted in this chapter aims to enrich the debate around platform governance. The question arises as to what extent existing legal frameworks already regulate innovative business models and to what extent a shift of paradigm is needed.

The chapter proceeds as follows. Section II examines the gatekeeping function of digital platforms. Section III discusses challenges posed to corporate governance as well as addresses the theoretical grounding of digital platform governance. Section IV analyses to what extent digital platforms owe fiduciary duties to users. Section V presents the findings regarding the role of law and regulation in mitigating conflicts of interest and regulating content. Section VI concludes.

II. THE GATEKEEPING FUNCTION OF ALGORITHM-DRIVEN DIGITAL PLATFORMS

In the financial markets, gatekeepers are independent professionals who pledge their reputational capital to protect the interests of dispersed investors.[5] Traditional gatekeepers are investment banks, auditors, securities analysts and credit rating agencies (CRAs).[6] The digitalisation era has heralded the emergence of new forms of information gatekeepers. This chapter focuses on the digital platforms that perform a function as information gatekeepers. Although digital platforms do not certify or verify statements, they serve as a channel to disseminate information. In fact, the more or less wide diffusion of information depends on their algorithms. It facilitates and enables the flow of information. The leading digital platforms have the ability to screen information and make it more or less visible to others. In so doing, they have a deterrent capacity.

In the capital markets, information is key. The leading CRAs have played a gatekeeping role.[7] They process a wide range of information and distil the

---

5 John C Coffee Jr, 'Gatekeeper Failure and Reform: The Challenge of Fashioning Relevant Reforms' (2004) 84 *Boston University Law Review* 301, 302, 308.

6 Jennifer Payne, 'The Role of Gatekeepers' in Niam Moloney, Eilís Ferran and Jennifer Payne (eds), *The Oxford Handbook of Financial Regulation* (OUP 2015) 255–6.

7 Aline Darbellay and Frank Partnoy, 'Credit Rating Agencies and Regulatory Reform' in Claire A Hill and Brett H McDonnell (eds), *Research Handbook on the Economics of Corporate Law* (Edward Elgar 2012) 274.

complexity of the financial world into simple rankings. The business models of information intermediaries have shifted for several reasons. In the market for financial information, technology and regulation have been two driving forces towards change. Indeed, two concurring trends have contributed to overhauling business models: (i) low-photocopying costs, the internet and the ensuing free-riding problem and (ii) regulation, regulatory incentives, including the use of financial information for regulatory purposes. In the 1930s, US securities regulation focused on investor protection by introducing mandatory disclosure requirements, thereby making financial information publicly available. This endeavour contributed to strengthening capital markets and direct finance, thereby gradually leading to enhancing disintermediation. In the 1970s, two concurring aspects led CRAs to shift from the issuer-pays business model to the investor-pays business model: (i) low-photocopying costs and (ii) regulatory references to credit ratings. In the twenty-first century, technology and to some extent regulation have paved the road towards evolving business models. In terms of technological advances, modern gatekeepers are algorithm-driven platforms. In terms of regulatory aspects, with respect to payment systems, the shift of business models has been encouraged by the EU policymakers and regulators. Indeed, the EU's revised Payment Services Directive (PSD2) has required that banks provide access to customer data to all authorised competitors such as FinTech actors.[8]

This section assesses these developments as follows. First, the demand for information stems from investors who tend to no longer be willing to pay for information due to technological changes and the ensuing free-riding problem. In fact, information is costly to produce but cheap to reproduce.[9] As a public good, information is non-rivalrous, i.e., more than one entity can possess the same information, non-excludable i.e., it takes effort to seek to limit sharing, and has zero marginal cost, i.e., once information is available, the cost of reproduction is often negligible.[10] This leads to the hope to free-ride on others' information and corresponding fear of being free-ridden by others.[11] In this sense, as technological advances have facilitated the rapid diffusion of information, it is increasingly difficult to charge beneficiaries. Second, the party

---

[8] Directive (EU) 2015/2366 of 25 November 2015 on payment services in the internal market, amending Directives 2002/65/EC, 2009/110/EC and 2013/36/EU and Regulation (EU) No 1093/2010, and repealing Directive 2007/64/EC (Payment Services Directive, PSD2) [2015] OJ L337/35.

[9] Carl Shapiro and Hal R Varian, *Information Rules: A Strategic Guide to the Network Economy* (Harvard Business School Press 1999).

[10] Rob Kitchin, *The Data Revolution: Big Data, Open Data, Data Infrastructures and Their Consequences* (Sage Publications 2014).

[11] Urs Birchler and Monika Bütler, *Information Economics* (Routledge 2007) 83.

that wants to disseminate information is increasingly willing to pay for it. In the case of CRAs, issuers started to pay high fees to be rated by the leading CRAs, partly owing to the regulatory privileges that they would be awarded in return.[12] Accordingly, business models have shifted, which may even be more profitable than previous business models.

Since technological advances have made information so easy to diffuse widely, this has resulted in the overhaul of business models in other industries as well. Indeed, users of information are no longer willing to pay for information. In the field of research and scientific knowledge, the promotion of open access has created incentives for editors to redesign their business models. Similar trends are present in the media and telecommunications sector as well as in the field of journalism. In terms of entertainment, users now have access to unlimited content for free.

Over the previous decades, concerns have been raised about the increasing role of digital platforms as information intermediaries. Digital platforms are firms that perform an intermediary function. The term platform is associated with tech companies operating in two-sided markets. Two-sided or multi-sided markets refer to platforms catering to two or more different user groups – i.e., sides of the market – with different but interdependent demands.[13] It is worthwhile noting that the choice of business models is crucial in platform markets as it is important to get both sides on board.[14] Algorithm-driven platforms operate as the new information gatekeepers. Gatekeepers manage the flow of information from issuers to users of information. Intermediaries perform a gatekeeping function in the sense that they process, screen and diffuse information to beneficiaries. Modern gatekeepers have become algorithmic. Accordingly, search engines and social media platforms are considered as algorithmic gatekeepers.[15]

Initially, traditional intermediaries performed a function to facilitate the production of information within a context of data scarcity. This function has evolved as information intermediaries tend to process and screen information within a context of data abundance.[16] With a view to coping with data abun-

---

[12] Aline Darbellay, *Regulating Credit Rating Agencies* (Edward Elgar 2013) 24.

[13] Thomas Hoppner, 'Defining Markets for Multi-Sided Platforms: The Case of Search Engines' (2015) 38(3) *World Competition Law and Economics Review* 349.

[14] Jean-Charles Rochet and Jean Tirole, 'Platform Competition in Two-Sided Markets' (2003) 1(4) *Journal of the European Economic Association* 990.

[15] Alejandro M Diaz, 'Through the Google Goggles: Sociopolitical Bias in Search Engine Design' in Amanda Spink and Michael Zimmer (eds), *Web Search, Multidisciplinary Perspectives* (Springer 2008) (relating to search engines as gatekeepers); Fabrizio Germano and Francesco Sobbrio, 'Opinion Dynamics via Search Engines (and other algorithmic gatekeepers)' (2020) 187 *Journal of Public Economics* 1.

[16] Kitchin (n 10).

dance rather than data scarcity, modern gatekeepers have used intelligent algorithms to process a considerable amount of information.

The influence of internet companies is significant at the international level. For instance, the world's largest and leading companies operate as so-called BigTech platforms. The most highly capitalised corporations are internet companies that generate revenue by collecting data from their users. Algorithms are designed to tailor information so that users receive personalised content. The business model that has been the most profitable is targeted advertising, i.e. processing user data to personalise advertising. Indeed, internet search engines provided by Google and social media platforms such as Facebook generate most of their revenue from targeted online advertising.[17] On the search side, intermediaries match users who are seeking information to information providers, whilst on the advertisement side, intermediaries match buyers to sellers, i.e., a two-sided matching mechanism supported by advertising.[18]

In fact, Google and Facebook are practically considered a duopoly in online advertising. It is not surprising that only a few players dominate the market. In platform markets, network effects incentivise actors to compete for growth. As a consequence, there are many issues relating to competition law, which are however not covered in this chapter. In short, digital markets are often concentrated due to these network effects.[19] Economies of scale may lead to a concentrated industry, resulting in natural oligopolies. Accordingly, there is a limited number of providers, which eventually may give rise to concerns in terms of homogenising market behaviour. Beyond the scope of this chapter, the question arises as to whether tailored content provided thanks to algorithms may offset these issues.

The digital marketplace for information gatekeepers encompasses different kinds of business models, which fall into two main categories as follows. First, digital platforms may provide their users with a free service and give them access to free content whilst being paid by their commercial customers that would like to disseminate information such as advertisement to the platform users, thereby benefiting from the reach of the platform. For instance, in the

---

[17] Hal R Varian, 'The Economics of Internet Search' in Johannes M Bauer and Michael Latzer (eds), *Handbook on the Economics of the Internet* (Edward Elgar 2016) 177, 184 (stating that the primary source of revenue of search engines comes from selling targeted advertisements and that Google ad auction is probably the largest auction in the world); Nicolas Petit, *Big Tech and the Digital Economy, The Moligopoly Scenario* (OUP 2020) 95, 106 (analysing the 10-K reports of the Big Tech and – among others – reporting that in 2017, Google generated a revenue of USD 95.4 billion on online advertising).

[18] Varian (n 17) 179.

[19] Emilio Calvano and Michele Polo, 'Market Power, Competition and Innovation in Digital Markets: A Survey' (2020) 19(9) *Information Economics and Policy*.

field of financial services, new intermediaries are involved as payment systems helping to reduce costs in the payment sector whilst sitting on a considerable amount of valuable data. Second, digital platforms may provide a free service in exchange for information about users whilst selling information to market participants willing to pay for it. In the field of finance, commission-fee business models depart from the traditional business model where financial intermediaries collect commission revenue in exchange for selling financial products and services. For instance, there is an ongoing shift from commission-driven financial advice to automated investment advice. Also, commission-free trading platforms may collect valuable information about retail investors, e.g., trading applications such as Robinhood. It is nevertheless worth mentioning that in terms of its business model, Robinhood's primary revenue source stems from payment for order flow (PFOF).[20] Robinhood receives payments from high-speed trading firms to which it sends customer's orders for execution. This differs from the digital platforms that monetise information about their users. In a nutshell, these various business models still have in common the fact that the users do not pay for the financial services. In some cases, the platform even collects data about its users that are of interest to third parties such as their commercial customers.

Digital platforms may bundle their existing services in online advertising with banking products.[21] They may leverage their superior information about consumer preferences, control shopping experiences and could rapidly achieve scale and scope in financial services, especially in market segments where network effects are present, such as payments and settlements.[22] In sum, all these business models centre around an algorithm-driven platform space, thereby promoting autonomy and flexibility amongst producers and consumers.[23] They seek to automate the match-making process and optimise the benefit of scaling, both in terms of the number of people a platform coordinates and the global reach across distances.[24] As a consequence of the role of digital platforms as the new gatekeepers of modern financial markets, investor protection can no longer focus exclusively on the disclosure of information

---

[20] PFOF accounted for 81 percent of Robinhood's first-quarter 2021 revenues, according to its SEC quarterly filing.

[21] Organisation for Economic Co-operation and Development (OECD), *Digital Disruption in Banking and Its Impact on Competition* (OECD 2020) 22.

[22] Ibid.

[23] Will Sutherland and Mohammad Hossein Jarrahi, 'The Sharing Economy and Digital Platforms: A Review and Research Agenda' (2018) 43 *International Journal of Information Management* 328, 331.

[24] Ibid., 333.

in the sense of information production but will also involve regulating how information is channelled.

III. CONFLICTS OF INTEREST AND CORPORATE GOVERNANCE MECHANISMS

Conflicts of interest are inherent to digital platform business models. This section addresses the corporate governance debate around the platform markets. Focus is laid on corporate governance issues amongst tech companies due to the special features they have. Defining the business environment in which firms operate is central to corporate governance outcomes. Accordingly, traditional governance models have been tested against the background of digital platform business models. Traditional corporate governance focuses on aligning the interests of managers with the interests of shareholders.[25] Digital platforms collect users' data for commercial purposes. Algorithms have been optimised to maximise the firms' revenue and profit based on the increased traffic they obtain on their platforms thanks to the tailored content they provide to users. [26] In so doing, they seek to achieve scale and scope and gain market share. In terms of commercial interests, digital platforms may first and foremost pursue the interest of their shareholders as well as the self-interest of their managers. Profitability may be achieved by using data towards their own commercial ends as well as selling data to commercial customers.

However, the traditional model of shareholder supremacy does not work in the digital marketplace. With respect to tech companies in which founders retain control even in the event the company goes public, shareholders cannot actively influence decision-making processes. In terms of the control structure, dual-class shares have extensively been used amongst tech companies.[27] What is even more notable is the issuance of shares without any voting rights at the stage of an initial public offering (IPO).[28] In this scenario, the traditional mechanism of corporate governance, which is based on the assumption that the shareholding is fragmented and that shareholders as a class can exercise control through their voting rights, fails to work. Further, it is necessary to

---

25 Jonathan R Macey, *Corporate Governance: Promises Kept, Promises Broken* (Princeton University Press 2008) 4.

26 Anupam Chander and Vivek Krishnamurthy, 'The Myth of Platform Neutrality' (2018) 2 *Georgetown Law Technology Review* 400, 404.

27 Two prominent examples are Google's parent company Alphabet Inc. as well Facebook Inc. Both tech giants have dual-class share structures that enabled their founders to retain voting control although they have gone public.

28 In 2017, Snap Inc. was the first company to issue non-voting shares at the IPO stage.

assess the distinctiveness of governance structures prevailing in high information asymmetry firms.[29] In the case of opaque business models and ensuing information asymmetries, shareholders tend to blindly trust managers, leading to *de facto* management control. The fact that the shareholder primacy model fails to work with respect to high information asymmetry firms is well illustrated in the banking sector.[30] In the event of heterogeneous expectations from shareholders, information conveyed by the market price can be misleading for the purpose of business policymaking.[31] In this respect, decision-making by managers on the basis of shareholder expectations is not deemed an optimal governance structure.[32]

Management shall steer the company in the interest of the enterprise as a whole. Conflicts of interest may emerge when parties have their own diverging interests and the agent engages in self-interested behaviour. According to the stakeholder-oriented approach to corporate governance, governance mechanisms shall be designed with a view to balancing the various interests at stake.[33] This involves taking into account a wide range of interests, including those of non-shareholder constituencies. Modern theories of corporate governance have laid emphasis on the need to apprehend the interests of various stakeholders. Whilst focusing on the interests of non-shareholder constituencies, corporate governance scholarship typically refers to the concept of employees as a class.[34] With respect to the digital marketplace, digital platforms have diverse stakeholder groups with different, sometimes even competing interests. Amongst others, the interests of the users of digital platforms give rise to specific issues. The interests of digital platforms and their commercial customers may be conflicting with the best interest of users.

Against this background, the question arises as to what is in the best interest of the users of digital platforms. The digital grand bargain consists of obtaining free communication services in exchange for pervasive data collection and

---

[29] Laura Field and Michelle Lowry, 'Bucking the Trend: Why do IPOs Choose Controversial Governance Structures and Why Do Investors Let Them?' (2019) Working Paper.

[30] William W Bratton and Michael L Wachter, 'The Case Against Shareholder Empowerment' (2010) 158 *University of Pennsylvania Law Review* 653.

[31] Ibid.

[32] Ibid.

[33] John Parkinson, 'Models of the Company and the Employment Relationship' (2003) 41(3) *British Journal of Industrial Relations* 481, 497–8.

[34] Luca Enriques, Henry Hansmann, Reinier Kraakman and Mariana Pargendler, 'The Basic Governance Structure: Minority Shareholders and Non-Shareholder Constituencies' in Reinier Kraakman et al. (eds), *The Anatomy of Corporate Law, A Comparative and Functional Approach* (3rd edn, OUP 2017).

analysis.[35] On the one hand, the promise of algorithm-driven platforms is to respond to users' demand for convenience and personalised in order to satisfy individual needs. On the other hand, risks stem from business models that collect data about their users and convert that data into microtargeted manipulations – for instance in the form of advertisements – aimed at influencing the behaviour of their users.[36] Such business models create perverse incentives, selling users' information to advertisers and manipulating users' attention so that they are more engaged and generate more profits by being more accessible to advertisers.[37] What makes the problem particularly tricky is that manipulations may be invisible to average users, for instance Google's way of displaying its partners first when making an online search.

In fact, owing to competitive pressures, the BigTech platforms tend to shape users' behaviour towards the ends of their commercial customers. Indeed, their revenue streams come from commercial customers that purchase prediction products.[38] The gatekeeping function of digital platforms may be compromised to a degree by the fact that it is typically paid by the party that seeks to disseminate information. As a result, their price mechanisms may end up favouring one over the other side of the platform, for instance incentivising them to minimise the information provided to users.[39]

Digital platforms operate on the basis of business models that claim human experience as free raw material for translation into behavioural data with a view to fabricating prediction products.[40] Competitive dynamics of these new markets drive to the intervention in user experience to herd behaviour towards profitable outcomes.[41] According to the economic logic that is at the core of the business model, they shift away from serving users to serving the interests of their shareholders and commercial partners. Incentives are misaligned. Owing to the disconnect between platforms and corporate governance, building on existing corporate governance frameworks is disturbed, thereby leading to a unique form of platform governance.[42]

---

[35] Jack M Balkin, 'Fixing Social Media's Grand Bargain' (2018) Aegis Series Paper No. 1814, 1–3.

[36] Yochai Benkler, Robert Faris and Hal Roberts, *Network Propaganda: Manipulation, Disinformation, and Radicalization in American Politics* (OUP 2018).

[37] Balkin (n 35) 10.

[38] Zuboff (n 3).

[39] Andrei Hagiu and Hanna Halaburda, 'Information and Two-Sided Platform Profits' (2014) 34 *International Journal of Industrial Organization* 25, 32.

[40] Zuboff (n 3) 8.

[41] Ibid.

[42] Mark Fenwick, Joseph A McCahery and Erik P M Vermeulen, 'The End of 'Corporate' Governance: Hello 'Platform' Governance' (2019) 20 *European Business Organization Law Review* 171.

The response may partly lie in designing appropriate corporate governance mechanisms. Giving new social responsibilities to digital platforms would ensure that they internalise the costs they impose on society, thereby creating legal incentives to develop professional cultures.[43] Owing to the special features of the digital platform markets, corporate governance mechanisms should be designed to be stakeholder oriented.

In this regard, it is crucial to examine what is in the best interest of users as a class. This is a challenging task. On the one hand, users may seek an enhanced user experience and welcome the personalisation of products and services. As digital platforms compete for users, they face constant pressure to innovate to enhance user convenience and achieve user satisfaction. In this regard, the quality of the platform is key. On the other hand, users have other interests that are not as easy to apprehend. The question arises as to whether users are able to assess and defend their long-term interests. There are important interests at stake that are more difficult to assess and that cannot be secured in the absence of coordination amongst users. Concerns have been raised about securing the interests of users as a class rather than individual user experience. Governance mechanisms have to be adopted to defend the interests of users as a class.

Corporate governance reforms are needed, especially given the fact that conflicts of interest impede effective governance. Additional challenges occur as empirical evidence has shown that technology entrepreneurs are able to spawn a bottom-up change in the regulatory framework with a view to accommodating their business model.[44] It is difficult to find the balance between the advancement of innovation and the need to protect consumers.[45] Further, the law sometimes shows lack of understanding of the rules of entrepreneurship as corporate law focuses on ownership and wealth.[46]

In the field of responsible AI, we have witnessed the proliferation of a plethora of standards, guidelines, codes of conduct and best practices, which are expected to be perfected through trial and error. They acknowledge the need to take into account the interests of various stakeholders. Self-regulation may partly address conflicts of interest. Broadly speaking, the incentive to self-regulate corporate governance depends on peer pressure. However, the experience with peer pressure can produce mixed outcomes.[47] Coupled with

---

[43] Balkin (n 35) 11.

[44] Amit Tzur, 'Uber Über Regulation? Regulatory Change Following the Emergence of New Technologies in the Taxi Market' (2019) 13 *Regulation & Governance* 340.

[45] Sofia Ranchordas, 'Does Sharing Mean Caring? Regulating Innovation in the Sharing Economy' (2015) 16(1) *Minnesota Journal of Law, Science & Technology* 413.

[46] Ibid.

[47] Klaus J Hopt, 'Comparative Corporate Governance: The State of the Art and International Regulation' in Andreas M Fleckner and Klaus J Hopt (eds), *Comparative*

international competition, market forces in favour of good corporate governance are enhanced by disclosure and comparability.[48] Algorithms should encode widely accepted social values and norms as the risk of relying on machine intelligence may contribute to a future of unaccountable corporate control.[49]

This falls within the debate over self-regulation *versus* command and control regulatory approach. As self-regulatory efforts will prove insufficient, a further-reaching regulatory response will likely be necessary. Here are some of the aspects that will need to be covered. First and foremost, the legal and regulatory frameworks may explicitly require the disclosure and mitigation of the types of conflicts of interest that are present in digital platform markets. Further, in order to ensure that management secures the interests of users, a proposal may be that users shall be represented in the boards of directors so that they are better involved in the decision-making process. Moreover, other measures may impose board composition such as requiring boards to reserve seats for independent board members as well as legal obligations to appoint independent directors to a specified number of board seats.[50] In addition, the largest digital platforms may have to constitute ethics committees as part of their governance structure. Finally, legal and regulatory provisions may explicitly require to pay due regard to the interests of users and to treat them fairly as well as to implement the requirement to assess and measure the fairness to users.

IV. CONFLICTS OF INTEREST AND FIDUCIARY DUTIES

Shifting business models have given rise to new sources of conflicts of interests relating to two-sided matching models. This section analyses to what extent gatekeepers owe fiduciary duties to the users of their services, thereby

---

Corporate Governance, A Functional and International Analysis (Cambridge University Press 2013) 91–2.

48 Ibid.

49 Omer Tene and Jules Polonetsky, 'Taming The Golem: Challenges of Ethical Algorithmic Decision-Making' (2017) 19 *North Carolina Journal of Law & Technology* 125.

50 For contrary opinions, see Sanjai Bhagat and Bernard S Black, 'The Non-Correlation Between Board Independence and Long-Term Firm Performance' (2002) 27 *Journal of Corporation Law* 231, 233; Lisa M Fairfax, 'The Uneasy Case for the Inside Director' (2011) 96 *Iowa Law Review* 127, 174–76; Antony Page, 'Unconscious Bias and the Limits of Director Independence' (2009) *University of Illinois Law Review* 237, 251–3 (describing how 'in-group' bias makes directors more likely to side with other directors).

focusing on private law aspects. Courts have defined fiduciary relationships as situations where one person places a special trust in another or where a special duty exists on the part of one person to protect the interests of another.[51] As defining elements, such relationships result in a superiority and influence over the other party as well as the inability of the other party to monitor the fiduciary.[52]

In this regard, the relationship between intermediaries and beneficiaries of digital services deserves further attention. It is worthwhile mentioning that the occurrence of conflicts of interest has been a typical legal issue in the financial sector. Indeed, intermediaries connecting issuers to investors are frequently subject to conflicts of interest. Moreover, new forms of information asymmetries have arisen since tech companies increasingly provide financial services. As the relationship between digital platforms and users is particularly loose in the realm of digital payments, it is important to consider whether fiduciary duties, such as the duties of loyalty and care, apply to the emerging digital financial services.[53]

With respect to two-sided markets, it is first and foremost crucial to understand that digital platforms may owe fiduciary duties to various beneficiaries that may potentially have diverging interests. On the one hand, the fact that they owe fiduciary duties to their commercial customers which pay for their services is an argument that may easily be made. On the other hand, it may further be argued that recognising the fiduciary duties of digital platforms towards their users may be a key component of responsible business practices in the digital era. Digital platforms would have a compelling reason to take into account users' interests if they faced higher liability risks. Indeed, higher litigation threats would provide digital platforms with incentives to intervene and for instance prevent fraud. Broadly speaking, the strict liability of gatekeepers makes sense when gatekeepers can effectively detect and prevent client misconduct.[54] In the event it is recognised that digital platforms owe fiduciary duties to both their commercial customers and their users, the question would arise as to how to tackle the problems relating to diverging interests, i.e., what fiduciary duty is stronger. Also, the risk is that digital platforms may just put waivers of their fiduciary relationship for users to click on in order to use their products or services. Owing to these issues, regulatory safeguards are definitely needed. The adequate response may indeed consist of regulatory inter-

---

51 *Wal-Mart Stores, Inc. v. AIG Life Insurance Co.*, 901 A.2d 106 (Del. 2006), *aff'g* 872 A.2d 611, 624 (Del. Ch. 2005).

52 *Burdett v. Miller*, 957 F.2d 1375, 1381 (7th Cir. 1992).

53 Rolf H Weber and Aline Darbellay, 'Legal Issues in Mobile Banking' (2010) 11 *Journal of Banking Regulation* 129, 130-131.

54 Coffee (n 5) 307.

vention on behalf of users that are unable to defend their own interests. Prior to analysing the role of regulation, it is nevertheless still important to assess to what extent fiduciary duties may be owed to users of digital financial services.

In common-law jurisdictions, concerns have been raised about conflicts of interest in the case of fiduciary relationships. Typically, the inquiry is dominated by tort law. In civil-law jurisdictions, rules on conflicts of interest are rooted in the mandate relationship, when an agent is empowered to act on behalf of the principal, which gives rise to a duty of care and loyalty.[55] A key difference between the two conceptual approaches is that when the legal analysis is based on a breach of fiduciary duties, this may attract a different remedy. This depends on whether the claims lead to either equitable remedies (i.e., injunctions, compensation, restitution), the recovery of limited contractual damages, or further-reaching tort damages, taking into account the fact that fiduciary duties involve special relationships of trust and confidence.[56] However, if the inquiry is based on the breach of a mandate, the cause of action is generally founded on contractual liability. At any rate, what remains most relevant for our analysis is that such relationships tend to give rise to conflicts of interest in the financial sector, for instance in the case of the relationship between a bank and its client.

The following part of the present chapter will develop the concept of fiduciary duties as conceived under US law. Since a major part of digital platforms are based in the US, this is the most relevant jurisdiction in this debate. In any case, as the two basic duties of fiduciaries are the duty of care and the duty of loyalty, there are overlaps between the concept of fiduciary duties and the duties arising out of the mandate agreement.

In the field of financial services, the above discussed issues regarding conflict of interest have notably given rise to concerns in the field of automated investment advice. Robo-advice platforms have been portrayed by the industry as having the purported ability to provide conflict-free advice.[57] Proponents claim that they remove the biases arising out of human involvement. From this standpoint, a shift away from commission-driven financial advice has been underway for some time because of regulatory pressure to address conflicts of

---

[55] Rashid Bahar and Luc Thévenoz, 'Conflicts of Interest: Disclosure, Incentives, and the Market' in Rashid Bahar and Luc Thévenoz (eds), *Conflicts of Interest, Corporate Governance and Financial Markets* (Kluwer Law International 2007) 3.

[56] Jack M Balkin, 'Information Fiduciaries and the First Amendment' (2016) 49(4) *UC Davis Law Review* 1183, 1207.

[57] Nicole G Iannarone, 'Computer as Confidant: Digital Investment Advice and the Fiduciary Standard' (2018) 93(1) *Chicago-Kent Law Review* 141, 149.

interest.[58] However, although automated investment advice offers significant benefits and may provide less biased financial advice than humans, they may still face conflicts of interest, by having the ability to direct massive capital flows, facing the risk of being subjected to influence on the algorithms used to allocate funds.[59] In principle, there is no need to amend the existing fiduciary standards for automated investment advice firms so that they qualify as fiduciaries.[60] Accordingly, robo-advisers should be subject to the same fiduciary standard that investment advisers have to comply with, requiring disclosure, avoiding conflicts of interest, acting in the customer's best interest.

In the field of emerging financial services provided by digital platforms, the question arises as to whether they owe a fiduciary duty to their users. In contractual relationships, there is no general obligation not to use the information other than for the users' interests. Duties arise only under specific circumstances. Broadly speaking, a fiduciary is an actor that has special obligations of loyalty and trustworthiness towards another party, thereby committing to act in the interests of the other party.[61] In fact, the fiduciary has the duty not to betray the trust or confidence that the beneficiary placed in it due to their relationship.

DeMott defines fiduciary duty in a way that may subject actors to fiduciary duties to other parties in relationships not conventionally characterised as fiduciary.[62] Whitt argues that the flexible nature of the common-law fiduciary doctrine can accommodate developing societal concerns such as digital platforms.[63] According to Balkin, information fiduciaries owe special duties with respect to the information they obtain in the course of their relationships with their clients, such as the duty to use the information for the client's benefit and not to harm the client.[64] Balkin explains to what extent online service providers may owe fiduciary duties to users, especially when users must trust and depend on online service providers, which, in turn, encourage users' trust and dependence.[65] According to Balkin, some types of online service providers are new classes of information fiduciaries in the digital age and their relation-

---

58 Benjamin P Edwards, 'The Rise of Automated Investment Advice: Can Robo-Advisors Rescue the Retail Market?' (2018) 93(1) *Chicago-Kent Law Review* 97, 107.

59 Ibid., 110–11.

60 Iannarone (n 57) 159; Edwards (n 58) 110.

61 Balkin (n 56) 1207.

62 Deborah A DeMott, 'Breach of Fiduciary Duty: On Justifiable Expectations of Loyalty and Their Consequences' (2006) 48(4) *Arizona Law Review* 925, 926.

63 Richard S Whitt, 'Old School Goes Online: Exploring Fiduciary Obligations of Loyalty and Care in the Digital Platforms Era' (2020) 36(1) *Santa Clara High Technology Law Journal* 75, 101.

64 Balkin (n 56) 1208–9.

65 Ibid., 1220.

ships with end-users are to be called fiduciary relationships.[66] Online service providers are information fiduciaries if they have induced trust with a view to getting people to use their services and if end-users reasonably expect that they will not misuse their data.[67] As the new information fiduciaries of the digital age, digital platforms owe special duties of care, confidentiality, and loyalty towards people whom the relationships place in special positions of vulnerability.[68]

More importantly, fiduciary duties may apply to digital platforms especially given the inability of users to self-protect their interests. Because of the vulnerability of end-users and their position of relative dependence, inability to monitor their conduct and preventing them from betraying our trust.[69] Due to the lack of transparency, algorithms can be black boxes, thereby impairing users' motivation and ability to verify that the algorithm's decision promotes their preferences.[70]

At any rate, the duties vary with the type of gatekeepers. Their fiduciary obligations should be tailored to the nature of the business and the reasonable expectations of consumers, i.e., more limited than those of lawyers, doctors and bankers.[71]

The two basic duties of fiduciaries are the duty of care and the duty of loyalty. Fiduciary duties are imposed by the law whenever beneficiaries have a justifiable expectation of loyalty.[72] As fiduciary duty's distinctive force, loyalty enables to provide some analytical structure to cases relating to the question of fiduciary duty outside the conventional or typical fiduciary categories.[73] Expectations of loyal conduct outside the conventional fiduciary categories are justifiable when the party is left unable to self-protect against the other party's misconduct owing to either the nature of the relationship or of the specific role occupied by the actor.[74] Indeed, the course of the relationship between the parties over time may form a basis of justifiable expectation of loyal conduct.[75] Relationships where one party has unique access to information highly material to the other party's decisions.[76] In *Groob,* the court ruled

---

66 Ibid., 1221.
67 Ibid., 1224.
68 Balkin (n 35) 12.
69 Balkin (n 56) 1222.
70 Michal S Gal and Niva Elkin-Koren, 'Algorithmic Consumers' (2017) 30(2) *Harvard Journal of Law and Technology* 309.
71 Balkin (n 35) 12.
72 See DeMott (n 62) 938.
73 Ibid., 956.
74 Ibid., 945.
75 Ibid., 941.
76 Ibid., 950.

that there is a need that the actor is aware of special trust reposed in it.[77] Also, the question arises as to whether the parties are in a principal-agent relationship. Agency relationships consist of a potential basis of analogical support for an expectation of loyal conduct. Problems may occur when the conduct is motivated by the agent's self-serving purposes as opposed to furthering the interests of the principal.

In the case of digital platforms, the relationship between digital platforms and users is analogous to a principal-agent relationship where there are asymmetries of power and information. As users are not sufficiently informed, they are unable to discipline digital platforms so that it is not possible to rely on the informed consumer choice model.[78]

In the age of surveillance capitalism, digital connection has become a means to others' commercial ends.[79] Conflicts of interest can cause damages to users. The risks stem from the fact that digital platforms may take advantage of another person's vulnerabilities to benefit themselves and harm the other persons.[80] The question arises as how to make digital platforms more responsive to the interests of their users. Users entrust digital platforms with sensitive information, thereby surrendering information to digital platforms. Their business model depends on trust. Successful platforms have induced trust amongst their users. When they do so, they hold themselves as information fiduciaries. It is not surprising that there shall be ensuing legal consequences.

V. THE PROMISE AND PERILS OF CONTENT REGULATION REGARDING INFORMATION GATEKEEPERS

In terms of the legal and regulatory responses to issues related to digital platforms, the first aspect relates to targeting digital platforms and holding them liable for disseminating misinformation. The second aspect consists of involving digital platforms in market surveillance. The question arises as to what extent digital platforms should screen content available on their platforms with a view to avoiding financial fraud and scams. The idea is that they may play a crucial role as self-regulatory entities. In this vein, legal provisions could mandate content moderation and require digital platforms to defer cases to criminal and supervisory authorities.

---

77 *Groob*, 843 N.E.2d.
78 Balkin (n 35) 5.
79 Zuboff (n 3) 2019.
80 Balkin (n 35) 4.

Both these concerns involve issues related to the regulation of information and its limitations. This section concerns the digital platforms that perform a gatekeeping function as information intermediaries. In this regard, the First Amendment of the US Constitution protects free speech. The US approach in the market for information has been characterised by a broad immunity from lawsuits. With respect to the comparable case of the credit rating industry, the leading CRAs have been historically relatively successful at shielding themselves from lawsuits by invoking the First Amendment protection.

In addition, Section 230 of the Communications Decency Act of 1996 (CDA) gives digital platforms broad immunity from liability for content posted through their platforms.[81] There are two sides of the same coin. On the one hand, protected intermediaries are largely immunised from secondary liability for most torts committed through their online platform.[82] On the other hand, Section 230 also allows digital platforms to moderate content when they publish third-party content, thereby accentuating their role as information gatekeepers. Without a horizontal application of free speech, digital platforms are allowed to freely regulate content posted by users, thereby potentially preventing content from being disseminated, especially given the fact that only a few BigTech platforms dominate the market. For instance, they establish guidelines that ban certain forms of speech from the platform and will accordingly not accept content that is against their own terms and conditions.[83]

This relates to the dissemination of information in the digital age. In the disintermediation and decentralisation process of finance, retail investors benefit from a direct access to the capital markets. The rapid dissemination of information also encompasses easily diffusing misinformation, which may in turn contribute to financial fraud and scams, for instance Ponzi schemes. Due to the aforementioned shifting business models, the party that wants to spread information is more likely to pay for it as opposed to the information beneficiaries. Given the economic logic that is at the core of the business models and ensuing conflicts of interest, financial fraud may under certain circumstances spread more quickly than legitimate business opportunities. This gives rise to concerns about the pyramiding effect of information diffusion. As algorithms are designed to observe patterns, this may reinforce market trends and even promote financial bubbles.

The fact that digital platforms are able to use data to detect scams and have the technical capabilities to go after scams makes the case for imposing on

81 Communications Decency Act of 1996 (CDA), 47 USC § 230.

82 Anupam Chander, 'The First Amendment as Killer App' (2016) 7 *Journal of Law, Technology & the Internet* 1, 4.

83 Chander and Krishnamurthy (n 26) 405–7.

them duties to moderate content.[84] If digital platforms face litigation threats, they would have incentives to increasingly monitor posts. From a technical perspective, they would be able to work on instruments to prevent misinformation from spreading and to take down fraudulent posts. For instance, liability has worked efficiently as an incentive to prevent copyright violations.

Nevertheless, from a legal perspective, there are constitutional limitations to the regulation of information. In the US, the contemporary First Amendment theory and doctrine do not block the path towards strong AI speakers' free speech protection.[85] At any rate, commercial speech is a form of communication that receives less robust protection under the First Amendment. In the landmark case of *Central Hudson,* the Supreme Court has ruled that the commercial speech doctrine applies to promotional advertising.[86] In fact, the commercial speech doctrine was created with a view to protecting the rights of listeners rather than speakers. As such, the focus is laid on the right of the public to receive information.

Nevertheless, the constitutional freedom of speech is not absolute. In commercial settings, the law often treats people as potentially uninformed and vulnerable.[87] Commercial settings outside the public discourse include commercial speech, professional or other fiduciary relationships. Commercial speech is not always constitutionally protected. In fiduciary relationships, the beneficiaries are also vulnerable and dependent on the other party. The core aspect is that they do not stand on equal footing. Clients are typically unable to monitor professional conduct and to prevent fiduciaries from abusing relationships of trust owing to asymmetry of skill and understanding.[88] In sum, digital platforms have a First Amendment right, yet they are held to a higher standard than ordinary individuals expressing their opinions as professional standards apply to them.[89]

With respect to Section 230 of the CDA, courts have recognised that this provision was not enacted to create a lawless no-man's-land on the internet.[90] Indeed, it should not provide a get-out-of-jail-free card for tech firms that publish third-parties' content on the internet.[91] Since Section 230 does not

---

84 Roger Allan Ford, 'Data Scams' (2019) 57 *Houston Law Review* 111, 172.

85 Toni M Massaro and Helen Norton. 'Siri-ously? Free Speech Rights and Artificial Intelligence' (2016) 110(5) *Northwestern University Law Review* 1169.

86 *Central Hudson Gas and Electric Corp. v. Public Service Commission*, 447 U.S. 557 (1980) *(Central Hudson).*

87 Balkin (n 56) 1215.

88 Ibid., 1216.

89 Balkin (n 35) 8.

90 *Fair Housing Council v. Roomates.Com*, LLC, 521 F.3d 1157, 1164 (9th Cir. 2008).

91 *Doe v. Internet Brands,* Inc., 824 F.3d 846, 853 (9th Cir. 2016).

provide immunity from liability for every digital platform's misconduct, the question arises as to what extent reprehensible conduct – such as facilitating financial criminal activity for its own profit at the expense of its users – may fall outside the scope of Section 230. In fact, recent court cases have rejected the Section 230 defence of BigTech companies such as Amazon, paving the way towards tech liability, for instance in the event of defective products sold by others on digital marketplaces, even though Amazon just acted as a matchmaker.[92]

For instance, there is the question of liability of digital platforms for the dissemination of fraud and scams. Scams take advantage of victims by causing them to act contrary to their own interests.[93] Digital platforms facilitate scams by making it easier and cheaper to find the most promising victims and to deploy the most effective scams.[94] The problem is that digital platforms lack incentives to detect scams because they increase their profits and revenues.[95]

Therefore, judicial oversight remains essential. In my opinion, liability threats are needed to the extent that they would give digital platforms incentives to identify and take down fraud and scams. This provides a rationale for holding digital platforms liable for scams committed through their platforms.[96] In the US, the judicial response may stem from recognising the gatekeeping role of digital platforms and the fact that they owe fiduciary duties to users. Also, further-reaching legal and regulatory developments will be needed as internal governance mechanisms will not provide a sufficient response to the current challenges. Regulatory intervention will indeed have to gain prominence in the digital marketplace.

Last but not least, our final question relates to the optimal level of deterrence. If algorithms are designed to avoid attention to outrageous content, the risk is to end up legitimising the control of users' minds. Indeed, consumer protection laws that seek to protect consumers against their own behavioural weaknesses give rise to concerns of institutionalised paternalism.[97] This results in a slippery slope that leads to the control of users' emotions and reinforces the control of users' minds and souls. Giving digital platforms the duty to supervise content may end up legitimising sliding towards an enhanced form

---

[92] For instance, *Bolger v. Amazon.com LLC,* 53 Cal.App. 5th 431 (2020); *Loomis v. Amazon.com LLC*, 63 Cal.App. 5th 466 (2021). Further, it is worth noting that social media firms may be subject to liability on an aiding-and-abetting theory under the Anti-Terrorism Act, see *Gonzalez v. Google, Inc.*, 2 F. 4th 871 (9th Cir. 2021).

[93] Ford (n 84) 137.

[94] Ibid., 147.

[95] Ibid., 115.

[96] Ibid., 175.

[97] Petit (n 17) 255.

of surveillance capitalism. The autonomy and freedom of users are at stake. Therefore, the challenge consists of striking the right balance between the various interests at stake.

VI. CONCLUSION

In sum, business models have evolved in the digital marketplace. Digital platforms have increasingly played a role as information gatekeepers. As they rely on algorithms to process and screen information, they have the ability to manage the flow of information available to users of digital services. This has given rise to new forms of conflicts of interest. Digital platforms have various stakeholders that may have diverging interests. Corporate governance mechanisms have to be redesigned with a view to taking into account the economic reality of digital platform business models.

In addition, digital platforms owe fiduciary duties to users of their services. This implies the need to take into account the interests of their users. This applies whenever they have induced trust amongst their users and they are aware of it. Also, this is particularly relevant to the extent that the users are unable to defend their own interests due to asymmetry of power and information and can thus not effectively monitor digital platforms. This is limited by the broad immunity from liability for third-party content. Nevertheless, such immunity is not absolute. Therefore, there is room to strike for the optimal level of deterrence.

6. Property and data: A confused relationship

Joseph Lee and Marc Van de Looverbosch

I. INTRODUCTION

The crypto-market is an emerging space for financial transactions. Different types of crypto-assets circulate on the internet offered by different operators in various jurisdictions. Policy makers, regulators, and courts are still in the process of coming to terms with this new system and developing approaches to its regulation. The aim of this chapter is to look at the relationship between crypto-assets taken as property, and data governance. Since crypto-assets are intangible it is difficult to know when to treat them as property, as information, or merely as data. For example, there is a clear distinction between a car (property), the registration number of the car in a system (data), and the identity of the person who owns the car (information). However, such distinctions are not so clear when thinking about a crypto-asset (data), registered on the blockchain (data), and the owner's details (also data). This can give rise to a number of obligations for the system operator: as proprietary custodian,[1] as data controller[2] and processor, as data owner, and as information gatekeeper.[3]

---

1 Eva Micheler, 'Custody Chains and Asset Values: Why Crypto-Securities are Worth Contemplating' (2015) 74(3) *Cambridge Law Journal* 505, 530, https://www.cambridge.org/core/journals/cambridge-law-journal/article/abs/custody-chains-and-asset-values-why-cryptosecurities-are-worth-contemplating/9C655568E79CE7998B43B6848309C121 accessed 2 September 2021.

2 Dr Michèle Finck, *Blockchain and the General Data Protection Regulation: Can Distributed Ledgers be Squared with European Data Protection Law?* (European Parliament, Study of Panel for the Future of Science and Technology (STOA), Scientific Foresight Unit, European Parliamentary Research Service (EPRS), July 2019) https://www.europarl.europa.eu/RegData/etudes/STUD/2019/634445/EPRS_STU(2019)634445_EN.pdf accessed 1 August 2021.

3 Rodrigo Coelho, Johathan Fishman and Denise Garcia Ocampo, *Supervising Cryptoassets for Anti-Money Laundering* (Financial Stability Institute Insights on Policy Implementation No. 31, April 2021) https://www.bis.org/fsi/publ/insights31.pdf accessed 1 August 2021.

To show the relationship between property and data in this crypto-space, we will first discuss the concept of payment tokens and asset tokens which are most commonly used in the current crypto-market. Secondly, we will introduce four cases involving crypto-assets, specifically cryptocurrency, in four different jurisdictions. Thirdly, we will discuss how confusion arises and whether there could be a better way to distinguish property and data in order to design an effective governance framework. In particular, we will discuss how the currently proposed EU regulation of markets in crypto-assets (MiCA)[4] addresses these issues.

II. PAYMENT TOKENS

Payment tokens such as Bitcoin and Ether, also termed exchange tokens, are used as a method of payment, and may be either unstable or stable.[5] Unstable tokens are not linked to any particular asset class recognised by the law and are created through the protocols of the 'mining' process.[6] An unstable token is an intangible, virtual object that can be used for payment as if it were gold or silver in the past.[7] There is no specific value affixed to this intangible object,[8] unlike fiat money or digital money, both of which have a set value. The value of a payment token is determined by supply and demand in the market and as a result, its price is variable with no stable benchmark to measure its intrinsic value.[9] As payment tokens are not issued by a central bank or a central authority, and there is no defined measure to stabilise their intrinsic value, stabilisation depends on what the participants in the consensus system (the nodes)

---

4 Dirk Zetzsche, Filippo Annunziata, Douglas Arner, and Ross Buckley, 'The Markets in Crypto-Assets Regulation (MiCA) and the EU Digital Finance Strategy' (2021) 16(2) *Capital Markets Law Journal* 203, 225, https://academic.oup.com/cmlj/article-abstract/16/2/203/6324188 accessed 2 September 2021.

5 G7 Working Group on Stablecoins, *Investigating the Impact of Global Stablecoins* (October 2019) https://www.bis.org/cpmi/publ/d187.pdf accessed 7 July 2020.

6 Joseph Lee and Florian L'heureux, 'A Regulatory Framework for Cryptocurrency', (2020) 31(3) *European Business Law Review* 423, 446.

7 Chia Ling Koh, 'The Rise of e-Money and Virtual Currencies: Re-discovering the Meaning of Money from a Legal Perspective' (Osborne Clarke, 2018) https://www.osborneclarke.com/wp-content/uploads/2018/07/The-rise-of-e-Money-and-virtual-currencies.pdf accessed 7 July 2020.

8 PWC, 'Cryptographic Assets and Related Transactions: Accounting Considerations under IFRS' (Research Report, 2019) https://www.pwc.com/gx/en/audit-services/ifrs/publications/ifrs-16/cryptographic-assets-related-transactions-accounting-considerations-ifrs-pwc-in-depth.pdf accessed 2 September 2021.

9 EY, 'The Valuation of Crypto-Assets: Minds Made for Shaping Financial Services' (2018) https://assets.ey.com/content/dam/ey-sites/ey-com/en_gl/topics/emeia-financial-services/ey-the-valuation-of-crypto-assets.pdf accessed 7 July 2020.

decide.[10] This can include revision of the original protocols used to create the tokens, which leads to the problem of 'forking' with the opportunity for market manipulation at the expense of anybody unable to participate meaningfully in the revision of the original protocols.[11] To counter the instability of unstable payment tokens, some stable coins have emerged, notable amongst them being Diem, which intends to issue tokens linked to underlying assets that can be used for payment within the network.[12] The aim is to stabilise the value of the issued tokens, possibly with a fixed price, so that people who purchase them with fiat currencies, use them as payment, or receive them as payments or gifts, would have some protection against fluctuations in value. However, as in other fiat currencies, payment tokens can also be used for purposes other than payment. They can be purchased as an investment by someone expecting the value to go up or to earn interest/dividends when in the custody of intermediaries such as exchanges or banks. They can also be used as a method of transmitting value, though not in retail payment transactions by consumers, for large payments between entities, or in investment. This ability is most likely to be used to facilitate exchanges in criminal activity, particularly if the tokens and the trading space are ungoverned.[13]

Current legal taxonomy and regulatory approaches to payment tokens remain sectoral rather than systematic. They are a taxable asset recognised as a 'unit of account' by the UK tax authority.[14] However, it is not clear how the UK tax authority intends to treat them in law, for instance, whether payment tokens can be held in trust and are capable of being passed down from the settler to the ultimate beneficiaries, or how tax rates can be applied to payment tokens that have no face value and a fluctuating intrinsic value.[15] A decision is needed on how legal taxonomy applies to crypto-assets. Whatever that decision is, the revenue authorities will have a keen interest in levying taxes on

---

[10] G7 Working Group on Stablecoins (n 5).

[11] Vitalik Buterin, 'Decentralised Protocol Monetisation and Forks' (*Ethereum Foundation Blog*, 30 April 2014) https://blog.ethereum.org/2014/04/30/decentralized-protocol-monetization-and-forks/ accessed 7 July 2020.

[12] The Libra Association Members, *Libra White Paper* (White Paper, 2020) https://libra.org/en-US/white-paper/ accessed 7 July 2020.

[13] Everette Jordan and others, *Risks and Vulnerabilities of Virtual Currency: Cryptocurrency as a Payment Method* (Public-Private Analytic Exchange Programme, 2017) https://www.dni.gov/files/PE/Documents/9—2017-AEP_Risks-and-Vulnerabilities-of-Virtual-Currency.pdf accessed 7 July 2020.

[14] HM Revenue & Customs, *Cryptoassets: Tax for Individuals* (Policy Paper of HM Revenue & Customs, 2019) https://www.gov.uk/government/publications/tax-on-cryptoassets/cryptoassets-for-individuals accessed on 7 July 2020.

[15] Ibid.

them, as a receipt of payment, an investment or a gift, either legal or illegal.[16] The tax authorities can levy taxes on gains that originate from money laundering, market abuse, insider dealing, or bribes.

As payment tokens have been used to facilitate exchanges associated with crime, money-laundering laws are necessary in order to cut off financing channels for activities such as the drug trade along the Silk Road.[17] In this context, money-laundering law has been the first set of laws to recognise the legal status of crypto-assets as money.[18] However, payment tokens are still not systematically recognised as money; Bitcoin, for instance, is not considered to be money in the Sale of Goods Act 1979.[19] When Bitcoin and similar tokens are treated as money, there are two implications. Firstly, since the law is targeted at money laundering, Bitcoin and other similar tokens are included within the parameters of anti-money-laundering regulations.[20] Secondly, it implies that the definition of money used by the anti-money-laundering law is not limited to payment tokens and may be extended to other tokens such as hybrid tokens.

The UK Payment Systems Regulator (PSR), which regulates credit card payments and digital third-party payment providers, does not issue guidance on how payment tokens are to be treated and recognised.[21] There is no reason why payment systems should not have the ability to process payment tokens and be subject to the oversight of the PSR. Although the market operations of payment tokens are different from those of fiat currency and e-money,[22] bringing processing payment tokens under the PSR would enhance the ability of operators to manage risk and promote innovation.[23]

---

[16] Peter Chapman and Laura Douglas, 'The Virtual Currency Regulation in the United Kingdom' in Michael Sackheim and Nathan Howell (eds), *The Virtual Currency Regulation Review* (The Law Reviews 2018) 310, 329.

[17] David Adler, 'Silk Road: The Dark Side of Cryptocurrency' *Fordham Journal of Corporate and Financial Law*, 21 February 2018) https://news.law.fordham.edu/jcfl/2018/02/21/silk-road-the-dark-side-of-cryptocurrency/ accessed on 7 July 2020.

[18] Peter Chapman and Laura Douglas (n 16).

[19] Laurie Korpi and Yasmine Dong, 'Unrivalled Insight into Global Digital Payments Regulation' (2015) https://gamblingcompliance.com/sites/gamblingcompliance.com/files/attachments/page/PaymentsCompliance%20-%20Payments%20Lawyer%20June%202015.pdf accessed 6 July 2020.

[20] Ibid.

[21] Financial Conduct Authority (FCA), *The Perimeter Guidance Manual, Chapter 15: Guidance on the Scope of the Payment Services Regulations* (PERG Handbook, 2017) <https://www.handbook.fca.org.uk/handbook/PERG/15.pdf> accessed 7 July 2020.

[22] Digital Watch Observatory, *Cryptocurrencies* (2020) <https://dig.watch/issues/cryptocurrencies> accessed 7 July 2020.

[23] Financial Conduct Authority (FCA), *Innovation in UK Consumer Electronic Payments: A Collaborative Study by Ofcom and the Payment Systems Regulator* (2014)

The Information Commissioner's Office, the UK's data protection regulator, also has jurisdiction over payment tokens when they contain personal information. The software design of payment tokens contains information about their origination in blocks on the DLT system, which means that personal information could be revealed.[24] Current encryption technology may not be effective in preventing violations of data protection and privacy.[25]

The discussion above shows that although regulators have begun to exert jurisdiction over payment tokens, they do not take a common approach to legal taxonomy. The way they share or divide their regulatory oversight largely relies on Memoranda of Understanding to avoid potential legal, organisational or operational conflicts in this sectoral regulatory sphere.[26] It is likely that payment tokens will continue to be regulated in this way and that a single regulator will not be able to determine the legal status of payment tokens and claim exclusive oversight. The way in which international regulators will coordinate will depend on how assets are legally classified.[27]

III. ASSET TOKENS

Asset tokens, also known as security tokens, represent underlying assets such as shares, bonds (debt), commodities, units of investment and rights to deal in those assets, such as options and futures.[28] They are issued by entities such as companies, but also by an individual or an association of individuals or entities.[29] If security tokens were treated as securities, it would bring them into the current legal and regulatory framework and securities law would apply

---

https://www.fca.org.uk/publication/research/ofcom-psr-joint-study.pdf accessed 7 July 2020.

[24] thinkBLOCKtank, *The Regulation of Token in Europe: National Legal & Regulatory Frameworks in Select European Countries* (2019) http://thinkblocktank.org/wp-content/uploads/2019/08/thinkBLOCKtank-Token-Regulation-Paper-v1.0-Part-C.pdf accessed 6 July 2020.

[25] PrivSec Report, 'Preventing Data Breaches and Assisting GDPR Compliance Using Encryption' (2017).

[26] J Dax Hansen, Sarah Howland and Will Conley, 'Digital Currencies: International Actions and Regulations' (2021) https://www.perkinscoie.com/en/news-insights/digital-currencies-international-actions-and-regulations.html accessed 5 September 2021.

[27] Apolline Blandin and others, 'Global Cryptoasset Regulatory Landscape Study' (University of Cambridge Faculty of Law Research Paper No. 23/2019) https://www.jbs.cam.ac.uk/wp-content/uploads/2020/08/2019-04-ccaf-global-cryptoasset-regulatory-landscape-study.pdf accessed 2 September 2021.

[28] Deloitte, 'Are Token Assets the Securities Tomorrow?' (2019) https://www2.deloitte.com/content/dam/Deloitte/lu/Documents/technology/lu-token-assets-securities-tomorrow.pdf accessed 8 July 2020.

[29] Ibid.

to the whole security trading cycle: issuing, trading, clearing and settlement. The current securities law covers the operations of the securities market. It recognises primary and secondary markets, and divides market players into infrastructure providers, issuers, intermediaries, institutional and retail investors, and domestic and foreign participants.[30] Securities law broadly divides into the prudential aspect of regulation with a focus on systemic aspect, and the conduct aspect with a focus on market integrity, investor protection, consumer protection, and market competitiveness.[31]

In addition to securities law, company law governs the internal affairs of a corporate organisation.[32] The major issues arising are capital maintenance for investor protection, particularly minority shareholders and outside creditors, governance of the organisation such as the decision-making process and the right to obtain redress, reorganisation, and dissolution of the organisation and dispute resolution.[33] Modern company law accommodates various types of companies, from closely held companies to publicly listed companies. Specific regimes have been created within the company law framework to service companies with different objectives and functions.[34] The aim is to ensure, on the one hand, that capital can continue to be aggregated efficiently through the collective effort of promoters, directors, shareholders, employees, and creditors, and, on the other hand, that benefits can be shared equitably amongst them.[35] New methods, processes and markets have been developed to facilitate

---

30 Baker McKenzie, 'Global Financial Services Regulatory Guide' (2016) https://www.bakermckenzie.com/-/media/files/insight/publications/2016/07/guide_global_fsrguide_2017.pdf?la=en accessed 7 July 2020.

31 Ibid.

32 Deborah Demott, 'Perspectives on Choice of Law for Corporate Internal Affairs' (1985) 48 (3) *Law and Contemporary Problems* 161, 198 https://scholarship.law.duke.edu/lcp/vol48/iss3/5/ accessed 4 September 2021.

33 Neal Watson and Beliz McKenzie, 'Shareholders' Right in Private and Public Companies in the UK (England and Wales)' (*Practical Law,* 1 July 2019) https://uk.practicallaw.thomsonreuters.com/5-613-3685?transitionType=Default&contextData=(sc.Default)&firstPage=true accessed 7 July 2020.

34 Business Roundtable, 'Principles of Corporate Governance' (*Harvard Law School Forum on Corporate Governance*, 8 September 2016) https://corpgov.law.harvard.edu/2016/09/08/principles-of-corporate-governance/ accessed 7 July 2020.

35 Paul Davies, *The Board of Directors: Composition, Structure, Duties and Powers* (Company Law Reform in OECD Countries: A Comparative Outlook of Current Trends, 2000).

the aggregation of capital, including private placement,[36] direct listing,[37] initial public offering,[38] private equity[39] and the newly emerged securities token offering (STO).[40] To ensure that benefits are shared equitably, various mechanisms have been introduced such as minority shareholder protection in closely held companies to corporate governance of listed and quoted companies. Besides these mechanisms, the takeover market has been developed as a way to monitor corporate performance rather than as a way to share the benefits of the company, mainly through the sale of the control premium to the bidders.[41]

Including security tokens under the company law framework poses a manageable legal risk for uncertainty but the problem is whether it would defeat the purpose of issuing asset tokens,[42] namely to ensure efficient capital aggregation and equitable sharing of benefits. In many STO projects, security tokens are offered on the open market to anyone who can access the internet; issue and purchase do not need the traditional financial intermediaries.[43] However, under the current company law framework, only certain companies can issue securities to the general public,[44] needing, for example, a clean three-year

---

36 Andrew Baum, 'The Future of Real Estate Initiative' (2020) University of Oxford Research, Said Business School, https://www.sbs.ox.ac.uk/sites/default/files/2020-01/Tokenisation%20Report.pdf accessed 7 July 2020.

37 Ran Ben-Tzur and James Evans, 'The Rise of Direct Listings: Understanding the Trend, Separating Fact from Fiction' (National Crowdfunding & Fintech Association (NCFA), 5 December 2019) https://ncfacanada.org/the-rise-of-direct-listings-understanding-the-trend-separating-fact-from-fiction/ accessed 7 July 2020.

38 Ryan Zullo, 'Can Tokenisation Fix the Secondary IPO Market?' (2020) https://www.eisneramper.com/tokenization-secondary-ipo-catalyst-0420/ accessed 7 July 2020.

39 R3, 'The Tokenisation of Financial Market Securities – What's Next? Including Research Report by Greenwich Associates: 'Security Tokens: Cryptonite for Stock Certificates'' (2019) https://www.r3.com/wp-content/uploads/2019/10/R3.Tokenization.Financial.Market.Securities.Oct2019.pdf accessed 7 July 2020.

40 Deloitte (n 28).

41 David Kershaw, *Principles of Takeover Regulation* (1st edn, Oxford University Press 2018) 44.

42 Ross Buckley et al, 'TechRisk' (March 2020) (1) *Singapore Journal of Legal Studies* 35; 'Initial Coin Offerings: Issues of Legal Uncertainty Report' (Comsure, 8 November 2019) https://www.comsuregroup.com/news/initial-coin-offerings-issues-of-legal-uncertainty-report-initial-coin-offerings-30-july-2019/ accessed 9 July 2020.

43 Jovan Ilic, 'Security Token Offerings: What Are They, and Where Are They Going in 2019?' (Medium, 18 March 2019) https://medium.com/mvp-workshop/security-token-offerings-sto-what-are-they-and-where-are-they-going-in-2019-cc075aea6313 accessed 7 July 2020.

44 S 755 of Companies Act 2006 provides that 'a private company limited by shares or limited by guarantee and having a share capital must not; (a) offer to the public any securities of the company, or (b) allot or agree to allot any securities of the company with a view to their being offered to the public'.

trading record.[45] Furthermore, the corporate governance rules in company law and the Corporate Governance Code place significant burdens on issuers who are often not able to afford the expense of governance services such as legal, compliance, and auditing costs.[46] Although 'Code as law' seems to be able to mitigate some of these costs through automation,[47] many areas would still require human intervention, especially where cognitive judgement is required to interpret rules that are based on policy objectives or where there are different acts to be balanced against one another.[48] The reason that STO is attractive to legitimate businesses is its ability to reach the entire internet community without infrastructure obstacles or national boundaries.[49] Bringing them under the current company law framework would compromise this benefit. As an example, the US's Howey test, when applied to DAO (an STO project), would prevent development in security token finance, and encourage underground STO markets.[50] Whilst many countries have created a specific legal and regulatory regime for STO and have provided trading platforms for the investment community, none has been successful.

It is time to reconsider the current legal, regulatory and market infrastructures for security tokens. How do they function? Can they change as required by developments in the market? Who has authority to create the law and to control its development? In particular, since the current legal and regulatory framework is the result of regulatory capture, to what extent are participants in today's security tokens market able to influence the law?

---

[45] LR 6.3.1R, FCA.

[46] Organisation for Economic Co-operation and Development (OECD), *Risk Management and Corporate Governance* (2014) http://www.oecd.org/daf/ca/risk-management-corporate-governance.pdf accessed 7 July 2020.

[47] Gabrielle Patrick and Anurag Bana, *Rule of Law Versus Rule of Code: A Blockchain-Driven Legal World*, (IBA Legal Policy & Research Unit Legal Paper, 2017).

[48] Smart Contracts Alliance: An Initiative of The Chamber of Digital Commerce, *Smart Contracts: Is the Law Ready?* (Smart Contract Whitepaper, 2018) https://lowellmilkeninstitute.law.ucla.edu/wp-content/uploads/2018/08/Smart-Contracts-Whitepaper.pdf accessed 7 July 2020.

[49] Deloitte (n 28).

[50] Lennart Ante and Ingo Fiedler, 'Cheap Signals in Security Token Offerings (STOs)' (2019) Blockchain Research Lab Working Paper Series No. 1, https://www.blockchainresearchlab.org/wp-content/uploads/2019/07/Cheap-Signals-in-Security-Token-Offerings-BRL-Series-No.-1-update3.pdf accessed 7 July 2020.

IV. THE FOUR CASES

The first case that is included in the selection, *MtGox*, is a milestone case from Japan, and arguably one of the first major judgments that attempts a civil law characterisation of Bitcoin. The second case that is discussed, *Hedqvist*, is the first European Court of Justice (ECJ) case on crypto-assets, specifically on the VAT exemption for Bitcoin. The third case, *Bitspread v. Paymium*, is a French one dealing with the property law characterisation of Bitcoin under French law. The fourth case, *AA v. Persons unknown and Bitfinex*, also deals with the proprietary status of cryptocurrencies, but this time in the context of a proprietary injunction under English law.

Whilst these cases may seem utterly diverse, they reveal a pattern that is still consolidating today. The pattern is converging on the treatment of Bitcoin and other crypto-assets as intangible property that can be privately owned and transferred. In *MtGox*, the Japanese court was reluctant to consider Bitcoin as property, due to the tangibility requirement inherited from German law. In *Hedqvist*, the ECJ ruled that Bitcoin could constitute a means of payment for purposes of the European VAT Directive, which perhaps shows that, in contrast with national civil laws, the VAT Directive would benefit from an update to include novel types of financial assets such as crypto-assets. The last two cases discussed, *Bitspread v. Paymium* and *AA v. Persons unknown and Bitfinex*, are more modern and more elaborate in their analysis of the property law characterisation of crypto-assets. They indicate the direction in which European case law is decidedly headed: the recognition of crypto-assets as transferable intangible property.

A. Japan: MtGox

1. Judgment of the Tokyo District Court, Civil Division 28, of 5 August 2015, MtGox[51]

Mark Karpelès was the founder of MtGox, one of the first major online bitcoin exchanges. One day, he discovered that the MtGox wallets which were supposed to hold around USD 400 million in bitcoins were empty.[52] Hackers had systematically syphoned off bitcoins from the exchange's cold wallets. About

[51] An unofficial English translation of the judgment is available at https://www.law.ox.ac.uk/sites/files/oxlaw/mtgox_judgment_final.pdf accessed 1 August 2021.

[52] A 'wallet' is a piece of software or hardware which enables storage of cryptocurrency. A wallet is said to be a 'cold wallet' if the wallet is kept offline. If the wallet is kept online, the wallet is called a 'hot wallet'. A 'cold wallet' is generally considered more secure than a 'hot wallet'.

a week after the discovery, on 28 February 2014, MtGox applied for creditor protection.

In an odd turn of events, 200,000 bitcoins, worth around USD 90 million at the time, were retrieved three weeks later, after scanning a wallet presumed empty. Unfortunately, this was not enough to steer the then largest bitcoin exchange in the world clear of insolvency. The Tokyo District Court declared MtGox Co., Ltd. bankrupt on 24 April 2014, thereby freezing the claims of creditors.

A key point in the overall design of financial systems is to ensure that assets held for an investor by an intermediary do not become assets of the intermediary. This point came to the fore in the MtGox case. One person, designated 'Plaintiff Z1' in the court documents, did not consider himself an ordinary creditor. Instead, he saw himself as the owner of bitcoins that just happened to be in possession of MtGox at the time it was declared bankrupt. So Plaintiff Z1 sued MtGox's bankruptcy trustee before the Tokyo District Court in order to obtain the return of the approximately 459 bitcoins he held in his MtGox account at the time of the bankruptcy declaration.

A major problem for Plaintiff Z1 was that Japanese law did not recognise ownership of crypto-assets at that time. In order to be the object of ownership under Japanese civil law, a thing needs to have two characteristics. First, the thing needs to be a tangible thing.[53] Secondly, the thing must be capable of being exclusively controlled.[54]

Plaintiff Z1 conflated these two characteristics in order to make the case that bitcoin can be the object of ownership. His argument was based on the following grounds.

a. The electronic record held on a number of computers embodies the bitcoin and is not merely a record of it;
b. Therefore, bitcoin has an existence;
c. (i) Therefore, it is possible to subject it to exclusive control; (ii) In addition, bitcoins can be the object of exclusive control due to the existence and functioning of the private key, without which unspent transaction outputs cannot be spent;
d. Because a bitcoin can be exclusively controlled, it is a tangible thing, capable of being the object of ownership.

---

[53] Article 85 of the Japanese Civil Code 1896; pp. 6, 7 of the English translation of the judgement discussed.

[54] Article 206 of the Japanese Civil Code 1896; pp. 6, 7 of the English translation of the judgement discussed.

The court was not convinced by the 'embodiment' argument in the first half of the plaintiff's argument. It had a strict reading of the corporeality requirement in Article 85 of the Japanese Civil Code, according to which even things that can be physically observed, such as electricity, heat and light, are excluded from being a 'tangible thing'.[55] Referring to Bitcoin's digital and internet-based nature, the court held that 'it is obvious that bitcoin has no corporeality which occupies space'.

The court also pointed out that the tangibility of a thing cannot be inferred solely from the possibility to exclusively control the thing, as Plaintiff Z1 seemed to be arguing in the fourth prong of his argument. Rather surprisingly, the court also held that bitcoins cannot be the subject of exclusive control. On the basis of a brief examination of how Bitcoin's mining process works, the court observed that 'the involvement of a person other than the parties is required in order to carry out the transaction'. In view of that observation, the court concluded that 'the person who manages the private key of his bitcoin address does not have the exclusive control of the remaining bitcoin balance on this address'.

To summarise, the Tokyo District Court dismissed Plaintiff Z1's claims, because Japanese law did not recognise the ownership of bitcoins.[56]

2. Recent developments

Things changed on 1 April 2017, when an amendment to the Japanese Payment Services Act came into effect.[57] The amendment added the notion of 'Virtual Currency' to the Payment Services Act. The term 'Virtual Currency' is defined as follows in the Payment Services Act:

> a. property value (limited to that which is recorded on an electronic device or any other object by electronic means, and excluding the Japanese currency, foreign currencies, and Currency-Denominated Assets; the same applies in the follow-

---

[55] An unofficial English translation of the Japanese Civil Code is available at http://www.japaneselawtranslation.go.jp/law/detail/?id=2057&printID=&re=02&vm=04.

[56] For further reading, see Ilya Kokorin, '"Hacked" Insolvencies of Crypto Exchanges' (Leiden Law Blog, 5 July 2018) https://leidenlawblog.nl/articles/hacked-insolvencies-of-crypto-exchanges; Louise Gullifer, Megumi Hara and Charles Mooney, 'English translation of the Mt Gox judgment on the legal status of bitcoin prepared by the Digital Assets Project' (*University of Oxford Commercial Law Centre Blog*, 6 February 2019) https://www.law.ox.ac.uk/research-subject-groups/commercial-law-centre/blog/2019/02/english-translation-mt-gox-judgment-legal; Marc Van de Looverbosch, 'Taming the Intangible: MtGox Judgment Translated into English' (Distributed Ledger Law, 14 February 2019). Accessed 1 August 2021.

[57] An unofficial English translation of the Japanese Payment Services Act is available at http://www.japaneselawtranslation.go.jp/law/detail/?id=3078&printID=&re=02&vm=04 .

ing item) which can be used in relation to unspecified persons for the purpose of paying consideration for the purchase or leasing of goods or the receipt of provision of services and can also be purchased from and sold to unspecified persons acting as counterparties, and which can be transferred by means of an electronic data processing system; and

b. property value which can be mutually exchanged with what is set forth in the preceding item with unspecified persons acting as counterparties, and which can be transferred by means of an electronic data processing system.

Expressly departing from the conclusion of the MtGox judgment, the definitions of both categories of Virtual Currency lead with the words 'property value'. Whilst the definitions are rather intricate, many crypto-assets, such as Bitcoin, Ethereum and Litecoin, seem to fall within the first category. Thus bitcoins are now considered a sort of 'property value' under Japanese law.

Additionally, cryptocurrency exchanges now have an obligation pursuant to Article 63-11 of the Payment Services Act to keep customers' money and cryptocurrency separate from their own assets. This segregation obligation carries criminal penalties and must be audited periodically by a certified public accountant.

But what if the exchange does not comply with the segregation obligation and subsequently goes bankrupt? What is the significance of the words 'property value' to an investor requesting the return of his/her cryptocurrency from the bankruptcy trustee? This remains a matter of debate in Japan.

3. The Coincheck hacking

To add insult to injury, Coincheck, one of Japan's largest cryptocurrency exchanges, was hacked in January 2018. This resulted in the theft of approximately USD 530 million worth of NEM tokens. Coincheck survived the attack and still operates today. However, in the aftermath of the theft, further revisions to the Payment Services Act as well as to the Financial Instruments and Exchange Act were enacted, including a newly introduced registration obligation for custodians of crypto-assets. These revisions further tightened the regulation of crypto custody in Japan.

B. EU: *Skatteverket v. Hedqvist*

1. Judgement of the European Court of Justice of 22 October 2015 in Case C-264/14, *Skatteverket v. David Hedqvist*

David Hedqvist's business idea was simple enough. He would buy bitcoins from whoever was willing to sell, and then resell them at a higher price via his own company's website: www.bitcoin.se. The difference between the purchase price and the sale price would constitute his company's earnings.

Mr Hedqvist soon realised that if the exchange service he provided would be subject to VAT, his business would be stillborn. So he decided to apply for a tax ruling with his home country's ruling commission, the Swedish Revenue Law Commission (Skatterättsnämnden).

In 2013, the Swedish Revenue Law Commission (SRLC) held that Hedqvist's bitcoin exchange service was not subject to VAT. The SRLC's reasoning was that bitcoin was a means of payment used in a similar way to legal means of payment. Traditional currency exchange services are exempt from VAT pursuant to Chapter 3, Paragraph 9 of the Swedish Law on VAT, which implements Article 135(1)(e) of the VAT Directive (Council Directive 2006/112/EC of 28 November 2006 on the common system of value added tax). Due to bitcoin's functional similarity to traditional currencies and considering the traditional currency exchange services exemption, services that offer exchange services between bitcoin and traditional currencies (such as the Swedish krona) should also be exempt.

The Swedish Tax Administration (Skatteverket) begged to differ with this finding of the SRLC. It appealed against the SRLC's decision to the Swedish Supreme Administrative Court, the Högsta förvaltningsdomstolen, which decided to stay the proceedings and refer two questions to the ECJ:

a. Is Article 2(1) of the VAT Directive to be interpreted as meaning that transactions in the form of what has been described as the exchange of virtual currency for traditional currency and vice versa, which is effected for consideration added by the supplier when the exchange rates are determined, constitute the supply of a service effected for consideration?
b. If so, must Article 135(1) [of that directive] be interpreted as meaning that the abovementioned exchange transactions are tax exempt?

The ECJ's answer to both questions was 'yes'.

It is easy to see how David Hedqvist's bitcoin exchange service constitutes the supply of a service for consideration (first question), so we will not expand on that. The second question and the ECJ's answer to that question are worthier of examination.

Three possible grounds for exemption were assessed under the second question: Article 135(1)(d), (e) and (f) of the VAT Directive.

The first exemption, in Article 135(1)(d), does not apply to bitcoin. This provision exempts 'transactions, including negotiation, concerning deposit and current accounts, payments, transfers, debts, cheques and other negotiable instruments, but excluding debt collection'. The ECJ held in respect of this provision that:

> [t]he 'bitcoin' virtual currency, being a *contractual means of payment*, cannot be regarded as a current account or a deposit account, a payment or a transfer.

> More-over, unlike a debt, cheques and other negotiable instruments referred to in Article 135(1)(d) of the VAT Directive, the 'bitcoin' virtual currency is a *direct means of payment* between the operators that accept it. (emphasis ours)

The third exemption, in Article 135(1)(f), does not apply to bitcoin either. This provision exempts 'transactions, including negotiation but not management or safekeeping, in shares, interests in companies or associations, debentures and other securities, but excluding documents establishing title to goods, and the rights or securities referred to in Article 15(2)'. The ECJ held in respect of this provision that: '[i]t is common ground that the "bitcoin" virtual currency is neither a security conferring a property right nor a security of a comparable nature'.

The second exemption, in Article 135(1)(e), however, does apply. This provision exempts 'transactions, including negotiation, concerning currency, bank notes and coins used as legal tender, with the exception of collectors' items, that is to say, gold, silver or other metal coins or bank notes which are not normally used as legal tender or coins of numismatic interest'.

The ECJ's reasoning in determining that the exemption of Article 135(1)(e) applies, was as follows:

a. The various language versions of Article 135(1)(e) of the VAT Directive differ from one another. Therefore, it cannot be determined without ambiguity whether that provision applies only to transactions involving traditional currencies or whether, on the contrary, it is also intended to cover transactions involving another currency.
b. Where there are linguistic differences, the scope of the expression in question cannot be determined on the basis of an interpretation which is exclusively textual. That expression must therefore be interpreted in the light of the context in which it is used and of the aims and scheme of the VAT Directive.
c. The exemption of Article 135(1)(e) envisages 'financial transactions'. As per the ECJ, financial transactions include, among others, 'transactions involving non-traditional currencies, that is to say, currencies other than those that are legal tender in one or more countries, in so far as those currencies have been accepted by the parties to a transaction as an alternative to legal tender and have no purpose other than to be a means of payment'.

The ECJ held that 'it is common ground that the "bitcoin" virtual currency has no other purpose than to be a means of payment and that it is accepted for that purpose by certain operators'. Thus, the exchange of bitcoin for traditional currencies, and vice versa, is a financial transaction.

d. The purpose of exempting financial transactions is to alleviate the difficulties connected with determining the taxable amount and the amount of VAT deductible which are allegedly inherent to such transactions.

The ECJ does not explain precisely which 'difficulties' it is referring to. We fail to see what makes it so much harder to levy VAT on financial transactions than on any other transaction. A more convincing argument for not levying VAT on financial transactions could be that the number of transactions would drastically decrease if VAT were to be levied on these transactions.

> e. The purported difficulties connected with determining the taxable amount and the amount of VAT deductible may be the same, whether it is a case of the exchange of traditional currencies, normally entirely exempt under Article 135(1)(e) of the VAT Directive, or the exchange of such currencies for virtual currencies with bi-directional flow, which — without being legal tender — are a means of payment accepted by the parties to a transaction, and vice versa. It therefore follows from the context and the aims of Article 135(1)(e) that to interpret that provision as including only transactions involving traditional currencies would deprive it of part of its effect.

For these reasons, bitcoin exchange services, such as the ones offered by David Hedqvist's company at www.bitcoin.se, are covered by the exemption from VAT of Article 135(1)(e) of the VAT Directive.

2. The ECJ's reasoning revisited

It is doubtful, to say the least, that bitcoin would today still be regarded as having 'no other purpose than to be a means of payment'. According to bitcoinfees.earn.com, the fastest and cheapest transaction fee for the median bitcoin transaction size at the time of writing amounted to about EUR 9.12 (c. USD 10.94). It seems irrational to use a payment medium with such high transaction fees, whilst numerous alternatives are available that charge zero transaction fees. Bitcoin is also a highly volatile asset. In the first half of 2021, Bitcoin's price has fluctuated from about USD 30,000 (in early January) to more than USD 63,000 (on 16 April) and back down to about USD 32,000 (at the end of June).[58] For these reasons, Bitcoin is currently primarily regarded as a speculative investment, not as a means of payment.

It could be deemed undesirable to subject transactions in bitcoin and other crypto-assets to VAT, as this would constitute (i) a non-deductible cost for private individuals, deterring private individuals from trading crypto-assets and reducing liquidity, and (ii) an administrative burden for entities that can deduct VAT, further deterring trading and reducing liquidity. To avoid this, it may be better to abandon the condition that non-traditional currencies must 'have no purpose other than to be a means of payment' in order for transactions in these currencies to be regarded as 'financial transactions' and fall within the

---

[58] See Coindesk https://www.coindesk.com/price/bitcoin accessed 1 August 2021.

scope of the exemption of Article 135(1)(e) of the VAT Directive. One may take the view that, as long as non-traditional currencies are accepted by the parties to a transaction as an alternative to traditional currencies, that transaction could be considered a 'financial transaction' for the purposes of the VAT exemption.

C. France: *Bitspread v. Paymium*

1. Judgment of the Commercial Court of Nanterre, France of 26 February 2020, *Bitspread v. Paymium*

On 26 February 2020, the Commercial Court of Nanterre, France handed down a judgment in the case of Bitspread versus Paymium. Bitspread is a crypto-asset trading and advisory company founded by a French national based in London. Paymium is a French Bitcoin ex-change. In May 2014, Bitspread opened an account on Paymium's trading platform at paymium.com. Between September 2014 and June 2016, Bitspread borrowed a total amount of 1,000 Bitcoin from Paymium. Bitspread then transferred some or all of the bitcoins so borrowed to its account on the crypto-asset trading platform Kraken.

All of these operations occurred prior to Bitcoin's first hard fork.[59] Bitcoin's very first hard fork, leading to a split of the bitcoin blockchain and the creation of Bitcoin Cash, occurred on 1 August 2017. It was alleged by Paymium during the proceedings before the Nanterre court that Bitspread received an amount of 1,000 Bitcoin Cash in its Kraken account as a result of the hard fork. Paymium alleged that it remained the owner of the bitcoins it lent to Bitspread and, consequently, that Paymium is also the owner of the Bitcoin Cash which Bitspread received from the hard fork, as they are the legal fruits of the bitcoins. Bitspread, on the other hand, refused to pay the Bitcoin Cash to Paymium, claiming they were Bitspread's property instead.

Another bone of contention was the interest due on the bitcoin loan. On 24 and 25 October 2017, Bitspread reimbursed the total principal amount of borrowed bitcoins. However, it did not pay any interest. At the outset, parties had agreed a 5 per cent annual interest rate, to be paid in Bitcoin.

On 26 October 2017, one day after reimbursement of the principal, Paymium informed Bitspread that an amount of 52 bitcoin in interest was due and outstanding. Some ten days later, Bitspread requested a withdrawal from its Paymium account in the amount of 53 bitcoin. Paymium refused this withdrawal, and replied with an overview of the amounts due by Bitspread, which included an amount of 1,000 Bitcoin Cash as well as the interest on the

[59] A 'hard fork' is essentially a split of the blockchain in two separate and distinct blockchains that each evolve independently from that moment on.

bitcoin loan, which now amounted to 45 bitcoin. One month later, Paymium sent Bitspread a notice of default and closed Bitspread's account. Bitspread replied with a formal notice requesting Paymium to return the amount of 53 bitcoin that was in the closed account. Paymium responded with a reiteration of its previous formal notice, adjusting the outstanding amount of the interest down to 42.49 bitcoin. Bitspread finally summoned Paymium to appear before the commercial court of Nanterre.

2. Custody or demand deposit

Bitspread demanded the repayment by Paymium of the 53 bitcoin in its closed account. It did so by arguing that Paymium was a depositary and the deposit was akin to a custody (depositum regulare). Thus, according to Bitspread, Paymium was under the obligation to return the 53 deposited bitcoins upon request in accordance with articles 1937 and 1944 of the French Civil Code.

Paymium denied this, stating that only chattels, i.e., tangible things, can be the object of a custody under French law. Because bitcoins are intangible, they cannot be the object of a regular deposit. Therefore, according to Paymium, Paymium was not a depositary and was not held to return the bitcoins.

The Commercial Court fully disregarded the question on whether or not Paymium was a depositary, and proceeded straight to the question whether Bitspread was the owner of the 53 bitcoins held by Paymium. From Paymium's statements the court inferred that Paymium did not contest that Bitspread was the owner of the 53 bitcoins in its account. The Court therefore held that Paymium must return the 53 bitcoins to Bitspread, implicitly holding that Bitspread was the owner of the bitcoins.

3. Loan for use or loan for consumption

The second legal issue that was at stake in the case before the Nanterre Commercial Court, was whether the bitcoin loan was a remunerated loan for use (*commodatum* in Latin, or '*prêt à usage*' in French) or an ordinary loan for consumption ('*prêt de consommation*' in French).

The key difference for the outcome of this case, is that a borrower under a loan for use regime is not entitled to keep the fruits of the borrowed object, being in this case the Bitcoin Cash, whereas a borrower under a loan for consumption is entitled to keep the Bitcoin Cash.

The court held that the Bitcoin loan was a loan for consumption, considering that Bitcoins are fungible and that using them entails their consumption. Fungibility is a feature of things which is assessed within the context of a given legal relation. Two things are fungible if they are interchangeable for the purposes of a legal obligation.[60] For instance: one 50 euro bank note is as good as any other 50 euro bank note for the purposes of paying for your groceries. 50 euro bank notes are thus said to be 'fungible' for the purposes of paying for groceries. When a party lends fungible things to another party, a presumption applies that the borrower can use the things borrowed, as long as the borrower returns the same quantity of things of the same kind and quality. The things originally borrowed and the things eventually returned to the lender are thus considered fungible for the purposes of honouring the borrower's obligation to return things.

A loan for consumption is defined in Article 1892 of the French Civil Code as 'a contract by which one of the parties delivers to the other party a certain quantity of things which are consumed by use, at the expense of the latter to return to him as much of the same kind and quality'. 'Consumption' in the context of this definition can refer both to material consumption, for instance a sandwich that is eaten, and to legal consumption, such as a sum of money that is paid in consideration for some goods acquired. Money can hardly be used without paying it away. '[T]he peculiarity of money [is] that its utility is solely derived from its exchange-value,' said John Maynard Keynes in his General Theory.

If 'consumable' things are lent, this implies that the loan is a loan for consumption. Consequently, the borrower becomes the owner of the things borrowed, because the borrower is authorised to use the things, and cannot use them without consuming them. This transfer of ownership is expressly confirmed in Article 1893 of the French Civil Code. The things borrowed and the things eventually returned in the context of a loan for consumption are fungible for the purposes of honouring the borrower's obligation to return things.

So to return to the judgment at hand, the Commercial Court ruled that Bitcoins are consumed when they are used, whether to pay for goods or services, to exchange them for foreign currency or to lend them. The Court considered that bitcoins are therefore consumable things, just like legal tender money, even if bitcoin is not legal tender.

Bitcoins are interchangeable, because they are of the same kind and quality in the sense that all Bitcoins are issued on the same distributed ledger and that they are mutually equivalent in terms of their value. Thus they are 'fungible' in the sense of Article 1347-1, second paragraph of the French Civil Code, such that a set-off can occur between bitcoin debts and credits.

---

[60] For a detailed legal analysis of fungibility under French law, see Stéphane Torck and Hervé Synvet, 'Essai d'une théorie générale des droits réels sur choses fongibles' (Doctoral thesis, Université Panthéon-Assas (Paris II), Paris, 15 December 2001) 627. or Pierre-Grégoire Marly, 'Fongibilité et volonté individuelle: étude sur la qualification juridique des biens', (Doctoral thesis, Paris: LGDJ, 2004) 365.

In accordance with the already mentioned Article 1893 of the French Civil Code, the borrower of bitcoins becomes the owner of these bitcoins. Because the borrower becomes the owner, he is also entitled to the fruits of the things borrowed. In the case at hand, Bitspread is thus legally entitled to the Bitcoin Cash received from the hard fork, so ruled the Commercial Court.

D. UK: *AA v. Persons unknown and Bitfinex* – Judgement of the High Court of Justice of 13 December 2019, *AA v. Persons unknown and Bitfinex, Re Bitcoin*

The Nanterre Commercial Court's decision on the ownership point is in keeping with recent developments in the UK.

In November 2019, The LawTech Delivery Panel issued a 'Legal statement on cryptoassets and smart contracts'. The Panel, consisting of, amongst others, members of the judiciary, academia and the technology sector, considered the question whether crypto-assets such as bitcoin can be characterised as personal property under English law.

The Panel concluded that (i) crypto-assets have all of the indicia of property, (ii) their novel or distinctive features do not disqualify them from being property, (iii) nor are crypto-assets disqualified from being property as pure information, or because they might not be classifiable either as things in possession or things in action, (iv) crypto-assets are therefore to be treated in principle as property, but (v) a private key is not in itself to be treated as property because it is information.

This conclusion was endorsed by Mr Justice Bryan in a decision dated 13 December 2019, in the case of *AA v Persons unknown and Bitfinex, Re Bitcoin*. The applicant, a Canadian insurance company, had been the victim of ransomware, causing all of the applicant's data and IT systems to become encrypted. It had paid Bitcoins to the attackers in order to regain control of its data and IT infrastructure.

The applicant sought a proprietary injunction against Bitfinex, being the platform on which the attackers held Bitcoin wallets to which part of the ransom was transferred. The fundamental question for the Court to consider for the purposes of the application was whether or not cryptocurrencies constituted a form of property capable of being the subject of a proprietary injunction.

Justice Bryan was of the opinion that the LawTech Delivery Panel's detailed legal analysis of the proprietary status of cryptocurrencies was 'compelling' and should be adopted by the Court. As such, Justice Bryan was satisfied – at least to the level required for the purposes of an application for interim relief – that Bitcoins constitute property, and are capable of being the subject of a proprietary injunction.

V. DIGITAL PROPERTY AND DATA GOVERNANCE

A. The Intersection

These cases demonstrate how confusion can easily arise when the relationship between property and data is not clearly defined, and that there can be an equivalent confusion between property law and data law. Confusion can result when the courts decide that a digital record on a system is purely data or information rather than property and when an operator who processes financial information for clients is designated a data services provider rather than a financial services firm. Such decisions can subsequently affect how governance, or more specifically data governance,[61] ought to be designed in order to protect the clients. In the *MtGox* case, the court recognised that *MtGox* operates a data processing system but did not recognise cryptocurrency as a property, because of the intangible nature of Bitcoin. This approach was also adopted in *Skatteverket v. Hedqvist*, but in the latter case, a distinction was made between the service of processing data and the service of processing financial transactions. In modern financial systems, especially digital finance, every financial transaction involves data processing.[62] It is therefore important to distinguish between the data processing that is involved in financial transactions and more general data processing that is not. The law in this area needs to be designed, on the one hand to protect the property in the transaction, and on the other to protect data in the transactions. Making such a distinction is important because the former not only involves transfer of property, but also safekeeping the property in the system.

One possible approach to crypto-assets is to see them as property consisting of data, distinct from data itself. Based on this approach, one can then recognise a non-fungible token (NTF)[63] of a painting as property consisting of

---

[61] Rene Abraham, Johannes Schneider and Jan Vom Brocke, 'Data Governance: A Conceptual Framework, Structured Review, and Research Agenda' (2019) 49 *International Journal of Information Management* 424, 438 https://www.sciencedirect.com/science/article/pii/S0268401219300787 accessed 4 September 2021; Marina Micheli and others, 'Emerging Model of Data Governance in the Age of Datafication' (2020) 1 *Big Data and Society* 1, 15 https://journals.sagepub.com/doi/full/10.1177/2053951720948087 accessed 4 September 2021.

[62] Peterson Ozili, 'Impact of Digital Finance on Financial Inclusion and Stability' (2018) 18(4) *Borsa Istanbul Review* 329, 340 https://www.sciencedirect.com/science/article/pii/S2214845017301503 accessed 4 September 2021.

[63] Michael Dowling, 'Is Non-Fungible Token Pricing Driven by Cryptocurrencies' (2021) 4 *Finance Research Letters* https://www.sciencedirect.com/science/article/pii/S1544612321001781?via%3Dihub accessed 4 September 2021.

data. This NTF is separate from the actual painting, from the copyright of the painting, from the copyright of the code design, and from the sets of data used.

The concept that a property may consist of data is not new; we have already seen how dematerialised securities operate in the financial market.[64] As securities are dematerialised and are no longer in paper form, their transfer takes place by data processing – adding digits or subtracting digits from accounts on the system. This is affirmed in *AA v. Persons unknown and Bitfinex* in which that court recognised that a crypto-asset was not only information but also property. In addition, the court also recognised that the private key which conferred exclusive control was information.[65] In other words, if the crypto-asset service provider is entrusted with the private key (data), it would be required to have data governance in place to protect the clients' property as well as to safeguard their data (private key). In this case, the court did not treat a private key that can give access to property (i.e., Bitcoin) as property, like an actual key to the safe. Similarly, in *Bitspread v. Paymium*, the court recognised Bitcoin as a property consisting of data on the register, and went further to decide that it can be 'consumed'.

B. Data Governance

Data governance defines how a crypto-asset provider should manage the data assets that it controls.[66] There are several aims of data governance. The provider should understand where datasets are (client's crypto-asset) and how to access them (which private key is to be used).[67] The provider should put in place effective processes to protect data from threats of inappropriate

---

[64] Jannice Käll, 'The Materiality of Data as Property' (2020) 61 *Harvard International Law Journal Frontiers* 1, 11 https://harvardilj.org/2020/04/the-materiality-of-data-as-property/ accessed 4 September 2021; Mimi Zou, 'Code, and Other Laws of Blockchain' (2020) 40(3) *Oxford Journal of Legal Studies* 645, 665 https://academic.oup.com/ojls/article/40/3/645/5900367?searchresult=1 accessed 4 September 2021; Jan Oster, 'Code is Code and Law is Law – The Law of Digitalization and the Digitalization of Law' (2021) 29(2) *International Journal of Law and Information Technology* 1, 17 https://academic.oup.com/ijlit/article/29/2/101/6313392 accessed 4 September 2021.

[65] Adam Petravicius, 'Is the Answer Less Privacy and Less Data Security?' (2006) 1(11) *Privacy & Data Security Law Journal* 968, 971 https://jenner.com/system/assets/publications/7692/original/PDSL_petravicius.pdf?1323181507 accessed 4 September 2021.

[66] Apolline Blandin and others (n 27).

[67] Lawrence Akka and others, *Legal Statement on Cryptoassets and Smart Contracts* (The LawTech Delivery Panel, 2019) https://35z8e83m1ih83drye280o9d1-wpengine.netdna-ssl.com/wp-content/uploads/2019/11/6.6056_JO_Cryptocurrencies_Statement_FINAL_WEB_111119-1.pdf accessed 1 August 2021.

release and access (hacking).[68] The provider should acquire and develop the right resources and skill sets to manage data. The provider should appreciate the importance of data stewardship, data ownership, data policies, and data standards. Data stewardship means that the provider does not own the data such as the crypto-assets, but instead is its caretaker.[69] The provider should ensure the quality, accuracy and security of the data.[70] Data ownership means that the provider owns the data and has responsibility for its creation and for defining its use in the organisation.[71] In this case, the provider should have data policies which include rules for the management of its data assets, such as enforcing authentication and access rights to data and compliance with laws and regulations. The provider should also ensure that there are precise criteria, specifications and rules for the definition, creation, storage and usage of data within an organisation.

C. The Proposed EU Regulation on Markets for Crypto-Assets (MiCA)

The distinction between property consisting of data, and data such as personal data is also reflected in the proposed EU MiCA.

1. Protection of client's property

Under EU MiCA, issuers of crypto-assets have a duty to maintain their systems and security access protocols in line with the appropriate EU standards. Furthermore, crypto-asset service providers holding crypto-assets which belong to their clients must ensure adequate protection of such crypto-assets,

---

68 Robby Houben and Alexander Snyers, *Cryptocurrencies and Blockchain: Legal Context and Implications for Financial Crime, Money Laundering and Tax Evasion* (Policy Department for Economic, Scientific and Quality of Life Policies of the European Parliament, July 2018) https://www.europarl.europa.eu/cmsdata/150761/TAX3%20Study%20on%20cryptocurrencies%20and%20blockchain.pdf accessed 1 August 2021.

69 Christine Borgman, 'Open Data, Grey Data, and Stewardship: Universities at the Privacy Frontier' (2018) 33(1) *Berkeley Technology Law Journal* 365, 412 https://www.btlj.org/data/articles2018/vol33/33_2/Borgman_Web.pdf accessed 4 September 2021.

70 Information Commissioner's Office, *Guide to the General Data Protection Regulation (GDPR)* (2018) https://ico.org.uk/media/for-organisations/guide-to-the-general-data-protection-regulation-gdpr-1-0.pdf accessed 1 August 2021.

71 Ivan Stepanov, 'Introducing a Property Right Over Data in the EU: The Data Producer's Right – An Evaluation' (2019) 34(1) *International Review of Computers & Technology* 65, 86 https://www.tandfonline.com/doi/full/10.1080/13600869.2019.1631621 accessed 4 September 2021.

in order to maintain their clients' full ownership rights.[72] This is especially the case in the event of the crypto-asset service provider's insolvency. In addition, the use of a client's crypto-assets is prohibited without the client's express consent, and adequate arrangements must be set in place to ensure the client's rights are respected.[73] As such, crypto-asset service providers have to ensure that the client's funds (crypto-assets) are held in an identifiable and separate account from the crypto-asset service provider's own accounts.[74] Should the crypto-asset service providers not respect these obligations, clients can file complaints against the crypto-asset service providers, pursuant to Article 64 MiCA.

2. Protection of clients' personal data

EU MiCA also addresses personal data issues. It states that all personal data concerning the client's assets which was shared with the competent authorities responsible for carrying out the obligations provided for in this regulation shall be considered confidential and subject to professional secrecy unless disclosure of such information is needed for legal proceedings.[75] Furthermore, the processing of personal data relating to this regulation must be carried out by competent authorities in accordance with the General Data Protection Regulation (GDPR).[76] Finally, crypto-asset service providers must ensure the protection and safeguarding of the security, integrity and confidentiality of information through their systems.[77]

3. Protection of clients' monetisation of their own data (monetary right to personal data)

MiCA does not deal specifically with the protection of data subjects' right to trade their own data. However, according to Article 5 paragraph 1 letter a GDPR, personal data must be processed lawfully, fairly and in a transparent

---

[72] Article 13 paragraph 1, letter d of the Proposal for a Regulation of the European Parliament and of the Council on Markets in Crypto-assets, and amending Directive (EU) 2019/1937 (MiCA).

[73] Financial Conduct Authority (FCA), *Guidance on Cryptoassets: Feedback and Final Guidance to CP19/3* (Policy Statement PS 19/22, July 2019).

[74] Article 63 paragraph 2 MiCA.

[75] Article 87 MiCA.

[76] Pursuant to Article 88 MiCA,

With regard to the processing of personal data within the scope of this Regulation, competent authorities shall carry out their tasks for the purposes of this Regulation in accordance with Regulation (EU) 2016/67968; With regard to the processing of personal data by the EBA and ESMA within the scope of this Regulation, it shall comply with Regulation (EU) 2018/172569.

[77] Article 61 paragraph 7 subparagraph 2 MiCA.

manner. Hence, monetising clients' personal data without their consent would not be a lawful, fair or transparent processing of personal data. In addition, according to letter b of the same paragraph of GDPR, personal data should only be collected for legitimate purposes. Making a profit by using a client's personal data would not be a legitimate purpose. If the crypto-assets provider uses a client's data to make gains, the client should be entitled to those gains. Furthermore, according to letter f of the same paragraph, the processing of personal data should ensure appropriate security of the personal data and protect it against unauthorised or unlawful processing. These conditions would not be met if a client's data were to be monetised without consent.

Similarly, the conditions for a lawful processing established under Article 6 GDPR would not be met if the crypto-asset provider monetises clients' data without their consent. Processing clients' data would not seem necessary for the performance of a contract, compliance with legal obligations, protection of vital interests, performance of a task, or any legitimate interests.

Pursuant to Article 18 paragraph 1 letter b GDPR, the data subject has the right to obtain restriction of processing from the controller if the processing is unlawful, which would be the case if the provider monetises a client's personal data. The right to erasure provided by Article 17 GDPR might not be the best option if the client wishes to stay with that same crypto-asset service provider. However, it would be doubtful that a client would wish to stay with a crypto-asset service provider if they unlawfully monetised their clients' data without their consent. The client as a data subject also has a right to object provided for at Article 21 GDPR.

VI. CONCLUSION

In this chapter, we have looked at how property and data are related to one another in the crypto-asset market. The discussion on payment tokens and asset tokens shows how property might be treated differently. This is reflected in the proposed EU MiCA. In most jurisdictions, crypto-assets are already being recognised, or are well under way to being recognised, as intangible assets that can be privately owned. The case law discussed shows that crypto-assets, or Bitcoin at the very least, can fit within existing civil law frameworks in the jurisdictions discussed (France, England and Japan). The cases also show that judges do not shy away from tackling difficult questions around the civil law status of crypto-assets. On the other hand, case law can only provide legal certainty around matters presented to the court in a given jurisdiction. On a wide range of legal issues connected with transactions in crypto-assets, the jury is still out. In addition, more often than not, dealings in crypto-assets span many jurisdictions. For these reasons, it is advisable for crypto-asset businesses (such as exchanges) to have in place detailed contractual arrangements with their clients that contain a 'choice of law' clause, and anticipate and mitigate uncertainty surrounding the legal treatment of crypto-assets to the greatest extent possible. The way that property and data relate to one another also highlights areas where data governance regulations will need to cover the protection of personal property that consists of data and the protection of personal data. The proposed EU MiCA has also made a distinction between the protection of data as personal property, and the protection of personal data. It is also important for policy makers to consider how personal data that can be 'purchased' and 'monetised' can be safeguarded, and to propose data governance to be adopted by crypto-asset providers who protect and manage the proprietary data for their clients.

7. Financial instruments: Transactions and consumer protection in Japan

Antonios Karaiskos[1]

I. INTRODUCTION

This chapter will mainly deal with the current state of consumer protection in Japan regarding financial instrument transactions. The primary focus is business-to-consumer (B2C) financial instrument transactions. The term 'financial instrument transactions' is not defined by Japanese law. However, based on legal provisions and related doctrine, one could define them as transactions in which the customer provides capital to a business, with the expectation of receiving capital in the future, under a specific agreement between the customer and the business.[2] Such an agreement can also be explained as the exchange of future cash flow with present cash flow. Examples are sales to consumers of stocks, corporate bonds, and investment trusts performed by securities companies. The extent of this notion continues to broaden, reflecting developments of new financial instruments and a diversification of marketing channels.[3]

In Japan, financial instruments transactions are regulated by various laws, creating a complex landscape. Case law related to consumer protection in the respective field has also accumulated, allowing for flexibility in securing a safe and sound financial instruments market for consumers. At the same

1 The author would like to thank Professor Dan Rosen (Chuo University) who kindly reviewed this chapter and provided valuable suggestions and comments. This work was supported by JSPS KAKENHI Grant Number 21K01269.

2 Art. 2 para. 1 of the Act on Sales, etc. of Financial Instruments (Art. 3 para. 1 of the Act on the Provision of Financial Services, once the amendment of the Act on Sales, etc. of Financial Instruments mentioned below at footnote 5 comes into force) contains a definition of the term 'sale of financial instruments'. The complexity of this definition is evident from the fact that it includes 11 items and cites various other laws.

3 Toshiro Ueyanagi, *Kin'yushohintorihiki to Shohisha [Financial Instruments Transactions and Consumers]*, in: Kunihiro Nakata and Naoko Kano (eds), *Kihonkogi Shohishaho [Basic Lectures of Consumer Law]*, Nihonhyoronsha, 2020, p. 212.

time, self-regulation plays an essential role, and alternative dispute regulation (ADR) has been supplementing judicial protection. Specific rules govern the solicitation for financial transactions to consumers. Amid a general trend toward deregulation, achieving a balance with adequate consumer protection in the field of financial instrument transactions has been a key concern.

Recent developments in the era of digitalisation and the increased use of artificial intelligence (AI) are posing new challenges. The use of AI in the financial sector, for example in the forms of Fintech and blockchain, creates new dynamics in Japanese law. The main two dynamics are, on the one hand—preservation of the existing system versus the necessity for new regulation and, on the other hand—business enhancement versus consumer protection.

This chapter will analyse the development and current state of financial instruments transactions in Japan, as well as future perspectives, focusing on consumer protection.

II. MAJOR LAWS RELATED TO THE REGULATION OF FINANCIAL INSTRUMENTS TRANSACTIONS

A. Major Laws

Several laws regulate consumer protection in financial instruments transactions. These laws can be largely divided into the following two categories. The first is laws regulating the rights and duties of businesses and consumers who are parties to such transactions. Examples are the Civil Code,[4] the Act on Sales

---

[4] Act No. 89 of 1896. Non-official English translations of major Japanese laws can be found at the website Japanese Law Translation (http://www.japaneselawtranslation.go.jp/?re=0 last accessed 16 December 2021) prepared by the Japanese Ministry of Justice. Provision translations of the Acts presented in this paper are in principle based on the ones in this website, with minor amendments when considered necessary.

The part of the Japanese Civil Code related to the law of obligations was amended in 2017, and the amended version came into force on April 1, 2020. Regarding this recent amendment, see amongst others Stefan Wrbka, *Japan's Civil Code Reform Plan – Seen from a Western Perspective*, Kyushu University Legal Research Bulletin, On-Line Edition, http://www.law.kyushu-u.ac.jp/programsinenglish/kulrb/stefan2.pdf last accessed 16 December 2021; Antonios Karaiskos, *Civil Code Reform in Japan: Is the New Regulation of Standard Contract Terms a Desirable One?*, in: Maren Heidemann and Joseph Lee (eds), *The Future of the Commercial Contract in Scholarship and Law Reform*, Springer, 2018, p. 73 et seq.; Hiroyuki Kihara, *Japan's Civil Code Reform and Consumer Protection, Asia University Law Review*, vol. 47, no, 1 (2012), p. 84 et seq.

etc. of Financial Instruments,[5] the Consumer Contract Act,[6] and the Insurance Act.[7] The second category involves laws providing for rules and supervision of businesses acting engaged in financial instruments transactions. Examples of such laws are the Financial Instruments and Exchange Act,[8] the Act on Investment Trusts and Investment Corporations,[9] the Insurance Business Act,[10] and the Commodity Derivatives Transaction Act.[11]

B. Main Characteristics and Relations of the Laws

Regarding the second category (laws regulating businesses acting engaged in financial instrument transactions), since these laws regulate business activities, infringements by businesses lead to sanctions by the supervising authority but do not in principle induce civil law effects. However, this does not mean that such infringements are completely irrelevant to civil lawsuits filed by victimised consumers. On the contrary, they are taken into consideration when determining the existence and extent of a business's tort liability to a consumer.[12]

---

5 Act No. 101 of 2000 (note: 'etc.' in the title of this Act and others in this chapter is part of the official Japanese title, and has therefore not been omitted in the English versions). This Act has been amended by Act No. 50 of 2020, and the amendment comes into force on November 1, 2021. The name of the Act will be changed to 'Act on the Provision of Financial Services'. As for the changes in its content, the core change will be the insertion of provisions regarding financial service intermediation businesses. The provisions treated in this chapter have not changed in content. Only changes in the numbers of provisions have occurred. Since at the time of writing of this chapter the previous numbering is still in effect, the new provision numbers are indicated in parentheses after the current ones.

6 Act No. 61 of 2000. Regarding the content of regulation and consumer protection by this Act, see amongst others, Masahiko Takizawa, *Consumer Protection in Japanese Contract Law*, Hitotsubashi Journal of Law and Politics, no. 37 (2009), p. 31 et seq.; Antonios Karaiskos, *Regulation of Unfair Contract Terms in Japan*, Waseda Bulletin of Comparative Law, vol. 28 (2010), p. 13 et seq.; Antonios Karaiskos, *Developments in the Regulation of Unfair Contract Terms in Japan*, in: Kunihiro Nakata and Naoko Kano (eds.), *Shohishaho no Gendaika to Shudantekikenrihogo [Modernisation of Consumer Law and Collective Redress]*, Nihonhyoronsha, 2016, p. 507 et seq.

7 Act No. 56 of 2008.

8 Act No. 25 of 1948.

9 Act No. 198 of 1951.

10 Act No. 105 of 1995.

11 Act No. 239 of 1950. For an overview of the laws related to financial consumer protection, see Hongmu Lee and Satoshi Nakaide, *Financial Consumer Protection in Japan*, in: Tsai-Jyh Chen (ed.), *An International Comparison of Financial Consumer Protection*, Springer, 2018, p. 265 et seq.

12 Tort liability in Japanese law is mainly regulated by Arts 709 et seq. of the Civil Code. According to Art. 709 (damages in torts), a person who has intentionally or negligently infringed any right of others, or legally protected interest of others, is liable to

A representative example is Article 16 of the Financial Instruments and Exchange Act. This provision provides liability for damages caused by a business that violates Article 15 of the same law, which prohibits transactions of securities for which notification has not yet come into effect and requires delivery of a prospectus. According to Article 16, a person who induces another person to acquire securities in violation of Article 15 is held liable to compensate the acquirer for damages arising from the violation. Thus, infringement of the business rule contained in Article 15 gives rise to the right to damages by the person who acquired the securities.

As for the relation between the laws belonging to the first category, that relate to civil law aspects, the Civil Code is the general law applying to all transaction types. The Consumer Contract Act is a special law to the provisions of the Civil Code related to manifestations of intention.[13] Similarly, the Act on Sales, etc. of Financial Instruments is a special law to the provisions of the Civil Code related to torts. In the cases that this chapter addresses, namely those in which the customer is a consumer, all these laws need to be taken into consideration. The level of difficulty for proving the requirements set in each of them differs. Comparative negligence may be taken into consideration by the court[14] and the length of the extinctive prescription could be at issue. As a result, the determination of which provisions of which law will be applied in the end is not a matter of merely theoretical importance.[15]

III. SELF-RESPONSIBILITY PRINCIPLE AND RIGHT TO SELF-DETERMINATION

Japanese civil law is based on the fundamental principle of private autonomy. In the context of financial instruments transactions between businesses and consumers, this means that since the consumer has decided on its own (based on its will) about the purchase of financial instruments, any loss that might arise from such a financial instrument should in principle be borne by the consumer (*caveat emptor*), unless exceptional circumstances exist. In order

---

compensate any damages resulting in consequence. Art. 710 provides for compensation for damages other than property. For an analysis of the Japanese tort law system, see Keizo Yamamoto, *Basic Features of Japanese Tort Law*, Jan Sramek Verlag, 2019.

[13] In German, 'Willenserklärung'.

[14] If the court is allowed to take comparative negligence into consideration, the amount of compensation of the victim for loss or damage will be decided by evaluating the existence and extent of its negligence.

[15] For details of these issues, see Nihonbengoshirengokai [Japan Federation of Bar Associations] (ed.), *Shohishaho Kogi [Lectures of Consumer Law]*, Nihonhyoronsha, 2018, p. 289–290 [Takeo Sakurai].

for this principle to apply, the conditions making possible a proper function of the right to self-determination by the consumer must exist. Only then can the consumer properly be held to bear the loss occurring from the transaction.[16]

In practice, many cases occur in which these conditions do not exist. This can happen when businesses abuse their superiority in the amount of information and negotiating power[17] and sell financial instruments to consumers by means of unfair solicitations. In cases like this where the prerequisites for the self-responsibility principle are not fulfilled, it is desirable to pass the risk onto the business, by imposing civil liability for such losses.

A look at the Japanese case law reveals that courts have admitted consumer claims for compensation in a large number of such cases. The legal basis used in such decisions is either tort liability of the employee who performed the solicitation (based on Civil Code Art. 709) or of the employee's company (based on Art. 715[18]), or contractual liability (Art. 415[19]). In some cases, courts have found nullity of the contract based on Article 95 of the Civil Code about mistake.[20] It needs to be emphasised, though, that in most court decisions

---

[16] Jisuke Nagao and others (eds), *Rekucha Shohishaho [Lectures of Consumer Law]*, 5th edn, Horitsubunkasha, 2011, p. 180 [Hiroyuki Kawachi].

[17] Japanese law expressly recognises the existence of such superiority of businesses. More specifically, Art. 1 of the Basic Act on Consumer Policies (Act No. 78 of 1968) and Art. 1 of the Consumer Contract Act, both relating to the purpose of the respective Acts, refer to a discrepancy (disparity) on the quality and quantity of information and in bargaining (negotiating) power between businesses and consumers.

[18] According to Art. 715 para. 1 Civil Code, a person who employs another person for a business undertaking is liable to compensate for damage inflicted on a third party by that person's employees with respect to the execution of that business. However, this does not apply if the employer exercised reasonable care in appointing the employee or in supervising the business, or if the damage could not have been avoided even if the employer had exercised reasonable care.

[19] Art. 415 Civil Code stipulates that if an obligor fails to perform consistent with the purpose of the obligation or the performance of an obligation is impossible, the obligee can claim compensation for loss or damage arising from the failure. However, this does not apply if the failure to perform the obligation is due to grounds not attributable to the obligor in light of the contract or other sources of obligation and the common sense in the transaction. The notion of 'common sense' included in this provision did not exist in the Civil Code before the revision of year 2017, and has been inserted by this revision in several provisions of the Civil Code, leading to discussions about lack of clarity of this newly introduced notion. For an analysis of this issue, see Hajime Nishiguchi, *Kaiseiminpo ni okeru 'Shakaitsunen' no Kenkyu – Hogengo no Shiten kara [Study of Common Sense in New Civil Law from the View of Forensic Linguistics]*, Chiiki Seisaku Kenkyu, vol. 22, no. 4 (2020), p. 1 et seq.

[20] According to Art. 95 para. 1 of the Civil Code, a manifestation of intention is voidable if it is based on either (i) a mistake wherein the person lacks the intention that corresponds to the manifestation of intention, or (ii) a mistake wherein the person making the manifestation of intention holds an understanding that does not correspond

holding a business liable for compensation, the existence of fault on behalf of the consumer is pointed out by the court and a reduction of compensation based on comparative negligence[21] is performed.[22] Unfortunately, this results in insufficient consumer protection against unfair solicitations of financial instrument transactions.

IV. INFORMATION DUTIES AND PRINCIPLE OF SUITABILITY

A. Information Duties

As mentioned above, Japanese law expressly recognises the disparity in information and bargaining power between businesses and consumers. This disparity often leads to situations in which consumers make decisions about the purchase of financial instruments based on insufficient information and material. In these situations, the principle of self-responsibility cannot apply. As a rectification, case law in Japan has imposed information duties on businesses, and the accumulation of such case law eventually led to the adoption of legislative measures.[23]

1. Case law related to information duties

A Tokyo High Court decision of November 27, 1996 is considered to be one of the leading cases related to information duties about financial instrument transactions.[24] The plaintiff asserted that an illegal solicitation by the defendant's employee led to the purchase of a warrant, and claimed damages based on tort.

The Tokyo High Court held that the securities company and its employees bore the duty to explain properly the benefits and risks of the securities transaction to ensure that the customer forms a correct understanding about the transaction and decides about it based on autonomous judgment. The properness of the explanation is evaluated in the light of elements such as the profession, age, knowledge, experience, and financial status of the customer.

---

to the truth with regard to the circumstances which the person has taken as the basis for the juridical act, and the mistake is material in light of the purpose of the juridical act and the common sense in the transaction.

21 The legal basis for this are Art. 418 Civil Code for contracts and Art. 722 Civil Code for torts.

22 Nagao and others (n 16), p. 180.

23 Ibid, p. 181.

24 Hanreijiho, no. 1587 (1997), p. 72 et seq.

According to the same decision, the legal basis for this explanation duty is good faith (Art. 1 para. 2 Civil Code).[25]

2. Provisions related to information duties

The accumulation of case law acknowledging the existence of information duties of businesses relating to consumers led to the enactment of legislation.

(a) Act on Sales, etc. of Financial Instruments (Act on the Provision of Financial Services)

Article 3 para. 1 of the Act on Sales, etc. of Financial Instruments (Art. 4 para. 1 of the Act on the Provision of Financial Services) provides that if a financial instrument provider intends to carry out sales of financial instruments on a regular basis, it must explain some important matters to customers at or before the time the sale is carried out. Important matters include the risk of incurring various types of loss as well as important portions of the structure of the transactions that generate the risk of loss.

According to para. 2 of the same article, the explanation prescribed in para. 1 must be provided in a manner and to the extent necessary for the customer to understand it, in light of the knowledge, experience, and financial status of the customer, and the purpose for the conclusion of the contract pertaining to the relevant sale of financial instruments. This provision incorporates wording similar to that used in the above-mentioned court decisions. The information duty imposed by this provision is not uniform to all customers but rather is 'tailor-made' to each specific customer.

A failure of the business to observe this information duty gives birth to civil liability. Article 5 of the Act (Art. 6 of the Act on the Provision of Financial Services) relates to liability for damages of a financial instrument provider. If a provider fails to explain important matters to the customer pursuant to the provisions of Article 3 (Art. 4 of the Act on the Provision of Financial Services) or provides a conclusive evaluation in violation of Article 4 (Art. 5 of the Act on the Provision of Financial Services),[26] the financial provider is liable for damages suffered by the customer.

---

[25] Art. 1 para. 2 Civil Code provides that the exercise of rights and performance of duties must be done in good faith. In some court decisions, Art. 644 Civil Code about the duty of care of mandatary is used as a legal basis. According to this provision, the mandatary bears the duty to administer the mandated business with the due care of a prudent manager in compliance with the main purport of the mandate.

[26] Art. 4 relating to the prohibition on the provision of conclusive evaluations by financial instruments provider, provides that if a financial instrument provider intends to carry out sales of financial instruments on a regular basis, the provider must not engage in the act of providing a customer with conclusive evaluations on uncertain

Customer protection by this provision is further supplemented by a presumption of loss established in Article 6 (Art. 7 of the Act on the Provision of Financial Services). If a customer claims compensation for damages pursuant to Article 5 (Art. 6 of the Act on the Provision of Financial Services), the amount of loss of principal is presumed to be the amount of loss incurred by the customer due to the failure of the financial instrument provider to explain important matters or due to providing a conclusive evaluation.[27] Although this presumption can be rebutted by the business, it assists the consumer procedurally by lightening the burden of proof that otherwise would be borne by it according to the general procedural provisions.

(b) Financial Instruments and Exchange Act

A similar provision has been inserted to the Financial Instruments and Exchange Act. Article 37-3 of the Act concerns delivery of a document prior to conclusion of contract. When a financial instrument business operator intends to conclude a contract for a transaction, it must, pursuant to the provisions of a Cabinet Office Ordinance, deliver to the customer a document in advance containing the matters laid down in the same provision. This does not apply to specific cases provided in the Cabinet Office Ordinance in which the legislature estimated the protection of investors is not hindered.

The matters that need to be contained in the document provided to the customer according to the provision of Article 37-3 include basic information regarding the transaction, for example—the trade name or name and address of the financial instrument business operator, an indication that it is such operator, its registration number, and an outline of the relevant contract for the transaction. In addition, disclosure such as the risk that a loss could be incurred due to fluctuations in the money rate, value of currencies, quotations on the financial instruments market, and other indicators is also required.

---

matters or with information that misleads the customer into believing the certainty of the uncertain matters with regard to the matters related to the relevant sales of financial instruments at or before the time that the sale of financial instruments is carried out.

[27] Art. 6 para. 2 (Art. 7 para. 2 of the Act on the Provision of Financial Services) explains the term 'amount of loss of principal' as used in para. 1. According to this provision, the same term means the amount that remains after deducting the amount obtained by adding the total of the amount of money received and the amount of money to be received by a customer as a result of the sale of financial instruments to the total disposal value of the property other than money or rights which has been acquired by the relevant customer as a result of the relevant sale of financial instruments and which the relevant customer has sold or otherwise disposed of, from the total of the amount of money paid and the amount to be paid by the customer as a result of the sale of financial instruments.

The wording of this provision, which requires the business to 'deliver a document' to the customer, creates the impression that it establishes a duty to deliver a document, somewhat different from the proper information duty mentioned in the case law presented above. However, its nature as an information duty becomes evident when one examines the Cabinet Office Ordinance referred to in the same provision. Article 117 paragraph 1 of the Cabinet Office Ordinance on Financial Instruments Business[28] concerns prohibited acts. It states that an act to conclude a contract for a financial instrument transaction is prohibited if the customer has not been provided with a prior explanation on the matters specified in Article 37-3, paragraph (1), items (iii)–(vii) of the Financial Instruments and Exchange Act upon delivery of the documents mentioned in the same provision of the Ordinance. This prior explanation needs to be provided in a manner and to the extent necessary for ensuring the customer understands such matters, in light of the customer's knowledge, experience, and financial status, and in light of the purpose of concluding the contract as a financial instruments transaction. Once again, a wording similar to that included in judicial decisions can be seen.

If the business fails to observe the duty imposed on it by the provision above, the supervising authority, namely the Financial Services Agency (FSA), can issue a business improvement order.[29] Further, if a person fails to deliver the documents requested according to the provisions presented above, he or she can be punished by imprisonment with work for not more than six months or by a fine of not more than 500 thousand yen (around 3.850 euro), or both.[30]

3. Challenges brought by Fintech

A large portion of services related to Fintech are provided online. The providers of such services are also required to fulfil the information duties when the parties are not present face-to-face.[31] The 'Comprehensive Guidelines for Supervision of Financial Instruments Business Operators, etc.' (January

---

[28] Cabinet Office Ordinance No. 52 of August 6, 2007.

[29] According to Art. 51 of the Financial Instruments and Exchange Act, when the Prime Minister finds it necessary and appropriate for the public interest or protection of investors, with regard to a financial instruments business's operation or its financial status, it can, within the scope of this necessity, order the financial instruments business to change the methods of business or take other necessary measures for improving its business operation or its financial status.

[30] Art. 205 (xii) and (xiii) of the Financial Instruments and Exchange Act.

[31] Atsumi Sakai Kyodo Horitsujimusho – Gaikokuhokyodojigyo Fintech Chimu [Atsumi & Sakai Law Office, Fintech team], Katsunobu Matsuda, Masato Niikura and Jun Takahashi (eds.), *Fintech no Bizinesusenryaku to Homu [Business Strategy and Legal Affairs of Fintech]*, Kinzai, 2017, p. 195.

2021)[32] drafted by the Securities Business Division, Supervisory Bureau, Financial Services Agency, include a rule about the disclosure of information in such circumstances. More specifically, item III-2-3-4 (1) (iv) of the Guidelines provides for the method of internet-based explanations, related to Article 117(1)(i) of the Cabinet Office Ordinance on Financial Instruments Business. This rule deals with the case of a financial instrument transaction conducted via the internet. In such a transaction, a financial instruments business operator will be deemed to have provided the explanations provided in a method and to an extent necessary for enabling the customer to understand, as specified under the above-mentioned Cabinet Office Ordinance, when the customer has read explanations shown on the computer display and indicated its understanding with a click of the button.

Although the Act on Sales, etc. of Financial Instruments (Act on the Provision of Financial Services) provides for the information duties of the financial instrument provider, additional information duties might be recognised by a court in the context of a specific dispute. The legal basis for such additional information duties is good faith, as provided in Civil Code Article 1 paragraph 2. Thus, Fintech businesses are in general advised to broadly disclose information about items that should be known by the customer beforehand, even if such items are not listed in the Act on Sales, etc. of Financial Instruments (Act on the Provision of Financial Services).[33]

B. Principle of Suitability

The principle of suitability is a rule that has been developed in the field of financial instruments transactions. In short, it demands that no solicitation be made to customers who are not suitable for the specific financial instruments for which the solicitation is to be made. As will be explained below, the actual content of this rule is a matter that has been widely discussed. As with the information duties analysed above, this rule has developed through decisions of Japanese courts and subsequently adopted by legislation.

1. Case law related to the principle of suitability

The first Supreme Court decision that a breach of the principle of suitability constitutes a tort was delivered on July 14, 2005.[34] The plaintiff claimed tort

32 Available in English translation at https://www.fsa.go.jp/common/law/guide/kinyushohin_eng.pdf last accessed 16 December 2021.

33 Masujima Masakazu and Hori Takane (eds.), *FinTech no Horitsu 2017–2018 [FinTech Laws 2017–2018]*, Nikkei BP, 2017, p. 488.

34 Saikosaibansho Minjihanreishu [Supreme Court Reports (Civil Cases)], vol. 59, no. 6, p. 1323 et seq.

damages, alleging that the defendant's employee performed a solicitation about a product that entailed extreme risk. It should be noted that this case was a B2B transaction. The Court ruled that when judging the suitability of a customer with regard to a specific financial product, investment experience, knowledge, purpose, and financial status are amongst the elements that need to be taken into consideration.[35]

2. Provisions related to the principle of suitability

The principle of suitability formulated by the Supreme Court in this case was enacted into legislation as follows.

(a) Financial Instruments and Exchange Act

Article 40 of the Financial Instruments and Exchange Act is titled Principle of Suitability. According to this provision, a financial instruments business must engage in its business in such a manner that the state of the operation of the business does not fall under any of the cases listed in the two items contained in the same provision.

Item (i) stipulates that where the financial instruments business operator conducts a solicitation with regard to a financial instruments transaction, such solicitation must not be conducted in a manner that is found to be inappropriate in light of the customer's knowledge, experience, financial status, or the purpose of concluding a contract, resulting in or likely to result in insufficient protection of the investors. The similarity to the wording of the Supreme Court decision mentioned above is obvious.

Further, according to item (ii) of the same provision, the following situations must not occur: a financial instruments business operator failing to ensure appropriate handling of customer information obtained in the course of the business; or where other circumstances are specified by a Cabinet Office Ordinance, the operation of the business being likely to go against the public interest or hinder protection of investors.

Administrative sanctions can be imposed against a business for breach of the principle of suitability, as stipulated by the provisions above.

In general, the provision of Article 40 of the Financial Instruments and Exchange Act is understood to refer to the principle of suitability in a *narrow* sense. The principle of suitability in a narrow sense means one that prohibits

---

[35] For an analysis of basic case law related to the principle of suitability, see Shintaro Kato and Teruhisa Nara, *Kin'yutorihiki no Tekigoseigensoku – Setsumeigimu wo Meguru Hanrei no Bunseki to Tenkai [Analysis and Developments of Judicial Precedents regarding the Principle of Suitability and Information Duties in Financial Transactions]*, Kin'yu – Shojihanrei [The Financial and Business Law Precedents], no. 1511 (2017).

solicitation for the sale of specific financial instruments to specific customers, even if the business has observed all information duties. The principle of suitability in a *broad* sense demands that businesses, when they solicit customers with regard to financial instruments, must perform the solicitation in conformity with the customer's knowledge, experience, and financial status; the purpose of investment; and similar factors. Whereas the narrow principle of suitability completely excludes the solicitation of specific financial instruments to specific customers, the broad version of the principle simply requires that the solicitation be in conformity with each customer and the financial instrument.

(b) Act on Sales etc. of Financial Instruments

An example of the principle of suitability in broad sense stems from Article 3 paragraph 2 of the Act on Sales, etc. of Financial Instruments (Art. 4 para. 2 of the Act on the Provision of Financial Services). As already mentioned, Article 3 paragraph 1 imposes an information duty on a business. Paragraph 2 of the same article provides that the explanation prescribed in paragraph 1 must be provided in a manner and to the extent necessary for the customer to understand it, in light of the knowledge, experience and financial status of the customer, and the purpose for the conclusion of the contract pertaining to the relevant sale of financial instruments.

Although this distinction between the principle of suitability in a narrow and in a broad sense is useful to a certain extent both in theory and practice, there has been strong debate as to whether it is proper, feasible, and necessary.[36]

(c) Self-regulatory Rules of the Japan Securities Dealers' Association

The Japan Securities Dealers' Association (JSDA) is an association functioning as a self-regulatory organisation (SRO) and as an interlocutor for the

[36] Regarding the principle of suitability in narrow and broad senses, see amongst other, Reizen Ou, *Tekigoseigensoku to Shihochitsujyo [Principle of Suitability and Private Law Order]*, Shinzansha, 2010; Masatoshi Kinoshita, *Kin'yushohin no Hanbai – Kan'yu Ruru to shite no Setsumeigimu to Tekigoseigensoku ni tsuite [Information Duties and Principle of Suitability as a Rule for Selling and Soliciting Financial Products]*, Hiroshima Hokadaigakuin Ronshu [Hiroshima University Law School Review], no. 5 (2009), p. 1 et seq.; Taiji Nagata, *Kyogi no Tekigoseigensoku no Shatei ni kansuru Joshotekikosatsu – Saikosaihanketsu to Kinpanho Rippoji no Gironjyokyo wo Tegakari ni [An Introductory Consideration of the Scope of the Principle of Suitability in Narrow Sense: Based on the Supreme Court Decision and the State of Discussions at the Time of Establishment of the Act on Sales, etc. of Financial Instruments]*, Himeji Hogaku [Himeji Dokkyo University Law Review], no. 59, p. 29 et seq.

securities industry.[37] As part of its activity, JSDA has issued self-regulatory rules and guidelines. Amongst them, the 'Rules Concerning Solicitation for Investments and Management of Customers, etc. by Association Members'[38] refer to the principle of suitability. Article 3 paragraph 3 of the Rules provides that when conducting sales of securities that are new for an association member, the member must fully understand the characteristics and risks of such securities and must not sell them if the association member cannot identify customers who are suitable for them. According to this rule, securities that are new for an association member must not be sold if no suitable customer can be identified. The judgement of whether such a customer can be identified or not will be made based on a reasonable prediction by the association member. Thus, the suitability criterion is an evaluation of whether such a customer can be expected to exist. On the contrary, in Article 40 of the Financial Instruments and Exchange Act, the criterion is each concrete customer who is actually being solicited.[39]

(d) Principles by the Financial Services Agency

The Financial Services Agency (FSA) is the government agency functioning as the financial regulator in charge of supervising banking, securities, and exchange.[40] On March 30, 2017, the FSA published the 'Principles for Customer-Oriented Business Operations', which were later amended on January 15, 2021.[41] According to principle no. 6 regarding the provision of services suitable for customers, a financial business must comprehend a customer's financial status, trading experience, knowledge, and trading purpose as well as needs. Further, a financial business must compose, sell, and recommend financial products that are suitable for the customer. Thus, this principle has made clear that financial businesses bear the duty to evaluate and know their customers, as well as the duty to offer products and services that conform to those customers.[42]

---

[37] For details, see its website in English, https://www.jsda.or.jp/en/about/index.html last accessed 16 December 2021.

[38] February 19, 1975. A tentative English translation can be found at https://www.jsda.or.jp/en/rules-guidelines/E03.pdf last accessed 16 December 2021.

[39] Ueyanagi (n 3), p. 219.

[40] For details, see its website in English, https://www.fsa.go.jp/en/index.html last accessed 16 December 2021.

[41] The amended version is available in Japanese at https://www.fsa.go.jp/news/r2/singi/20210115-1/02.pdf last accessed 16 December 2021.

[42] Ueyanagi (n 3), p. 219.

C. Other Relevant Provisions

Apart from the already presented provisions on information duties and the principle of suitability, additional provisions aim at ensuring the disclosure of correct information to customers and contributing more generally to consumer protection.

1. Consumer Contract Act

The Consumer Contract Act permits a consumer to rescind the manifestation of an intention to be bound by the offer of a contract or by the acceptance of an offer for such a contract in situations such as when the consumer has misunderstood or was distressed by certain actions of the business. The Act also enables a consumer to have clauses fully or partially declared null and void, if they exempt a business from liability for damages or otherwise unfairly harm the interests of consumers (Art. 1). According to Article 4 paragraph 1 of the Act, consumers can rescind their manifestation of intention to be bound by the offer of a consumer contract or by the acceptance of such an offer. This right exists if a business's acts in soliciting the consumer to enter into the consumer contract, set forth in items provided in the same article, cause the consumer to be under the mistaken belief set forth in the same items, and lead the consumer to manifest the intention to be bound by the offer of that consumer contract or by the acceptance of such an offer. Item (i) of the same paragraph grants such a right to rescind when the business has conveyed something that diverges from the truth with regard to an important matter, and has misled the consumer to believe that what has been conveyed is true.

These provisions require that the mistaken belief of the consumer was caused in the 'soliciting' of the consumer by the business. Previously, there was debate about whether advertisements that are not addressed to a specific consumer but rather to the consumer public in general, fall under the notion of 'soliciting'. The issue was resolved by a Supreme Court decision of January 24, 2017.[43] The Court held that the fact that a solicitation by a business is addressed to several unspecified consumers by means of advertisement does not automatically exclude such a solicitation from the notion of 'soliciting' under the Consumer Contract Act. In the era of Fintech, this means that Fintech businesses need to observe the requirements of these provisions when advertising their services.[44]

---

43 Hanreijiho, no. 2332 (2017), p. 16 et seq.
44 Atsumi & Sakai Law Office and others (n 31), p. 249 et seq.

2. Other provisions of the Financial Instruments and Exchange Act

Articles 36–45 of the Financial Instruments and Exchange Act contribute to the provision of correct information to customers and to fair and transparent financial instruments transactions. For example, Article 36 provides for a duty of sincerity to customers. Article 36-2 establishes the duty of financial businesses to post signs in the format specified by a Cabinet Office Order in a place that is accessible to the public at each of their business offices or other offices. Article 36-3 prohibits name lending. Article 37 regulates advertising of financial instruments. Article 37-2 imposes on financial businesses the obligation to clarify the conditions of transactions in advance. Article 37-3 provides for the delivery of documents prior to the conclusion of a contract. Article 37-4 provides for the delivery of documents upon the conclusion of a contract. Article 38 prohibits providing a customer with false information in connection with the conclusion of a financial instrument transaction contract or in connection with the solicitation thereof ((i)). The same article also prohibits providing a customer with a conclusive assessment of a matter that is uncertain or with information that could mislead the customer into believing that a matter that is uncertain is actually certain, thereby soliciting the customer to conclude a financial instruments transaction contract ((ii)).[45]

Article 17 of the Act lays down rules on the compensatory liability of a person using a prospectus containing a false statement. Statements subject to this provision are those in a public offering or secondary distribution of securities specifically provided for in the same Act or of securities for which disclosure has already been made. According to the same provision, a person is liable if he or she causes securities to be acquired whilst using a prospectus that contains a false statement about a material particular, omits a statement as to a material particular that is required to be stated, or omits a statement of material fact that is necessary to prevent it from being misleading; or is using materials that contain a false or misleading representation about a material particular or omit a representation of material fact that is necessary to prevent being misleading. In such cases, this person is liable to provide compensation for damage sustained by someone who acquires the securities without knowing that the statement is false or has been omitted, that the representation is false or misleading, or that a representation has been omitted. This does not apply if the person who would be liable proves he or she did not know, and even in the exercise of reasonable care could not have known, that the statement was false or had been omitted, or that the representation was false or misleading.

---

[45] Similar prohibitions are also set by Art. 300 Insurance Business Act, Art. 214 and Art. 214-3 Commodity Futures Act.

Finally, Article 22 provides for the compensatory liability of the officers of a company submitting a registration statement that contains false statements. According to paragraph 1 of the same article, the officers of a company are liable if a securities registration statement contains false statements about a material particular, omits a statement as to a material particular that is required to be stated, or omits a statement of material fact that is necessary to prevent it from being misleading. The liability of the officers of the company lies in compensating someone who, without knowing that the statement is false or has been omitted, acquires or disposes of securities issued by the person submitting the securities registration statement other than through a public offering or secondary distribution, for damage arising from the statement being false or having been omitted.

These last two provisions of Articles 17 and 22 also ensure the disclosure of proper information to customers, thereby enhancing consumer protection in financial instruments transactions.

V. PROHIBITION OF UNREQUESTED SOLICITATION

In Japan, numerous incidents have occurred involving businesses that perform improper solicitations of financial instruments to consumers, resulting in consumers suffering nuisance and considerable economic loss. The damage caused from retail foreign exchange trading in 2004 drew public attention and led to the introduction of a prohibition of unrequested solicitation for financial instrument transactions.[46] Article 38 (iv) of the Financial Instruments and Exchange Act prohibits visiting or telephoning a customer who is not asking to be solicited for the conclusion of a financial instrument transaction contract, and soliciting such a customer to conclude a financial instrument transaction contract. In cases of breach of this prohibition, business improvement orders or business stay orders can be issued. Further, Article 38 (v) prohibits soliciting a customer to conclude a financial instrument transaction contract without obtaining confirmation from the customer, prior to solicitation, as to whether or not the customer is willing to be solicited.[47]

---

[46] Ueyanagi (n 3), p. 220.

[47] See also Art. 214 (vii) and (ix) Commodity Derivatives Act. For details of the regulation of unrequested solicitation in Japan in general, see Antonios Karaiskos, *Regulation of Unrequested Solicitation in Japan: The Way Toward a Do-Not-Call and Do-Not-Knock System?*, in Kansai University Review of Law and Politics, no. 38 (2017), p. 21 et seq.; Antonios Karaiskos, *Fukosei na Torihikihoho to Shihonriron – EU-ho to no Hikakuhotekikosatsu [Unfair Commercial Practices and Private Law Theory: A Comparative Analysis with EU Law]*, Horitsubunkasha (2020), p. 5 et seq.

During the deliberation process for the reform of the Act on Specified Commercial Transactions[48] in 2015, there were discussions about introducing a general regulation of unrequested solicitation. However, no consensus could be reached, in large part due to strong resistance by business circles. Thus, the prohibition above related to financial instruments has an exceptional character in the landscape of Japanese law.

VI. PROCEDURAL ISSUES FOR DISPUTE RESOLUTION

Japan, like other countries, has various means of dispute resolution arising from financial instruments transactions, each of which demonstrates advantages and disadvantages for the customer.

A. Negotiation

Negotiation allows for an early resolution of the relevant disputes. Since in many cases, details of the related businesses are unknown or their financial situations are unstable, temporary measures aiming at the preservation of their property are often required.[49]

B. Litigation

Litigation is, in general, the main way to resolve disputes. In view of the quite commonly unstable financial situation of the businesses related, the practice of including amongst the defendants the person who made the solicitation of the financial instruments or the company officers is not rare. The aim of this practice is to ensure satisfactory collection of claims in the case of successful litigation.

In general, it is estimated that most lawsuits related to financial instruments are dismissed. This tendency is even stronger in disputes involving new financial products. Some of the main factors leading to this result are said to be the fact that the burden of proof is borne by the plaintiff, the lack of a disclosure procedure similar to that in the US, and the lack of experience of judges about investment activities. Further, courts are willing to reduce the compensation paid to the victim because of comparative negligence. Moreover, enforcement

---

[48] Act No. 57 of 1976.

[49] Nihonbengoshirengokai [Japan Federation of Bar Associations] (n 15), p. 315.

of decisions granting compensation is difficult when the financial situation of the business is unstable. All these matters create additional obstacles.[50]

In this context, it is notable that a consumer organisation collective litigation system is available for consumer issues in Japan. This system is constructed by two procedural categories, namely injunction and redress for damage. Injunction lawsuits can be filed by qualified consumer organisations.[51] Further, lawsuits for redress for damage can be filed by specified qualified consumer organisations.[52] The later procedure consists of two steps. The first step deals with a declaratory judgment as to the business's obligation to pay. In the second step, the amount of money payable to each consumer is determined.[53] This system was introduced in 2013 by the Act on Special Measures Concerning Civil Court Proceedings for the Collective Redress for Property Damage Incurred by Consumers,[54] and is expected to contribute to collective consumer redress in Japan.[55]

C. Alternative Dispute Resolution

Alternative dispute resolution (ADR) offers a choice for early resolution with the participation of persons experienced in the relevant field. Regarding financial instruments, both general ADR applying to all types of disputes and ADR specific to this field are available.[56]

---

50 For details see ibid., p. 289.

51 22 organisations currently accredited throughout Japan. See the relevant list in Japanese, at https://www.caa.go.jp/policies/policy/consumer_system/collective_litigation_system/about_qualified_consumer_organization/list/ last accessed 16 December 2021.

52 Four organisations currently accredited throughout Japan. See the relevant list in Japanese at https://www.caa.go.jp/policies/policy/consumer_system/collective_litigation_system/about_qualified_consumer_organization/list_of_specified/%20 last accessed 16 December 2021.

53 For details, see online leaflet prepared in English by the Consumer Affairs Agency (CAA), at https://www.caa.go.jp/en/policy/consumer_system/pdf/consumer_system_190402_0001.pdf last accessed 16 December 2021.

54 Act No. 96 of 2013.

55 However, at the same time, the limited scope of application of this Act does not allow for a broad use. More specifically, mental suffering. Lost profits, consequential damage and physical injury are excluded from its scope of application.

56 For details about the ADR offered for consumer disputes in Japan, see Antonios Karaiskos, *Consumer Disputes and Consumer Dispute Resolution in Japan*, Journal of Law and Society (2017), p. 1 et seq.

General ADR is offered for example by means of civil mediation, or by institutions such as the National Consumer Affairs Center (NCAC),[57] the Local Consumer Affairs Centers,[58] and arbitration centres of Bar Associations.

ADR specifically for financial disputes (financial ADR) was fully introduced with the amendment of the Financial Instruments and Exchange Act and other Acts in 2010. Currently, the relevant Acts contain provisions about the designation of dispute resolution organisations.[59] Accordingly, institutions such as FINMAC (a dispute resolution body created by Japan Securities Dealers' Association and the Financial Futures Association of Japan[60]), the Japanese Bankers Association,[61] the Life Insurance Association of Japan,[62] and the Marine and Fire Insurance Association of Japan[63] offer their services as designated dispute resolution organisations.[64]

Currently, the Japanese government is deliberating about the digitalisation of the court procedures.[65] This development might enhance the digitalisation of ADR procedures too, in the form of introducing online dispute resolution (ODR) procedures. Should this be realised, AI will likely be used as a first step for the resolution of disputes, before human intervention. Further, it is expected that big data collected in ODR procedures will also be utilised for the prevention of future disputes.[66]

---

[57] NCAC serves as a core institution for consumer affairs by utilising consumer related information from local consumer affairs centers, to prevent and minimise consumer detriment. Further, it supports consumer consultation services at local consumer affairs centers, and conducts ADR procedures to resolve consumer disputes. For details, see the website of NCAC in English, http://www.kokusen.go.jp/ncac_index_e.html last accessed 16 December 2021.

[58] Local Consumer Affairs Centers are established by local authorities throughout Japan. In these Centers, consumer consultants having passed the relevant state exam offer their services without charge.

[59] For example, Art. 37-7 Financial Instruments and Exchange Act stipulates the obligation of financial instrument businesses to conclude a contract with a designated dispute resolution organisation.

[60] https://www.ffaj.or.jp/en/ last accessed 16 December 2021.

[61] https://www.zenginkyo.or.jp/en/ last accessed 16 December 2021.

[62] https://www.seiho.or.jp/english/ last accessed 16 December 2021.

[63] https://www.sonpo.or.jp/en/about/outline.html last accessed 16 December 2021.

[64] Nihonbengoshirengokai [Japan Federation of Bar Associations] (n 15), p. 316.

[65] For details, see Kazuhiko Yamamoto, *Minjisaibantetsuzuki no IT-ka no Juyoronten – Hoseishinchukanshian no Soten [Important Issues regarding the Digitalization of Civil Court Procedures: Points at Issue in the Interim Proposal by the Legislative Council]*, Yuhikaku, 2021.

[66] Kazuhiko Yamamoto, *Shohisha to Minjitetsuzukiho [Consumers and Civil Procedure]*, in: Kunihiro Nakata and Naoko Kano (eds.), *Kihonkogi Shohishaho [Basic Lectures of Consumer Law]*, Nihonhyoronsha, 2020, p. 348.

VII. CONCLUDING REMARKS

This chapter has analysed the current state of consumer protection regarding financial instrument transactions. The analysis has revealed the complex landscape in Japan with multiple laws applying and regulating various aspects. At the same time, we can discern some basic ideas on which this system is founded. One such idea is ensuring that the self-responsibility principle and the right to self-determination, which are fundamental to civil law in general, can properly function in this field too. An important role is played by information duties that rectify the imbalance between businesses and consumers. The principle of suitability adds to this protection by making sure that a solicitation is made in a manner proper to each specific customer. At the same time, various other provisions strengthen consumer protection in the field of financial instrument transactions, with the prohibition of solicitation in specific cases and ADR playing an important role.

As mentioned in the beginning of the chapter, the increased use of AI, for example in the forms of Fintech and blockchain, is creating new dynamics in Japanese law. The chapter has addressed some aspects of these dynamics in the field of financial instrument transactions. It remains to be seen what developments these new dynamics will bring to financial services in general. The future perspectives in Japan are still unclear. What is certain is that the developments in this context are worthy of further observation and analysis.

8. Data governance by insurance companies in Singapore

Christopher Chao-hung Chen

I. INTRODUCTION

Data governance is of immense importance in the insurance industry. On the one hand, insurers need to use a considerable amount of data to evaluate the exposure and magnitude of the risks insured. They can then decide whether to accept the risk and can determine the appropriate amount of the premiums to be charged to the insured. Insurers also require data to assess claims, make proper investment decisions and detect frauds. On the other hand, insurers also possess a significant amount of data regarding their customers and the risks that they are insured for. In addition to collecting personal information from customers when they apply for policies, insurers also collect a lot of data through insurance claims (e.g., accidents or customers' health information). The latter might enable powerful behavioural analyses to be carried out in association with people's lives and conducts. In short, data usage and its applications are extremely prevalent in the insurance industry. Therefore, the importance of data for insurers cannot be overstated.

With the rise of financial technology (FinTech), how insurers should manage data acquisition and usage becomes an ever more important issue especially when insurers start to use big data, artificial intelligence (AI) and machine learning for the operation and management of their insurance businesses. The mismanagement of data may lead to potential legal liabilities due to the personal-data protection laws and cyber security laws that are applicable in a country. It may also raise regulatory concerns about the fitness of an insurer, its internal control and its adherence to conduct of business standards.

The objective of this chapter is to explore potential data governance issues in the insurance context. This chapter examines the existing legal and regulatory regimes in Singapore – a leading international financial centre and insurance hub in Asia – with regard to data governance by insurance companies. In particular, this chapter considers three perspectives: (1) issues regarding the use of big data by insurers, (2) insurers' usage of customer data and (3) the potential outsourcing risk related to the transfer of customer data. Finally, the chapter briefly examines the general personal data protection laws and regulations issued by the Monetary Authority of Singapore (MAS) with regard to data governance by insurers.

The remainder of the chapter is arranged as follows: First, section II briefly introduces how the arrival of new insurance technology (InsurTech) might improve the insurance services and business operations of insurers as well as mitigate the potential risks arising from the misuse and mismanagement of the data held by insurers. Next, section III further examines the existing legal regimes in Singapore in relation to data governance by insurers. Then, section IV provides a general reflection on the existing regulations in Singapore on data governance by insurers. Finally, section V concludes the chapter.

II. DEMAND FOR DATA GOVERNANCE IN THE INSURANCE SECTOR

A. Sources of Data for Insurers

In general, insurance is a contract under which one party (insured) agrees to pay a sum of money (i.e., insurance premiums) to the other party (i.e., the insurer) in exchange for the latter promising to provide funds upon the occurrence of certain events (i.e., the insured events).[1] In essence, insurance is a contract that allows the insured to transfer their risk exposure to the insurer in the form of the latter's monetary compensation or indemnity for losses. The traditional insurance model operates on the principle of pooling risks from customers with varying degrees of risk levels.[2] Insurers then charge premiums to different customers based on their profiles to reflect the level of risk insured. Then, after issuing the policies, insurers need to actively manage their assets to meet the future insurance payout and generate profit as well.[3] Hence, there is

---

[1] See *Prudential Insurance Co v Commissioners of Inland Revenue* [1904] 2 KB 658, 663-664 (per Channel J).

[2] Randy E. Drumm, David L. Eckles and Martin Halek, 'An Examination of Adverse Selection in the Public Provision of Insurance' (2013) 38(2) *The Geneva Risk and Insurance Review* 127, 137–9; Hajime Miyazaki, 'The Rat Race and Internal Labor Markets' (1977) 8(2) *The Bell Journal of Economics* 394; Michael Spence, 'Product Differentiation and Performance in Insurance Markets' (1978) 10 *Journal of Public Economics* 427, 440; Francis Cheng, 'Time to Review Risk Pooling in Health Insurance' *The Straits Times* (5 December 2015) https://www.straitstimes.com/forum/letters-in-print/time-to-review-risk-pooling-in-health-insurance accessed 25 May 2021.

[3] Lin Lin and Christopher Chen, 'The Promises and Perils of InsurTech' [2020] *Singapore Journal of Legal Studies* 115, 118.

a strong demand for having a more precise assessment for insurance risk and asset management.[4] To achieve this goal, more precise data is necessary.

Insurers can acquire data from various sources. First, they can acquire general statistics and data related to the risks insured. For instance, they could seek general information about traffic accidents, crime rates and the health of the population from the government or other sources to understand the general level of risk exposure in a society. Insurers can also draw upon data collected through insurance claims. The data could be further divided into sub-groups to further understand the behavioural patterns of the population. For example, based on past cases and statistics, insurers can acquire a general idea regarding the number of car accidents involving drivers of different genders and from different age groups. In another example, insurers might want to know certain geographic and geological information, such as whether a property is located close to a known fault line, if they provide coverage to households against earthquakes. Through such data, insurers can obtain an idea of the risk insured and charge different premiums accordingly to reflect the risk exposure.

Second, a significant amount of the data come from the customers. Public data and general statistics may describe the risk in a particular society or a place as a whole, but they do not perfectly reflect the true level of risk exposure individually. Some information is often privy only to the insured person (e.g., their health information) in principle. This creates a general problem of the existence of asymmetric information between an insured individual/object and the insurer. To address this issue, the various insurance laws of the world often impose a pre-contractual duty on the insured person (or the person who applies for the insurance) to disclose material information about the insured or the risk to the insurer, although the exact formulation of the duty may vary from country to country.[5]

To acquire information, insurers commonly require an applicant or the insured person (together hereinafter referred to as 'insured' for simplicity) to fill in certain information in a physical or digital proposal form (or application form). A proposal or application form could include numerous questions for various purposes. For instance, the application form (as of March 2021) for the life insurance policy offered by NTUC Income, a Singaporean insurer, includes questions regarding the insured and their basic personal information (such as their name, identification number, birthday, nationality, etc.), occupation,

---

4 These three categories broadly correspond to the risk factors identified in the regulations: see Insurance (Valuation and Capital) Regulations 2004 (No S 498/2004), sch 2.

5 See, e.g., Marine Insurance Act s 18 (Singapore) or Insurance Act 2015, ss 2–8 (UK).

contact information and payment instructions.[6] The form also requests certain tax declarations (especially when the insured is a foreigner) and information related to any politically exposed persons or sources of funds for anti-money laundering purposes.[7] In the application form, the insured also has to state payout and distribution options (and, therefore, some banking information), in the case that the insured passes away or survives the policy period, depending on the policy terms.[8] Moreover, the insurer's proposal form also requests information about the insured's other insurance policies and past insurance history.[9] More importantly, the insurer asks for information about a person's body (e.g., height and weight), lifestyle (e.g., whether they smoke or drink alcohol) and participation in risky behaviours (e.g., parachuting). In addition, they also ask about certain medical aspects (e.g., past visits to a doctor or past medical tests, etc.) and whether the insured has been diagnosed with certain diseases (e.g., Alzheimer's disease) in the past.[10] The same insurer may also request for additional health information (such as whether the individual has tested positive for COVID-19).[11] The data acquired through this process allows insurers to paint a picture of the insured's life, which they use to determine the level of risk exposure for that particular individual.

Third, new technology may allow insurers to acquire additional data from other sources. The insurers may potentially access an insured's social media if it is public and searchable. This may allow them to obtain information about an insured's life that is beyond that provided through the proposal form. Further, the sensors used in motor vehicles or wearable devices may provide more insight into a person's conduct and activity than the general statistics and proposal form can offer (e.g., the driving styles of an insured or the number of steps that the person walks per day). There will be a huge amount of sensor data as a result of the installation of billions of sensors 'that will be giving off valuable information'.[12] Information from sensors may also be used for

[6] See NTUC Income website, https://www.income.com.sg/kcassets/1ccadcd8-fdec-4a13-bd2b-6fa9439cb97a/Life%20Insurance%20with%20Medical%20Undewriting%20(Aug20).pdf accessed 31 March 2021.

[7] Ibid.

[8] Ibid.

[9] Ibid.

[10] Ibid.

[11] See NTUC Income website, https://www.income.com.sg/kcassets/89694651-ad26-4ccd-9284-95dfdd5b33a8/Additional%20Medical%20Questionnaire.pdf accessed 25 March 2021.

[12] Paul Schulte and Gavin Liu, 'FinTech is Merging with IoT and AI to Challenge Banks: How Entrenched Interests Can Prepare' (2018) 20(3) *The Journal of Alternative Investments* 41, 45.

business insurance (e.g., for fire insurance) to have better monitoring and assist insurers with assessing the reasons for the corresponding losses.

In summary, insurers need plenty of information to perform proper risk evaluation. They could rely on the general statistics about a society and the information provided by the insured through the proposal forms and questionnaires. Insurers now may also have other resources to obtain more information about the insured (e.g., social media) or may collect additional data from electronic devices where appropriate. The availability of such data can obviously help insurers make better and more accurate decisions. For example, instead of counting on rough proxies, such as gender or age, to determine the risk exposure for motor vehicles, insurers can now investigate into a driver's lifestyle and driving habits to formulate a more precise assessment of the corresponding risk.[13] In theory, having more data should improve efficiency and consumer welfare (e.g., lower premiums for some people).[14] However, the use of big data may also result in potential risks, which are examined in the next section.

B. Potential Risks of Using Big Data

Despite the apparent tangible benefits that having a greater amount of data may bring to the insurance industry, there are also potential problems associated with the use of big data regardless of whether the information is obtained from traditional sources or through new technology-based tools.

First, the accuracy of the data is always a problem. There is a chance that an insured tells a lie or provides partial, obscure or incomplete information during the application process. Sometimes, an insured could simply be innocent, as no one can disclose things that they actually do not know about. But when there is an apparent concern of having their insurance application rejected, it is safe to assume that the person could be attempting to hide certain facts (e.g., pre-existing medical conditions). Even in the digital era, the information acquired through social media or other online sources may not be entirely accurate. As illustrated the deep-fake technology or fake news, not all information seen on the Internet may be true; some could be fabricated on purpose, and pictures could be altered using software. It is also not difficult to imagine that people could manipulate sensor data if they have the knowledge and means to do so.

---

[13] Lin and Chen (n 3) 122.
[14] Lin and Chen (n 3) 122.

Second, data analytics may be biased and may not reflect the actual reality. Data biases may come from sampling, measurement and algorithm risks.[15] Any bias in the data and modelling of algorithms could affect the validity of the model and its outcome and, henceforth, the trained results obtained using artificial intelligence.[16] If an insurer makes a decision based on a prejudiced outcome, it could create further prudential issues (e.g., incorrect premiums) or conduct issues (e.g., incorrect profiling of a customer).[17]

Third, there are issues of data dependence. As Lin and Chen argue, '[i]naccurate, biased, or manipulated information threatens to compromise the accuracy of insights used by insurance companies to plan, operate and grow their businesses'.[18] Whether the obtained data is of good quality may be questionable unless the data sources and their coding structure can be more thoroughly analysed. Robust auditing and transparency are necessary for ensuring the traceability and accountability of the data usage and learnings.[19]

Fourth, there could be further issues related to data discrimination even in the big data era. It might raise potential concerns regarding fairness and equality. For instance, for motor insurance, additional data obtained from social media or sensors may help an insurer classify an insured as presenting low risk, without which the person would otherwise be allocated to a traditional high-risk group (e.g., young male). Therefore, the insured could enjoy a lower premium for their insurance. However, the same approach can also result in an insured paying higher premiums if their behavioural pattern suggests that they present higher risk than the traditional modelling suggests. In an extreme situation, it is possible that certain people from the high-risk group may not be able to acquire insurance due to high risk or high premiums.[20] How the industry should deal with this potential prejudicial effect must be subjected to further scrutiny by the public in a given market.[21]

---

15 Bernhard Babel et al., 'Derisking Machine Learning and Artificial Intelligence', McKinsey & Co (February 2019), 4 https://www.mckinsey.com/business-functions/risk/our-insights/derisking-machine-learning-and-artificial-intelligence accessed 25 March 2021.

16 Lin and Chen (n 3) 127–8.

17 Ibid., 128.

18 Ibid.

19 Nicholas Boyle et al., 'Technology and Disruption in the Insurance Sector', DLA Piper (21 May 2019) https://www.dlapiper.com/en/uk/insights/publications/2019/05/technology-and-disruption-in-the-insurance-sector/ accessed 25 March 2021.

20 Financial Stability Board, 'Artificial Intelligence and Machine Learning in Financial Services' (2017), 31–32 https://www.fsb.org/2017/11/artificial-intelligence-and-machine-learning-in-financial-service/ accessed 7 April 2021.

21 Lin and Chen (n 3) 126.

In sum, regardless of whether the data is acquired using the traditional method or new technology, there is always a general problem of data accuracy and comprehensiveness. Big data and artificial intelligence may also create new biases with respect to data collection and data analytics. In addition, there could be general social problems associated with data discrimination that may need considerable value judgment in a given society. The subsequent sections of this chapter further examine and comment on the data governance framework used for insurers. The chapter primarily uses Singapore as the target region of study.

III. DATA GOVERNANCE FRAMEWORK OF INSURERS IN SINGAPORE

At the moment, there is no unified data governance regime that is specifically prescribed in the insurance regulations of Singapore. In this part, this chapter offers a general overview of the potential legal and regulatory rules that may govern the usage of customer data by insurers in Singapore. The chapter then offers a reflection and review on the current state of the Singaporean laws related to insurance data governance in Part IV.

A. Personal Data Protection Laws in Singapore

In the 21st century, the importance of personal data protection has risen to the fore. In many countries, there are dedicated personal data protection laws that regulate when a person or a firm can acquire such data and how it can be used appropriately, and Singapore is no exception. Passed by the Parliament in 2012, the Personal Data Protection Act 2012 (PDPA)[22] created the Personal Data Protection Commission (PDPC) as the chief regulator of personal data protection in Singapore.[23]

By definition, 'personal data' means any data (whether true or not) associated with an individual that can be used to identify the individual or any data and other information to which an organisation has or is likely to have access.[24] A piece of information is considered personal data if it allows its owner to be identified.

Under the PDPA, an insurer has to consider what a reasonable person would find appropriate when dealing with personal data.[25] An insurer is also required

---

22 No 26 of 2012.
23 Personal Data Protection Act 2012 s 5.
24 Ibid., s 2 ('personal data').
25 Ibid., s 11(1).

to develop and implement data protection policies and processes to ensure compliance with the PDPA.[26] Largely, the collection, use and disclosure of personal data is dependent on the customer's consent.[27] In addition, even with their consent, an insurer can collect, use or disclose a customer's personal data only for purposes that a reasonable person would consider appropriate and those that the customer has been informed of.[28]

Once an insurer collects an individual's personal data, it has to exert reasonable effort to ensure that the data collected is accurate and complete if it is likely to be used to make a decision that might affect the person.[29] An insurer should make reasonable arrangements to protect all personal data in its possession or under its control and prevent unauthorised access to or the use of the data.[30] A breach of the PDPA could result in criminal penalties and civil liability.[31]

There are further rules that assist insurers in relation to the PDPA. Under the Act, an insurer can collect personal data about an individual without their consent from a source other than them if the collection, use or disclosure of that personal data is necessary for evaluative purposes.[32] By statutory definition, 'evaluative purpose' includes 'for the purpose of deciding whether to insure any individual or property or to continue or renew the insurance of any individual or property'.[33] An insurer is also allowed to collect, use or disclose personal data about an individual as it is for conferring an interest on the individual under a benefit plan or for administering the benefit plan.[34] A 'benefit plan' includes 'an insurance policy, a pension plan, an annuity, a provident fund plan or other similar plans'.[35] In other words, the collection and use of personal data by an insurer for insurance purposes is considered legitimate under Singapore's PDPA, and insurers could collect data from other sources without the insured's consent for such purposes. This allows more leeway for insurers to collect and use a customer's personal data.

As a consequence, all insurers in Singapore have created their own personal data protection or privacy policy and have incorporated relevant consent provisions in their documentation. On the one hand, a consent provision could be

26 Ibid., s 12.
27 Ibid., s 13.
28 Ibid., ss 18 and 20.
29 Ibid., s 23.
30 Ibid., s 24.
31 Ibid., s 48C et seq.
32 Ibid., s 17(1) and First Schedule part 3 para 2.
33 Ibid., s 2 ('evaluative purpose').
34 Ibid., First Schedule part 3 para 7.
35 Ibid., s 2 ('benefit plan').

inserted into the proposal form in the first place. Therefore, a customer may have already, knowingly or unknowingly, provided their consent for their personal data to be collected and used when applying for insurance. For instance, the proposal form for the life insurance offered by NTUC Income, one of the largest life insurers in Singapore, contains the following provision:[36]

> By providing the information and submitting this application, I/we [i.e. Insured] give my/our consent to NTUC Income Insurance Co-operative Limited, its representative, agents (collectively "Income"), relevant third parties, referred to in Income's Privacy Policy which can be found at http://www.income.com.sg/privacy-policy and/or appointed distribution partners to collect, use, and disclose the information (including any updates) *for the purposes of processing and administering this insurance application or transaction, providing me with financial advice and/or recommendation on products and services, managing my relationship and policies with Income, including sending me corporate communications and notices on updates and servicing, research and data analytics, and in the manner and for the purposes described in the Income's Privacy Policy.*
>
> Where personal data of a third party (for example, information of my spouse, child, ward or parent) is provided by me/us, I/we represent and warrant that I/we have obtained the consent of the third party to provide Income with their personal data for this application or transaction.
>
> For the purpose of this application, I/we also authorize, agree and consent (whether this application is accepted or refused):
>
> a. Income to collect from and/or disclose to any medical source, insurance office, reinsurer, or organisation any relevant information to do with me/us; and
> b. Income or any of its approved medical examiners or laboratories to perform the necessary medical assessment and tests for Income to underwrite and evaluate my/our health status or condition in relation to this application and any claim in connection with this policy.
>
> [Emphasis added]

This chapter is not intended to criticise the use of this kind of consent provision. Insurers, of course, should have a privacy policy that describes its commitment to the protection of a customer's personal data and privacy.[37] However, by signing the proposal form (which is normally incorporated into the insurance policy by way of an entire agreement clause within the same), a customer permits the insurer not only to use their personal data for the insurance appli-

---

[36] See NTUC Income, 'Life Insurance Application with Medical Underwriting', 19 https://www.income.com.sg/kcassets/1ccadcd8-fdec-4a13-bd2b-6fa9439cb97a/Life%20Insurance%20with%20Medical%20Undewriting%20(Aug20).pdf accessed 24 March 2021.

[37] For example, see NTUC Income, 'Privacy Policy' https://www.income.com.sg/privacy-policy accessed 24 March 2021; Great Eastern Life Assurance, 'Privacy Statement' (for General Public) https://www.greateasternlife.com/bn/en/privacy-and-security-policy.html accessed 24 March 2021.

cation and acquire their medical records but also to provide financial advice or recommendations of products (i.e., to promote other insurance or investment products). The provision also asks the customer to confirm that they have acquired the consent of the concerned individual when a third party's (e.g., a spouse) data is involved. Similar consent provisions are commonly found in the proposal forms of other insurers.[38]

Last, we should also note that the personal data protection laws from other major markets could create a strong extraterritorial effect. In other words, firms in Singapore may have to follow not only Singapore's PDPA but also follow the laws of other major markets if they have higher standards that the Singaporean firms. One such example is of the General Data Protection Regulation (GDPR) issued by the European Union.[39] Article 3 defines the jurisdiction scope of the GDPR as 'the processing of personal data in the context of the activities of an establishment of a controller or a processor in the Union, regardless of whether the processing takes place in the Union or not'.[40] The GDPR also applies to the processing of the data of persons from EU by a controller or processor outside the Union if the processing activities are related to the offering of goods and services to the 'data subjects' in the EU or to the monitoring of their behaviours that take place within the Union.[41] This chapter does not intend to discuss the jurisdiction scope and interpretation of the GDPR in detail. Nevertheless, if a non-EU company plans to acquire personal data of people living in EU countries, the GDPR may be applicable. It is probably sufficient to trigger its application if a non-EU entity offers goods and services to people in the EU (even though there could be other non-European customers) or if the entity is monitoring the behaviours of people within the EU.[42]

Consequentially, the GDPR has a significant extraterritorial effect. If the EU standards are higher than the local ones, it is possible that a firm has to adopt the higher standard as common practice in order to reduce compliance costs. If so, the GDPR literally sets the tone for global data protection policy. As a trading hub, there is a considerable likelihood that companies or service

[38] For example, Great Eastern Life Assurance, 'Adult Proposal Form – Direct Channel' https://www.greateasternlife.com/content/dam/great-eastern/sg/homepage/personal-insurance/our-products/life-insurance/direct-great-term/direct-purchase-proposal-form.pdf accessed 24 March 2021; Axa Singapore, 'Smart Drive Private Application Form' https://www.axa.com.sg/pdf/our_solutions/car/smart-drive/smartdrive_application_form.pdf accessed 24 March 2021.

[39] Regulation (EU) 2016/679 (GDPR).

[40] GDPR Art 3(1).

[41] GDPR Art 3(2).

[42] See Deloitte, 'GDPR Top Ten #3: Extraterritorial applicability of the GDPR' https://www2.deloitte.com/ch/en/pages/risk/articles/gdpr-extraterritorial-applicability.html accessed 25 March 2021.

providers in Singapore may have to deal with people in the EU, thereby exposing them to the GDPR.

In summary, the PDPA of Singapore established the fundamental principles and regulations regarding when and how an entity can collect, use and disclose personal information about an individual. Largely, the collection, use or disclosure of personal data is dependent on the individual's consent when the data is used for legitimate purposes. For insurers, the PDPA allows them to collect and use personal data about an individual for insurance evaluation purposes or for the management of their insurance benefits. In addition to local laws, we should also note the potential extraterritorial effect of the personal data protection laws of other countries, notably the EU's GDPR. For instance, an insurer in Singapore might have to comply with the GDPR if it collects information from European customers or receives customers' personal information from its European parent company. Whether it must comply with the GDPR depends on the circumstance and detailed legal analysis. However, the potential legal risk from exterritorial application of the GDPR on insurers in Singapore should not be ignored.

B. MAS FEAT Principles

In 2018, the MAS published the *Principles to Promote Fairness, Ethics, Accountability and Transparency (FEAT) in the Use of Artificial Intelligence and Data Analytics in Singapore's Financial Sector* (the FEAT Principles).[43] As per this policy document, the MAS collects 'a set of generally accepted Principles for the use of artificial intelligence and data analytics ('AIDA') in decision-making in the provision of financial products and services'.[44] The FEAT principles are created not only with inputs from the financial industry but also in collaboration with other relevant stakeholders.[45] Since this document only uses the term 'principles', instead of 'notices' or even 'guidelines', it is not considered mandatory. Rather, these principles are intended to provide some guidance when insurers use AIDA for offering insurance-related services[46] in order to 'improve business processes, mitigate risks and facilitate stronger decision-making'.[47]

---

43 MAS Principles to Promote Fairness, Ethics, Accountability and Transparency https://www.mas.gov.sg/publications/monographs-or-information-paper/2018/FEAT accessed 25 May 2021 (MAS FEAT Principles).

44 Ibid., para 1.1.

45 Ibid., para 1.3.

46 Ibid., para 2.1.

47 Ibid., para 1.1.

There are a few key principles that insurers need to consider before using AIDA. The first is fairness. Further, the use of technology needs to be justifiable so that '[i]ndividuals or groups of individuals are not systematically disadvantaged through AIDA-driven decisions unless these decisions can be justified'.[48] Moreover, the use of personal attributes as factors for an AI-driven decision also needs to be justified.[49] Furthermore, the data and models used for AI-based decisions must be regularly reviewed and validated for accuracy and relevance to minimise unintentional biases and ensure that the models behave as designed and intended.[50]

The second principle is associated with ethics. Insurers need to show that their use of AIDA aligns with the firm's ethical standards, values and code of conduct.[51] AIDA-driven decisions should also be held to at least the same ethical standards as human-driven decisions.[52]

The third principle is about accountability and has two aspects. For internal accountability, the use of AIDA in decision-making needs to be approved by an appropriate internal authority.[53] A firm also cannot use externally sourced AIDA models for any reason.[54] The firm should also raise the level of awareness regarding these regulations amongst the board and senior management.[55] For external accountability, the FEAT principles require that the data subjects are provided with channels to enquire about, submit appeals for and request reviews of the AIDA-driven decisions that affect them.[56] A firm is also required to consider the verified and relevant supplementary data provided by the data subjects when performing a review of the AIDA-driven decisions.[57]

The last principle is transparency. To improve public confidence in AI, its use has to be proactively disclosed to the data subjects as a part of the general communication with them.[58] Customers should be provided with, upon request, clear explanations regarding what data is used to make AIDA-driven decisions about the data subjects and how this data affects said decisions.[59]

48 Ibid., para 4.1.
49 Ibid., para 4.2.
50 Ibid., paras 4.3 and 4.4.
51 Ibid., para 4.5.
52 Ibid., para 4.6.
53 Ibid., para 4.7.
54 Ibid., para 4.8.
55 Ibid., para 4.9.
56 Ibid., para 4.10.
57 Ibid., para 4.11.
58 Ibid., para 4.12.
59 Ibid., para 4.13.

They should also be provided with, upon request, clear explanations about the consequences that the AIDA-driven decisions may have for them.[60]

The principles correspond to the concerns about data mentioned in the previous section on the potential prejudicial and discriminatory effect of using big data and AI inappropriately. A bigger question is then about how to ensure whether a firm is effectively putting the principles into practice. This chapter provides some general discussion regarding this in section IV.

C. Cyber Hygiene

Data governance is also related to cyber security and technology risk management for an insurer. In the 21st century, where many functions or services are digitalised, the safety of the computing system is of utmost importance.

To some extent, data security must also be supported by people's conduct. However safe a system and however strong a firewall, one can breach data security if a manager, employee or customer inadvertently gives away their access to an account or system. For this purpose, the MAS has issued the *Notice on Cyber Hygiene*[61] as a way to improve the security of digital systems.

First, the MAS requires that an insurer (and other financial institutions) must ensure that every administrative account related to an operating system, database, application, security appliance or network device is secured to prevent any unauthorised access to or the use of such accounts.[62] Second, an insurer must apply security patches in a timely manner to address any vulnerability in every system.[63] Third, there has to be a written set of security standards for every system to make sure that they all conform to the established security standards.[64] In addition, an insurer must set up an appropriate network parameter defence to restrict unauthorised network traffic[65] and implement measures to protect the systems from malware.[66]

At the consumer end, whilst the MAS cannot directly regulate a customer's conduct, at least the financial regulator can improve an insurer's security measures to allow customers' access to any system or account. In Singapore, the regulator requires multi-factor authentication for not only administrative

---

60 Ibid., para 4.14.

61 MAS Notice on Cyber Hygiene (Notice 655) https://www.mas.gov.sg/-/media/MAS/Notices/PDF/MAS-Notice-655.pdf last accessed 26 March 2021. (MAS Notice on Cyber Hygiene)

62 Ibid., para 4.1.

63 Ibid., para 4.2.

64 Ibid., para 4.3.

65 Ibid., para 4.4.

66 Ibid., para 4.5.

accounts but also all accounts used for accessing customer information through the Internet.[67] A common way to establish multi-factor authentication is to require a person or customer who wants to log onto a system to enter not only their username and password but also an additional passcode that is sent to their registered mobile phone or that is generated by a security device. By controlling the access and improving the security required to access a system, the robustness of data security can be made stronger.

D. Technology Risk Management

Similar to cyber hygiene, a broader subject is an insurer's technology risk management. MAS's *Technology Risk Management Guidelines* (TRM Guidelines) were expanded in January 2021 to provide more detailed guidance on the TRM framework and measures in the digital era.[68] As noted by the MAS, '[d]igital transformation in the financial sector can be broadly characterised by the adoption of new technology and the use of existing technology in innovative ways to achieve greater automation and enrich financial service offerings'.[69] The MAS also identifies cyber risk as one of the main sources of technology risk.[70] Thus, unlike the previous version of the TRM Guidelines, which focused more on recovering the critical systems of a bank or insurer, the current 2021 version places an immense amount of emphasis on cyber risk management.

In general, an insurer needs to establish sound and robust technology risk governance and oversight and maintain cyber resilience.[71] The board and senior management are eventually responsible for establishing the policy, strategy and governance framework for TRM in a firm.[72] 'The board of directors and senior management should ensure a Chief Information Officer, Chief Technology Officer or Head of IT, and a Chief Information Security Officer or Head of Information Security, with the requisite expertise and experience, are appointed.'[73]

An insurer should ensure that 'stringent security practices are in place to safeguard and protect any sensitive data the vendor has access to over the

---

67 Ibid., para 4.6.

68 MAS Technology Risk Management Guidelines (last updated in January 2021) https://www.mas.gov.sg/-/media/MAS/Regulations-and-Financial-Stability/Regulatory-and-Supervisory-Framework/Risk-Management/TRM-Guidelines-18-January-2021.pdf last accessed 26 March 2021 (MAS TRM Guidelines).

69 Ibid., para 1.2.

70 Ibid., para 1.3.

71 Ibid., para 1.4.

72 Ibid., para 3.1.

73 Ibid., para 3.1.3.

course of [an IT project]'.[74] An insurer should also institute a policy and strategy for backing up data regularly.[75] To maintain data confidentiality and integrity, an insurer should adopt cryptographic algorithms to encrypt their data.[76] Regarding data centres, an insurer needs to ensure data centre resilience. A firm should conduct a 'threat and vulnerability risk assessment' (TVRA) for its data centres to identify potential vulnerabilities and weaknesses as well as establish the protection needed to safeguard the data centres.[77]

Moreover, an insurer should develop 'comprehensive data loss prevention policies and adopt measures to detect and prevent unauthorised access, modification, copying, or transmission of its confidential data' whilst taking into consideration the data in motion, the data at rest and the data in use.[78] The insurer should also require any third-party service providers to maintain the same level of security protection and the same security standards.[79] Systems should have strong access control to prevent fraudsters from gaining access to confidential data. Security measures should also be in place to prevent and detect unauthorised Internet services that allow users to communicate or store confidential data (e.g., through social media or file sharing).[80] An insurer should also restrict the use of sensitive production data in a non-production environment.[81] They are also required to install network security devices (such as firewalls) to secure their network and connections with third parties.[82] Finally, an insurer should regularly conduct security testing to identify and remediate exploitable loopholes and weaknesses in their systems.[83]

E. Outsourcing and Customers' Data

If an insurer outsources certain functions to a third-party service provider (TPSP) for data analysis or other services, there is a good chance that some data, including some personal data or the insurer's collected information, may have to be transferred to or shared with the TPSP. It may be as simple as using a third-party cloud storage facility, which would involve customers' data being moved from the insurer to the third-party's cloud storage. Further,

74 Ibid., para 5.3.2.
75 Ibid., para 8.4.1.
76 Ibid., paras 10.1.1 and 10.1.2.
77 Ibid., para 8.5.
78 Ibid., para 11.1.1.
79 Ibid., para 11.1.2.
80 Ibid., 11.1.5.
81 Ibid., 11.1.6.
82 Ibid., 11.2 et seq.
83 Ibid., Appendix A.

data may also have to be transferred for other applications of technology, such as electronic know-your-customer processes, fraud detection or anti-money laundering analytics, if outsourced to a TPSP. There could also be a higher risk when outsourcing to an offshore TPSP. Hence, managing outsourcing risk has become an important issue in the FinTech era.

In Singapore, the MAS has issued the *Guidelines on Outsourcing*[84] ('outsourcing guidelines') to provide guidance to insurers and other financial institutions for managing outsourcing and controlling outsourcing risks. The management of TPSPs is also a part of the TRM practices.[85] In general, the MAS relies on the board of directors' (and senior management) oversight and outsourcing agreements to manage outsourcing. In this way, the regulator relies on internal control and private ordering to control outsourcing activities but without overly restricting when and how an insurer can outsource certain functions.

There are certain key points in the outsourcing guidelines. First, the board of directors and the senior management are in charge of managing outsourcing activities and must thus be aware of the potential risks involved.[86] They are also required to set up a proper outsourcing policy and evaluate the ability and capacity of a TPSP before awarding it an outsourcing contract.[87] The appropriate due diligence has to carried out before outsourcing any work.[88] An insurer should also create a structure for managing and controlling all outsourcing agreements.[89] For offshore outsourcing, an insurer should also carefully consider the risks associated with the country in which the TPSP is located.[90]

Second, the terms of an outsourcing agreement are of utmost importance, which sets out the rights and obligations of both parties. The MAS requires an insurer to have a written agreement that evidences the contractual terms with a TPSP.[91] The contract should clearly address the risks identified through the risk assessment and due diligence processes.[92] The contract should also clearly specify the notification of adverse events, dispute resolution, termination and sub-contracting, etc.[93]

---

84 MAS, Guidelines on Outsourcing https://www.mas.gov.sg/regulation/guidelines/guidelines-on-outsourcing accessed 25 March 2021 (MAS Guidelines on Outsourcing).

85 MAS TRM Guidelines para 3.4.

86 MAS Guidelines on Outsourcing para 5.3.1.

87 Ibid., paras 5.3.1, 5.8.2 and 5.9.7.

88 Ibid., para 5.4.1 et seq.

89 Ibid., para 5.8.1.

90 Ibid., para 5.10.1.

91 Ibid., para 5.5.1.

92 Ibid., para 5.5.2.

93 Ibid., para 5.5.4.

Third, the MAS aims to ensure that outsourcing should not become an impediment to regulatory oversight and supervision.[94] Thus, it requires that an outsourcing agreement should allow not only the outsourcing insurer but also the regulator to carry out audits, and the TPSP is also required to submit reports to the MAS upon request.[95]

Fourth, data security is of utmost importance. The MAS notes that the security of a TPSP is extremely important for maintaining public confidence.[96] An insurer should proactively identify and specify the confidentiality and security requirements in an outsourcing agreement, which should also clearly state the responsibility of a TPSP regarding data security.[97] In addition, the customers' information should be disclosed to a TPSP only on a need-to-know basis.[98] An insurer should also continuously review the associated process and practice to ensure data security.[99] Moreover, on an ongoing basis, an insurer should ensure a third party to employ a high standard of care and diligence in terms of the protection of data confidentiality and integrity.[100]

Last, specifically in relation to customer data, the MAS requires that, when using cloud-based services, an insurer should actively take steps to address the risks associated with data access and security. In addition, the insurer should also ensure 'that the service provider possesses the ability to clearly identify and segregate customer data using strong physical or logical controls'.[101] Furthermore, the insurer should require the TPSP to 'have in place robust access controls to protect customer information, and such access controls should survive the tenure of the contract of the [cloud services]'.[102]

It is worth noting that 'customer information', as per the outsourcing guidelines, means 'information that relates to its customers, and [this includes] customers' accounts, particulars, transaction details and dealings with the financial institutions, but does not include any information that is public, anonymised, or encrypted in a secure manner such that the identities of the customers cannot be readily inferred'.[103] According to the definition provided in the outsourcing guidelines, an insurer should have more liberty to transfer information to a TPSP if the customers' information has been anonymised or

94 Ibid., para 5.9.
95 Ibid., paras 5.9.2, 5.9.3 and 5.10.2(b).
96 Ibid., para 5.6.1.
97 Ibid., para 5.6.2.
98 Ibid., para 5.6.2.
99 Ibid., para 5.6.2.
100 MAS TRM Guidelines 3.4.3.
101 MAS Guidelines on Outsourcing para 6.7.
102 Ibid., para 6.7.
103 MAS Guidelines on Outsourcing para 3.1.

encrypted in a secure manner with the effect of the de-identification of the data. This apparently gives insurers a lot more leeway for taking advantage of the large amount of data they possess, assuming they can safely anonymise the data in a secure manner. Whether this approach is robust enough to face threats from talented hackers and computer engineers remains to be seen. The chapter discusses this point further in section IV.

F. Summary

Section III has demonstrated that Singapore's approach to data governance for insurers comes from various sources. On the one hand, personal data protection laws remain the cornerstone on any issue related to the collection, use and disclosure of personal data. Whilst there are some exemptions to assist insurers for evaluation purposes, insurers still need to govern personal data pursuant to Singapore's PDPA. On the other hand, how insurers can use data (if not strictly confined to personal data) is also governed by the regulatory rules and guidance issued by the MAS, which serves as the financial regulator. Whilst there are no uniform guidelines or regulations, there are various rules that may have an effect on insurers' data governance, including the FEAT Principles, TRM guidelines, outsourcing guidelines and cyber hygiene rules.

In short, a two-pronged approach seems to have been adopted by the MAS at the moment in relation to an insurer's use of data. On the one hand, in relation to the use of big data and artificial intelligence (AI) by insurers, the MAS counts on the FEAT principles to offer some guidance on how insurers can use AI. Since they are just principles, they are not considered mandatory, and there is some leeway for insurers to decide how best to use AI and the data they collect. This is an illustration of principle-based regulations. Since we do not possess exhaustive knowledge regarding how big data and AI can be used and what the potential problems might be, this is perhaps the most efficient solution for the time being.

On the other hand, the MAS also considers data governance from risk management angles. With the popular use of the Internet and smartphones, cyber security (in addition to personal data protection) has become a major issue with regard to the new applications of technology in finance. Hence, it is obvious that the MAS places a significant amount of emphasis on enhancing the security of systems and on how insurers should ensure system security. With a high possibility of a part of insurers' business operations being outsourced to third-party technology firms, the MAS has also published extensive outsourcing guidelines to regulate how insurers should manage outsourcing arrangements and preserve regulatory power.

IV. REFLECTION ON SINGAPORE'S CURRENT APPROACH TO INSURANCE DATA GOVERNANCE

This section provides some general reflection on Singapore's current approaches to insurance data governance. Largely, this section further analyses certain data governance issues for Singaporean insurers from two primary perspectives: (1) how insurers may acquire and use data for the operation of insurance business and (2) how they may use the customer data acquired through their insurance companies for other uses. Regarding the first issue, this chapter questions, in general, whether the current consent-based approach to the collection and use of personal data is ideal. It also considers how more transparency in data usage and governance can be achieved and how the associated guidelines can be enforced. Regarding the second issue, we examine whether the anonymisation and encryption of the data is enough to allow insurers to transfer personal data to other parties.

A. Consent-based Provision: Too Wide?

Under Singapore's PDPA, there are two main controls for the collection, use and disclosure of personal data: a person's consent and a legitimate reason for collecting, using or disclosing said data. For the latter, Singaporean law has clearly mentioned that insurers can collect and use personal data for insurance assessment. The former requirement is met by having an insured or a customer sign a proposal form (or similar document) that contains a consent provision. As we have illustrated with an example above,[104] the consent provision is generally drafted ambiguously to broaden the scope of a customer's consent and give more flexibility to insurers with respect to collecting and using a customer's data.

However, like all other standard contracts used in the consumer context, there could be some general problems. First, a consumer may have no choice but to accept the consent provision. In the insurance market, retail consumers have no real bargaining power over the terms of a proposal form or insurance policy. In addition, the consent provision is often stated in the middle of a long proposal form. Considering the content, the provision is often in small print. Hence, the standard consent provision for personal data protection purposes may face similar problems as the exclusion clauses in boilerplate standard contracts. Eventually, this could raise further consumer protection and fairness concerns.

---

[104] See section III.A above.

If a customer does not like the consent provision, they could, of course, choose to find another insurance company for their insurance needs. In other words, customers may seek other alternatives in the market. In the end, the market force can decide which kind of consent provision is most acceptable to customers. However, this argument hinges upon the fact that other insurance products are equal. Some insurance products may largely be the same to allow insurers to compete in terms of pricing (e.g., minimum third-party risk motor insurance) or other additional services (e.g., free towage). For other insurance products, the policies offered by different insurance companies are not necessarily fungible (e.g., many health or hospitalisation policies or investment-linked policies). This means that the decision to choose another insurer is more complicated than a choice between different personal data consent provisions. In addition, if most insurers have similar provisions, a customer may be left with either a broadly drafted consent provision that allows the possible inappropriate use of their personal data or, simply, no insurance. Hence, the market power probably cannot work perfectly to curb the use of broad personal data consent by insurers.

There should be fewer problems if insurers largely confine the collection and use of personal data purely to insurance assessments or claim processing. However, as the sample provision discussed above has shown, this may have a potentially wide application for other financial guidance (e.g., for investment products). It is also arguable whether such consent should be effective in allowing insurers to use the data collected for other profits (e.g., allowing other TPSPs to use the data (if anonymised and encrypted)).

This chapter does not make the bold suggestion that we should reform the consent-based personal data protection regime, as seen in many countries. This is a much larger topic that is beyond the scope of this chapter. However, this chapter suggests that regulators should conduct a thorough empirical survey on how personal data protection consents are drafted and how personal data can be used by insurers in practice. Such research would provide more evidence regarding what regulators should do to either improve the personal data protection regime or strengthen, more specifically, the use of personal data by insurers in Singapore.

B. Enforcement of Guidelines and Principles

As section III has shown, the MAS has adopted a less intrusive approach to regulating the governance of data by insurers. On the one hand, the MAS issued the FEAT principles to serve as guidance when insurers use big data and AI in the provision of services. On the other hand, the MAS has issued guidelines related to TRM and outsourcing. However, regardless of whether they are called principles or guidelines, they remain less mandatory than other regulatory instruments such as regulations or notices. As per the MAS, they are the 'best practice standards' that govern the conduct of financial firms.[105] A breach of these guidelines does not in itself amount to an offence and attract a civil penalty, although it could be a factor when the MAS assesses a firm's compliance standards.[106] The cyber hygiene rules are more mandatory in nature, but they are mainly associated with the management of the administration accounts and security measures of an insurer's computing system. Thus, these rules do not directly regulate data governance.

This chapter does not challenge the approach taken by the MAS. After all, with the pace of technological innovation and application in the past two decades, a rigid and mandatory approach may not meet the reality of the market and could stifle innovation if drafted too narrowly. However, the use of less intrusive guidelines also raises a further question: how do regulators know whether an insurer has complied with the set principles and standards? In other words, the issue is about how these guidelines should be enforced. Even though they are not meant to be mandatory, a guideline is still expected to be followed.

There could be two general issues related to the enforcement of the guidelines. The first is a major issue regarding the information held by regulators. Without sufficient knowledge, regulators can hardly do anything until something bad happens. Traditionally, regulators could have various tools to acquire knowledge from an insurer. On the one hand, insurers have to file annual returns and financial reports periodically.[107] Moreover, the MAS could also conduct investigations and on-site inspections if necessary.[108] However, regulators can usually only react after it receives information on breach of rules or guidelines or when there are serious incidents. This means that, normally, regulators can only do something after a breach of the guidelines has occurred.

To ensure that insurers can properly carry out operations on a continuous basis, it is necessary to depend on a firm's strong internal control system. The approach of relying on the guidelines implies that regulators rely on an insurer's self-regulation, i.e., a form of *meta* regulation.[109] This is also reflected in the various guidelines mentioned in section III that require various degrees of

---

[105] MAS, Supervisory Approach and Regulatory Instruments https://www.mas.gov.sg/regulation/MAS-Supervisory-Approach-and-Regulatory-Instruments accessed 2 April 2021.

[106] Ibid.

[107] Insurance Act (Cap 142) s 36 (Singapore).

[108] Insurance Act ss 40 to 40C (Singapore).

[109] For a broad general discussion on meta regulations, see Julia Black, 'Paradoxes and Failures: "New Governance" Techniques and the Financial Crisis' (2012) 75 *Modern Law Review* 1037.

board and senior management oversight for relevant policies, strategies and regular reviews. Whether such an approach is effective at ensuring compliance with the principles and guidelines is worth a long-term research project.

Second, sometimes, an enforcement issue may arise from the lack of clarity of certain standards. For instance, the FEAT principles require insurers to provide more transparency regarding the use of AI. However, it is unclear as to when and how insurers should make a disclosure to their customers. Is it sufficient to have a general (and, often, vague) statement about how an insurer can use AI for analysing customers' data? Or should an insurer provide more details about how an algorithm works and explain its potential impact to customers? Perhaps, at this stage, regulators do not have enough examples or cases to decide what the best course of action should be. However, with the ever-increasing use of data analytics by insurers, regulators should adjust and rethink how the transparency requirement can be improved for better communication with customers.

In summary, this chapter does not oppose the reliance on more self-regulation and guidelines in insurance data governance. This should improve efficiency with regard to the use of data and the design of a suitable governance structure inside a firm. However, from the regulator's point of view, how to ensure the strength and effectiveness of an insurer's internal control system with regard to data governance and how to improve information transparency for regulators may be issues that regulators have to monitor and then devise suitable solutions for in the future with greater use of data and technology in the provision of insurance services.

C. Packaging Insurance Data and Anonymity

Apart from collecting and using customers' data for insurance assessment, insurers also possess a large amount of personal data (e.g., accidents, injuries, health records, etc.). A further question is about to what extent can insurers package and allow a third party to use this data for profits or for further value enhancement (e.g., for further machine learning for other purposes). It is common sense that an insurer should not transfer data to a third party if the data is considered personally identifiable (i.e., personal data) unless they have the consent of the customer. Even with the consent, such a transfer also needs to satisfy the legitimate interest requirement.[110] Hence, it is perhaps too difficult for an insurer to sell the personal data it possesses to a third party under the current Singaporean laws.

---

[110] See section III.A for the discussion of the Personal Data Protection Act in Singapore.

What if the data is anonymised? As mentioned above, under the MAS's outsourcing guidelines, 'customer information' does not include any information that is 'public, anonymised, or encrypted in a secure manner such that the identities of the customers cannot be readily inferred'.[111] This implies that an insurer has more liberty to transfer customer data to a third party for outsourcing purposes if said data is anonymised or encrypted in a manner that de-identifies the information. In other words, if the data cannot be linked to an individual customer, the MAS seems to allow its transfer to third parties for, at least, the outsourcing of certain operations or services. It is unclear how much an insurer can do with anonymised data that is not personally identifiable, and the general presumption remains that insurers should have more freedom to use the information as they like. If so, this should facilitate additional value enhancement for insurers with regard to the insurance-related data collected from customers.

There could be two general problems that regulators should look out for in the future. First, there is a general question regarding whether anonymised data is truly anonymised. The MAS's approach seems to be based upon the assumption that the anonymisation or encryption of data cannot be reversed to make the data identifiable. Even if the data is encrypted to ensure anonymity, one may always wonder how likely it is that the encryption code can be broken to enable the recovery of the identity of the customers. Much would depend on the encryption technology used and the skills of advanced hackers in terms of breaking such codes. It also depends on how 'anonymity' is actually perceived. It is certainly not sufficient to simply hide the names and identification numbers (if applicable). However, it is also not news that people may reverse-engineer the data to re-create the profile of a customer if sufficient data is available. This then translates into a general risk management question: do we have sufficient tools to address these potential risks?

Second, a more theoretical question is about the ownership of the data. Customers can perhaps claim that their personal data, even if anonymised, is still their own. This is also the basis of the consent-based personal data protection regime. However, insurers can perhaps also claim that the anonymised data is theirs, especially in combination with other data proprietary to or collected by the insurers from other sources. If the anonymised data belongs to the insurers only, theoretically, insurers should have the freedom to use their own property as they wish. This chapter cannot address the debate about the ownership of personal data (even anonymised) in the digital era. But we should take note that the ownership of data might eventually provide a solid theoretical basis for any legal regime.

---

[111] MAS Guidelines on Outsourcing para 3.1.

Ultimately, it would depend on the attitude and philosophy of the financial regulator. A prudent outlook might indicate a more cautious approach in relation to anonymised customer data. In contrast, if the regulator is confident about the encryption technology and the level of anonymity adopted by an insurer, allowing insurers to have more ways to use the vast volume of data they hold may be more efficient for generating greater returns not only for insurers but also for other TPSPs or even for the welfare of the consumers. The real effect of this should be subject to further studies of the market. The MAS currently seems to be aligned with the more liberal approach; but this may change soon if the underlying anonymity requirement is not robust enough to ensure the protection of personal data.

V. CONCLUSION

In conclusion, data governance is of utmost importance in the insurance sector, as insurers rely on a significant amount of data from various sources for making insurance-related decisions. The arrival of InsurTech makes data governance ever more important to address potential concerns such as fairness, accuracy and bias. In Singapore, insurance regulations do not provide a uniform framework to regulate the collection and use of data by insurers. On the one hand, the PDPA still provides the basis of the general protection of personal data. On the other hand, the MAS has issued certain guidelines, such as the FEAT principles, TRM guidelines or outsourcing guidelines, to address data governance from different angles.

Whether Singapore's approach is robust enough to meet the growing pace of technological innovation and data analytics remains to be seen. At one stage, perhaps, data governance should be further incorporated into an insurer's internal control and risk management framework. However, at this stage, this chapter generally accepts that the MAS's approach is more flexible and should not hinder further financial innovation in the market. Nevertheless, this chapter identifies three key problems overall: the validity of the consent-based personal data protection regime; the enforcement of the associated guidelines and principles; and the robustness of the anonymisation or encryption of the consumer data if insurers are allowed to make better use of the data they possess and share the same with third parties.

9. Data governance in AI: Board duties and liability

Jan Lieder and Philipp Pordzik

I. INTRODUCTION

The digital disruption of all areas of life is increasingly affecting corporate law. Whilst the legal assessment of automated processes has dominated the discourse up to now, the emergence of Artificial Intelligence (AI) means that there is an increasing need to deal with the legal coverage of autonomous entities.[1] The closely related issue of Data Governance in AI, however, has been left in the shadows.[2] This chapter aims to outline the board responsibilities in the area of Data Governance and to identify liability risks. To this end, the practical correlation of AI and Big Data will first be addressed (under II). Then, the term 'Data Governance' will be examined in more detail (under III), in order to look at the existence of the board's duties in the area of Data Governance (under IV). Finally, the chapter concludes with a summary of the main results (under V).

1 Jan-Erik Schirmer, 'Rechtsfähige Roboter?' (2016) 71 JZ 660; Philipp Hacker, 'Verhaltens- und Wissenszurechnung beim Einsatz von Künstlicher Intelligenz' (2018) 9 RW 243; Florian Möslein, 'Digitalisierung im Gesellschaftsrecht: Unternehmensleitung durch Algorithmen und künstliche Intelligenz?' (2018) 39 ZIP 204; Gunther Teubner, 'Digitale Rechtssubjekte?' (2018) 218 AcP 155; Robert Weber, Alexander Kiefner and Stefan Jobst, 'Künstliche Intelligenz und Unternehmensführung' (2018) 29 NZG 1131; Dimitrios Linardatos, 'Künstliche Intelligenz und Verantwortung' (2019) 40 ZIP 504; Ulrich Noack, 'Organisationspflichten und -strukturen kraft Digitalisierung' (2019) 183 ZHR 105; Dirk Zetzsche, 'Corporate Technologies – Zur Digitalisierung im Aktienrecht' [2019] AG 1; Marcus Becker and Philipp Pordzik, 'Digitalisierte Unternehmensführung' [2020] ZfPW 334.

2 For a first approach see Gerald Spindler, 'Zukunft der Digitalisierung – Datenwirtschaft in der Unternehmenspraxis' (2018) 71 DB 41.

II. CORRELATION BETWEEN AI AND BIG DATA

In order to underline the importance of Data Governance, a cursory introduction to the functioning of AI as well as the resulting need for large data sets is needed.

A. Artificial Intelligence

AI can be broadly defined as the ability of artificial entities to achieve set goals.[3] A particular implication is the possibility of functionality enhancements through machine learning. Due to their effectiveness, artificial neural networks have proven to be a central driver of development. The functional principle of these systems finds its model in nature. Like natural neurons, artificial neurons work together to solve complex tasks. To do this, they are arranged in different layers, which are at different levels of abstraction. Hidden layers for further data processing up to the output layer regularly follow an input layer. As the number of hidden layers increases, the performance of the artificial neural network increases as well. Therefore, multi-layered artificial neural networks (deep neural networks) have become established.[4]

The learning effect can be achieved by means of different learning methods. In supervised learning, an evaluation of results allows recalibrations based on error feedback. The result evaluation is possible because the algorithm not only knows the inputs, but also the correct outputs.[5] With unsupervised learning, no such error feedback takes place. Here, the algorithm's task is to recognise categories and correlations within the input data and, on this basis, to generate a model that enables predictions.[6]

Various differentiations and terminologies have been proposed for the classification of such systems.[7] The essential criterion for legal assessment is the degree of autonomation. In this regard, strong AI and weak AI have to

---

[3] John Armour and Horst Eidenmüller, 'Selbstfahrende Kapitalgesellschaften?' (2019) 183 ZHR 169, 172.

[4] The network architecture described is called the multilayer feed-forward model. For a visualization see Bradley Boehmke, 'Feedforward Deep Learning Models' (UC Business Analytics R Programming Guide) http://uc-r.github.io/feedforward_DNN accessed 3 March 2021; For other topologies see Simon Haykin, *Neural Networks and Learning Machines* (3rd edn, Pearson 2009) 21 ff.

[5] Ethem Alpaydin, *Maschinelles Lernen* (2nd edn, De Gruyter 2019) 12, 23 ff.

[6] Alpaydin (n 5) 12 ff; For more on learning processes, see also Haykin (n 4) 47 ff.

[7] Cf Anand Rao, 'A Strategist's Guide to Artificial Intelligence' (2017) 87 strategy+business 1, 4 ff; Hacker (n 1) 252 ff; Armour and Eidenmüller (n 3) 172.

be distinguished. Currently, there is no strong AI.[8] There is no system really imitating a human being, such as a so-called superintelligence. Only weak AI is applied today. These are single technologies for smart human-machine interactions. Weak AI focuses on the solution of specific application problems based on the methods from maths and computer science, whereby the systems are capable of self-optimisation.[9]

Artificial neural networks are not only dependent on data sets that are as precise and extensive as possible during the training phase, but they are also predestined to process such data sets due to their data processing capacities. This is why data is being described as the 'resources of the 21st century'.[10] In this context, the term 'Big Data' stands as a symbol for the promises and challenges of technological change.[11]

B. Big Data

Big Data is generally distinguished from classic data sets by three characteristics. They are high volume data sets that are generated and transferred at high velocity and are composed of a high variety of data types and sources. The complexity of these data overwhelms the data processing capacity of traditional systems. However, advanced analysis methods make it possible to recognise unrecognised correlations and causalities in previously impenetrable piles of data and thus generate added value for businesses with high-quality source data.[12]

---

8 Cf Noack (n 1) 107; Ulrich Noack, 'Der digitale Aufsichtsrat' in Barbara Grunewald, Jens Koch and Jörgen Tielmann (eds), *Festschrift für Eberhard Vetter* (Dr. Otto Schmidt 2019) 497, 500 for a different use of this wording, see Lutz Strohn, 'Die Rolle des Aufsichtsrats beim Einsatz von Künstlicher Intelligenz' (2018) 182 ZHR 371 ff.

9 See Antwort der Bundesregierung, 'Erarbeitung einer KI-Strategie der Bundesregierung' BT-Drucks. 19/5678, 2.

10 Chancellor Angela Merkel quoted after Alexander Armbruster, 'Merkel: Daten sind die Rohstoffe des 21. Jahrhunderts' *Frankfurter Allgemeine* (Frankfurt, 12 March 2016) https://www.faz.net/aktuell/wirtschaft/cebit/angela-merkel-fordert-mehr-modernisierte-digitale-technologien-14120493.html accessed 3 March 2021.

11 Cf Dirk Mewis, 'Big Data für die Diagnose' *Frankfurter Allgemeine* (Frankfurt, 11 June 2019) 0X1; Steffen Mau, 'Wir wollen es ja selber' *Die Welt* (Berlin, 03 July 2019) 21; from the legal literature, e.g., Boris Paal and Moritz Hennemann, 'Big Data im Recht, Wettbewerbs- und daten(schutz)rechtliche Herausforderungen' (2017) 70 NJW 1697; Gerald Spindler and Andreas Seidel, 'Die zivilrechtlichen Konsequenzen von Big Data für Wissenszurechnung und Aufklärungspflichten' (2018) 71 NJW 2153.

12 In detail Samuel Fosso Wamba and others, 'How 'big data' can make big impact' (2015) 165 *Int. J. Prod. Econ.* 234, 235; see also Luca Enriques and Dirk Zetzsche, 'Corporate Technologies and the Tech Nirvana Fallacy' (2019) ECGI Working Paper

III. DATA GOVERNANCE

Dealing with Big Data presents companies with fundamentally new challenges. Against this background, the demand for Data Governance in companies is becoming increasingly popular.[13] Legal scholarship, however, has found it difficult to enter into the discourse on the requirements of Data Governance.[14] This may be explained by the fact that the term 'Data Governance' is already used in many different versions.[15] This finding is sometimes even used as an explanation for the lack of Data Governance structures in companies. The conceptual vagueness alone is supposed to discourage them from dealing with this topic, the importance of which should not be underestimated.[16]

In an extensive meta-analysis of the use of the term 'Data Governance', however, it has recently been possible to establish a common foundation and, building on this, to develop a definition of Data Governance. According to this, Data Governance specifies a cross-functional framework for managing data as a strategic enterprise asset. In doing so, Data Governance specifies decision rights and accountabilities for an organisation's decision-making about its data. Furthermore, Data Governance formalises data policies, standards, and procedures and monitors compliance.[17] Data management is to be distinguished from this as the day-to-day realisation of Data Governance.[18]

N° 457/2019, 15 ff https://papers.ssrn.com/sol3/papers.cfm?abstract_id=3392321] accessed 3 March 2021; Zetzsche (n 1) 3.

[13] Vijay Khatri and Carol Brown, 'Designing Data Governance' (2010) 53 Communications of the ACM 148; Tibor Koltay, 'Data Governance, data literacy and the management of data quality' (2016) 42 *International Federation of Library Associations and Institutions Journal* 303; Paul Brous, Marijn Janssen and Riikka Vilminko-Heikkinen, 'Coordinating Decision-Making in Data Management Activities: A Systematic Review of Data Governance Principles' (*HAL*, 16 November 2017) https://hal.inria.fr/hal-01636460/document accessed 3 March 2021; Rene Abraham, Jan vom Brocke and Johannes Schneider, 'Data Governance: A Conceptual framework, structured review, and research agenda' (2019) 49 *International Journal of Information Management* https://www.researchgate.net/publication/334653735_Data_Governance_A_conceptual_framework_structured_review_and_research_agenda accessed 3 March 2021; Alevita Krotova and Jan Eppelsheimer, 'Was bedeutet Data Governance' (*DEMAND* 2019) https://www.iwkoeln.de/fileadmin/user_upload/Studien/Gutachten/PDF/2019/Gutachten_Data_Governance_DEMAND_Template.pdf accessed 3 March 2021.

[14] For a first approach, see Spindler (n 2).

[15] See also the meta-analysis in Abraham, vom Brocke and Schneider (n 13).

[16] Alevita Krotova and Jan Eppelsheimer (n 13) 4.

[17] Abraham, vom Brocke and Sven Schneider (n 13).

[18] Ibid.

IV. DATA GOVERNANCE AND BOARD DUTIES

Against the backdrop of the increased importance of data as an asset of every company, questions arise as to which responsibilities should be attributed to boards of directors in the area of Data Governance. Due to diverging corporate governance regimes, however, it is first necessary to determine the normative point of reference. In continental European jurisdictions, just like Germany, a dual board structure is the prevailing system with a management board running the day-to-day business of the firm and a supervisory board monitoring the business decisions of the management board. In Anglo-American jurisdictions, like the US and the UK, the two functions of management and supervision are combined within one unitary board – the board of directors.[19] Hereafter, the regulatory framework under German law will be taken as a basis.

A. Board Duties in the Area of Data Governance

In the absence of a statutory regulation of Data Governance, the normative starting point for executive board duties in the area of Data Governance is the duty of care as outlined in § 93(1)(1) German Stock Corporation Act (*Aktiengesetz – AktG*).[20] Members of the management board must exercise the due diligence of a responsible and conscientious businessperson in their management activities. This is not only a definition of the standard of care for directors' liability, but also a general clause-like description of the duties of care, from which situation-specific individual duties can be derived.[21] The duty of care is complemented by the guarantee of discretionary powers under § 93(1)(2) *AktG*. According to this, management board members satisfy their duty of care if, when making an entrepreneurial decision, they could reasonably assume that they were acting in the best interests of the company based on appropriate information.[22]

---

19 For a comparative overview, see Jan Lieder, *Der Aufsichtsrat im Wandel der Zeit* (JWV 2016), 636 ff.

20 *Aktiengesetz* of 6 September 1965, last amended by Art 15 of the Act of 22 December 2020.

21 Jens Koch, '§ 93 Rn. 5' in Uwe Hüffer and Jens Koch (eds), *Beck'scher Kurz-Kommentar zum Aktiengesetz* (14th edn, C.H. Beck 2020); Holger Fleischer, '§ 93 Rn. 15' in Martin Henssler (ed), *Beck-online Großkommentar zum Aktienrecht* (1 February 2021, C.H.Beck 2021).

22 In detail recently Christoph Seibt, 'Neuvermessung der "angemessenen Informationsgrundlage" (§ 93(1) Satz 2 AktG) unter VUCA-Rahmenbedingungen' in Alfred Bergmann, Michael Hoffmann-Becking and Ulrich Noack (eds) *Festschrift für Ulrich Seibert* (Dr. Otto Schmidt 2019) 825 ff.

1. Duty of legality and duty of legality control

The cardinal duties of a management board include the duty of legality and the duty of legality control as special characteristics of board-related duties of care. Whilst the former obliges the board of directors to comply with all company-related legal requirements, the latter requires the creation of structures to prevent violations of the law at subordinate levels.[23]

In dealing with Big Data, the requirements of antitrust law are of particular relevance, which in German law have recently been explicitly extended to trade in and control over data.[24] The regulatory requirements on data protection, namely the General Data Protection Regulation (GDPR),[25] also prompt firms to have a close look at the data which is handled and stored in the company, and how data is used at any level of the corporation.

However, the board's duties in the area of Data Governance go far beyond mere compliance with mandatory law. It is precisely these unwritten board duties that harbour considerable liability risks due to the lack of normative contours, which is why special attention should be paid to them.[26]

2. Ensuring data quality

This begins with the demand to guarantee sufficient data quality,[27] even if the research on guaranteeing quality standards in the use of Big Data is still in its infancy.[28] In the press, unclean data is even being touted as a special advan-

---

[23] Gerald Spindler, '§ 93 Rn. 86 ff, 115' in Wulf Goette, Mathias Habersack and Susanne Kalss (eds), *Münchener Kommentar zum Aktiengesetz* (5th edn, C.H. Beck 2019); Jens Koch, '§ 93 Rn. 6, 6c' in Uwe Hüffer and Jens Koch, *Beck'scher Kurz-Kommentar zum Aktiengesetz* (14th edn, C.H. Beck 2020).

[24] See Spindler (n 2) 42 ff.

[25] Regulation (EU) 2016/679 of the European Parliament and of the Council of 27 April 2016 on the protection of natural persons with regard to the processing of personal data and on the free movement of such data, and repealing Directive 95/46/EC (General Data Protection Regulation) [2016] OJ L 119/1.

[26] See Spindler (n 2) 42 ff.

[27] Thomas Hoeren, 'Thesen zum Verhältnis von Big Data und Datenqualität, Erstes Raster zum Erstellen juristischer Standards' (2016) 19 MMR 8 ff; Weber, Kiefner and Jobst (n 1) 1132 ff.

[28] For more information see Barna Saha and Divesh Srivastava, 'Data Quality: The other Face of Big Data' (2014 IEEE 30th International Conference on Data Engineering, 19 May 2014) <https://ieeexplore.ieee.org/stamp/stamp.jsp?tp=&arnumber=6816764> accessed 3 March 2021; Ismael Caballero, Manuel Serrano and Mario Piattini, 'A Data Quality in Use Model for Big Data (Position Paper)' in Marta Indulska and Sandeep Purao (eds), *Advances in Conceptual Modeling* (Springer 2014); Noraini Abdullah and others, 'Data Quality in Bag Data: A Review' (2015) 7 *International Journal of Advances in Soft Computing and its Applications* http://home.ijasca.com/data/documents/IJASCA-SI-070302_Pg16-27_Data-Quality-in-Big-Data-A-Review.pdf accessed 3 March 2021; David Becker, Bill McMullen and Trish Dunn

tage of Big Data.[29] Although policymakers are not quite ready to accept this, they are finding it difficult to lay down concrete requirements. The European Commission's White Paper on AI, for example, contains requirements aimed at providing reasonable assurances that the use of the products or services that the AI system enables is safe. Safety could be ensured, for example, by requirements guaranteeing that AI systems are trained on data sets that are sufficiently broad and cover all relevant scenarios needed to avoid dangerous situations. Requirements to take reasonable measures aimed at ensuring that such subsequent use of AI systems does not lead to outcomes displaying prohibited discrimination are also taken into consideration. These could entail in particular obligations to use data sets that are sufficiently representative, especially to ensure that all relevant dimensions of gender, ethnicity and other possible grounds of prohibited discrimination are appropriately reflected in those data sets.[30] A more precise requirement can be found in Article 5(1)(d) GDPR, according to which personal data should be accurate and, where necessary, kept up to date. However, universal quality standards cannot be derived from the GDPR. In view of this, it is not surprising that the existence of corresponding board obligations has so far only been marginally illuminated.

(a) Recognition of the board's duty

With regard to the business judgment rule (§ 93(1)(2) *AktG*),[31] according to which management board members are privileged if they can reasonably assume to act in the best interests of the company on the basis of adequate information, one may argue the board of directors must ensure that its information is of sufficient quality.[32] This argument is convincing in such situations where AI is granted its own decision-making powers. Otherwise, the board could evade its responsibility to provide information by delegating decisions

---

King, 'Big Data, Big Data Quality Problem' (2015 IEEE International Conference on Big Data (Big Data), 28 December 2015) https://ieeexplore.ieee.org/stamp/stamp.jsp?tp=&arnumber=7364064 accessed 3 March 2021; Li Cai and Yangyong Zhu, 'The Challenges of Data Quality and Data Quality Assessment in the Big Data Era' (2015) 14 Data *Science Journal* Article 2 https://www.researchgate.net/publication/277943983_The_Challenges_of_Data_Quality_and_Data_Quality_Assessment_in_the_Big_Data_Era accessed 3 March 2021; Jorge Merino and others, 'A Data Quality in Use model for Big Data' (2016) 63 Future Generation Computer Systems 123 ff.

29 Helmut Martin-Jung, 'Warum wir Big Data verstehen müssen' *Süddeutsche Zeitung* (Munich, 9 October 2015) https://www.sueddeutsche.de/wirtschaft/digitale-datenflut-warum-wir-big-data-verstehen-muessen-1.2685115 accessed 3 March 2021.

30 European Commission, 'White Paper on Artificial Intelligence – A European approach to Excellence and Trust' COM (2020) 65 final, 16.

31 See under IV.A.

32 See Weber, Kiefner and Jobst (n 1) 1132 ff.

to AI. However, this justification does not appear to be sustainable if such delegation is not the case, as the criterion of an adequate information basis precisely specifies the duties of care in decision-making situations. Nevertheless, it cannot be assumed that data quality assurance could be completely disregarded outside of decision-making situations. It would hardly be compatible with the due diligence of a responsible and conscientious businessperson to undermine the functionality of an AI application by insufficient data quality after the entrepreneurial decision to use it. From the entrepreneurial decision to use AI follows, therefore, the responsibility of the board of directors to ensure adequate data quality.

Figure 9.1 *Data quality*

(b) Requirements

In order to measure the content of this obligation, findings from research on data quality can be used.[33] However, data quality is not accessible to an abstract determination, but must be measured from the user's perspective. The quality of data is thus defined in terms of its 'fitness for use'. Data are of high

---

[33] For more information Leo Pipino, Yang Lee and Richard Wang, 'Data Qualitiy Assessment' (2002) 45 Communications of the ACM 211; Cinzia Cappiello, Chiara Francalanci and Barbara Pernici, 'Data quality assessment from the user's perspective' [2004] Information Quality in Informational Systems 68; Carlo Batini and others, 'Methodologies for Data Quality Assessment and Improvement' (2009) 41 ACM Computing Surveys Article 16; explicitly to Big Data Caballero, Serrano and Piattini (n 28); Saha and Srivastava (n 28); Abdullah and others (n 28); Cai and Zhu (n 28); Becker, McMullen and King (n 28); Merino and others (n 28).

Table 9.1 Data quality

Accessibility	not only refers to the difficulties of obtaining data, but also includes the comprehensibility and usability of data in a technical sense.
Timeliness	describes the data being up to date.
Relevance	indicates the abstract applicability and usefulness of data in its overall context for the intended task.
Accuracy	is defined as the closeness of data values to known reference values considered correct.
Integrity	characterises the structural completeness of a dataset. This includes in particular the standardisation of the data values according to a data model or data type.
Consistency	concerns the degree to which correlated data is correct and complete. In the fields of databases, it usually means that the same data that are located in different storage areas should be considered to be equivalent. This is the case when data have an equal value and the same meaning or are essentially the same.
Completeness	indicates the extent to which a given data collection includes data describing the corresponding set of real-world objects.

quality if they meet the needs of the user.[34] A multi-dimensional concept has become established for a more accurate determination, which is presented in Figure 9.1 and Table 9.1 for a better overview.[35]

Due to the contextual nature of the concept of quality, this widely agreed concept is only subject to marginal discrepancies in the exact description of the individual dimensions. Nevertheless, the essential content can be described as generally recognised.[36]

Based on this concept, the quality of data can reliably be determined.[37] Therefore, it can also be used as a starting point for defining the content of the obligation to ensure adequate data quality.[38] From the fundamental realisation that the quality of data is measured by its suitability for its concrete application, it follows that the objectives pursued with the use of data must be formulated as precisely as possible. An ideal data set, measured against that objective, would then fully meet the requirements of all quality dimensions. However, directors can hardly be required to guarantee ideal data sets, as such data sets are unlikely to be obtained in the reality of business on a regular basis. In view of the specific requirements in dealing with AI, the required ideal data quantity

34 Cappiello, Francalanci and Pernici (n 33); cf Cai and Zhu (n 28) 2.

35 Cf with marginal differences Pipino, Lee and Wang (n 33) 212; Cappiello, Francalanci and Pernici (n 33) 68 ff; Abdullah and others (n 28) 19 ff; Cai and Zhu (n 28) 5 ff.

36 Cf Pipino, Lee and Wang (n 33) 212; Cappiello, Francalanci and Pernici (n 33); Abdullah and others (n 28) 19 ff; Cai and Zhu (n 28) 5 ff.

37 Abdullah and others (n 28) 19 ff.

38 Referring to Cai and Zhu (n 28) 7 ff.

and the appropriate data quality may clash.[39] Therefore, the executive board must be granted entrepreneurial discretion in determining the appropriate data quality, which allows it to consider individual objectives. For this purpose, it is necessary to weight the quality dimensions according to their relevance for the pursued objective and to define minimum requirements to be achieved in each case. For example, the timeliness and accuracy of personal data will be given more weight than their integrity or completeness if the data is only to be used for personal advertising. Based on the weighting of the quality dimensions and the definition of internal targets, an evaluation baseline can be formulated that defines appropriate data quality. In addition, the specific circumstances must be taken into account. If the data is to be used to prepare important decisions, higher demands must inevitably be placed on the data quality than for more insignificant objectives. The actual review of the data quality is then directed towards this evaluation baseline. It must be taken into account that each quality dimension requires its own testing processes, which is why testing time and costs can diverge considerably.[40] Therefore, with regard to the required monitoring intensity, only appropriate data assessment in view of the planned use of the data must be ensured. The executive board must also be granted entrepreneurial discretion for this process in order to be able to consider the specific circumstances.

The requirement to ensure data quality can thus be summarised as follows. First, boards need to be precise about the objectives of data use. Based on this, the quality dimensions must be weighted according to their relevance, and the minimum requirements to be achieved must be defined. These are entrepreneurial decisions, which is why the board must be granted discretion in this regard. The quality of the data is then to be measured against the evaluation baseline obtained in this way, whereby the definition of the audit intensity is also an entrepreneurial decision by the board of directors.

3. Ensuring data security

Whilst the board's obligations to ensure adequate data quality have so far received only sporadic attention by legislators, the board's obligations regarding data security have been given higher recognition.[41] Thus, various

---

[39] See Weber, Kiefner and Jobst (n 1) 1133.

[40] Cai and Zhu (n 28) 7 ff.

[41] Cf Sean Hipworth, 'Corporate Compliance in the Computer Age' (2015) 20 *J. Tech. L. & Pol'y* 209; Harris Yegelwel, 'Cybersecurity oversight: A cautionary tale for directors' (2015) 20 *J. Tech. L. & Pol'y* 229; Kim Mehrbrey and Marcus Schreibauer, 'Haftungsverhältnisse bei Cyber-Angriffen' (2016) 19 MMR 75; Lawrence Trautman and Peter Ormerod, 'Corporate Directors' and Officers' Cybersecurity Standard of Care: The Yahoo Data Breach' (2017) 66 *Am. U. L. Rev.* 1231; Natalie Daghles,

content-related and addressee-related obligations have been introduced with largely similar content. The GDPR, as a content-related obligation, requires increased protection of the integrity and confidentiality of personal data through appropriate technical or organisational measures. This basic requirement is considered so relevant that it is repeated throughout various provisions of the GDPR.[42] The German legislator has also paid attention to the protection of personal data through similar provisions for service providers in the areas of telecommunications and telemedia.[43] Addressee-related obligations to ensure data security concern not only operators of critical infrastructures[44] but also providers of online marketplaces, online search engines and cloud computing services[45] as well as the regulated financial industry.[46] However, it would be wrong to see these legal obligations as comprehensive. Their explicit standardisation is justified by the special relevance of the protected data as well as the increased importance of the respective companies for the welfare of the community. This does not exclude an obligation of the executive board to ensure data security in the interest of the company.

(a) Recognition of the board's duty

In view of the increased importance of data, there is an established consensus that the existence of a duty to ensure data security cannot be denied.[47] Paradigmatic for this finding is an attack on Yahoo, in which millions of users' data was stolen with the consequence that the purchase price for the company

'Cybersecurity-Compliance: Pflichten und Haftungsrisiken für Geschäftsleiter in Zeiten fortschreitender Digitalisierung' (2018) 71 DB 2289; Noack (n 1); Sarah Schmidt-Versteyl, 'Cyber Risks – neuer Brennpunkt Managerhaftung?' (2019) 72 NJW 1637; Alexander Kiefner and Benedikt Happ, 'Cyber-Security als rechtliche Herausforderung für die Unternehmensleitung und Unternehmensorganisation' [2020] BB 2051.

42 See Art. 5(1)(f) GDPR; Art. 25 GDPR; Art. 32 GDPR.

43 See § 109 German Telecommunications Law (*Telekommunikationsgesetz – TKG* of 22 June 2004, last amended by Article 319 of the Act of 19 June 2020); § 13(7) German Telemedia Law (*Telemediengesetz – TMG* of 26 February 2007, last amended by Article 1 of the Law of 19 November 2020).

44 See §§ 8a(1); 2(10) German Law on the Federal Office for Information Security (*Gesetz über das Bundesamt für Sicherheit in der Informationstechnologie – BSIG* of 14 August 2009, last amended by Art. 73 of the Act of 19 June 2020).

45 See §§ 8c(1); 2(11) *BSIG*.

46 See § 25a(1)(3)(5) German Banking Act (*Gesetz über das Kreditwesen – KWG* of 9 September 1998, last amended by Art. 4 of the Law of 9 December 2020); § 80 German Securities Trading Law (*Gesetz über den Wertpapierhandel – WpHG* of 9 September 1998, last amended by Art. 8(1) of the Law of 9 December 2020).

47 Mehrbrey and Schreibauer (n 41) 79 ff; Daghles (n 41) 2290; Noack (n 1) 124 ff; Schmidt-Versteyl (n 41) 1640; Kiefner and Happ (n 41).

was reduced by 350 million USD in a subsequent sale to Verizon.[48] However, preventive measures are also expected from smaller companies, even if digitalisation still plays a less significant role there.[49] Normatively, the duty to ensure data security is understood to be part of the general duty of care. In view of the extensive computer networks in companies, a complete disregard of data security can no longer be considered compatible with the diligence of a responsible and conscientious businessperson.[50] This is even more true if the data are assets that generate added business value due to their use in AI processes.

(b) Requirements

In line with the legislative requirements for data security, the adoption of appropriate organisational and technical measures to protect existing data is required as a matter of principle.[51] However, it is difficult to derive operational criteria from this statement alone. Further legislative points of reference are needed in order to fill the requirement of appropriate organisational and technical measures with life.

A first reference point is provided by provisions for the regulated financial industry, namely § 25a(1)(3) German Banking Act (*Gesetz über das Kreditwesen – KWG*). The provision requires appropriate and effective risk management, which is described in more detail. It contains a multi-dimensional concept consisting of preventive measures to avert danger (preparedness), preparatory measures to counter danger (response) and the establishment of an internal control system (control). These requirements are intended to safeguard the entrusted assets and ensure the proper functioning of banking transactions and financial services.[52] Data are recognised as assets of a company. In light of their importance for business activities, this legislation can be considered a more generally applicable guideline for diligent business management. The legislative concept for the regulated financial industry can be utilised to outline the content of the director's obligation to take appropriate organisational and technical measures to protect existing data.[53]

---

48 Schmidt-Versteyl (n 41) 1638; further Trautman and Ormerod (n 41).

49 Noack (n 1) 126.

50 Kiefner and Happ (n 41); as well Noack (n 1) 124 ff; referring to § 91(2) *AktG* in general Schmidt-Versteyl (n 41) 1639; Mehrbrey and Schreibauer (n 41) 79 ff; Daghles (n 41) 2290.

51 Noack (n 1) 127.

52 Ulrich Braun, '§ 25a Rn. 34' in Karl-Heinz Boos, Reinfrid Fischer and Hermann Schulte-Mattler (eds), *Kommentar zu Kreditwesengesetz, VO (EU) Nr. 575/2013 (CRR) und Ausführungsvorschriften* (C.H. Beck 2016).

53 For a similar structure cf Kiefner and Happ (n 41).

At the same time, measures to ensure data security fulfil the structural requirements of the provisions for the early detection of developments jeopardising the continued existence of the company according to § 91(2) *AktG*, which must be observed in any case if the data is sufficiently relevant. The management board must take suitable measures for the identification of risks threatening the existence of the company and exercise continuous control with the help of a monitoring system.[54] These measures were originally intended as a reaction to corporate crises in the 1990s in order to prevent developments that could endanger the existence of the company.[55] Specifically, the management board must establish a risk management system and establish unambiguous responsibilities. Furthermore, it must set up a close-knit reporting system that is documented accordingly. It must be ensured that all relevant departments, from the responsible person to the respective hierarchical management levels including directors, are informed of existing risks in order to be able to initiate appropriate measures to control these risks. The risk management system must be documented so that it can also be communicated within the company. The disclosure of organisational regulations, the measures taken and procedures is an integral part of optimising the risk management system of a company.[56]

Drawing on these requirements, guidelines can be defined to ensure compliance with the obligation to take appropriate organisational and technical measures to protect existing data. It must be taken into account that the appropriateness of the measures can only be assessed in relation to the situation. Therefore, the management board is to be granted entrepreneurial discretion to determine appropriate measures, if it could reasonably assume to act in the best interests of the company based on appropriate information.[57] At the same time, this finding marks the starting point of a diligence-based guarantee of data security. An adequate basis of information – as a prerequisite for the privilege of non-liability – requires risk analysis as the foundation for further measures.[58] Without such risk analysis, the management board is precluded from claiming entrepreneurial discretion.[59] To this end, the vulnerabilities in data security must be identified and the probability of unauthorised access

[54] Gerald Spindler, '§ 91 Rn. 15' in Wulf Goette, Mathias Habersack and Susanne Kalss (eds), *Münchener Kommentar zum Aktiengesetz* (5th edn, C.H. Beck 2019); Holger Fleischer, '§ 91 Rn. 36' in Martin Henssler (ed), *Beck-online Großkommentar zum Aktienrecht* (C.H.Beck 2021).

[55] Holger Fleischer, '§ 91 Rn. 36' in Martin Henssler (ed), *Beck-online Großkommentar zum Aktienrecht* (C.H.Beck 2021).

[56] LG München I NZG 2008, 319, 320.

[57] Mehrbrey and Schreibauer (n 41) 79 ff; Schmidt-Versteyl (n 41) 1640; Kiefner and Happ (n 41) 2052.

[58] Schmidt-Versteyl (n 41) 1641; Kiefner and Happ (n 41) 2052.

[59] Kiefner and Happ (n 41) 2052.

quantified by comparing its vulnerabilities with known threats. A risk profile can then be created on this basis. The probability of unauthorised access must be correlated with its expected impact. Risk analysis is supposed to draw a correct and complete picture of the risks affecting the company, based on which preventive measures can be taken to deal with the risks.[60]

After the board has obtained an adequate basis of information, the determination of appropriate measures for risk prevention is a business decision. Ultimately, this is a cost-benefit analysis that depends on a number of different factors and includes a determination of the company's risk acceptance.[61] These criteria also apply to the requirements for an appropriate emergency concept. Its objective is to strengthen the resilience of the company in the event of unauthorised data access. In addition to measures to contain negative effects, this also includes measures to continue business operations as quickly as possible. The company should not be forced to react, but should be put in a position to act proactively. In addition to obtaining information promptly, special attention should be paid to accessing precisely defined reporting channels in order to avoid frictional losses in acute situations.[62]

The *IT-Grundschutz-Kompendium* of the German Federal Office for Information Security (*Bundesamt für Sicherheit in der Informationstechnik*) may serve as a point of reference for determining appropriate measures.[63] This comprehensive work not only lists typical vulnerabilities, but also includes a roadmap to counter them appropriately. It is subject to a continuous updating process to take new developments and threats into account.[64] Its prominent position in the discourse on security concepts in companies can also be attributed to the use of international standardisation. For example, using an ISO 27001 certificate based on the *IT-Grundschutz-Kompendium*, companies can prove that the implemented information security measures comply with recognised international standards.[65] The *IT-Grundschutz-Kompendium* consists

---

[60] On the whole Kiefner and Happ (n 41) 2052.

[61] Kiefner and Happ (n 41) 2052; for the catalogue of measures as well Noack (n 1) 127 ff; Schmidt-Versteyl (n 41) 1641.

[62] For the contingency plan in detail Kiefner and Happ (n 41) 2055 ff.

[63] As well Noack (n 1) 128; Schmidt-Versteyl (n 41) 1641; for a compendium see *Bundesamt für Sicherheit in der Informationstechnik*, 'IT-Grundschutz-Kompendium' (2019), https://www.bsi.bund.de/SharedDocs/Downloads/DE/BSI/Grundschutz/Zertifikat/ISO27001/Zertifizierungsschema.pdf?_blob=publicationFile&v=6 accessed 3 March 2021.

[64] Noack (n 1) 128.

[65] *Bundesamt für Sicherheit in der Informationstechnik*, 'IT-Grundschutz-Kompendium' (2019), https://www.bsi.bund.de/SharedDocs/Downloads/DE/BSI/Grundschutz/Zertifikat/ISO27001/Zertifizierungsschema.pdf?_blob=publicationFile&v=6 accessed 3 March 2021.

of process and system modules, which are assigned to different layers such as 'organisation and personnel' or 'IT systems' to simplify the matter.[66] In order to meet the requirements of the *IT-Grundschutz-Kompendium*, the appropriate modules must be selected and implemented following analysis of the individual situation. For this purpose, there are usually detailed implementation instructions that explain suitable security measures.[67] This modular system facilitates the creation of a company-specific concept for guaranteeing data security, which should always satisfy requirements to diligently determine appropriate measures for protecting data security.[68]

Finally, the board is obliged to continuously monitor the measures taken.[69] The enormous speed of technological progress must be taken into account, which makes the obligation to ensure data security a dynamic task.[70] Whether the strict requirements for recognising developments that threaten the existence of the company are to be followed, even if such developments are not to be feared according to the findings of the risk analysis, is subject to the discretion of the management board. Given the reversal of the burden of proof for management board members in the event of an allegation of a breach of their duty of care, detailed documentation of the measures taken based on risk analysis is recommended in any case.[71]

B. Delegability of Board Duties in the Area of Data Governance

Whilst the duty to ensure data security is widely described as a 'managerial responsibility',[72] there is no such explicit assignment for the duty to ensure data quality. Nevertheless, it is considered one of the original board duties.[73] This refers to the internal constitution of the joint stock corporation and the legal admissibility of delegating tasks in Data Governance.

1. Corporate governance[74]

The management board has the authority to run the corporation on a day-to-day basis. Management tasks comprise any actions of the management board of

---

66 Bundesamt für Sicherheit in der Informationstechnik (n 63) Chapter 2.
67 Ibid., Chapter 1.5.
68 In conclusion as well Noack (n 1) 128; Schmidt-Versteyl (n 41) 1641.
69 As well Schmidt-Versteyl (n 41) 1641; Kiefner and Happ (n 41) 2053.
70 Kiefner and Happ (n 41) 2053.
71 Schmidt-Versteyl (n 41) 1641.
72 Gerald Spindler, 'Gesellschaftsrecht und Digitalisierung' (2018) 47 ZGR 1, 40; Noack (n 1) 124.
73 Weber, Kiefner and Jobst (n 1) 1132 ff.
74 The following remarks are based on the presentation in Becker and Pordzik (n 1) 342 ff.

a factual or legal nature, which are undertaken on behalf of the company.[75] However, in corporate reality it is not possible for the management board members to carry out all measures in person.[76] As a result, it is generally recognised that the board can delegate management tasks to individual board members (horizontal delegation) or to subordinate employees (vertical delegation).[77]

If the board of directors can transfer its collective responsibility for management tasks and delegate them to individual board members or subordinate employees, this does not mean that the legal responsibility itself is transferred to the delegates. The management board cannot escape its responsibility: Where tasks are delegated, directors are liable for violations of the applicable duties.[78] Mistakes on the part of the delegates are not to be attributed to the board. These delegates act within the scope of duties of the company, not of the

---

[75] Cf Michael Kort, '§ 77 Rn. 3' in Michael Kort, Mathias Habersack and Max Foerster (eds), *Großkommentar zum Aktiengesetz* (5th edn, De Gruyter 2015); Jens Koch, '§ 77 Rn. 3' in Uwe Hüffer and Jens Koch, *Beck'scher Kurz-Kommentar zum Aktiengesetz* (12th edn, C.H. Beck 2018); Gerald Spindler, '§ 77 Rn. 6' in Wulf Goette, Mathias Habersack and Susanne Kalss (eds), *Münchener Kommentar zum Aktiengesetz* (5th edn, C.H. Beck 2019).

[76] Ernst Geßler, 'Der Betriebsführungsvertrag im Licht der aktienrechtlichen Zuständigkeitsordnung' in Robert Fischer and others (eds), *Festschrift für Wolfgang Hefermehl* (C.H. Beck 1976) 263, 273; Oliver Hegnon, 'Aufsicht als Leistungspflicht – Umfang persönlich wahrzunehmender Aufsichtspflichten von Geschäftsleitern bei vertikaler Arbeitsteilung aus gesellschafts- und strafrechtlicher Sicht' (2009) 2 CCZ 57; Georg Wiesner, '§ 22 Rn. 17' in Michael Hoffmann-Becking (ed), *Münchener Handbuch des Gesellschaftsrechts* (5th edn, C.H. Beck 2015); Marcus Weber, '§ 77 Rn. 27' in Wolfang Hölters (ed), Kommentar *zum Aktiengesetz* (3rd edn, C.H. Beck 2017).

[77] Instead of all Michael Kort, '§ 76 Rn. 32a' in Michael Kort, Mathias Habersack and Max Foerster (eds), *Großkommentar zum Aktiengesetz* (5th edn, De Gruyter 2015); Marcus Weber, '§ 76 Rn. 8' in Wolfang Hölters (ed), *Kommentar zum Aktiengesetz* (3rd edn, C.H. Beck 2017); Jens Koch, '§ 76 Rn. 8, § 77 Rn. 15' in Uwe Hüffer and Jens Koch, *Beck'scher Kurz-Kommentar zum Aktiengesetz* (C.H. Beck 2018); In addition, there is the right to delegate to third parties outside the company within certain limits. (*Outsourcing*), in this regard see Michael Kort, '§ 76 Rn. 50' in Michael Kort, Mathias Habersack and Max Foerster (eds), *Großkommentar zum Aktiengesetz* (5th edn, De Gruyter 2015); Gerald Spindler, '§ 76 Rn. 18 ff' in Wulf Goette, Mathias Habersack and Susanne Kalss (eds), *Münchener Kommentar zum Aktiengesetz* (5th edn, C.H. Beck 2019); Holger Fleischer, '§ 76 Rn. 73' in Martin Henssler (ed), *Beck-online Großkommentar zum Aktienrecht* (C.H. Beck 2020).

[78] Eberhard Schwark, 'Spartenorganisation in Großunternehmen und Unternehmensrecht' (1978) 142 ZHR 213, 219; BGH NJW 2001, 969, 971 (regarding Ltd.); Holger Fleischer, 'Zur Leitungsaufgabe des Vorstands im Aktienrecht' (2003) 24 ZIP 1, 7; Daniel Froesch, 'Managerhaftung – Risikominimierung durch Delegation' (2009) 61 DB 722, 724; Franck Schmidt-Husson, '§ 6 Rn. 10, 12' in Christoph

management board.[79] Therefore, the behaviour of the board members remains the starting point for liability: Their duty to fulfil their tasks is transformed into a residual duty of supervision because of the delegation.[80] This group of duties is described as a duty to carefully select, instruct and supervise the delegate.[81] The intensity of the corresponding duties depends on the type of delegated task and the circumstances of the individual case.[82]

From a conceptual point of view, the law distinguishes between 'management' and 'leadership' of the company, which is the responsibility of the management board according to § 76(1) *AktG*. Leadership is understood to be a distinct sub-category of management, which is characterised by the exercise of the original entrepreneurial leadership function of the management board.[83] In addition to the duties mandatorily assigned to the board as a whole by law, this includes fundamental decisions such as the determination of the

---

Hauschka, Klaus Moosmayer and Thomas Lösler (eds), *Corporate Compliance* (C.H. Beck 2016).

[79] Holger Fleischer, 'Vorstandsverantwortlichkeit und Fehlverhalten von Unternehmensangehörigen – von der Einzelüberwachung zur Errichtung einer Compliance-Organisation' [2003] AG 291, 292; BGH AG 2011, 876 Rn. 17; Andreas Cahn, 'Business Judgement Rule und Rechtsfragen' [2015] Der Konzern 105, 106 ff; Klaus Hopt and Markus Roth, '§ 93 Rn. 384' in Heribert Hirte, Peter Mülbert and Markus Roth (eds), *Großkommentar zum Aktiengesetz* (De Gruyter 2018); Jens Koch, '§ 93 Rn. 46' in Uwe Hüffer and Jens Koch, *Beck'scher Kurz-Kommentar zum Aktiengesetz* (14th edn, C.H. Beck 2020).

[80] Schwark (n 78) 216 ff; BGHZ 133, 370, 377 ff (regarding Ltd.); BGH NJW 2001, 969, 971 (regarding Ltd.); Fleischer (n 78) 7, 9; Fleischer (n 79) 292; Froesch (n 78) 724; Hegnon (n 76) 58; Franck Schmidt-Husson, '§ 6 Rn. 12' in Christoph Hauschka, Klaus Moosmayer and Thomas Lösler, *Corporate Compliance* (C.H. Beck 2016); Gerald Spindler, '§ 93 Rn. 170' in Wulf Goette, Mathias Habersack and Susanne Kalss (eds), *Münchener Kommentar zum Aktiengesetz* (5th edn, C.H. Beck 2019).

[81] Cf in general BGHZ 127, 336 (347) (regarding Ltd.); BGH WM 1971, 1548, 1549; Fleischer (n 78) 8 ff; Cahn (n 79) 106 ff; Klaus Hopt and Markus Roth, '§ 93 Rn. 162' in Heribert Hirte, Peter Mülbert and Markus Roth (eds), *Großkommentar zum Aktiengesetz* (De Gruyter 2018); Hans Christoph Grigoleit and Lovro Tomasic, '§ 93 Rn. 38' in Hans Christoph Grigoleit (ed), *Kommentar zum Aktiengesetz* (C.H. Beck 2020).

[82] Making the intensity of the obligation dependent on the circumstances of the individual case BGH NStZ 1986, 34; Fleischer (n 79) 293 ff; Klaus Hopt and Markus Roth, '§ 93 Rn. 163' in Heribert Hirte, Peter Mülbert and Markus Roth (eds), *Großkommentar zum Aktiengesetz* (De Gruyter 2018).

[83] Fleischer (n 78) 2; Michael Kort, '§ 76 Rn. 29 ff' in Michael Kort, Mathias Habersack and Max Foerster (eds), *Großkommentar zum Aktiengesetz* (5th edn, De Gruyter 2015); Gerald Spindler, '§ 77 Rn. 17' in Wulf Goette, Mathias Habersack and Susanne Kalss (eds), *Münchener Kommentar zum Aktiengesetz* (5th edn, C.H. Beck 2019); Holger Fleischer, '§ 76 Rn. 73' in Martin Henssler (ed), *Beck-online Großkommentar zum Aktienrecht* (C.H. Beck 2020); different and for far-reaching equa-

company's targets or business policy.[84] The leadership authority of the board of directors is limited by the purpose of the company as defined in the company's articles of association as well as the company's objectives.[85] In contrast to the simple management tasks, delegation of leadership decisions is not permitted either vertically or horizontally.[86] They represent the core area of the board's activity, and may therefore not be delegated to anyone else.[87]

However, this restriction is limited to the core area of the board's activities, i.e., the exercise of leadership responsibility as such. Auxiliary activities preparing or supporting these decisions are not covered by this prohibition.[88] The board as a whole fulfils its leadership responsibility by deciding in a well-considered manner and within its own responsibility on the drafts pre-

tion of the terms Johannes Semler, *Leitung und Überwachung der Aktiengesellschaft* (Heymanns 1996) Rn. 3–6.

84 Fleischer (n 78) 5; Andreas Cahn and Hans-Joachim Mertens, '§ 76 Rn. 4' in Ulrich Noack and Wolfgang Zöllner (eds), *Kölner Kommentar zum Aktiengesetz* (3rd edn, Heymanns 2010); Marcus Weber, '§ 76 Rn. 10' in Wolfang Hölters (ed), *Kommentar zum Aktiengesetz* (3rd edn, C.H. Beck 2017).

85 Michael Kort, '§ 76 Rn. 45' in Michael Kort, Mathias Habersack and Max Foerster (eds), *Großkommentar zum Aktiengesetz* (5th edn, De Gruyter 2015); Jens Koch, '§ 82 Rn. 9' in Uwe Hüffer and Jens Koch, *Beck'scher Kurz-Kommentar zum Aktiengesetz* (14th edn, C.H. Beck 2020); on terminology see Stephan Harbarth, '§53 Rn. 186' in Holger Fleischer and Wulf Goette (eds), *Münchener Kommentar zum GmbH-Gesetz* (C.H. Beck 2018).

86 For common opinion see Semler (n 83) Rn. 11 ff, 22 ff; Fleischer (n 78) 2; Andreas Cahn and Hans-Joachim Mertens, '§ 76 Rn. 45' in Ulrich Noack and Wolfgang Zöllner (eds), *Kölner Kommentar zum Aktiengesetz* (3rd edn, Heymanns 2010); Meinrad Dreher, 'Nicht delegierbare Geschäftsleiterpflichten' in Stefan Grundmann and others (eds), *Festschrift für Klaus J. Hopt* (De Gruyter 2010) 517, 519 ff; Ernst Thomas Emde, 'Gesamtverantwortung und Ressortverantwortung im Vorstand der AG' in Peter Mülbert and others (eds), *Festschrift für Uwe H. Schneider* (Dr. Otto Schmidt 2011) 295, 301; Michael Kort, '§ 76 Rn. 34' in Michael Kort, Mathias Habersack and Max Foerster (eds), *Großkommentar zum Aktiengesetz* (5th edn, De Gruyter 2015); Holger Fleischer, '§ 76 Rn. 9' in Martin Henssler (ed), *Beck-online Großkommentar zum Aktienrecht* (C.H. Beck 2020).

87 Fleischer (n 78) 2; Andre Turiaux and Dagmar Knigge, 'Vorstandshaftung ohne Grenzen? – Rechtssichere Vorstands- und Unternehmensorganisation als Instrument der Risikominimierung' (2004) 56 DB 2199, 2205; Holger Fleischer, '§ 76 Rn. 9' in Martin Henssler (ed), *Beck-online Großkommentar zum Aktienrecht* (C.H. Beck 2020).

88 Fleischer (n 78) 6; Froesch (n 78) 724; Michael Kort, '§ 76 Rn. 49' in Michael Kort, Mathias Habersack and Max Foerster (eds), *Großkommentar zum Aktiengesetz* (5th edn, De Gruyter 2015); Gerald Spindler, '§ 76 Rn. 18' in Wulf Goette, Mathias Habersack and Susanne Kalss (eds), *Münchener Kommentar zum Aktiengesetz* (5th edn, C.H. Beck 2019).

pared by those who produced them.[89] Ultimately, these auxiliary activities in the run-up to or after the leadership decision, which must be taken by the entire board as a whole, are management tasks that can be delegated in accordance with the principles outlined above. Taking into account the constitution of the joint stock corporation, the differentiation with regard to the permissibility of delegation is between the (delegable) management tasks and the (non-delegable) leadership decisions.[90]

2. Data governance as leadership decision

Finding the demarcation between management tasks and leadership decisions is a complex task. In order to avoid an inflation of leadership tasks that overwhelms the management board, the assumed significance of an action cannot be used to infer its qualification as a leadership task.[91] One example of this is energy supply. Even though a company's activities are hardly conceivable without energy supply, it has never been conceived of as a leadership task that cannot be delegated.[92] In order to give contour to the concept of leadership tasks, reference is therefore made to economic findings.[93]

Leadership decisions are characterised by three features. They are of immediate importance for the existence and future of the company, can only be made from within the company as a whole, and may not be delegated in the

---

[89] Fleischer (n 78) 6 emphasises the difference between delegable 'decision shaping' and independent 'decision taking'; Froesch (n 78) 724; Dreher (n 86) 527 ff; Gerald Spindler, '§ 76 Rn. 18' in Wulf Goette, Mathias Habersack and Susanne Kalss (eds), *Münchener Kommentar zum Aktiengesetz* (5th edn, C.H. Beck 2019). Jens Koch, '§ 76 Rn. 8' in Uwe Hüffer and Jens Koch, *Beck'scher Kurz-Kommentar zum Aktiengesetz* (14th edn, C.H. Beck 2020).

[90] Froesch (n 78) 724; Hegnon (n 76); Michael Kort, '§ 76 Rn. 32a' in Michael Kort, Mathias Habersack and Max Foerster (eds), *Großkommentar zum Aktiengesetz* (5th edn, De Gruyter 2015); Gerald Spindler, '§ 76 Rn. 14' in Wulf Goette, Mathias Habersack and Susanne Kalss (eds), *Münchener Kommentar zum Aktiengesetz* (5th edn, C.H. Beck 2019); Jens Koch, '§ 76 Rn. 8' in Uwe Hüffer and Jens Koch, *Beck'scher Kurz-Kommentar zum Aktiengesetz* (14th edn, C.H. Beck 2020); sceptical about the differentiation and instead referring on the relevant circumstances of the case Christoph Seibt, 'Dekonstruktion des Delegationsverbots bei der Unternehmensleitung' in Georg Bitter and others (eds), *Festschrift für Karsten Schmidt* (Dr. Otto Schmidt 2009) 1463, 1476 ff.

[91] Noack (n 1) 125.

[92] Ibid.

[93] Gerald Spindler, '§ 76 Rn. 15' in Wulf Goette, Mathias Habersack and Susanne Kalss (eds), *Münchener Kommentar zum Aktiengesetz* (5th edn, C.H. Beck 2019); Holger Fleischer, '§ 76 Rn. 15' in Martin Henssler (ed), *Beck-online Großkommentar zum Aktienrecht* (C.H. Beck 2020); Jens Koch, '§ 76 Rn. 9' in Uwe Hüffer and Jens Koch, *Beck'scher Kurz-Kommentar zum Aktiengesetz* (14th edn, C.H. Beck 2020).

interest of the company.[94] On this basis, a typological approach has become established, whereby modern definitions also fall back on the early initial formula.[95] According to this, typical leadership tasks are the determination of corporate policy in the long term, the coordination and control of important subdivisions as well as the filling of management positions. In addition, decisions on the business and financial risks to be accepted as well as the control and orientation of the company's activities are defined as leadership tasks.[96]

Based on these criteria, information technology tasks are increasingly being defined as leadership tasks within the direct responsibility of the board of directors.[97] The profound technological change and the increased importance of the use of technology for the future of the company are made reference to in legal literature.[98] Whilst data processing used to be a static process in the sense of better record keeping, omnipresent networking and the increasing technical independence of data processing procedures conjure up entrepreneurial risks that can be described as a core leadership task.[99] Decisions in Data Governance require complex consideration processes for the control and orientation of corporate activities, which at the same time define the risk profile of the company. Therefore, these can only be made by the board collectively.

This does not mean, however, that the board of directors may not make use of any support in the fulfilment of its Data Governance duties. Both the delegation of preparatory tasks and the delegation of decision-implementing

---

[94] Erich Gutenberg, *Unternehmensführung: Organisation und Entscheidungen* (1st edn, Dr. Th. Gabler 1962) 60 ff.

[95] Holger Fleischer, '§ 76 Rn. 15, 18' in Martin Henssler (ed), *Beck-online Großkommentar zum Aktienrecht* (C.H. Beck 2020).

[96] With marginal differences Gerald Spindler, '§ 76 Rn. 15 ff' in Wulf Goette, Mathias Habersack and Susanne Kalss (eds), *Münchener Kommentar zum Aktiengesetz* (5th edn, C.H. Beck 2019); Holger Fleischer, '§ 76 Rn. 15' in Martin Henssler (ed), *Beck-online Großkommentar zum Aktienrecht* (C.H. Beck 2020); Jens Koch, '§ 76 Rn. 9' in Uwe Hüffer and Jens Koch, *Beck'scher Kurz-Kommentar zum Aktiengesetz* (14th edn, C.H. Beck 2020).

[97] Michael Kort, '§ 76 Rn. 37' in Michael Kort, Mathias Habersack and Max Foerster (eds), *Großkommentar zum Aktiengesetz* (5th edn, De Gruyter 2015); Noack (n 1) 125; Jens Koch, '§ 76 Rn. 9' in Uwe Hüffer and Jens Koch, *Beck'scher Kurz-Kommentar zum Aktiengesetz* (14th edn, C.H. Beck 2020); On the responsibility for information Gerald Spindler, '§ 76 Rn. 15' in Wulf Goette, Mathias Habersack and Susanne Kalss (eds), *Münchener Kommentar zum Aktiengesetz* (5th edn, C.H. Beck 2019); Holger Fleischer, '§ 76 Rn. 18' in Martin Henssler (ed), *Beck-online Großkommentar zum Aktienrecht* (C.H. Beck 2020).

[98] Michael Kort, '§ 76 Rn. 37' in Michael Kort, Mathias Habersack and Max Foerster (eds), *Großkommentar zum Aktiengesetz* (5th edn, De Gruyter 2015); Noack (n 1) 125.

[99] Noack (n 1) 125.

tasks remain possible in horizontal as well as vertical terms, since these are to be classified merely as management tasks. This can be a practical necessity, especially for technically sophisticated issues in the area of Data Governance. However, an obligation to delegate, in particular to establish a separate management board department 'Data Governance' cannot be justified under company law.[100] In any case, the final decision must remain with the board as a collegial body. This division of responsibilities also reflects the differentiation between Data Governance as a leadership task and data management as the day-to-day implementation of Data Governance.

3. Requirements for the qualification of board members

This competence order affects the standard of qualification for board members, who must be able to fulfil the tasks assigned to them with the diligence of a reasonable and conscientious businessperson. This requires them, in particular, to attain a level of technical knowledge that enables them to deal with Data Governance in a sound manner.[101] In this context, the requirements for their qualification are as dynamic as the technological development itself. Therefore, a combination of introductory information and regular in-depth information to convey current developments is considered desirable.[102]

It is not required for directors to have a detailed understanding of operational measures. It is sufficient if the board may reasonably assume to act in the best interests of the company based on adequate information. To this end, it is not precluded from having recourse to expert advice. The Federal Court of Justice precisely defined the requirements in form of the so-called ISION-Principles. According to these principles, the board of directors may rely on expert advice if it obtains advice from an independent professional who is qualified to resolve the question, provided with a comprehensive description of the company's circumstances, provided with the necessary documents, and if the board subjects the information provided to a plausibility check.[103]

Depending on the situation, however, higher requirements may have to be met.[104] In companies where Data Governance is of great importance due to their business activities, particularly in AI, this may be the case for the board in its entirety. Individual board members may also be exposed to increased requirements if, for example, they are to be granted responsibility for Data

---

[100] Ibid.; however suggesting this Schmidt-Versteyl (n 41) 1640.

[101] Kiefner and Happ (n 41) 2053.

[102] Ibid., 2053.

[103] BGH NZG 2007, 545 Rn. 16ff.

[104] Cf on the personal requirements also Gerald Spindler, '§ 84 Rn. 41' in Wulf Goette, Mathias Habersack and Susanne Kalss (eds), *Münchener Kommentar zum Aktiengesetz* (5th edn, C.H. Beck 2019).

Governance by way of horizontal delegation. In this respect, a blanket definition of the qualification requirements for board members is impossible. As board members can be liable for damages to the company due to acceptance fault (*Übernahmeverschulden*) if they do not meet the minimum requirements appropriate to the situation, legal practitioners can only be advised to pay special attention to questions of Data Governance.[105]

V. CONCLUSION

Data Governance is becoming increasingly important with technological progress, especially in the context of AI. This results in specific obligations for the board of directors that go beyond the mere obligation to comply with legal requirements. In particular, the management board is obliged to ensure adequate data quality and data security. With regard to leadership duties of the management board, these duties cannot be delegated. Only the preparation of leadership decisions and their subsequent implementation may be delegated. Therefore, the requirements for the qualification of board members are increasing. As a minimum requirement, the board members must always be able to subject expert advice to a plausibility check. Therefore, a combination of introductory and in-depth information on current technical developments is advisable. Depending on the situation, however, higher requirements may also have to be met.

[105] On liability Susanne Kalss, '§ 76 Rn. 184' in Wulf Goette, Mathias Habersack and Susanne Kalss (eds), *Münchener Kommentar zum Aktiengesetz* (5th edn, C.H. Beck 2019).

10. Data production by market infrastructures and AI developments

Manuela Geranio

I. INTRODUCTION

Information has always been at the core of financial institutions and financial markets activity. The same well-known definition of market efficiency (strong, semi-strong and weak) revolves around the concept of how information is incorporated into prices.[1]

In the last decade the digitalisation of many industries of the global economy, the increased availability of cloud computing resources and the emergence of artificial intelligence techniques has driven the demand for data in an unprecedented way.[2]

Traditionally, data used by financial operators to make decisions and trade on the markets can be grouped into three main categories. There are macroeconomic data, produced by public information agencies (such as the economy's growth rate, unemployment rate, etc.). Given the general interest in such information, its production cost is usually covered by public funds. Financial operators then access this information at a cost through specialised data vendors which intermediate the distribution of data between sources and users and offer additional services (such as time series, combination with other indicators, etc.).

There are corporate data, produced by the companies themselves (such as balance sheet data), by commissioned third parties (such as rating companies) or by financial analysts that elaborate on raw data to produce forecasts either for their use or to sell. Cost of producing the raw data is typically borne by the companies. The cost of further analysis falls on investing companies that

---

1 Eugene Fama, 'Efficient Capital Markets: A Review of Theory and Empirical Work' (1970) 25 *The Journal of Finance* 383, 417.

2 Robin Wigglesworth and Eric Platt, 'S&P Global's $44bn deal shows data is the oil of the 21st century', [2020] *Financial Times* https://www.ft.com/content/cd99579c-e01f-4a71-a124-e9c03598e5b9 accessed 15 January 2021.

use in-house analysts or purchase external consulting services. Corporate information may also be disseminated to the public by data vendors and media companies.

Then there are trading data or market data, relating to the prices and quantities at which traders are willing to trade on trading platforms. Trading data are produced by stock exchanges and other trading platforms and disseminated either by the same proprietary data sources or by data vendors. In terms of variety, it ranges from simple standard and individual services and content (e.g., professional workstations) to complex data flows and sophisticated data processing platforms serving multiple business areas.

In recent years a fourth category of information has emerged: alternative data. These are granular and real time data referred to a specific company that are not derived from firm disclosures or traditional documents (like analyst reports, investors' presentations, etc.) but from alternative sources including point-of-sale transactions, satellite images, and clickstream data. The use of alternative data is rapidly increasing due to the broader and more complex analysis possibilities offered by artificial intelligence and its anticipatory value.[3] Main providers of alternative data producers are fintechs, although incumbent data vendors are also entering the sector.

Amongst the different categories, nowadays market data represents the largest expense item for financial operators. On the one side, most trading systems must be fed with large amounts of high frequency data to work effectively. In fact, traders' demand for market data can be considered quite rigid. On the other side, the generation and diffusion of market data is concentrated in a few entities that have a de facto monopoly on supply. Against this backdrop, market data prices in recent years have increasingly diverged from their cost of production and have risen frequently in all major financial marketplaces, with only partial intervention by regulatory agencies at least until now.

The aim of the next pages is to shed some light on the actual market data debate, leaving commentary on alternative data to the final part.

II. MARKET DATA PRODUCERS: TRADING VENUES

Financial market infrastructures, a definition that includes official stock exchanges as well as the multitude of alternative platforms which are now-

---

[3] M Lopez De Prado and A Lipton, Three quant lessons from Covid 19, March 2021 https://www.fma.org/assets/docs/virtualseminar/DePrado_Three%20Quant%20Lessons%20from%20COVID-19%20%28presentation%20slides%29.pdf accessed 19 February 2021.

adays available for securities trading, produce and distribute large parts of data used by the financial players. Such data may refer to trading activity per se (pre- and post-trade data), to information concerning listed companies (announcements, periodic financial results, etc.) or to indexes and benchmarks which are disseminated by and large in the financial community.

The importance of data has impressively grown in the last two decades, as financial operators adopted algorithmic trading to elaborate strategies and place orders.[4] These algorithms require large amount of data feeds in real time, so both trading companies and market infrastructures largely invested in the technology needed to access and provide such information flow.

Market data also became an important revenue flow for trading venues.[5] As shown by Figure 10.1, in 2017 market data revenues averaged more than 100 million EUR amongst European stock exchanges, with some marketplaces more active than others.

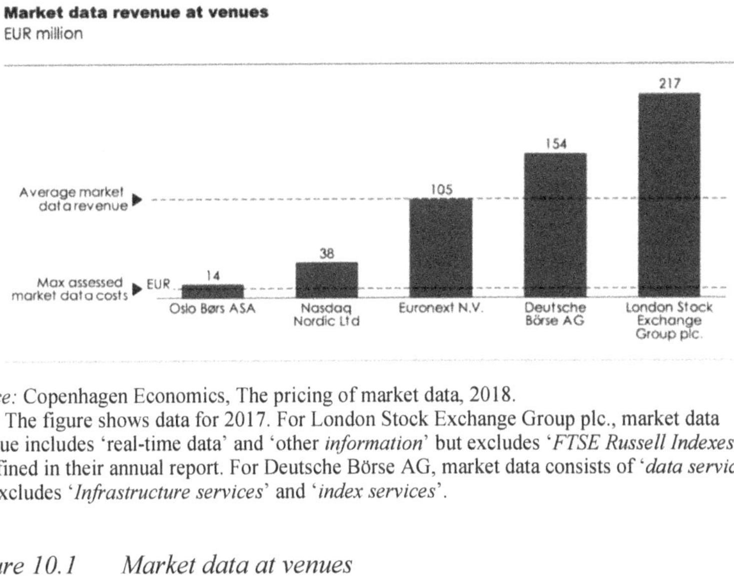

Source: Copenhagen Economics, The pricing of market data, 2018.
Note: The figure shows data for 2017. For London Stock Exchange Group plc., market data revenue includes 'real-time data' and 'other *information*' but excludes '*FTSE Russell Indexes*' as defined in their annual report. For Deutsche Börse AG, market data consists of '*data services*' and excludes '*Infrastructure services*' and '*index services*'.

Figure 10.1 Market data at venues

---

4 ESMA, MiFID II/MiFIR Review Report No. 1, On the development in prices for pre- and post-trade data and on the consolidated tape for equity instruments, 2019 (ESMA70-156-1606) https://www.esma.europa.eu/sites/default/files/library/mifid_ii_mifir_review_report_no_1_on_prices_for_market_data_and_the_equity_ct.pdf accessed 19 July 2021.

5 Copenhagen Economics, The pricing of market data, [2018] https://www.copenhageneconomics.com/publications/publication/pricing-of-market-data accessed 19 February 2021.

One of the most representative examples is the case of the LSE group, where in 2020[6] data and analytics represented by far the largest source of revenues (39 per cent of the total, 66 per cent if also FTSE and Russell Indexes businesses are included), followed by capital markets revenues (16 per cent of the total) and post trade services (13 per cent of the total).

Data on trading activity sold by exchanges can be divided into two main categories: pre-trade data and post-trade data. The former originates from orders and quotations inserted by market players, such as the order book with prices and quantities available to be traded. The latter refers to executed deals, that is prices and quantities effectively exchanged. In terms of revenues, pre-trade data represents the largest part of the business, being an essential feed for traders to elaborate their strategies. Post-trade data instead represent a minor part in terms of revenues, even if such data is disseminated to a much wider community to provide backoffice service, to price portfolios, produce indexes and benchmarks (see Figure 10.2).

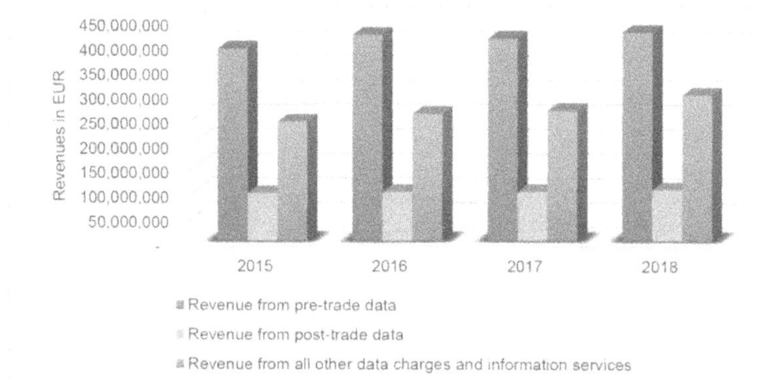

Source: ESMA, 2019.

Figure 10.2 Development of trading venues' revenues from market data, 2015–18

6 London Stock Exchange Group plc, Annual Report 2020 https://www.lseg.com/investor-relations/presentations-and-webcasts/annual-reports accessed 19 February 2021.

Data from exchanges is typically sent through proprietary channels to final users (traders, investment banks, asset managers) or data vendors (such as Bloomberg and Refinitiv) that resell it to final users. Data may be distributed with various levels of latency, from nanoseconds to delayed formats, depending on the user's need. The level of disclosure may also vary, as data may refer to the full order book or just to a partial order book (e.g., the Best Bid and Offer prices, BBO). Post-trading data is usually released free of charge with a delay of a few minutes.

In particular, in the United States securities regulators mandated the formation of a consolidated tape to provide real-time information on BBO and every trade execution in US equity markets. The US exchanges jointly own the Consolidated Tape Association and the Consolidated Quote Association; they share revenue from the tape depending upon the volume of trades and the production of quotes in each market. In addition, most US exchanges also directly sell their market data at premium fees to traders that are interested to receive data feeds at higher speed, that is anticipation with respect to the tape.

In Europe, regulators are currently evaluating the opportunity to create a mandatory consolidated tape (see section IV, C). According to MiFID, exchanges and trading platforms can freely sell their proprietary data provided that data fees are set with 'a reasonable relationship to the cost of producing and disseminating that data'.[7]

In Asian markets like China and Hong Kong trading is still almost totally concentrated on official exchanges, which sell market data under the supervision of national regulatory agencies. Instead in Japan the development of off-exchange trading has led to the emergence of privately managed consolidated tape initiatives.

Another dimension of data pricing is the type of use: display data are offered to be consumed on screens, whilst non-display data are licensed for further elaboration by market participants, including market analysis and automated trading. The surge of algo trading has dragged the demand for non-display data and induced data producers to multiply the fees charged based on data usage (see section IV).

In order to have a more comprehensive picture of traders' operativity in market infrastructures, connectivity services should also be taken into consideration. Indeed, access to trading and data can take place through different technical methods to which correspond different speed and costs.

Trading on a market platform is typically reserved to exchanges' members. As such, for investors there are three ways to access an exchange marketplace:

---

7 ESMA70-156-1606, 2019.

traditional brokerage service providers; direct market access; and sponsored access.

Traditional brokerage service providers act as middlemen between buyers and sellers: they obtain quotes from market makers, offer the best quote (one value prices at any given time) to the trader that will then decide to accept or not.

Direct market access refers to access to the electronic facilities and order books of financial market exchanges that facilitate daily securities transactions. With direct market access a member firm can allow a customer to submit orders to the trading system under the member firm's trading codes and via the member firm's order management systems. Direct market access requires a sophisticated technology infrastructure and is often owned by sell-side firms. Some buy-side firms may also use direct market access to place trades themselves rather than relying on market-making firms and broker-dealers to execute trades.

Sponsored access is a direct technical connection that enables a non-member firm (the sponsored user) to access the order books directly under an existing member firm's (the sponsoring firm) trading code. Differently from direct market access, sponsored access allows a sponsored user to submit orders under a member firm's trading code to the trading system without passing through a member firm's order management systems; instead their orders pass through a series of validation checks provided by the exchange whilst orders are monitored by the member firm in real-time.

III. MARKET DATA DISSEMINATION: THE ROLE OF DATA VENDORS

Users of market data might opt to buy data directly from exchanges (and in such case they also have to consider the costs of hardware for transporting, processing, storing, and distributing that data) or from a data provider which may handle technology and service requirements (including the relative cost in its fees).

In 2019 financial market data and news expenditure has reached a record high of 32.0 billion dollars at the worldwide level.[8] The Americas contributed to 48 per cent of market data spending, followed by EMEA with 33 per cent and Asia with 19 per cent. The year-on-year growth was similar in the various

---

[8] Burton-Taylor International Consulting, Financial Market Data/Analysis Global Share & Segment Sizing [2020] https://burton-taylor.com/financial-market-data-analysis accessed 19 February 2021.

geographical areas, with a rate of over 5 per cent compared to the previous year. Structural and cyclical factors are behind this growth.

Real-time trading and data spending represent the largest share of total spending. This can be justified by the preponderance of high-frequency trading that characterises all major financial markets. However, strong demand for pricing, reference and valuation data is also emerging as market users have to fulfil risk and compliance mandates. Similarly, portfolio management and analytics services are progressively growing, motivated by the search for unconventional correlations and innovative solutions to respond to the diffusion of passive management products. This latter market segment is also one of the main consumers of data, if only because of the size it has now reached.

From a cyclical point of view, the volatility induced by the Covid-19 pandemic motivated a greater use of data, especially from mobile sources as people were forced to work from home (+50 per cent, according to provider Refinitiv[9]). The surge of financial markets and trading volumes reported in 2020 supported an even higher demand for data, with a particular interest for new sources that can provide a trading advantage starting form social media and sentiment data.

The growing data spending trend encompasses all major subsectors in the financial industry (see Figure 10.3 below). Investment management has always been the larger spender (approximately one-third of the total), followed by fixed income and equity trading.

In terms of players, Bloomberg is by far the major global market data vendor (33 per cent of total market share in 2019), followed by Refinitiv (21 per cent) and S&P Global (6 per cent).[10]

IV. OWNERSHIP AND PRICING OF TRADING DATA

There is an open debate on the ownership of market data, especially after the demutualisation and privatisation of stock exchanges.[11] On the one side, exchanges claim intellectual property rights in market data since data and trading are interpreted as a 'joint product': it is not possible to generate one without the other. In order to consolidate their claim, exchanges usually require market participants to transfer any ownership right on data to the marketplace itself. Moreover, based on the joint product principle, exchanges

9 Shanny Basar, 'Record demand for data due to Covid-19' (Markets media, 24 April 2020) https://www.marketsmedia.com/record-demand-for-data-due-to-covid-19/ accessed 19 February 2021.

10 [2020] Burton-Taylor International Consulting (n 8).

11 Manuela Geranio, *Evolution of the Exchange Industry* (Springer, 2016).

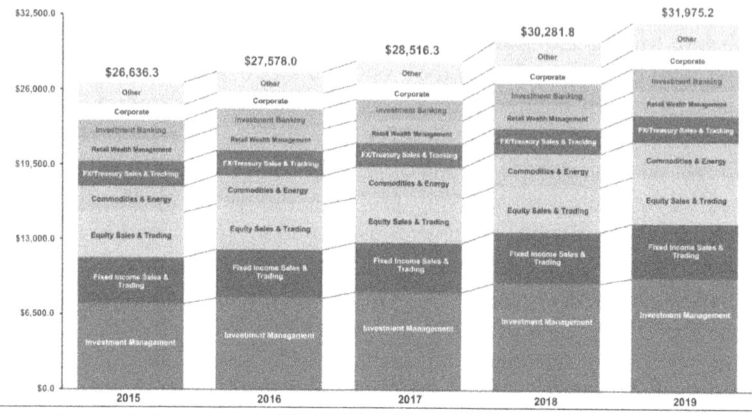

Source: Burton-Taylor International Consulting, Financial Market Data/Analysis Global Share & Segment Sizing [2020] https://burton-taylor.com/financial-market-data-analysis accessed 19 February 2021.

Figure 10.3 Global market data revenue analysis by segments of users

typically attribute part of the cost of the trading platform to data production, including them as an item of data fees.

On the other side, opponents say that the fact that exchanges add a time stamp is not enough to claim intellectual property. Indeed, the input for trading data is provided by market participants trading on that market and the effort made by trading venues in the presentation of market data are minimal.[12]

Such debate is strictly interlinked with the pricing of data fees. Theoretically, being a by-product of the trading activity, the cost of producing and disseminating data should be low and standardised amongst marketplaces. In other words, there should be a reasonable relationship between fees and costs.

In practice, market data fees have soared in recent years and vary substantially amongst exchanges.[13] Moreover, the comparison amongst marketplaces is not trivial, since charging schemes are complex and varied.

Pricing for data includes at least four types of fees:[14]

---

[12] Oxera, The design of equity trading markets in Europe, 2019.

[13] ESMA70-156-1606, 2019.

[14] Robert Anderson, 'Overview of Market Data Fees: What You Need to Know When Planning Your Market Data Infrastructure' (Markets media, 7 October 2020) https://a-teaminsight.com/overview-of-market-data-fees-what-you-need-to-know-when-planning-your-market-data-infrastructure/?brand=tti accessed 19 February 2021.

- *access fee* or 'technical connection fee': it is a flat fee for the access to a given data feed (unaffected by the number of users but charged for each specific data product). Some exchanges include data access in the membership fee package. This fee is usually higher for direct access connection (to receive the data directly from an exchange via an extranet connection, co-location, or other direct access mechanism) than for indirect connection (via the internet or a feed from a third-party source);
- *usage fee*: it is charged per-display, or per screen that visualises the data according to several dimensions, such as the type of user (professional or private);
- *non display fee*: it is applied for the use of real time data in a not display manner, such as trading applications like execution algorithms, market making or index creation;
- *redistribution licence fee*: it must be paid whenever market data, display or non-display, is redistributed to a system, person, or business other than the one that initially purchased the data (for example when a broker shows market data to a client or a vendor sells the market data information to a third party).

Data users complain about the lack of harmonisation, the complexity and the frequent updates on criteria to charge fees established by each trading venue. They claim that the increase in prices consist not only of direct fee rises for existing products, but also included the introduction of fees for services which were previously provided free of charge.

Since data flows are indispensable to run many businesses, from trading to asset management, to the fulfilment of regulation requirements (like e.g., the EU best execution rules), the demand for data is inelastic. On the offer side stock exchanges maintain a privileged position in market data production and vending. They have a consolidated expertise and the technological infrastructure needed to collect, manage and disseminate information. Moreover, even if trading volumes partially shifted to alternative trading platforms, stock exchanges maintain their pivotal role in pricing formation and referencing. As a result, trading venues keep de facto a monopolistic position in data vending. The risk that they apply prices well above the cost of production is real, also considering the reduction they suffered in other business lines (i.e., trading fees especially for traditional venues, a consequence of the competition by alternative trading platforms).

A. The View of Academics

The growth in the cost of data may adversely affect one of the core functions of an exchange, that is to provide price discovery for listed shares.[15] This function is a relevant one because market prices drive capital allocation.[16] A better price discovery process should lead to a more efficient allocation of capital and ultimately to enhanced growth in the real economy. According to Alan and Schwartz[17] price discovery is a public good because end-users include a wide range of people who do not necessarily take part in trading activity. Indeed, prices set on exchanges are used as benchmarks for derivatives pricing, mutual fund quotes valuation, dark pool pricing. The price discovery function can be compared to a lighthouse signalling to all boats the entrance to the harbour, no matter if the boats are charged for the service or not.

Cespa and Focault[18] show that there is a conflict between the efficiency of price discovery and profit maximisation by exchanges. What is more, this conflict might influence the quality of the price discovery process. For profit exchanges supply information at various speeds, charging a higher fee to traders who receive price information more quickly. These traders are typically proprietary trading firms that will use the information to put into practice high frequency trading strategies, in some cases on the same stock exchange platform. As such, these firms will also pay a trading fee to the exchange. Exchanges then face a trade-off between two sources of expected revenue: from the sale of price information and from trading. Lowering the price to access quick information may enlarge the pool of traders willing to buy this service; what is more, this move should also upgrade the price discovery process, since all players would observe prices in real time. By the same token, a more efficient pricing process would rapidly reduce profit opportunities for proprietary trading firms and high frequency traders, resulting in lower transaction fees for the exchange.

Therefore, for the purpose of maximising profits, exchanges may find the optimal solution in keeping fees high for faster information services to attract high-frequency traders, who will be the only players able to take advantage of them. All other traders will receive slightly delayed information and pay

[15] Maureen O'Hara M, 'Presidential Address: Liquidity and Price Discovery' (2003) 58(4) *Journal of Finance* 1335.

[16] Avanidhar Subrahmanyam and Sheridan Titman, The Going-public Decision and the Development of Financial Markets (1999) 54(3) *Journal of Finance* 1045.

[17] Nazli Sila Alan and Robert A Schwartz, 'Price Discovery: The Economic Function of a Stock Exchange' (2013) 40(1) *Journal of Portfolio Management* 124.

[18] Giovanni Cespa and Thierry Focault, 'Sale of Price Information By Exchanges: Does it Promote Price Discovery?' (2014) 60(1) *Management Science* 148.

smaller fees. As a consequence, electronic exchanges are segmenting traders and related information services and prices according to their sensitiveness to the fast information advantage. This segmentation resembles the process that occurred in physical exchanges between member traders (physically present inside the exchange) and non-member traders (who connected to the exchange by fax and telephone). The former used to buy a seat to get a time advantage on information that would be used in trading strategies, whilst the latter would accept paying smaller fees to receive information from the exchange with a slight delay. Similarly, nowadays proprietary trading firms and high frequency are willing to pay higher fees to get faster access to information. In addition, they often agree to additional fees in order to co-locate their servers closer to the trading engine and thus pass faster orders to the trading platform. Other traders maintain the cheaper standardised information dissemination system established by regulation. Up to this point, the strategy of exchanges could simply be considered a profit maximising approach, similar to service segmentation that occurs in other infrastructure industries such as transportation (i.e., different pricing and services offered by a high-speed train as opposed to a traditional train). However, in the case of exchanges, the segmentation policies adopted in information vending can result in negative externalities. The reason for this, according to Cespa and Focault, is that the advantage exchanges give to a restricted number of traders will lower the quality of price discovery, thus justifying the need for regulatory intervention on the sale of price information.

A complementary view is offered by Easley, O'Hara and Yang,[19] which documented that allowing exchanges to sell price information benefits exchanges and harms liquidity traders. Moreover, selling price data increases the cost of capital and volatility, worsens market efficiency and liquidity, and discourages the production of fundamental information.

In their model, traders acquire market data and fundamental data as complementary resources needed to manage their activity. If the price of market data is high, traders have less incentive not only to buy market data but also to buy or produce fundamental information. This in turn may harm price informativeness, increase both the cost of capital and return volatility, and lower liquidity. In a word, the aggressive sale of market data by exchanges worsens the market quality.

Easley et al. recognise that it is costly for exchanges to provide market data (so they may not be disseminated for free) but they also reaffirm the 'public

[19] David Easley, Maureen O'Hara and Liyan Yang, 'Differential Access to Price Information in Financial Markets' (2016) 51(4) *Journal of Financial and Quantitative Analysis* 1071.

good' nature of data since the use of it by one trader does not preclude another trader from using the same data (prior use of the data might affect the value of the data to subsequent traders, but that does not make the data a private good). They highlight that competition on trading services may lead exchanges to subsidise order submission (by 'rebates') in order to generate the valuable price information that they sell. In this case the market conditions improve but not enough to ensure the absence of monopolistic conduct.

In the recent past some market entrants (such as BATS and other multilateral trading systems) adopted free data distribution policies to attract traders to use their trading platforms. Taking the reasoning to the extreme and recognising that information is a public good and its production costs are joint with those incurred for trading, all potential users could be allowed access to this information almost free of charge, in order to attract trading flows.

Overall academic research agrees on the need for a stricter regulation of the data selling business. Allowing exchanges to sell data is undesirable because such activity reduces market quality and the perception of transparency by traders, who might decide to stop trading altogether. Ding, Hanna and Hendershott[20] provide empirical evidence on the effects on transparency and fairness of the US equity markets, generated by the parallel use of publicly provided market data and faster direct data feeds from the exchanges. For the most traded shares, price dislocations between the two information channels occur several times a second and typically last 1–2 milliseconds. The short duration of dislocations makes relative costs negligible for investors who trade infrequently, whilst the frequency of the dislocations makes them costly for frequent traders.

B. The View of Market Participants

In the debate amongst market participants similar themes arise, reporting that soaring costs of data is limiting the market access for smaller investors and brokers, leaving only algo traders and big players capable to access them. In turn, this could lead to the concentration of the market in the hands of a few big counterparties, reducing information, liquidity and the efficiency of the market.

In 2018 SIFMA (Securities Industry and Financial Markets Association, a trade association that represents securities brokerage firms, investment banking institutions, and other investment firms in the US) published research on how NYSE market data fees changed for retail and institutional trading

---

[20] Shengwei Ding, John Hanna and Terrence Hendershott, 'How Slow is the NBBO? A Comparison with Direct Exchange Feeds' (2014) 49 *Financial Review* 313.

firms.[21] The analysis considered both proprietary 'non-core' data as well as 'core' market data, that is information administered by the Consolidated Tape Association. In the period 2010–18 proprietary data fees have soared the most, registering increases between +600 per cent and +1100 per cent. Consolidated tape data fees also have grown, although at a much lower rate (+5 per cent, still higher than the inflation). These increases derive primarily from the substantial doubling of access fees, the inclusion of new fees (non-display and redistribution fees) and additional practices that have multiplied costs (such as the segregation of access fees for multiple products). Despite cost increases, both retail and institutional firms have continued to buy both proprietary and consolidated tape data, resulting in significant expense increases for firms and their clients. The lack of change in demand to the increase of prices was partly attributed to the proliferation of charges that trading firms incur to satisfy transparent execution and compliance rules.

SIFMA also criticised the US national market system for the dissemination of real-time trade and quote information in equity securities as it fails to deliver the high-speed standards needed nowadays by market participants. The association then proposed the adoption of a more effective model to reduce latency and bring the US consolidated tape architecture in line with competitive private market solutions.

Also in Europe the investment industry highlighted the material challenge arising from higher data costs to the effective functioning of markets. In a joint publication dated 2020, EFAMA (European Funds and Asset Management Association), ICSA (International Council of Securities Associations) and Managed Funds Association, claimed that exchanges utilise their market power to increase market data prices with the consequence of limiting market data access, data distribution and competition.[22] Indeed, soaring market data spending force many data consumers to reduce data purchase to a minimum level, excluding certain markets segments, such as smaller companies and foreign markets. The consequences are less informed markets, weaker competition, higher costs for investors and potential higher cost of capital, especially for smaller companies. Therefore, asset management associations recommend that governments and regulators establish core principles to address the problem. In particular they sustain that the price of market data and connectivity must be based on the efficient costs of producing and distributing

---

[21] SIFMA and Expand, an Analysis of market data fees, October 2018, https://www.sifma.org/wp-content/uploads/2019/01/Expand-and-SIFMA-An-Analysis-of-Market-Data-Fees-08-2018.pdf accessed 9 March 2021.

[22] Efama, Icsa, Managed Funds Association, Global Memo Market Data Costs (2020) https://www.efama.org/newsroom/news/joint-associations-global-memo-market-data-costs-1, accessed 9 March 2021.

the market data plus a reasonable mark-up (as opposed to the value market participants derive from market data). Such cost should be measured against a recognised cost benchmark. In addition, trading venues should standardise market data contract definitions, terms and interpretations and market data licensing contracts should be simplified, in order to ease administration and reduce the need for audit practices.

On the opposite side, exchanges assert that there is no need to regulate data-vending activity because they should be free to manage such services as they do with trading. Indeed trading and market data are joint products, so their pricing should be defined accordingly. Quoting a recent declaration by the World Federation of Exchanges 'stock-market data exists only because exchanges create it and has value because of the use that market participants can make of it and because of the care that exchanges take in creating it'.[23]

Market infrastructures highlight the significant investments necessary to jointly offer high-quality trading and price-discovery services, which require state-of-the-art technological equipment as well as adequate safeguards in terms of market supervision and cyber resilience.

They recognise that they provide a public good in ensuring price discovery, whilst stressing that 'public good' does not mean 'free' for all. The provision of slightly delayed data to the general public for free is considered a proper compromise in order to satisfy their wider social function. At the same time, they claim the right to keep on pricing market data according to the commercial appetite of professional market users.

From a legal perspective, exchanges cannot claim copyright on closing prices as they are merely 'a record of fact or the product of a mathematical adjustment to a fact'.[24] Copyright instead requires originality or at least some contribution of ideas or skill to the written or recorded expression of the work. In part, the prospect could be different if the data were inserted in a database. The latter, however, would have to possess elements of originality and skill in its construction in order to be protected by copyright law. In practice most databases provided by the exchanges are simple lists and therefore do not meet this condition.

However, the absence of copyright has not prevented many stock exchanges from taking advantage of their position to insert restrictive clauses on the use and redistribution of data.

---

23 World Federation of Exchanges, Market data prices, 2019, https://www.world-exchanges.org/our-work/research accessed 23 September 2020.

24 EDI, 'Closing Prices and Other Stock Exchange Data: Copyright and Competition Law Issues', 2020, https://www.exchange-data.com/closing-prices-and-other-stock-exchange-data-copyright-and-competition-law-issues accessed 9 February 2021.

In the EU a case of abusing a dominant position and acting in a way that unlawfully impedes competition in the internal market could emerge if a stock exchange used its near-monopoly position to set restrictive clauses and prices unrelated to the cost of data production in order to protect and cross-subsidise its business.

Another issue that is becoming increasingly sensitive, especially in the US, concerns terms and conditions in contracts by which an exchange authorises a third-party vendor to redistribute data through to end-users. The risk could be that exchanges are exploiting access to data to impose contractual terms that are oppressive or designed to inhibit competition. The SEC is currently working on this topic, in order to 'increase competition and transparency, which will improve data quality and data access for all market participants'.[25]

C. The View of Regulators

After receiving complaints about costs from investment firms, traders and hedge funds, regulators in the US, UK and Europe are looking at market data prices and practices. However, despite supervisory intervention, nothing beyond guidance has been published yet.[26]

In the US the first requests for intervention to the SEC had already been made in 2006 by some internet companies (Google, Yahoo, etc.) who complained of an increase in the fees applied by the exchanges to enable the dissemination of market data to the public.[27]

Since then, the SEC has taken a number of steps to monitor more closely the evolution of market data distribution and costs, not taking direct action until October 2018. On that occasion the agency rejected a fee increase applied by NYSE and Nasdaq with the motivation that the exchanges had not justified the price increases. In June 2020 the US court of appeals for the district of Columbia overturned the ruling, stating that fee increases cannot be challenged by the government after they have taken effect.[28]

---

[25] SEC, SEC adopts rules to modernize key market infrastructures (Press release, 9 December 2020) https://www.sec.gov/news/press-release/2020-311 accessed 15 January 2021.

[26] Tom Groenfeldt, 'Regulators Continue Reviews of Market Data Pricing, Little Action' (*Forbes*, 18 December 2020) https://www.forbes.com/sites/tomgroenfeldt/2020/12/18/regulators-continue-reviews-of-market-data-pricing-little-action accessed 15 January 2021.

[27] Jed Horowitz, 'Internet Firms Seek SEC Review Of Stock Exchanges' Data Fees' (*Wall Street Journal*, 14 November 2006) https://www.wsj.com/articles/SB116345157444821918 accessed 15 January 2021.

[28] Dave Michaels and Alexander. Osipovich, 'Stock Exchanges Win Legal Battle with SEC over Data Fees' (*Wall Street Journal*, 5 June 2020) https://www.wsj.com/

Although this initial intervention was not in fact successful, since then the SEC became more willing to intervene on the data issue. Indeed, the US regulator issued guidance for trading venues to assist them in ensuring that proposed or increased fees are consistent with the relevant requirements that fees are reasonable, equitably allocated, not unfairly discriminatory, and not an undue burden on competition. In October 2019 it also proposed a new rule requiring trading venues to seek industry feedback about any proposed fee changes, before those fees could be charged. A proper rule became effective as of November 2020, so that exchange fee changes now must be approved by the SEC after public opinion hearing.

In 2020 the SEC also proposed changes to modernise the infrastructure for collecting, consolidating and disseminating NMS market data by the introduction of a faster decentralised model, in order to reduce the disadvantages of the consolidated tape data versus exchange proprietary data. At the moment (2021) they are also reconsidering the governance of NMS plan and the redistribution of related fees to exchanges providing market data with the aim of giving investors better data on fair and reasonable terms, as well as generally promoting the integrity and efficiency of the US equity markets.[29]

Although the regulatory measures have yet to show their effects, the debate on the cost of data became relevant and central in the US markets, with regulators amongst main stakeholders.

Recently, EU regulators and supervisors also started to pay more attention to the topic.[30] The regulatory framework is already quite clear in this regard. According to MiFID II, trading venues must publicly provide separate pre- and post-trading data on a reasonable commercial basis and must ensure non-discriminatory access to the information. Pre-trade transparency obligations require trading venues to make information about the trading opportunities publicly available. Post-trade transparency obligations require trading venues to make the price, volume and time of the executed transactions publicly available, as close to real time as is technically possible.

Market data must be available without being bundled with other services, its price should be based on the cost of production and dissemination (which may include an appropriate share of joint costs for other services as well as a reasonable margin) and trading venues must disclose the price for providing

articles/court-overturns-sec-decision-to-reject-fee-increases-for-exchanges-data-feeds-11591383268 accessed 15 January 2021.

[29] SEC, 'Testimony on "Oversight of the Securities and Exchange Commission" Before the U.S. Senate Committee on Banking' (Housing, and Urban Affairs by Chairman Jay Clayton, 17 November 2020) https://www.sec.gov/news/testimony/clayton-sec-oversight-2020-11-17 accessed 15 January 2021.

[30] ESMA70-156-1606, 2019.

market data along with the terms and conditions in an easy and accessible way for the public. MiFID II also set out the framework for the establishment of a consolidated tape for equities, even if no private provider proposed for such service to date.

Prompted by market users' complaints about data fees increase, in July 2019 ESMA launched a public consultation on the development in prices for pre- and post-trade data and on the possible introduction of a consolidated tape. In a following report, published in December 2019, the EU market supervisor concluded that MiFID II had not so far delivered on its objectives to reduce the price of market data and increase their transparency. Then, in February 2020 the EU Commission launched a public consultation on MiFID II/MiFIR review which included the possible establishment of an EU consolidated tape and the affirmation of the principle that market data should be charged based on the costs of producing and disseminating it and not on the value the data represents to users.

In November 2020 ESMA issued a consultation paper seeking input from market participants in relation to its draft guidelines on the MiFID II / MiFIR obligations on market data. Such guidelines require market data providers to have a clear and documented methodology for setting the price of market data. The final report and guidelines are expected to be released by mid-2021.

In 2020 the FMA also launched a call for input to UK market users in order to better understand how data and advanced analytics are being accessed and used, the value offered to market participants and whether data are being competitively sold and priced. In particular the areas researched concern trading data, benchmarks and market data vendor services. Results are expected to come in 2021.

V. THE MANAGEMENT OF MARKET DATA

The 'market data' market presents a high level of complexity, given the plurality of products and services and their continuous evolution.[31]

Demand is clearly growing, from multiple industries and for different reasons, including regulatory compliance and the search for new information sources from big data. At the same time, the supply of single products is characterised by a few suppliers with a low level of competition; mergers and acquisitions between major players are further reducing the room for alternative providers.

---

[31] Alessandra Lanterna, 'Market Data: cosa sono e perché è importante saperli gestire' (Parva Consulting, 2020) https://parvaconsulting.com/it/market-data-cosa-sono-e-perche-e-importante-saperli-gestire accessed 17 January 2021.

Prices are constantly rising: in recent times market data prices increased, on average, between 2 and 10 per cent per year. In addition, contracts regulate the rights and duties of the subscribers in an increasingly detailed and stringent manner. In particular, data sellers hold a right of audit, that is the right to inspect how data are used by the subscribers and to apply severe penalties in case of non-compliance. The financial community has only recently begun to question the business practices imposed by market data providers, without yet achieving concrete results.

Adding to this general panorama there are growing management issues coming from the use of market data, amongst which the fragmentation of purchasing procedures and contractual management across numerous organisational structures; the need to monitor all acquired services and their evolution over time; the evolving knowledge of products and related contractual requirements; the definition of internal policies for the allocation of expensive products and services; the general coordination and vision for the market data management.

For such reasons larger financial institutions are introducing specialised managers to properly define their market data policy and supervise its implementation. Main benefits of such approach derive from the centralisation of negotiations and purchases, the creation of a dedicated monitoring centre for data consumption, the consolidation of contractual and technical knowledge to the benefit of the entire firm. However, smaller companies may find it more difficult or lack sufficient scale to dedicate specific resources to data management, and therefore ultimately fail to optimise the use of an increasingly crucial resource.

VI. ARTIFICIAL INTELLIGENCE AND FINANCIAL MARKET DATA

The finance industry has been one of the earlier investors in artificial intelligence and big data technologies, with a 15 per cent contribution to the total investments at the world level.[32]

In particular, algo trading and high-frequency traders can be considered pioneers in the implementation of automated applications that analyse huge amounts of data and elaborate market strategies. Such an approach shifted data

[32] JP Morgan, 'Big Data and AI Strategies: Machine Learning and Alternative Data Approach to Investing' (2017) https://cpb-us-e2.wpmucdn.com/faculty.sites.uci.edu/dist/2/51/files/2018/05/JPM-2017-MachineLearningInvestments.pdf accessed 17 November 2020.

consumption in the traditional trading data market towards non-display market data products with high granularity and low latency.

In recent times, financial market investors also increased the demand for alternative data that are able to anticipate traditional sources of information in order to generate innovative and profitable trading signals. In particular, alternative data may be retrieved from individuals either from their social media use (posts and tweets, useful to capture the public sentiment) or from their geolocation data (that allow to infer customer preferences from frequented stores). A second group of data comes from business processes (credit card payments and trade flows data) or logistic reports and sensors (geolocation outside stores to infer the company performance). A third source of information comes from government sources like satellite images (to judge the state of the economy) or weather reports (to forecast the demand for a specific product or industry). These new sources of information are typically tested and combined in a sentiment analysis framework to trade equities, bonds, currencies, etc.[33]

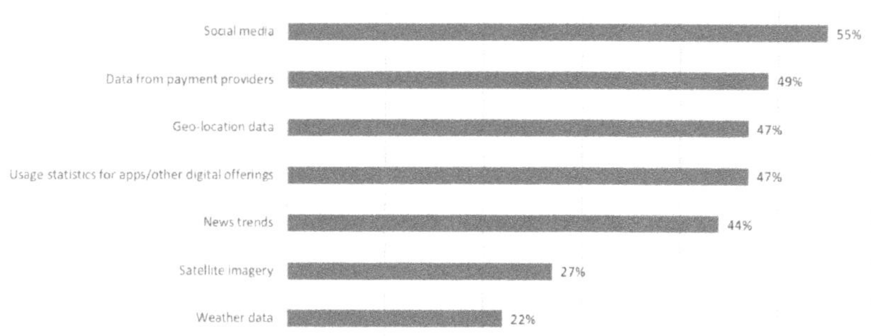

Source: World Economic Forum and Cambridge University, 'Transforming Paradigms A Global AI in Financial Services Survey' (2020) https://www.weforum.org/reports/transforming-paradigms-a-global-ai-in-financial-services-survey accessed 15 December 2020.

Figure 10.4 Usage rate level of AI in investment activity

A survey published in 2020 by the World Economic Forum and Cambridge University[34] on a total of 151 respondents (54 per cent fintechs and 46 per cent incumbent financial institutions) from 33 countries reports on the usage inten-

[33] Quinlan and Associates Research, Alternative Alpha, September 2017 https://www.quinlanandassociates.com/wp-content/uploads/2017/09/Quinlan-Associates-Alternative-Alpha.pdf accessed 15 December 2020.

[34] World Economic Forum and Cambridge University, 'Transforming Paradigms A Global AI in Financial Services Survey' (2020) https://www.weforum.org/

sity of alternative data types in investment activity (see Figure 10.4). Social media data are used by 55 per cent of investors, whilst weather and satellite data are used by less than one-third.

According to the same source, at present portfolio risk management is the most active area of AI implementation with an adoption rate of 61 per cent, followed by portfolio structuring (58 per cent) and asset price forecasting (55 per cent). Looking at the future, market infrastructures and portfolio managers convene on the strong potential of AI to generate new revenue through new products and processes. In particular, AI will contribute greatly to asset volatility forecasting and sustainable investment selection, and to a lesser extent, to asset price forecasting (see Figure 10.5). It is worth noting that access and quality of data used to feed AI application is perceived as critical by 60 per cent of respondents.

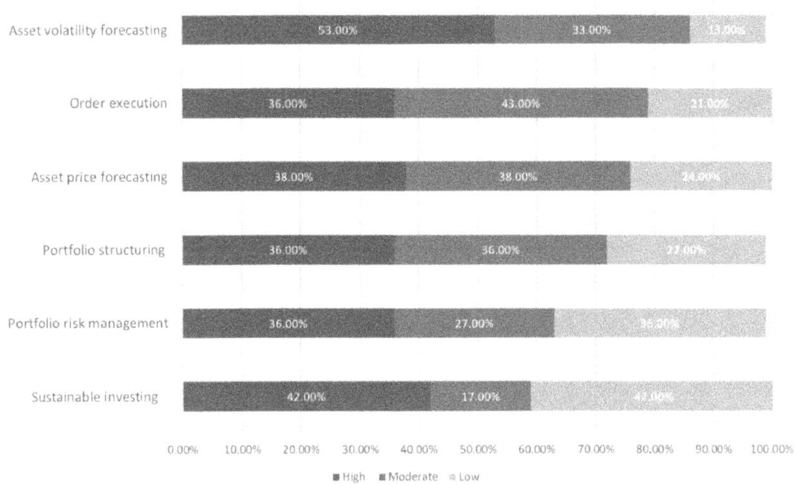

Source: World Economic Forum and Cambridge University, 'Transforming Paradigms A Global AI in Financial Services Survey' (2020) https://www.weforum.org/reports/transforming-paradigms-a-global-ai-in-financial-services-survey accessed 15 December 2020.

Figure 10.5 *Expected long term impact of AI in investment returns by use case*

---

reports/transforming-paradigms-a-global-ai-in-financial-services-survey accessed 15 December 2020.

The market for alternative data providers is quite fragmented at the moment (more than 500 players according to a study produced by JP Morgan[35]) and includes providers of raw data, as well as providers of signals and reports. Many exchanges entered into partnerships or acquisitions to incorporate these new technologies and expertise, trying to exploit a first-mover advantage in combination with their central role in the market.

For example, in December 2018 Nasdaq acquired Quandl, a major provider of alternative data, to integrate its technology into an analytics hub inside the exchange global information services division. In its strategic plan 2022 Euronext recognised the need to undertake new investments in the artificial intelligence field to address new data needs and opportunities. In a wider sense, the merger between LSE and Refinitiv can also be interpreted as a move to enlarge and integrate the traditional offer of trade data by exchanges to respond to the new data demand using their consolidated distribution channels.

Global spending on artificial intelligence is expected to double over the next four years, growing from $50.1 billion in 2020 to more than $110 billion in 2024.[36]

By now it is not easy to predict who will conquer primacy in the alternative data market. The competition is certainly more open, given the wide number of providers and the higher contestability of alternative data in comparison with market-originated data. Market infrastructures and data vendors that will integrate their traditional offer with alternative data can take advantage from AI adoption by their retained customers and consolidate their position in the sector even more.

The task of regulators will be to ensure that prices and the way in which information is distributed do not disadvantage certain categories of investors over others and do not guarantee monopoly rents for the sole benefit of major data providers.

VII. CONCLUSION

The market for trading and financial markets data has been growing dramatically in recent years. The production and distribution of such data is structurally concentrated in the hands of a few players, primarily the stock exchanges and some global data vendors. Pre-trade data, in particular, represent one of the main sources of revenue for stock exchanges, many of which increased prices and adopted stricter commercial policies for providing data. Regulators

---

35 JP Morgan, 2017 (n 32).

36 International Data Corporation, Worldwide Artificial Intelligence Spending Guide, August 2020.

are watching the evolution of the industry, concerned about possible rent seeking to the detriment of smaller financial players and market quality. The development of artificial intelligence is also fuelling demand for alternative data aimed at providing original and valuable investment insights. On this front, production is wider and more diversified, at least at the present time, thanks to the greater contestability of data and the plurality of operators who are investing in the sector. However, even in this area, the scale of investment required and the ability to rapidly implement innovation will dictate a selection amongst financial players.

11. Cybersecurity certification and compliance in financial services[1]

Radim Polčák

I. INTRODUCTION

At first, we will briefly look at the situation in financial services regarding cybersecurity readiness. Unlike in the case of other sorts of essential service providers, it was relatively common that financial institutions were well prepared for cybersecurity challenges far before cybersecurity became even societally and politically relevant. The regulatory developments, namely represented by Directive (EU) 2016/1148 concerning Measures for a High Common Level of Security of Network and Information Systems across the Union (NIS Directive),[2] were then met in the financial sector mostly with mixed attitudes and reservations. We will see that such reservations were quite understandable, because the new legal regulatory framework did not bring, in many respects, greater cybersecurity into the financial sector, but rather only introduced new compliance duties and procedures as well as new reporting and transparency obligations. When analysing the regulatory logic of the EU cybersecurity law, we will mostly focus on performance-based regulatory models. Performance-based rules which are used namely in the NIS Directive and its subsequent implementations in the EU member-states, are typical by defining only general aims, whilst making it mandatory for the regulated subjects to develop and implement their own rules, procedures or measures reflecting particular properties of respective information systems.

This unorthodox regulatory approach, which can be seen also e.g., in Regulation (EU) 2016/679 on the Protection of Natural Persons with Regard to the Processing of Personal Data and on the Free Movement of such Data

---

[1] This chapter is based on the research undertaken under project No. CZ 02.1.01/0.0/0.0/16_019/0000822.

[2] Directive (EU) 2016/1148 of the European Parliament and of the Council of 6 July 2016 Concerning Measures for a High Common Level of Security of Network and Information Systems across the Union [2016] OJ L194/1 (NIS Directive).

(General Data Protection Regulation, GDPR),[3] aims at maximum efficiency of particular security measures, because they shall always be tailor-made and thus they should be mostly suitable for respective systems or networks. However, as the law lays down here only very general rules and principles, it might also lead to overall uncertainty of the regulated subjects. In that respect, we will see that the relative freedom that performance-based rules leave for financial institutions might turn here into fatal uncertainties as to whether the individually developed complex combinations of security measures and compliance procedures actually meet those vaguely defined legal requirements. We will then discuss the extent to which such uncertainties can be mitigated in the financial sector by the certification mechanism that was introduced by the Cybersecurity Act. We will critically review the mechanism of creation and implementation of certification schemes as well as the corresponding institutional framework. Besides the prospective functioning of the certification system as such, we will also look at the possibilities of intra-institutional alignment of cybersecurity certificates with other compliance measures that are used in associated fields such as protection of personal data, AML etc. We will then finally focus on the question as to whether cybersecurity certificates should be awarded to particular products or rather to their vendors. We will note that objective certification (i.e., certification of products) is not entirely fit to serve the purpose in case of complex information systems or technological solutions – i.e., those that are very common in the financial sector. Instead, we will argue for subjective certification (i.e., certification of vendors or providers) that can provide in the case of complex systems for greater flexibility together with overall trust and compatibility with general priorities of public and national security.

II. CYBERSECURITY IN FINANCIAL SERVICES

Information security has always represented an essential agenda for financial institutions. Even in the old Rome, the *argentarii* or *mensarii* paid utmost attention, besides the security of the actual bearers of value, to securing records and communications that documented various financial transactions.[4] It is then no wonder that cybersecurity was diligently tackled by the financial sector from the very first moment when respective records and communica-

---

[3] Regulation (EU) 2016/679 of the European Parliament and of the Council of 27 April 2016 on the Protection of Natural Persons with Regard to the Processing of Personal Data and on the Free Movement of such Data, and repealing Directive 95/46/EC (General Data Protection Regulation, GDPR).

[4] A complex picture of financial services in ancient Greece and Rome is provided in monograph Guillard, E. *Les banquiers atheniens et romains: trapezites & argentarii* (Paris: Guillaumin & Cie, 1875). The book is also available online via books.google.

tions started being processed electronically.[5] The key methodological issue in securing electronic processing of financial data is in proper understanding and implementation of the method of virtualisation. This method, that has been known and used for centuries, is based on changing formal elements of certain phenomenon whilst preserving its core.

The purpose of replacing formal properties of various phenomena with new forms is primarily to resolve problems that are connected to the form as such. As a new form is introduced, new problems emerge. Virtualisation is then successful simply if the problems that had disappeared together with departure from the old form were more substantial than those that emerged with the new form.

The reason why virtualisation of various phenomena became so frequent and popular with the introduction of information technologies is that computers allow for unprecedented virtualising in terms of scale and depth. If any phenomenon allows for being virtualised by digitisation, such virtualisation is throughout, because the respective phenomenon loses its central formal aspect, i.e., physical embodiment. At the same time, the whole process, i.e., switching from physical to digital, can be instant and often also relatively inexpensive. Moving a physical enterprise into a digital form (i.e., virtualising it) might be even faster and less costly than moving it from one physical location to another.

Virtual enterprise is also used as an illustrative example of virtualisation by Pierre Lévy, a leading theoretician of virtuality.[6] In a regular, or physical, enterprise, people work in offices, gather at the coffee machine, go for lunch during the break, etc. If an enterprise gets virtualised (by typically moving respective operations online), the problems that entirely or mostly disappear are, e.g., bills for electricity or heating, sexual harassment or at-work injuries. As we have just experienced exactly that type of virtualisation with the current lockdowns, we are now quite well aware of the problems that might newly emerge such as a decline in efficiency, motivational issues, etc. The current

---

[5] Concerns of financial institutions regarding cybersecurity are, inter alia, driven also by popular demand. Financial transactions in online purchases and e-banking are steadily considered as the most risky by users of information society services – see e.g., Seungeun Lee, C., Hye Kim, J., 'Latent groups of cybersecurity preparedness in Europe: Sociodemographic factors and country-level contexts' (2020) 97 *Computers & Security* 5. Another, even more obvious, reason is the impact of cybersecurity incidents to operations and trade value of financial institutions – see Gao, L., Calderon, T. G., Tang, F., 'Public companies' cybersecurity risk disclosures' (2020) 38 *International Journal of Accounting Information Systems* 1.

[6] The method of virtualisation is explained in detail in monograph Lévy, P. *Qu'est-ce que le virtuel?* (Paris: La Découverte, 1995). More internationally known is Lévy's later book Lévy, *P. Becoming Virtual* (New York: Plenum Trade, 1998).

experience also shows that for certain enterprises, virtualisation works well and is being kept even after the mandatory lockdowns, whilst others return to physical presence at work.

Lévy specifically stresses that virtual is not an opposite to real.[7] Virtualised phenomena, if they manage to keep their core (or essence), are as real as their non-virtualised counterparts. Unfounded distinguishing between traditional and virtualised facts often represents a problem in legal procedures, e.g., when courts try to handle electronic documents. However, the financial sector seems to be getting virtualisation right from the very beginning, as values or transactions are treated here with the same care and respect regardless of whether they are fixed on gold, paper or information society services.[8] The fact that financial institutions correctly understood the idea and method of virtualisation can be seen also on their approach to cybersecurity. The financial sector was amongst the first fields, together with national security and intelligence, where serious investments to systemic securing of IT infrastructures initially began.[9]

The overall situation as to readiness and willingness of various fields of critical infrastructure to develop and implement cybersecurity measures was quite spectacular across Europe. Whilst the financial sector was, as noted above, mostly ready, other industries, public and private, varied from readiness to ignorance to resistance.[10] The first EU member-state that developed a complex cybersecurity legislation was the Czech Republic.[11] The 2014 Cybersecurity Act[12] came into force approximately two years before the NIS Directive and later acted as a role model for other member-states and even for the Directive as such.

In the near five-year development process of the Czech Cybersecurity Act, relevant stakeholders' different standings were clearly highlighted. The financial sector and most of the public sector were jointly opposing the introduction

---

7 See Lévy, 'P. Welcome to Virtuality' (1997) 8(1) *Digital Creativity* 3.

8 See e.g., Claessens, S., Glaessner, T. C., Klingebiel, D. 'Electronic finance: A new approach to financial sector development?' (2002) World Bank discussion paper No. 431, https://openknowledge.worldbank.org/handle/10986/14075 accessed 20 June 2021.

9 See Dupont, B., 'The cyber-resilience of financial institutions: significance and applicability' (2019) 5(1) *Journal of Cybersecurity* 1.

10 See Kasper, 'EU cybersecurity governance -stakeholders and normative intentions towards integration' in A. Harwood, M., Moncada, S., Pace, R., *The future of the European Union: demisting the debate* (University of Malta. Institute for European Studies, 2020), 166, available also online at um.edu.mt.

11 The legislative history of the Czech cybersecurity law is summarised, incl. English translations of relevant statutes, at nukib.cz.

12 See the Act No. 181/2014 Sb., on Cyber Security and change of related acts (Act on Cyber Security), available in English at nukib.cz.

of a new legal regulatory framework, yet for very different reasons. The reasons for the financial sector were primarily the aforementioned actual readiness and lack of interest in yet another public interference in financial services. To the contrary, the public sector resisted the newly developing laws mostly due to overall tragic situation regarding vendor lock-ins and other problems in public procurement in IT that were, quite correctly, believed to be amplified by the introduction of new cybersecurity obligations.[13]

Quite surprisingly, and unlike in the financial and public sector, most of the Czech private sector welcomed and even actively supported the introduction of the new cybersecurity laws. The reason was that officials who represented large corporations from energy, heavy industry, food and other industries, were mostly security or IT specialists who were well aware of the need for cybersecurity measures. In many of the respective corporations, however, investment requests made by these specialists, were often being declined as they were overly burdening and dispensable.[14] In that respect, the introduction of mandatory legal requirements and consequent inclusion of cybersecurity investments into compliance procedures of these corporations meant that these investments were no longer to be neglected or omitted.[15]

Although cybersecurity is not new to the financial sector as a security agenda, it is relatively new as a regulatory agenda.[16] The difference between the technical and regulatory nature of cybersecurity might not be entirely evident but distinguishing these two aspects of cybersecurity is essential to a successful understanding and efficient implementation of various regulatory tools, including the recently introduced mechanism of cybersecurity certifications (see below).

The introduction of legal cybersecurity obligations, most of which are of *ex ante* nature, meant an organisational dilemma for financial institutions. Before

---

13 For a more detailed study on contracting issues in public cybersecurity, see Nussbaum, B., Park, S. A., 'Tough decision made easy?: local government decision-making about contracting for cybersecurity' in Janssen, M., Ae Chun, S., Weerakkody, V. dg.o 18: 19th Annual International Conference on Digital Government Research, New York: Association for Computing Machinery, 2018.

14 See also Michels, J. D., Walden, I. how safe is safe enough? Improving cybersecurity in Europe's critical infrastructure under the NIS Directive, Queen Mary School of Law Legal Studies Research Paper No. 291/2018, available at ssrn.com, abstract No. 3297470, p. 5.

15 For a comprehensive analysis of investment logic of cybersecurity, see Gordon, L.A., Loeb, M. P., Lucyshyn, W., Zhou, L., 'Increasing cybersecurity investments in private sector firms' (2015) 1(1) *Journal of Cybersecurity* 3.

16 A summary of new regulatory instruments in the EU law is provided in Didenko, A. N. 'Cybersecurity regulation in the financial sector; prospects of legal harmonisation in the EU and beyond' (2020) 25(1) Uniform Law Review 125.

cybersecurity got a regulatory component, it was dealt with by banks, clearing houses and other institutions as a technical and security agenda.[17] That does not mean that a legal or organisational component was not present at all, but it was mostly related to liability. If regulatory obligations were present, they mostly related either to relatively independently developed internal corporate rules or to rules imposed as a result of standards[18] and practices required by financial regulators or providers of insurance.

When legal duties arose, cybersecurity got another, and relatively new, dimension of compliance and liability.[19] This situation when technical and legal agenda interact is obviously not new. A similar case is with safety at work, protection of personal data, etc. Financial institutions are however quite specific by having had their technical and organisational cybersecurity highly developed and functioning, including respective institutional backing, far before the emergence of various regulatory obligations.[20] That made it easier for financial institutions to comply with newly introduced legal requirements, because in most cases, the actually implemented security solutions were far beyond the legally required minimum standards. At the same time, it introduced organisational dilemmas, such as which of the existing branches of financial institutions (IT, security, compliance) should be ultimately in charge of this relatively attractive and new regulatory agenda.

The question regarding the inclusion of cybersecurity into some of the existing organisational branches of financial institutions might seem just as a managerial issue and an easy fix. In fact, it has been a source of hard tensions and inefficiencies that remain unresolved for years. Aligning cybersecurity with other compliance-based agendas, namely personal data protection[21] and

---

[17] See e.g., Calliess, C., Baumgarten, A., 'Cybersecurity in the EU: the example of the financial sector: a legal perspective' (2020) 21 *German Law Journal* 1149.

[18] See ibid., 1159.

[19] See e.g., Odermatt, J., 'The European Union as a cybersecurity actor' in Blockmans, S, Koutrakos, P. (eds), *Research Handbook on EU Common Foreign and Security Policy* (Edward Elgar Publishing, 2018) 354.

[20] Even the NIS Directive notes in its recital (13) that:

> Operational risk is a crucial part of prudential regulation and supervision in the sectors of banking and financial market infrastructures. It covers all operations including the security, integrity and resilience of network and information systems. The requirements in respect of those systems, which often exceed the requirements provided for under this Directive, are set out in a number of Union legal acts(…)

A list of sector-specific standards and regulations is provided in Calliess and Baumgarten (n 17), 1165.

[21] See Cole, M. D., Schmitz, S., 'The Interplay Between the NIS Directive and the GDPR in a Cybersecurity Threat Landscape' (2019) University of Luxembourg Law Working Paper No. 2019-017, available at ssrn.com, abstract No. 3512093.

protection of other regulated information (insider trading, stock market data, AML etc.) thus represents a highly sought-after service from providers of corporate consulting and advisory services.

III. PERFORMANCE-BASED REGULATION

Cybersecurity, together with protection of personal data, substantially differs from other information-related security agendas. The main difference is in the primary use of performance-based rules instead of regular behavioural rules. In AML, classified information, stock market data rules and other areas, regulated subjects are under the standard behavioural regulation that defines particular regulatory duties. These duties, if not entirely precisely specified, are then particularly interpreted by respective regulators or courts. As a result, there is a set of rules that originate with the state and are to be implemented by regulated subjects.

Unlike that, performance-based rules do not define particular obligations. Instead, the law only makes it mandatory for regulated subjects to develop their own rules in-house.[22] Legal regulation in that case mostly defines general scopes, principles and goals for development of internal regulatory instruments and deployment of organisational[23] or technical measures. Particular rules for these measures are then individually developed by each regulated subject, depending on their individual circumstances. A good example of the use of performance-based rules is the speed limit on German highways. Everywhere else in Europe, there apply behavioural rules and they set clear and predictable legal obligations for drivers of passenger cars not to exceed, say, 130 km/h. Unlike that, in Germany, the law lays down a speed limit in the sense that one can drive as fast as it is safe. It thus imposes a duty for each driver to realistically assess their car, driving abilities as well as all other relevant conditions and circumstances, and to set their own speed limit. On the one hand, it is burdensome to the drivers, because it requires them to diligently and wisely consider a number of relevant factors, but, on the other hand, it allows for everybody to efficiently use their assets and abilities.

---

22 For a general discussion of performance-based regulation, see Coglianese, C., 'The limits of performance-based regulation' (2017) 50(3) *University of Michigan Journal of Law Reform* 525.

23 These include, at the first place, measures to prevent individual failures that represent most frequent passive cause of cybersecurity incidents – see Donaldsa, C., Osei-Bryson, K.-M., 'Cybersecurity compliance behavior: Exploring the influences of individual decision style and other antecedents' (2020) 51 *International Journal of Information Management* 1.

One might argue that a speed limit on a highway is one thing, but cybersecurity of a billion-euro worth system that processes financial data is another. As the model of performance-based rules is relatively vague and general, it is in many respects far from ideal. Regulated subjects might critically lack particular regulatory guidance and certainty when implementing performance-based rules. However, agendas such as cybersecurity or protection of personal data do not practically (or pragmatically) allow for any other regulatory model due to their complexity and diversity.

If behavioural rules were to be developed for a cybersecurity regulatory agenda, in the financial sector or elsewhere, they would need to elaborate on some typical use-case (or a couple of typical use-cases) as a model for particular regulatory action. Behavioural rules would then be designed to work for the use case and would provide for certain and efficient regulation as long as particular practical situations would fit the scope of the use case or fall close to it. In cybersecurity, there is, however, no such typical use-case or two, but the law tries to cover here extreme variety of applications, processes or technologies that are not even known to the state. Consequently, the law would have to develop thousands, or even more, different sets of behavioural rules for different typical situations in order for the rules to be efficient. Another reason for the use of performance-based rules in cybersecurity regulation is institutional. The state has neither technical competences nor regulatory potential to efficiently develop security measures for respective information systems.[24] Partly, it is due to the problem of the above complexity and variety of respective systems that the state is unable to comprehend and process. Even more important is then the difference between the state and the regulated subject with regards to the regulatory tools that can be used for efficiently securing respective information infrastructures.[25] As the state is obviously limited in the European legal culture by general principles of rule of law and proportionate protection of fundamental rights,[26] its options in terms of implementation of technical measures or activities of responsible staff are incomparably weaker than are the competences of an owner of respective equipment and employer of respective staff. In the Czech Republic, there is an old saying that a shirt is always closer to a person than the coat. In this case, it can translate in the way that it is always more efficient when particular rules are developed by the owner/employer who is not just closer to the regulated substance in terms

[24] See e.g., Kesan, J. P., 'Private internet governance' (2003) 35 *Loyola University Chicago Law Journal* 87.

[25] See Berrejka, M., 'A case for government promoted multi-stakeholderism' (2012) 10 *Journal on Telecommunications & High Technology Review* 2.

[26] See Christen, M., Gordijn, B., Weber, K., van de Poel, I., Yaghmaei, E. 'A review of value - conflicts in cybersecurity' (2017) 1(1) *Orbit* 1–19, 6.

of technical knowledge, but also as to the toolbox of available authoritative measures.

The specific nature of performance-based rules is also reflected in the way of sanctioning of respective breaches. Performance-based rules only define basic scope and principles for the development of particular in-house regulatory, technical and organisational solutions and so the situation of regulated subjects is relatively uncomfortable. The law does not particularly say here what it actually requires, whilst there is a risk that if these fuzzy requirements are not met, sanctions might follow. However, the logic of sanctioning of performance-based rules is not based on an ideal normatively prescribed behaviour that is compared to the actual behaviour of regulated subjects. The law does not envisage here an ideal behaviour, because no such ideal objectively exists. Particular conditions for development and implementation of cybersecurity greatly differ amongst regulated subjects and so there is no ideal set of security measures or internal policies. Thus, a sanctioning authority does not answer a question as to whether the regulated subject did it right (because there is no such thing as 'right'), but rather whether it was not done wrong in given circumstances.

IV. ENVIRONMENTAL APPROACH TO CYBERSECURITY

Cybersecurity, as a regulatory agenda, can either be tackled through individual liability or as an environmental regulation.[27] The liability-based approach was typical namely for regulatory attempts that were popping up in the United States at the beginning of the second decade of this century.[28] The main idea of this approach was that if a combination of regulatory and technical measures makes a perpetrator less anonymous and easier to find and sanction, it provides for an efficient prevention of emergence of cybersecurity incidents.

The advantage of this approach is that it utilises the strength and motivational effects of criminal, administrative or private legal liability. In that sense, it can be quite efficient in motivating particular individuals either by deterring them from intentional malicious conduct or making them more diligent as to possible negligence that might cause cybersecurity incidents. The downside of the liability-based approach is that it requires implementation of regulatory and technical measures that would enhance transparency of individual behav-

---

[27] For a detailed study of possible regulatory models, see Shackelford, S., 'Toward cyberspace: Managing cyberattacks through polycentric governance' (2013) 62 *American University Law Review* 1273.

[28] See e.g., Sales, N. A., 'Regulating cyber-security' (2013) 107 *Northwestern University Law Review* 1503.

iour online and so it would limit or avoid possibilities of anonymous online acting.[29] Concerns as to possible negative effects of lowering the level of privacy protection of users of information society services[30] were also the main reason for this approach not being finally fully adopted in the US. Interestingly for the situation in the EU, the main criticism regarding possible negative effects to privacy was not motivated by concerns over privacy or personal data as such in the US, but rather by possible risks for freedom of speech. That is because an inherent component of freedom of speech is the freedom to speak anonymously.[31]

The latter approach which aims at creating a secure environment was thus for many reasons more viable in the US as well as in Europe.[32] Regulatory tools are in that case not aimed at liability for cybersecurity incidents but rather at duties that can provide for an environment that is overall resilient to these incidents.[33] A good parallel of the environmental approach is the regulatory agenda of fire prevention. It consists mostly of obligations of relevant stakeholders (owners of buildings, enterprises, etc.) to implement technical and organisational measures that prevent the appearance and emergence or fires and, in case of an actual fire, also measures that enable its efficient handling. There is, at the same time, a regulatory regime for individual liability for fires, but that is relatively separate and backed by different institutional setups. If a fire emerges, it is the task for firefighters and fire authorities to get it under control and prevent its reappearance. A task for the police and state prosecutors is then to find the arsonists, gather evidence and bring them to justice. Similar to that, the task for the cybersecurity institutions is to enforce preventive cybersecurity measures and mitigate impact of cybersecurity incidents. Prosecuting perpetrators (hackers or negligent users) is then a task for the relatively independently acting law enforcement.

The advantage of the environmental approach is the relatively small or nearly no exposure of privacy of users of respective services. Consequently, the level of political sensitivity of specific cybersecurity laws is in that case also relatively low. In addition, the legal obligations apply primarily on provid-

---

[29] See Rid, T., Buchanan, B., 'Attributing cyber attacks' (2015) 38 *Journal of Strategic Studies* 4.

[30] See also Macnish, K. van der Ham, J., 'Ethics in cybersecurity research and practice' (2020) 63 *Technology in Society* 3.

[31] See e.g., Steinhauer, J. 'Senate rejects measure to strengthen cybersecurity', *New York Times*, 11 June 2015.

[32] See Tran, J. L., 'Navigating the Cybersecurity Act of 2015' (2016) 19 *Chapman Law Review* 483.

[33] See Christou, G., 'The collective securitisation of cyberspace in the European Union' (2019) 42 *West European Politics* 278.

ers of information infrastructure which means that the target group is relatively well defined, easily accessible and in most cases potent in terms of ability to develop and implement respective security measures. The disadvantage of the environmental approach is in the risk of inefficiency of regulatory measures. The regulatory pressure to possible perpetrators is not direct but goes mostly through security measures that are implemented by the providers of services or owners of respective infrastructure.

It is also quite difficult for the lawmakers to design the desired security measures in a way that actually and efficiently prevent the emergence of cybersecurity incidents. Here, the parallel with fire prevention does not entirely work, because there is extensive and relatively stable knowledge of risks related to fires and so the preventive measures can be on point and efficient. Unlike that, the overall cybersecurity landscape is everchanging and new sorts of risks and threats constantly appear. All of the above problematic factors of the environmental approach make it difficult to define particular obligations as to the structure and content of security measures. Moreover, there is no typical regulatory use case, because there is extreme variety of target information systems in terms of size, value, types of processed data etc. As a result, there is practically no other way to implement a functioning and future-proof environmentally oriented regulation in cybersecurity than through performance-based rules of relatively high level of abstraction.

V. THE NIS DIRECTIVE

The main regulatory tool in cybersecurity at the EU level is the NIS Directive.[34] It came out in 2016 as a basic regulatory instrument that was aimed at establishing cybersecurity as a new European regulatory agenda and laying down a fundamental structure of protective and cooperative duties, most of which have the form of performance-based obligations (see above).

The NIS is an EU directive which means that it has to be transposed into the laws of the member-states. As a result, the implementation of the NIS directive differs from one member-state to another.[35] That does not represent an issue for most regulated subjects, because the infrastructures that have to implement

---

[34] See the Directive (EU) 2016/1148 concerning measures for a high common level of security of network and information systems across the Union. The Directive is currently under a review and the "NIS 2.0" has recently been published – see the web announcement by Cybersecurity & Digital Privacy Policy (Unit H.2) at https://digital-strategy.ec.europa.eu/ accessed 14 December 2021.

[35] The EU Commission publishes a continuously updated list of national implementations of the NIS Directive at https://ec.europa.eu/ accessed 14 December 2021under the title 'State-of-play of the transposition of the NIS Directive.'

respective cybersecurity measures or report cybersecurity incidents (see below), such as electricity, health or electronic communications, are mostly local. However, differences amongst the national implementations of the NIS Directive might matter to financial institutions that often operate across the common market and for whom it is a matter of cost efficiency whether to establish one or many compliance structures for different branches. The primary personal scope of application of the NIS Directive is defined through the term of 'essential service operators', whereas essential service means '(…) a service which is essential for the maintenance of critical societal and/or economic activities, the provision of that service depends on network and information systems and an incident would have significant disruptive effects on the provision of that service'.

The definition of essential services practically covers what national laws of the member-states mostly refer to as 'critical infrastructure', yet it is limited only to the infrastructures whose functioning is dependent on information technologies.[36] The term 'critical infrastructure' could not be used here, because it is already taken in the European law.[37]

Financial institutions are covered in the list of essential services in paragraphs 3 and 4 of the Annex III of the NIS Directive. Under 'banking', there are listed credit institutions in the meaning of the Art. 4(1) of the Regulation (EU) No 575/2013 and 'financial market infrastructures' contain operators of trading venues as defined in Art. 4(24) of the Directive 2014/65/EU and central counterparties as defined in Art. 2(1) of the Regulation (EU) No 648/2012.

Besides essential services, the NIS Directive covers also 'digital services' that are recently[38] defined, not very conveniently, in Art. 4(5) together with Art. (4)(17–19) and Annex III of the NIS Directive, and Art. 1(1)(b) of Directive (EU) 2015/1535, as information society services of the following sorts: online marketplaces, search engines and cloud computing services. In addition, Art. 16(11) states that most important obligations for digital services that are listed under Chapter V of the NIS Directive, do not apply to micro- and small enterprises.[39] In any case, not many financial institutions will fall under

---

[36] See also Michels and Walden (n 14), 9.

[37] See Council Directive 2008/114/EC on the identification and designation of European critical infrastructures and the assessment of the need to improve their protection.

[38] The planned NIS 2.0 will mostly likely abandon the category of 'digital services' as such and will instead only introduce different classes of essential services – see the web announcement on NIS 2.0 by Cybersecurity & Digital Privacy Policy (Unit H.2) at https://digital-strategy.ec.europa.eu/ accessed 14 December 2021.

[39] See Commission Recommendation 2003/361/EC concerning the definition of micro-, small- and medium-sized enterprises.

any of the sub-categories of 'digital services'. Even if a financial service is provided by a non-SME through an online marketplace, it will most likely not be regarded as a 'digital service', because it will mostly fall outside the scope of the definition of 'information society services'.[40] In that regard, it is important to note the current case-law of the Court of Justice of the EU that clarifies the definition of the information society service and implements the main criterion of level of control over respective transactions.[41] As regular online marketplaces with financial services are either run directly by providers of these services, or their providers have nearly full control over defining elements of respective transactions, they would be regarded as financial service providers rather than providers of services of information society.

The NIS Directive lays down a requirement for the member-states to establish two main sorts of general obligations for those financial institutions that fall under the scope of the definition of essential services, i.e., to introduce cybersecurity measures and to report cybersecurity incidents. Substantively more important than these two obligations is the duty to design and implement cybersecurity measures. The NIS Directive requires the member-states to ensure that 'operators of essential services take appropriate measures to prevent and minimise the impact of incidents affecting the security of the network and information systems used for the provision of such essential services, with a view to ensuring the continuity of those services'.[42]

This provision is obviously a little bit too metaphorical even for a performance-based rule. Consequently, the laws of the member-states do not solely transcript it but rather further define categories of cybersecurity measures and in some cases even particular duties that should be implemented by essential service operators.[43] A common approach among the member-states is to use statutory law for definition of basic duties and categories of cybersecurity measures, whilst bylaws and other sub-statutory regulatory instruments provide for more detailed breakdown of technical requirements, minimum standards, etc.

---

[40] See Art. 1(1)(b) of the Directive (EU) 2015/1535 laying down a procedure for the provision of information in the field of technical regulations and of rules on Information Society services.

[41] See Case C-434/15 *Asociación Profesional Elite Taxi v. Uber Systems Spain, SL* and Case C-390/18 *Airbnb Ireland.*

[42] See Art. 14(2) of the NIS Directive.

[43] For a more detailed theoretical breakdown of various security measures, see Michalec, O. A., van der Linden, D., Milyaeva, S., Rashid, A. Industry Responses to the European Directive on Security of Network and Information Systems (NIS): Understanding policy implementation practices across critical infrastructures, in Proceedings of the Sixteenth Symposium on Usable Privacy and Security, USENIX, 2020, p. 301.

In general, security measures can be basically divided between technical and organisational measures. Technical measures include preventive and reactive tools like access control, incident detection, use of encryption, etc. Organisational measures cover mostly compliance tools including asset identification, HR management, training, legal issues (including management of relations with contractors of respective systems) or internal rules. Depending on the scope and depth of national implementations of the NIS Directive, most of the member-states also require essential service operators to provide for documentation of respective technical and organisational measures.

The structure of basic performance-based duties of essential service operators and the subsequent obligations to document their fulfilment are in essence very similar to the requirements of the GDPR.[44] In the regulatory agenda of protection of personal data, controllers also have a duty to know which data they process and how, they must implement appropriate security measures and they also have to demonstrate the fulfilment of legal obligations by sufficient documentation. The only important difference between the regulatory architecture of personal data protection and cybersecurity is that the GDPR is process-oriented, whilst the NIS Directive is object-oriented. The main element of the regulatory logic of the GDPR is a process in which personal data are involved. In that sense, every process has to be individually described, assessed, documented and secured. To the contrary, the regulatory logic of the NIS Directive uses as the main element not a process but rather an object which means a system or a network. Essential service operators are thus not required to document and secure individual processes that are critically important for respective essential services but are rather obliged to identify and secure whole critically important systems and networks.

Another set of obligations for essential service operators relate to notifications of cybersecurity incidents.[45] These duties are again designed in a very similar manner in the NIS Directive and the GDPR.[46] Essential service operators are required to have means for detection of cybersecurity incidents and the laws of the member-states also provide for particular behavioural (in this

---

44 For a more detailed comparison of the regulatory regime of the NIS Directive and the GDPR, Markopouloua, D., Papakonstantinoua, V., De Hert, P., 'The new EU cybersecurity framework: The NIS Directive, ENISA's role and the General Data Protection Regulation' (2020) 35 *Computer Law & Security Review* 1.

45 See ibid., p. 4.

46 See also Cole, M. D., Schmitz, S., 'The Interplay Between the NIS Directive and the GDPR in a Cybersecurity Threat Landscape' (2019) University of Luxembourg Law Working Paper No. 2019-017, 2019, available at ssrn.com, abstract No. 3512093, p. 10.

case not performance-based) duties to report these incidents to the respective national CSIRT.[47]

The reporting duties in protection of personal data mostly have the function of notifying data protection authorities of wrongdoings and alerting data subjects of possible risks to their privacy. In comparison to that, the duty to report cybersecurity incidents to a national CSIRT plays a very different role. Having real-time knowledge about security situations in critically important parts of national information infrastructure is an essential precondition for the ability of security forces to efficiently protect that infrastructure from damage or disruption. It is, unlike in the case of personal data protection, relatively common that individual essential service operators have neither technical or legal means, nor the know-how to handle serious or large-scale security incidents. Reporting in these cases means that national security is alerted and can get actively involved in protecting respective parts of the national critical infrastructure. However, the above situation when essential service operators report cybersecurity incidents to national CSIRTs in order to get efficient assistance in incident handling is not common for financial institutions, especially for the larger ones. Namely banks are in general very hesitant to give away any data about anything going wrong in them, including information about their systems being attacked or malfunctioning. Despite incident data being kept by the national CSIRTs strictly confidential, banks still tend to consider this kind or reporting risky in its own right. Moreover, as noted above, financial institutions have often relatively high levels of their own cybersecurity arrangements and so there is, sometimes validly, scepticism of the banks as to the ability of the national CSIRTs to handle security incidents more efficiently than the banks' own cybersecurity professionals or contractors.

VI. THE CASE FOR CYBERSECURITY CERTIFICATION

There is, again, not a big difference between the regulatory logic of the NIS Directive and the GDPR as to the fundamental *ex ante* orientation of the regulatory mechanism.[48] Both regulatory frameworks are not primarily using *ex post* liability as a desired method of normative motivation of regulated subjects but rather *ex ante* compliance. Essential service operators are thus expected not to sit and wait until some sanctionable incident pops up but, as described above, they are normatively motivated to identify and describe their assets, design and implement technical and organisational security measures

---

47 See Recital 32 and Art. 12 of the NIS Directive.

48 See Markopouloua, Papakonstantinoua and De Hert (n 44).

and, primarily as a matter of prevention, report cybersecurity incidents. At the same time, the laws of the member-states cannot be too specific about what in particular should be done in every system or network – namely because there is a great diversity as to their size, purpose, functioning, security exposures, etc. That is, as we noted above, exactly the case for performance-based rules that only generally define the desired effects of regulation and leave it for regulated subjects, who are best positioned to know what and how it is needed, to develop their own internal rules and measures.

The problem is then obviously in the combination of the need for clear and particular compliance-oriented corporate solutions and the inevitably general nature of performance-based rules. Regulated subjects (essential service operators) are obliged here to develop their own particular cybersecurity solutions upon very general legal obligations. It implies that it is extremely difficult for essential service operators to verify whether their security solutions really meet the respective legal requirements.

Whenever there are vague rules that count with *ex ante* compliance solutions, there is a natural demand for an analogical *ex ante* official review mechanism. It is just logical that regulated subjects call for a procedure that would provide for an official review of particular implementations of general regulatory duties, because absence of such procedure leads to fatal legal uncertainty. Without an official review mechanism, even a diligent and caring regulated subject is left on its own to design and implement all security measures without particular authoritative guidance, and then to only sit and wait for possible *ex post* authoritative inspections and possible sanctions.

The above uncertainty can be mitigated in cybersecurity namely by commercial assurance that is mostly provided by vendors or respective cybersecurity solutions or external providers of consulting services.[49] Having a contractually-based assurance as to the compliance of implemented cybersecurity measures is, however, far from ideal. At first, an inspection by a cybersecurity authority can turn up at the time when financial ability of respective auditors or vendors to compensate for sanctions and subsequent damages for non-compliance, can be already gone. Secondly, and quite importantly for financial institutions as well as many other essential service operators, the possibility that a cybersecurity authority orders e.g., termination of functioning of a non-compliant system or network might represent an objectively unacceptable (and even uninsurable) risk. Thirdly, even the mere fact that the cybersecurity authority might, due to the object orientation of the NIS Directive,

---

[49] Didenko speaks about 'licensing' of cybersecurity services that provides assurance of certain standards – see Didenko (n 16), 180.

investigate the design and functioning of respective systems or networks as such, might represent a serious problem for some financial institutions.

In general, there are two ways to resolve the above demand for officially backed certainty as to compliance of in-house measures – codes of conduct or certificates (eventually audits). The code of conduct model is implemented in the GDPR and there were originally quite high hopes that various sectors would initially develop their own particular solutions that would act, upon an approval by respective data protection authorities, as particular guidelines and models for in-house compliance solutions.

However, it has not worked so far – partly probably because of a less-than-ideal initial institutional approach by the relevant data protection authorities and partly due to inappropriate hesitation or even ignorance of relevant stakeholders. The European cybersecurity law initially did not contain any particular compliance-friendly ex-ante solution at all. The NIS directive only envisaged in Art. 15(2) that essential service operators will have a duty to document and demonstrate their cybersecurity measures by a 'security audit carried out by the competent authority or a qualified auditor'.

The NIS Directive does not go any further in specifying details as to which or how authorities should conduct these audits. Thus, only a very few member-states implemented specific official auditing procedures, some others laid down, directly or indirectly, an acknowledgment of existing official or commercial auditing schemes,[50] and some left the issue of ex ante assurance as to the compliance of cybersecurity measures without any regulatory attention.

It is quite understandable that many member-states chose not to instantly develop new auditing schemes. The scope of the NIS Directive is relatively broad and so developing and implementing a good quality cybersecurity auditing procedure would have required significant efforts and investments. At the same time, a new kind of official stamping would automatically bring new challenges as to possible market impact, corruption risks, etc. Some segments of the financial sector, typically banking, can even in cases when no specific cybersecurity auditing schemes were adopted, partly rely on existing auditing procedures that often contain some aspects of confidentiality, data security or cybersecurity and are developed and run by central banks or national financial regulators.[51] Despite the regulatory framework of the financial sector being relatively independent on cybersecurity regulation, the national cybersecurity

---

[50] For a comprehensive overview, see Sivan-Sevilla, I., 'Europeanisation on demand: the EU cybersecurity certification regime between market integration and core state powers (1997–2019)' (2020) *Journal of Public Policy* 10.

[51] The relations between sectoral regulations and the NIS Directive are discussed in Ducuing, C., 'Understanding the rule of prevalence in the NIS directive: C-ITS as a case study' (2021) 40 *Computer Law & Security Review* 1.

authorities regularly acknowledge these audits and assume upon them compliance also with the requirements of national implementations of the NIS Directive.

VII. EUROPEAN CYBERSECURITY CERTIFICATION FRAMEWORK

The much-anticipated ex ante official compliance regime for cybersecurity on the EU-level and was finally brought by the Cybersecurity Act.[52] The aim of the Act is to establish a framework for certification of IT products, services and even for 'processes' that would be backed by official authorities and mandatorily acknowledged across the common market. The central element of the newly established certification framework are certification schemes.[53] These are to be issued by the European Commission and should contain detailed specification of particular products, services or 'processes', technical or other (e.g., organisational) requirements as well as details regarding the certification procedure, peer reviews, properties of the certificates, etc. Once a certification scheme is issued (currently, two schemes are at an advanced stage of drafting and a dozen more are being prepared), the Act guarantees that respective certificates will be valid across the European Economic Area. Moreover, the Act lays down in Art. 57 a priority of EU certification schemes over existing national schemes – official or commercial.[54] Thus, existing nationally recognised cybersecurity certificates will remain valid, but if the same sort of product, service or process falls under the EU certification scheme, its new officially recognised certification has to be done according to the new EU scheme.

The above implies that there are two key processes in the new system of EU cybersecurity certification – the adoption of a certification scheme and then, obviously, the mere certification. The Commission adopts the 'Union rolling work programme for European cybersecurity certification' that outlines areas in IT products, services or processes that are fit for being subject of certification under the Act. The rolling work programme, which is due to be updated every three years, then acts as a main basis for the Commission to request ENISA to develop a particular certification scheme. The Act, however,

[52] See Regulation (EU) 2019/881 on ENISA (the European Union Agency for Cybersecurity) and on information and communications technology cybersecurity certification and repealing Regulation (EU) No 526/2013 (Cybersecurity Act) (Text with EEA relevance).

[53] See Arts 49–54 of the Cybersecurity Act.

[54] See e.g., Sivan-Sevilla (n 50).

also envisages a possibility for the Commission to request ENISA to prepare a scheme that falls outside the rolling work programme.[55]

Another body that may request ENISA to prepare a certification scheme is the European Cybersecurity Certification Group (ECCG). It consists of representatives of national cybersecurity certification authorities (see below). The role of the ECCG, as a representation of relevant authorities of the member-states, is relatively important, yet not decisive. The ECCG might request ENISA to draft a new certification scheme and it may also further collaborate and comment on drafts, but neither these requests nor opinions are binding for ENISA. The Act states in Art. 49(6) that 'ENISA shall take utmost account of the opinion of the ECCG' but later it clarifies that '[t]he opinion of the ECCG shall not bind ENISA, nor shall the absence of such an opinion prevent ENISA from transmitting the candidate scheme to the Commission'. Similarly, Art. 40(2) states that 'ENISA may prepare candidate scheme' upon a request by the ECCG, not 'shall prepare', as stated when the Act refers to the requests made by the Commission. The Act then only adds that 'If ENISA refuses such a request, it shall give reasons for its refusal. Any decision to refuse such a request shall be taken by the Management Board.' In any case, the current experience of preparing the two initial candidate schemes shows that the cooperation between ENISA and the ECCG is smooth, mutually respectful and overall working, so there is no reason to expect tensions or problems any time soon.

Another body that plays a role in the process of identification of agenda for certification schemes is the Stakeholder Cybersecurity Certification Group.[56] It consists of members of relevant stakeholders (mostly industry and academia) that are selected by the Commission upon an open call and subsequent recommendation by ENISA. The SCCG is mostly a consultative body and has no binding powers. However, its role as a representative of the cybersecurity community has already proven in the process of preparation of the rolling work programme. By having a consultative role here, the SCCG has a quite significant possibility to affect which products, services or processes will fall under the spotlight for possible development of future certification schemes. The SCCG has also already proved itself as a useful source of practical and doctrinal expert feedback for ENISA in the process of defining the particular scope and content of currently drafted certification schemes.[57]

---

[55] See Art. 48(2) of the Cybersecurity Act.

[56] See Art. 22 of the Cybersecurity Act.

[57] Currently, there are two candidate schemes - the EUCC Candidate Scheme for ICT Products, which is set to replace the existing SOG-IS certification, and the Scheme on Cloud Services (EUCS). Both candidate schemes are published at https://www.enisa.europa.eu accessed 14 December 2021.

Once the certification schemes are passed by the Commission, the actual certification will be carried out by particular Conformity Assessment Bodies (CAB). These might be public or private institutions that will demonstrate sufficient professional and material background against the requirements of respective schemes and get accredited by some of the national accreditation bodies. The process of accreditation of CABs will utilise existing institutional and procedural framework laid down by Regulation (EC) No 765/2008, so the Cybersecurity Act adds here only a new substantive accreditation agenda to the existing national accreditation bodies. The Cybersecurity Act counts with three assurance levels of certification schemes – basic, substantial and high[58] – depending on the level of risk for which respective IT products, services or processes are destined. Basic level will probably serve for most consumer products including mobile communication devices, household IoT products, etc. High level certificates will be most likely used in critical applications, including vital systems of essential service operators. High level certificates can be awarded only by public CABs, whilst certification for substantial and basic levels of assurance will be carried out also by private CABs. Basic certificates, in addition, will also be available for self-certification through statements of conformity.[59] Vendors of IT products or providers of services for which basic certification will be available, will in that case issue a statement of conformity and file technical documentation with the respective national cybersecurity authority. By such a statement, they assume responsibility for compliance of their product or service with respective certification schemes which is in essence a similar approach to the 'CE' marking in consumer products.

Each member-state has designated a 'cybersecurity certification authority'[60] also referred to simply as 'cybersecurity authority'. These are mostly specialised administrative bodies or, especially in smaller member-states, security authorities with general jurisdiction on whose competence the respective member-state entrusted the regulatory agenda of cybersecurity. As the institutional structure in public and national security greatly differs among the member-states, the nature of cybersecurity certification authorities designated under the Cybersecurity Act ranges from public security to national security to intelligence or even military. Cybersecurity certification authorities have a central role in the deployment and operational functioning of the EU cybersecurity certification framework. At first, they supervise, document and sanction the whole process of accreditation of CABs and certification of products, ser-

---

58 See Art. 52(1) of the Cybersecurity Act.

59 See Art. 53 of the Cybersecurity Act.

60 See Art. 58 of the Cybersecurity Act.

vices or processes in respective member-states. The cybersecurity certification authorities thus have a range of powers including extensive investigative and supervisory competences or the authority to revoke certificates.[61] They can even themselves act as CABs, yet for that activity, their conformity assessment units need a standard accreditation analogically to other CABs.

The Act also envisages a specific procedure for some schemes where CABs will require not only the accreditation issued by the national accreditation authority but also a prior authorisation by the national cybersecurity certification body. This mechanism will most likely be used namely in high level certification and will mean that CABs will in order to be allowed to certify products, services or processes need not only the accreditation by the national accreditation body, but also authorisation by the national cybersecurity certification authority. The Act envisages in its recital that cybersecurity certifications will become a widely used compliance and assurance tool for a broad range of products, services or processes. Once the framework as such gets going and certification schemes start being issued, it is likely that cybersecurity certificates will instantly be used in a variety of critical applications as well as in consumer products. At the moment, neither the Cybersecurity Act, nor the NIS Directive, make it mandatory on the EU level for regulated subjects (essential service operators or others) to use certified products, services or processes.

National cybersecurity authorities already acknowledge or even require various cybersecurity certificates or audits. Even the regulated subjects, as well as their sectoral supervisory authorities or insurance providers, demand this form of *ex-ante* assurance of compliance of cybersecurity measures with regulatory or industry standards. Even the NIS Directive as well as the Cybersecurity Act envisage the possibility for the Commission to implement mandatory use of cybersecurity certificates in particular areas or industries.

In any case, we can expect that if new EU certification schemes are rightly positioned, they will become widely used not primarily upon the authority of the Commission but rather by the naturally generated demand from responsible authorities as well as from essential service operators.

VIII. CHALLENGES AHEAD

The regulatory framework of EU cybersecurity certification is very flexible. It allows for certification schemes to cover all sorts of cybersecurity-related aspects of IT in the public and private sector, including those that are yet to be discovered. The advantage of such opened and flexible framework is that it can

---

[61] See Art. 55 of the Cybersecurity Act.

remain relatively stable over time, whilst the Commission has enough space to shape particular standards and even to react to future challenges including deployment of autonomous technologies in various sectors. The downside of such regulatory flexibility is a lack of balancing and control mechanisms of the regulatory powers of the Commission. The possibilities of the Commission to craft and enforce certification schemes is limited mostly procedurally, i.e., by the role of ENISA in preparing the certification schemes and then by the comitology process[62] for their final adoption. However, there are only a very few options for a substantive review of the schemes by the Court of Justice or for individual member states to intervene, especially in cases when an EU scheme will be e.g., seen by them as too benevolent.

It is legitimate to ask in that sense, whether a substantive review of certification schemes would ever be needed in a situation when certification is not compulsory. That, at first, might change over the upcoming years, with the member-states and the Commission itself starting to require *ex ante* compliance measures in a number of IT-related sectors like electronic communications, e-health etc. Secondly, the priority of the EU certification might lead to a situation where a more benevolent EU certification scheme prevails over an even stricter national scheme.[63] A recent example of the EU executive being a bit too benevolent, especially to offshore providers of information society services, are the adequacy decisions made by the Commission regarding processing of personal data by US businesses under the Safe Harbour deal and later under the Privacy Shield agreement.[64] Both adequacy decisions, which are executive regulatory tools of the Commission in the field of security of personal data,[65] were annulled by the Court of Justice for being benevolent beyond the substantive requirements of data protection laws.[66] The Cybersecurity Act, however, contains only a very few and vague provisions (moreover, mostly found in the recital) that would not even allow for a similar substantive review.

---

[62] See Arts 49(7) and 66(2) of the Cybersecurity Act, together with Regulation (EU) No 182/2011 laying down the rules and general principles concerning mechanisms for control by Member States of the Commission's exercise of implementing powers.

[63] See Art. 57(1) of the Cybersecurity Act.

[64] The decision of the CJEU on the Privacy Shield (see below) is still too fresh for a proper doctrinal coverage. For a throughout analysis of the Safe Harbour case, together with some wise predictions, see Kuner, C., 'Reality and illusion in EU Data Transfer Regulation post Schrems' (2017) 18 *German Law Journal* 881.

[65] See Art. 44 of the GDPR.

[66] For the annulment of the Safe Harbour adequacy decision, see Case C-362/14 *Maximillian Schrems v Data Protection Commissioner*. For the annulment of the Privacy Shield adequacy decision, see Case C-311/18 *Data Protection Commissioner v Facebook Ireland Limited and Maximillian Schrems*.

Similar in essence, yet of the opposite nature, is the risk of undue benevolence on the level of the member-states. Any possibility of differentiated approach in a regulatory agenda that covers the whole common market inevitably creates an opportunity for some member-states to opt for a benevolent approach and attract vendors or providers who then use such member-states as a base from which they cater the whole common market. In that sense, the Cybersecurity Act provides for quite a comprehensive mechanism of possible peer-review in the certification process as well as for the review or revocation mechanism of cybersecurity certificates. Still, it might be, depending only on care and attention of the Commission and ENISA, easier or harder to get the same certificate, only depending on where the certification process takes place.

A big challenge for the ENISA, as well as for the ECCG and the SCCG, will be determining the general scope of cybersecurity certification schemes. The currently drafted schemes show that ENISA will most likely be inspired by existing industrial standards. Also, there is obvious and clearly understandable influence of existing European IT certification bodies which means that certification schemes will be primarily developed by ENISA as checklists of required features of respective IT products or services. At the same time, the experience shows that it might not be the key to securing information systems or networks to determine the security features of a particular product or service, but rather the credibility of the vendor or provider.[67] Certifying (or auditing) not primarily products or services but rather vendors and providers has many advantages. At first, a secure provider might update respective technology or service and users will not have to wait with its deployment for the end of the certification process. Moreover, many technologies and services are so complex that ex-ante checklists make only little sense when it comes to their complex security. Thirdly, some IT products or services, when procured and implemented, inevitably bring vendor lock-ins. It might then be quite a matter of security concerns as to by whom is the respective essential service operator locked-in, regardless of security of respective information systems or networks as such.

Subjective certification is, compared to technological certificates, relatively underestimated and underdeveloped in the EU. Moreover, the EU Commission has neither its own coherent security agenda[68] nor institutions, such as intel-

---

[67] See e.g., Balding. C. 'Huawei Technologies' links to Chinese State Security Services' 2019, available at https://ssrn.com/abstract=3415726 together with Urgessa, W. G. 'Multilateral cybersecurity governance: Divergent conceptualizations and its origin' (2020) 36 *Computer Law & Security Review* 5.

[68] See e.g., Odermatt, J., 'The European Union as a cybersecurity actor' in Blockmans, S., Koutrakos, P. *Research Handbook on the EU's Common Foreign and Security Policy,* Eward Elgar Publishing, 2018, p. 360.

ligence or security bodies, to properly implement it. All of that makes it difficult to establish a valid subject-based cybersecurity certification under the Cybersecurity Act.[69] It seems not to be an issue, because the cybersecurity certification will not cover security, law enforcement or military IT applications. However, even the functioning of consumer electronic communications, information society services, or even IT-related financial services like e-banking, etc., might be a matter of imminent concern for public or national security.

IX. CONCLUDING REMARKS

In this chapter, we discussed the case for *ex ante* obligations of financial institutions in cybersecurity. We noted that the situation in the financial sector regarding cybersecurity readiness is relatively better in comparison with other classes of essential services. Financial institutions have also extensive experience with compliance-based regulatory mechanisms which makes it easier for them to process and implement the performance-based regulatory model of the NIS Directive. Relative advancement of financial institutions is also in some respects problematic when it comes to the inclusion of the financial sector into national and European cybersecurity framework. It will certainly take some time and efforts namely to establish trusted relations between financial institutions and cybersecurity bodies and other relevant authorities from outside of the financial sector. We also noted that one of the key features of the EU cybersecurity regulatory framework is the environmental approach and emphasis on performance-based ex-ante preventive obligations. In that respect, we discussed namely certification as a regulatory tool that is designed to tackle actual resilience against cybersecurity incidents as well as certainty of regulated subjects regarding compliance with regulatory requirements.

As the regulatory framework of cybersecurity certification is quite general and flexible, its success will depend, at first, on quality of certification schemes drafted by ENISA and passed by the Commission. Secondly, the way the envisaged institutional backing will be established and namely how efficient the communication between relevant bodies and authorities will be – namely the ENISA, ECCG, SCCG, national cybersecurity certification authorities, accreditation bodies and CABs, will be crucially important. At the level of financial institutions, the success of cybersecurity certification and other compliance tools will mostly depend on the ability of these institutions to align cybersecurity agenda with other compliance schemes such as personal

[69] The developing role of the EU in the agenda of cybersecurity is summarised in Belaz, A. 'The changing role of the EU in cybersecurity' (2019) 2 *Safety and Security Scineces Review* p. 17.

data protection, sectoral regulation regarding information security, AML or compliance with international sanctioning mechanisms. In any case, as repeatedly noted above, the current standing of the financial sector is very good, so there is a good prospect that financial institutions can act as role models for other sectors and can even take initiative in development and deployment of certification schemes and other compliance mechanisms.

12. The European Union and the promotion of values in its external relations – the case of data protection

Julia Schmidt

I. INTRODUCTION

Digitalisation will revolutionise many areas of our lives, bringing with it many innovations with plenty of opportunities for businesses and jobs. At the same time, digitalisation, which depends on the availability and the free flow of accurate data, poses new challenges for the protection of fundamental rights. The EU's approach to Artificial Intelligence (AI) as one of the key developments within digitalisation highlights the EU's ambition to establish itself as a competitive international actor as far as AI technologies and innovations are concerned and that is exploring new potential markets.[1] But apart from economic interests and the desire to prevent third states from creating barriers to the free flow of data across borders and undue digital protectionism, the EU is determined to shape the international framework for the deployment of AI based on a European approach, including a high standard of data protection.[2] The EU has expressed its desire to influence the international debate and to cooperate with others based on EU rules and values.[3] EU political statements such as the Commission's White Paper on Artificial Intelligence, highlight the potential risks of AI for some of the values the EU is founded on, in particular for its fundamental rights.[4] In response to these risks, the European Commission has expressed its conviction that 'international cooperation on

[1] European Commission White Paper, On Artificial Intelligence – A European approach to excellence and trust COM(2020) 65 final [hereinafter *White Paper on AI*] 3–6.

[2] European Commission, 'Building Trust in Human–Centric Artificial Intelligence' (Communication) COM (2019) 168 final [hereinafter *Building Trust in Human-Centric AI*], 2; *White Paper on AI* (n 1) 1, 8, 9.

[3] *White Paper on AI* (n 1) 8.

[4] *White Paper on AI* (n 1) 11.

AI matters must be based on an approach that promotes the respect for fundamental rights, including dignity, pluralism, inclusion, non-discrimination and protection of privacy and personal data and [that] it will strive to export its values across the world'.[5]

With regards to the protection of personal data, the EU already seems to be well-established in its ambition to promote its values and interests to the outside world and has positioned itself as key standard setter.[6] The EU's General Data Protection Regulation (GDPR) which primarily 'lays down rules relating to the protection of natural persons with regard to the processing of personal data and rules relating to the free movement of personal data',[7] based on the protection of fundamental rights and freedoms, most notably the right to the protection of personal data,[8] can be a powerful tool in this regard. The GDPR contains two legal regimes that directly facilitate the global reach of the EU's approach to the protection of personal data. According to its Article 3, which outlines the territorial scope of the GDPR, the GDPR 'applies to the processing of personal data in the context of the activities of an establishment of a controller or a processor in the Union, regardless of whether the processing takes place in the Union or not' and it also extends the EU's legal data protection regime to companies established outside the EU where the processing of data is related to the offering of goods or services to data subjects in the EU or to the monitoring of the behaviour of individuals in the EU.[9] In addition, the GDPR includes a dedicated chapter on the 'Transfers of personal data to third countries or international organisations' based on the notion that the protection of data enjoyed by individuals living in the EU should travel with data.[10]

The latter regime becomes of importance in the context of the EU's trade relationship with third states. The EU-Japan Economic Partnership Agreement (EPA) which entered into force on 1 February 2019 has been complemented by a reciprocal finding by the European Commission and Japan that an adequate level of data protection is ensured in the EU and in Japan on 17 July 2018.[11]

---

5 *Commission White Paper on AI* (n 1) 9 [references omitted from quote].

6 Kuner C, 'The Internet and the Global Reach of EU Law' in M Cremona and J Scott (eds), *EU Law Beyond EU Borders: The Extraterritorial Reach of EU Law* (2019 OUP) 112, 130.

7 Regulation (EU) 2016/679 of the European Parliament and of the Council on the protection of natural persons with regard to the processing of personal data and on the free movement of such data, and repealing Directive 95/46/EC (General Data Protection Regulation) [2016] OJ L119/1 [hereinafter *GDPR*], Article 1(1).

8 Article 1(2) GDPR.

9 Article 3(1), (2) GDPR.

10 GDPR, Chapter V.

11 European Commission, 'Questions & Answers on the Japan Adequacy Decision' (Factsheet) MEMO/18/4503, available at https://ec.europa.eu/commission/presscorner/

This has been celebrated by the EU as the creation of the 'world's largest area of safe data flows', highlighting that 'European companies will benefit from uninhibited flow of data with this key commercial partner, as well as from privileged access to the 127 million Japanese consumers' [..., affirming] that, in the digital era, promoting high privacy standards and facilitating international trade go hand in hand'.[12] In 2019, the Commission formally adopted the Japan Adequacy Decision which provides the basis for the lawful travel of personal data from the EU to Japan.[13]

The chapter will investigate the role of data protection in the EU's external relations and the external reach of the GDPR with a particular focus on the EU's trade relationships. It will be shown that the promotion of data protection is inspired by some of the general drivers that can be found behind the EU's intent to promote its values and interests to the outside world but that the promotion of data protection is also indicative of novel developments as far as the EU's ambition to set and influence international standards and norms are concerned. This ambition influences not only which values the EU promotes in the context of data protection when a choice could be made between values internal or external to the EU, but it also impacts on the procedure and methods the EU has chosen to do so. In contrast to the EU's well-established practice of including human rights clauses in its trade agreements, adequacy decisions as one possible basis for the lawful transfer of data to a third country, appear to constitute a stricter form of conditionality, as the level of data protection required by the EU is moved outside of the sphere of negotiation between the parties to a trade agreement, serving as a non-negotiable benchmark.[14]

The chapter will start by looking at the EU's promotion of 'trustworthy AI' as a policy objective and of the importance of the protection of personal data as a recognised European fundamental right in this regard. This will be followed by a brief assessment of the global reach of the GDPR, before the legal framework for the cross-border transfer of data to third states will be addressed. Particular emphasis will be put on the substantive and procedural questions raised by adequacy decisions in light of recent case law developments and in

---

detail/en/MEMO_18_4503 accessed 06/09/2021 [hereinafter *Q&A Japan Adequacy Decision*], 1.

[12] European Commission, 'The European Union and Japan agreed to create the world's largest area of safe data flows' (Press Release) IP/18/4501.

[13] Commission Implementing Decision (EU) 2019/419 pursuant to Regulation (EU) 2016/679 of the European Parliament and of the Council on the adequate protection of personal data by Japan under the Act on the Protection of Personal Information (Text with EEA relevance) [2019] OJ L 76/1.

[14] Other possible bases for a transfer of data abroad are available if appropriate safeguards have been provided and will be addressed in section IV below.

light of the increasingly important link between cross-border data transfers and international trade agreements. Section V will turn to the unique features of the EU's promotion of the protection of personal data when compared to its traditional approach of promoting its values and interests as part of the missionary principle. The final section of the chapter will address the advantages of the GDPR system for the effective promotion of the EU's high standard of data protection when compared to the EU's traditional approach of including a general human rights conditionality in its trade agreements. Throughout the discussion, the EU's relationship with Japan in the context of trade as well as in the context of data will be put into focus.

II. TRUSTWORTHY AI AND THE IMPORTANCE OF DATA PROTECTION

The EU started to put increased focus on AI in 2017 as part of its commitment to a 'Digital Europe' and its 'Digital Single Market Strategy'.[15] From the beginning, the EU's economic interests in AI but also the potential risks of AI for the values the EU is founded on took central stage in the debate. The European Council invited the European Commission 'to put forward a European approach to artificial intelligence' and also asked it to develop 'the necessary initiatives for strengthening the framework conditions with a view to enable the EU to explore new markets through risk-based radical innovations and to reaffirm the leading role of the industry' but already raised awareness

[15] European Commission, 'Communication from the Commission to the European Parliament, the Council, the European Economic and Social Committee and the Committee of the Regions on the Mid-Term Review on the implementation of the Digital Single Market Strategy: A Connected Digital Single Market for All' (10.5.2017) COM(2017) 228 final, 21-22; European Council, European Council meeting of 19 October 2017, Conclusions (Brussels, 19 October 2017) EUCO 14/17 [hereinafter *European Council Conclusions October 2017*) paras 9–12; European Commission, Communication from the Commission to the European Parliament, the European Council, the Council, the European Economic and Social Committee and the Committee of the Regions, 'Artificial Intelligence for Europe' (Brussels, 25.4.2018) COM (2018) 237 final [hereinafter *Artificial Intelligence for Europe*], 3. A digital single market has been defined as a market 'in which the free movement of goods, persons, services and capital is ensured and where individuals and businesses can seamlessly access and exercise online activities under conditions of fair competition, and a high level of consumer and personal data protection, irrespective of their nationality or place of residence', see European Commission, Communication from the Commission to the European Parliament, the Council, the European Economic and Social Committee and the Committee of the Regions, 'A Digital Single Market Strategy for Europe' COM(2015) 192 final, 3.

for the need to ensure 'a high level of data protection, digital rights and ethical standards'.[16]

The European Commission's Communication on 'Artificial Intelligence for Europe' of April 2018 calls on the EU to ensure that AI is developed and applied in an ethical and legal framework, highlighting the significance of the values the EU is founded on, the Charter of Fundamental Rights of the European Union,[17] as well as the GDPR for the protection of individuals in the EU.[18] The values the EU is founded on include, 'the respect for human dignity, freedom, democracy, equality, the rule of law and respect for human rights'.[19] The Commission's 2020 White paper on AI which in general 'supports a regulatory and investment oriented approach with the twin objectives of promoting the uptake of AI and of addressing the risks associated with certain uses of this new technology' outlines different policy options in order to achieve the mentioned objectives.[20] Importantly, it calls for AI to be 'trust-worthy, ethical and human centric'.[21] All three concepts are interlinked but the Commission regards 'trustworthiness of AI' as central for the creation of a 'human-centric approach to AI'.[22] Trustworthy AI is considered by the Commission to build on the values the EU is founded on, as well as on compliance with the law binding the EU, (in particular EU fundamental rights as well as international human rights law,[23]) the respect for ethical principles, as well as robustness.[24] One of seven identified key re-requirements to create trustworthy AI is data governance and privacy.[25] In order to create trust in the processing of data, the need of individuals to feel in control of their personal data, as well as their need

---

[16] *European Council Conclusions October 2017* (n 15) para 11.

[17] Charter of Fundamental Rights of the European Union [2016] OJ C202/389 [hereinafter *EU Charter*].

[18] *Artificial Intelligence for Europe* (n 15) 2, 13–14.

[19] Consolidated Version of the Treaty on European Union [2016] OJ C 202/1 [hereinafter *TEU*], Article 2 TEU.

[20] *White Paper on AI* (n 1) 1.

[21] *White Paper on AI* (n 1) 21.

[22] *Building Trust in Human-Centric AI* (n 2) 1.

[23] The EU is not a party to most international human rights treaties but it is bound by international human rights as far as they represent customary international law.

[24] *Building Trust in Human-Centric AI* (n 2) 2, 3. The latter three components of a trustworthy AI have been developed by the High-Level Expert Group on AI which has been set up by the Commission. Independent High-Level Expert Group on Artificial Intelligence set up by the European Commission, 'Ethics Guidelines for Trustworthy AI' (8.4. 2019), available at https://ec.europa.eu/digital-single-market/en/news/ethics-guidelines-trustworthy-ai accessed 06/09/2021 [hereinafter *Ethics Guidelines for Trustworthy AI*], 5–7.

[25] The other key requirements include: human agency and oversight; technical robustness and safety; transparency; diversity, non-discrimination and fairness; societal

to be assured that their data will not be used in a way that is harmful to them has been identified.[26]

With the GDPR, the EU already possesses a regulatory framework that not only facilitates the free flow of personal data within the EU but which also provides for a high level of data protection, often promoted by the EU as a basis for trust.[27] Finding the right balance between the free movement of data, an economic interest and the protection of fundamental rights, which represent EU values, is however not always an easy task and has at times been approached differently by the European Commission and the Court of Justice of the European Union (CJEU), as discussed below.

The GDPR reflects the significance the EU has attributed to the protection of personal data and the respect for privacy as recognised and codified fundamental rights enshrined in the EU Charter.[28] The preamble of the latter explicitly acknowledges the need 'to strengthen the protection of fundamental rights in the light of changes in society, social progress and scientific and technological developments by making those rights more visible in the Charter'.[29] As part of the fundamental right codified in Article 7 EU Charter, '[e]veryone has the right to respect for his or her private and family life, home and communications'. According to Article 8(1) EU Charter, '[e]veryone has the right to the protection of personal data concerning him or her'.

In addition, the right to data protection has been included in the TFEU as one of the provisions having general application,[30] and thereby joins other key values the EU seeks to promote in its policies such as non-discrimination,[31] as well as consumer[32] and environmental protection.[33] The recognition by the EU of data protection as a stand-alone fundamental right next to the protection of privacy is worth mentioning, as human rights treaties in general do not contain special provisions on data protection and rather tend to consider the protection

---

and environmental well-being; and accountability. *Building Trust in Human-Centric AI* (n 2) 4-6. See also *Ethics Guidelines for Trustworthy AI*, ibid., 14–20.

[26] *Building Trust in Human-Centric AI*, ibid., 5.

[27] Preamble, recital 7 GDPR.

[28] Articles 7 and 8 EU Charter. See also Article 1(2) GDPR according to which the GDPR 'protects fundamental rights and freedoms [...] and in particular [... the] right to the protection of personal data'.

[29] Preamble, recital 4 EU Charter.

[30] Consolidated Version of the Treaty on the Functioning of the European Union [2016] OJ C 202/1 [hereinafter TFEU], part one, title two; Article 16.

[31] Article 10 TFEU.

[32] Article 12 TFEU.

[33] Article 11 TFEU.

of personal data as forming part of the right to privacy.[34] The case law of the CJEU (formerly ECJ) established that:

> [...] access to a natural person's personal data with a view to its retention or use affects the fundamental right to respect for private life guaranteed in Article 7 of the Charter, which concerns any information relating to an identified or identifiable individual. Such processing of data also falls within the scope of Article 8 of the Charter because it constitutes the processing of personal data within the meaning of that article [...].[35]

For an interference with the right to privacy, '[...] it does not matter whether the information on the private lives concerned is sensitive or whether the persons concerned have been inconvenienced in any way [...]'.[36] In *Opinion 1/15*, the CJEU held that the 'right to the protection of personal data requires, inter alia, that the high level of protection of fundamental rights and freedoms conferred by EU law continues where personal data is transferred from the European Union to a non-member country'.[37]

The protection guaranteed by both fundamental rights enshrined in Articles 7 and 8 EU Charter is not absolute and the right to privacy as well as the right to the protection of personal data have to 'be considered in relation to their function in society'.[38] A limitation of the right to the protection of personal data has to respect the conditions outlined in Article 8(2) EU Charter which requires that 'data must be processed fairly for specified purposes and on the basis of the consent of the person concerned or some other legitimate basis laid down by law', it has to respect the essence and thus cannot jeopardise the core of the right to the protection of personal data and finally, it has to comply with the principle of proportionality.[39]

III. THE GLOBAL REACH OF THE GDPR

With its high standard of data protection, the GDPR has the capacity to generate trust in the protection of personal data as far as processing activities and the free movement of personal data within the EU and across EU Member State

---

[34] H Kranenborg 'Article 8' in S Peers et al (eds), *The EU Charter of Fundamental Rights: A Commentary* (Hart Publishing 2014) paras 08.21, 08.57–08.61.

[35] Case C-311/18 *Data Protection Commissioner v Facebook Ireland Limited and Maximillian Schrems*, ECLI:EU:C:2020:559 [hereinafter *Schrems II*], para 170.

[36] C-293/12 *Digital Rights Ireland and Seitlinger and Others*, ECLI:EU:C:2014:238, para 33.

[37] Opinion 1/15, ECLI:EU:C:2017:592, para 134.

[38] *Schrems II* (n 35) para 172.

[39] Article 52(1) EU Charter.

borders is concerned. On this background, the GDPR is not only considered as 'an important element of ensuring trust in AI' but also as an 'anchor of trust in the single market for data'.[40] The ambition to create a 'single market for data', also referred to as a 'single European data space', which is 'open to data from across the world',[41] is essential for the EU's ambition to become a competitive actor in the sphere of AI. Nevertheless, if the protection of personal data would be limited to the territory of the EU, it would be easy to undermine the EU's strict standard of data protection to the detriment of data subjects in the EU.

The GDPR, which replaced Directive 95/46/EC and entered into force in 2018, has been attributed with a broad territorial scope and applies irrespective of 'whether the processing of [personal] data takes place in the Union or not', as long as the data is processed 'in the context of the activities of an establishment of a controller or a processor in the Union'.[42] In addition, the GDPR extends to controllers and processors not established in the EU, as far as 'the processing of personal data of data subjects who are in the Union' is concerned and where the processing activities are related to either the offering of goods or services to data subjects in the Union; or to 'the monitoring of their behaviour as far as their behaviour takes place within the Union'.[43] Thus, the GDPR has the potential to create a level playing field between companies established in one of the EU Member States and companies established outside of the EU as far as data protection requirements are concerned.[44] This is not only beneficial from a fundamental rights perspective but also in light of economic considerations and for the competitiveness of the EU. A lower level of required

---

40 European Commission, 'Coordinated Plan on Artificial Intelligence' (Communication) COM (2018) 795 final [hereinafter *Coordinated Plan on AI*], 6.

41 European Commission, 'A European Strategy for Data'(Communication) COM (2020) 66 final, 4.

42 Article 3(1) and preamble, recital 22 GDPR. Thereby the GDPR reflects the ECJ's broad interpretation of the territorial scope of the GDPR's predecessor, Directive 95/46/EC of the European Parliament and of the Council on the protection of individuals with regard to the processing of personal data and on the free movement of such data [1995] OJ L 281 /31, in *Google Spain*. Case C 131/12 *Google Spain SL and Google Inc. v Agencia Española de Protección de Datos (AEPD) and Mario Costeja González*, ECLI:EU:C:2014:317, paras 53–56. In 2019, the CJEU clarified the territorial scope of de-referencing requests. See Case C-507/17 *Google LLC, successor in law to Google Inc. v Commission nationale de l'informatique et des libertés (CNIL)*, ECLI:EU:C: 2019:772, paras 51–52, 59–66.

43 Article 3(2) GDPR.

44 M Gömann, 'The New Territorial Scope of EU Data Protection Law: Deconstructing a Revolutionary Achievement' (2017) 54 *Common Market Law Review* 567, 588; European Commission, 'Exchanging and Protecting Personal Data in a Globalised World' (Communication) COM (2017) 7 final [hereinafter *Exchanging and Protecting Personal Data in a Globalised World*], 3.

protection outside of the EU could come at a cheaper cost, thereby granting an economic advantage to foreign companies that are in competition with EU companies.

IV. TRANSFER OF DATA TO THIRD STATES AND THE CONTINUITY OF DATA PROTECTION: THE CASE OF ADEQUACY DECISIONS

If the EU's data protection law would only apply to the situations enumerated in Article 3 GDPR, the data protection offered to individuals in the EU could easily be circumvented. Especially international trade requires the movement of data from and to states that are not Member States of the EU.[45] Like its predecessor, the GDPR responds to this risk with a dedicated chapter on the 'Transfer of personal data to third countries or international organisations'.[46] Thus, the EU's data protection framework which reflects the importance it attributes to the protection of fundamental rights, not only applies to its single market but is also extended to the EU's external trade relationships. The new trade and investment policy proposed by the European Commission in 2015 emphasises in the context of digital trade that '[r]ules on the processing of personal data are not negotiated in, or affected by, trade agreements'.[47] The non-negotiability of data protection in the EU's external trade relations as a policy objective[48] finds its legal foundation in the GDPR and has been adhered to in practice.[49]

When it comes to the lawful transfer of data to third states, a distinction can be drawn between those states that ensure an adequate level of data protection as evidenced by an adequacy decision adopted by the European Commission,[50]

---

[45] See preamble, recital 101 GDPR.

[46] GDPR, Chapter V. See also Article 44 GDPR. On the relationship between Chapter V of the GDPR and Article 3 GDPR, see C Kuner, 'Article 44' in C Kuner (ed), *The EU General Data Protection Regulation (GDPR): A Commentary* (OUP 2020) 755, 758.

[47] European Commission, 'Trade for All: Towards a More Responsible Trade and Investment Policy' (2015), available at https://ec.europa.eu/trade/policy/in-focus/new-trade-strategy/ accessed 06/09/2021 [hereinafter *Trade Strategy*], 12.

[48] *Exchanging and Protecting Personal Data in a Globalised World* (n 44) 6.

[49] For a discussion on cross-border data flows under international trade law which is outside the scope of this chapter, see S Yakovleva and K Irion, 'Pitching Trade against Privacy: Reconciling EU Governance of Personal Data Flows with External Trade' (2020) 10 *International Data Privacy Law* 201–21.

[50] Article 45(1), (3) GDPR.

and non-EU Member States without an adequacy decision.[51] With regard to the latter, the transfer of data is still possible, 'if the controller or processor has provided appropriate safeguards, and on the condition that enforceable data subject rights and effective legal remedies for data subjects are available'.[52] Thus, it is the responsibility of the controller or processor to 'take measures to compensate for the lack of data protection in a third country'.[53] Binding corporate rules and standard data protection clauses adopted by the European Commission qualify as appropriate safeguards, as well as 'standard data protection clauses adopted by a supervisory authority or contractual clauses authorized by a supervisory authority'.[54] As a further option, and in the absence of an adequacy decision or appropriate safeguards, a transfer of data outside the EU may lawfully take place on the basis of derogations for specific situations enumerated in Article 49 GDPR.

According to Christopher Kuner, adequacy decisions provide the highest standard of data protection, as appropriate safeguards based on Article 46 GDPR would need to be designed for specific transfers or types of transfers and therefore could not shield against certain risks which would need to be addressed by the Commission in the context of an adequacy decision assessment, as outlined in Article 45(2) GDPR.[55] Derogations on the basis of Article 49 GDPR are held to provide the lowest standard of protection.[56] In *Schrems II*, delivered in July 2020, the CJEU seems to have narrowed the gap of protection as far as appropriate safeguards are concerned as it held that for '[...] the factors to be taken into consideration in the context of Article 46 of that regulation correspond to those set out, in a non-exhaustive manner, in Article 45(2) of that regulation'.[57]

Adequacy decisions can be adopted by the Commission to attest that a third state provides an adequate level of protection in general but they may also be restricted to a specific territory or to a specific sector within a third state.[58] In the following emphasis will be put on the discussion of adequacy decisions that apply to a third state. In determining with which key trading partners an

---

51 Article 46(1) GDPR. According to preamble, recital 102 GDPR, international agreements may also regulate 'the transfer of personal data including appropriate safeguards for the data subjects'. Nevertheless, Chapter V of the GDPR does not further elaborate on this option. See C Kuner C, 'Article 45' in Kuner (n 46), 771, 777.

52 Article 46(1) GDPR.

53 Preamble, recital 108 GDPR.

54 Articles 46(2), 47 GDPR; preamble, recital 108 GDPR.

55 C Kuner, 'Article 45' (n 51), 774; C Kuner, 'Article 46' in Kuner (n 46), 797, 802.

56 C Kuner, 'Article 45' (n 51) 774; C Kuner, 'Article 49' in Kuner (n 46), 841, 846.

57 *Schrems II* (n 35) para 104. See also para 105.

58 Article 45(1) GDPR; preamble, recital 103 GDPR.

adequacy dialogue should be pursued, the Commission will be guided by the following criteria:

> (i) the extent of the EU's (actual or potential) commercial relations with a given third country, including the existence of a free trade agreement or ongoing negotiations;
> (ii) the extent of personal data flows from the EU, reflecting geographical and/or cultural ties;
> (iii) the pioneering role the third country plays in the field of privacy and data protection that could serve as a model for other countries in its region; and
> (iv) the overall political relationship with the third country in question, in particular with respect to the promotion of common values and shared objectives at international level.[59]

In its adequacy assessment, the Commission needs to be guided by the 'fundamental values the EU is founded on, in particular human rights'.[60] The CJEU has consistently held that Article 45(1) GDPR has to be read in the light of Articles 7, 8 and 47 of the EU Charter.[61] According to Article 45(2) GDPR, the Commission is asked to consider the following elements, with regards to the third state's domestic substantive and procedural legal framework as well as its international commitments:

> (a) the rule of law, respect for human rights and fundamental freedoms, relevant legislation, both general and sectoral, including concerning public security, defence, national security and criminal law and the access of public authorities to personal data, as well as the implementation of such legislation, data protection rules, professional rules and security measures, including rules for the onward transfer of personal data to another third country [...] which are complied with in that country [...], case-law, as well as effective and enforceable data subject rights and effective administrative and judicial redress for the data subjects whose personal data are being transferred;
> (b) the existence and effective functioning of one or more independent supervisory authorities in the third country [...], with responsibility for ensuring and enforcing compliance with the data protection rules, including adequate enforcement powers, for assisting and advising the data subjects in exercising their rights and for cooperation with the supervisory authorities of the Member States; and
> (c) the international commitments the third country [...] has entered into, or other obligations arising from legally binding conventions or instruments as well as from its participation in multilateral or regional systems, in particular in relation to the protection of personal data.

---

59 *Exchanging and Protecting Personal Data in a Globalised World* (n 44) 8.
60 Preamble, recital 104 GDPR.
61 See, e.g., *Schrems II* (n 35) para 198. Article 47 EU Charter contains the right to an effective remedy and to a fair trial.

The Commission can only adopt an adequacy decision if it finds that the legal order of the third state ensures an adequate level of protection. As clarified by the ECJ in *Schrems*:

> [e]ven though the means to which that third country has recourse [...] may differ from those employed within the European Union in order to ensure that the requirements stemming from Directive 95/46 read in the light of the Charter are complied with, those means must nevertheless prove, in practice, effective in order to ensure protection *essentially equivalent* to that guaranteed within the European Union.[62]

Although this clearly indicates that an identical standard of protection is not required, leaving some room for discretion for the Commission, the Court held that:

> [...] in view of, first, the important role played by the protection of personal data in the light of the fundamental right to respect for private life and, secondly, the large number of persons whose fundamental rights are liable to be infringed where personal data is transferred to a third country not ensuring an adequate level of protection, the Commission's discretion as to the adequacy of the level of protection ensured by a third country is reduced, with the result that review of the requirements stemming from Article 25 of Directive 95/46, read in the light of the Charter, should be strict [...].[63]

By analogy, the Court's reasoning can be transferred to today's Article 45 GDPR.

An adequacy decision adopted by the Commission with regards to a third state is legally binding,[64] and in essence has the effect of authorising the transfer of personal data to the third state in general so that no specific authorisations are needed.[65] In light of their importance for guaranteeing a level of protection of personal data which is essentially equivalent to the EU's standard, informed by the intention 'to ensure the continuity of that high level of protection where personal data is transferred to a third country',[66] adequacy decisions need to provide a mechanism for periodic review.[67] The Commission

---

[62] C-362/14 *Maximillian Schrems v Data Protection Commissioner*, ECLI:EU:C:2015:650 [hereinafter *Schrems*], para 74. Emphasis added by the author. Directive 95/46/EC of the European Parliament and of the Council on the protection of individuals with regard to the processing of personal data and on the free movement of such data [1995] OJ L 281 /31. The 'essentially equivalent' requirement also applies to the GDPR. See preamble, recital 104 GDPR; *Schrems II* (n 35) para 94.

[63] Schrems (n 62) para 78.

[64] Article 288(4) TFEU.

[65] *Schrems II* (n 35) para 171, Article 45(1) GDPR.

[66] *Schrems II* (n 35) para 93.

[67] Article 45(3) GDPR.

is under the obligation to continuously monitor developments in the third state which could affect the functioning of an adequacy decision, which in turn feeds into the periodic review.[68] In cases where a third state no longer ensures an adequate level of protection, the Commission shall amend, repeal or suspend the adequacy decision.[69]

The Commission and the CJEU do not always agree on the approach to be taken when weaknesses in the level of protection are revealed and the right balance needs to be found between economic interests and the protection of fundamental rights. Such was the case with regards to Decision 2000/520, the so-called Safe Harbour Decision adopted by the Commission.[70] The Safe Harbour Adequacy Decision did not apply to the US as a third state in general, but rather to organisations established in the US that comply with the 'Safe Harbour Principles' set out in its Annex 1.[71] In 2013, the Commission reported the need to address problems with regards to 'transparency of privacy policies of Safe Harbour members, effective application of Privacy Principles by companies in the US, and effectiveness of the enforcement'.[72] In addition, the Commission voiced concerns about 'the large scale access by intelligence agencies to data transferred to the US by Safe Harbour certified companies [...in light of] the continuity of data protection rights of Europeans when their data in [sic] transferred to the US'.[73] Although the Commission found that these weaknesses would create competitive disadvantages 'for European companies compared to those competing US companies that are operating under the [Safe Harbour] scheme but in practice not applying its principles',[74] as well as 'a negative impact on the fundamental right to data protection of EU citizens',[75] the Commission chose not to revoke the Safe Harbour Decision and instead to strengthen it.[76] In exercising its discretion, the Commission

[68] Article 45(3), (4) GDPR.

[69] Article 45(5) GDPR.

[70] Commission Decision 2000/520/ EC pursuant to Directive 95/46/EC of the European Parliament and of the Council on the adequacy of the protection provided by the safe harbour privacy principles and related frequently asked questions issued by the US Department of Commerce [2000] OJ L 215/7.

[71] Commission Decision 2000/520/ EC, article 1.

[72] European Commission, 'Communication from the Commission to the European Parliament and the Council on the Functioning of the Safe Harbour from the Perspective of EU Citizens and Companies Established in the EU' COM (2013) 847 final [hereinafter *Report on the Functioning of Safe Harbour*], 18.

[73] *Report on the Functioning of the Safe Harbour*, ibid.

[74] European Commission, 'Rebuilding Trust in EU-US Data Flows' (Communication) COM (2013) 846 final [hereinafter *Rebuilding Trust in EU-US Data Flows*], 6.

[75] Ibid., 7.

[76] Ibid.

prioritised economic interests over fundamental rights concerns based on the justification that the revocation of Safe Harbour 'would adversely affect the interests of member companies in the EU and in the US'.[77]

When the Safe Harbour Decision was challenged in *Schrems*, the ECJ found it to be invalid.[78] Before the ruling was delivered, the European Commission had already started to talk with US authorities in order to strengthen the Safe Harbour regime in light of the recommendations included in its 2013 report.[79] Following the ECJ's ruling in *Schrems*, the talks intensified and led to the 'EU-US Privacy Shield'.[80] Although the Privacy Shield adequacy decision passed three annual reviews of the Commission, it was nevertheless declared invalid in *Schrems II*.[81] In particular, the CJEU held that in finding

> [...] that the United States ensures an adequate level of protection for personal data transferred from the Union to organisations in that third country [including intelligence services] under the EU-US Privacy Shield, the Commission disregarded the requirements of Article 45(1) of the GDPR, read in the light of Articles 7, 8 and 47 of the Charter.[82]

The *Schrems* cases demonstrate that the respect for fundamental rights is a condition for the lawfulness of data transfers to third states. In its adequacy assessment, the European Commission is not required to establish a standard of protection in a third state that is identical to the EU standard as a precondition for the lawful transfer of data to a third state, but the standard of protection offered by the latter nevertheless has to be 'essentially equivalent'. The importance the EU legal system has attributed to the protection of personal

---

[77] Ibid.

[78] *Schrems* (n 62) para 106. See also paras 86–98. For a detailed discussion of *Schrems*, see L Azoulai and M van der Sluis, 'Institutionalizing Personal Data Protection in Times of Global Institutional Distrust: *Schrems*: Case C-362/14, *Maximillian Schrems v. Data Protection Commissioner*, joined by *Digital Rights Ireland*, judgment of the Court of Justice (Grand Chamber) of 6 October 2015, EU:C:2015:650' (2016) 53 *Common Market Law Review* 1343–72.

[79] Commission Implementing Decision (EU) 2016/1250 pursuant to Directive 95/46/EC of the European Parliament and of the Council on the adequacy of the protection provided by the EU-U.S. Privacy Shield (Text with EEA relevance) [2016] L 207/1, introduction, recital 12.

[80] Commission Implementing Decision (EU) 2016/1250, introduction, recital 12. For a discussion of the EU-U.S. Privacy Shield, see S Bu-Pasha, 'Cross-border Issues under EU Data Protection Law with Regards to Personal Data Protection' (2017) 26 *Information & Communications Technology Law* 213, 223–27.

[81] European Commission, 'Report from the Commission to the European Parliament and the Council on the Third Annual Review of the Functioning of the EU-U.S. Privacy Shield' COM (2019) 495 final, 1; *Schrems II* (n 35) para 201.

[82] *Schrems II* (n 35) para 198.

data of individuals significantly limits the Commission's discretion. Economic considerations and the importance of international trade with key strategic partners are not supposed to lower the bar. As of February 2021, the European Commission has adopted thirteen adequacy decisions that are currently in force.[83]

V. CROSS-BORDER DATA TRANSFER AND INTERNATIONAL TRADE AGREEMENTS

Data protection will have to be considered in the context of finding agreement on a trade deal but it cannot be part of a trade-off for other preferences between the potential trading partners. It has been reported in December 2016 that a dispute over data created an unforeseen obstacle in the trade negotiations between the EU and Japan,[84] which nevertheless could be overcome and led to the signing of the EPA.

The adoption of the Japan adequacy decision by the Commission became possible once Japan agreed to apply additional safeguards to the data of Europeans with the aim of decreasing the differences between the Japanese and EU systems of data protection.[85] Japan's agreed improvements include the provision of a higher level of protection to the onwards transfer of data of Europeans to another third state, as well as the establishment of a system to handle and to resolve complaints which will be supervised by the Japanese data protection authority, in order to guarantee 'that potential complaints from Europeans as regards access to their data by Japanese law enforcement and national security authorities will be effectively investigated and resolved', for example.[86]

The EPA itself addresses data in its general provisions and provides that '[n]othing [...] shall affect the right of a Party to define or regulate its own levels of protection in pursuit or furtherance of its public policy objectives in areas such as: [...] personal data [...]'.[87] According to the so-called rendez-vous clause, the 'Parties shall reassess within three years of the date

---

83 For an up-to date overview see, European Commission, Adequacy Decisions, available at https://ec.europa.eu/info/law/law-topic/data-protection/international-dimension-data-protection/adequacy-decisions_en accessed 06/09/2021.

84 A Mucci et al, 'Data Fight Emerges as Last Big Hurdle to EU-Japan Trade Deal: Brussels Closes in on its Biggest Trade Agreement' *Politico*, available at https://www.politico.eu/article/eu-japan-trade-deal-caught-up-in-data-flow-row-cecilia-malmstrom/ accessed 6/9/2021.

85 *Q&A Japan Adequacy Decision* (n 11) 1.

86 Ibid., 1.

87 Article 18.1(2)(h) EPA.

of entry into force of this Agreement the need for inclusion of provisions on the free flow of data into this Agreement'.[88] The EPA is accompanied by a Strategic Partnership Agreement (SPA) with which the Parties pursue to 'contribute jointly to the promotion of shared values and principles, in particular democracy, the rule of law, human rights and fundamental freedoms'.[89] According to its Article 39, the 'Parties shall enhance cooperation with a view to ensuring a high level of protection of personal data'.[90] As discussed above, if Japan stopped providing a standard of data protection that is essentially equivalent to the EU standard of protection, the Japan adequacy decision would need to be amended, repealed or suspended based on the regulatory framework provided by the GDPR, irrespective of the specific content and requirements created by the EPA and the SPA which will be further discussed below.

In the context of the ongoing negotiations for a free trade agreement between the EU and Indonesia, the current 'EU proposal for provisions on Cross-border data flows and protection of personal data and privacy', follows a similar pattern as the EU-Japan EPA and provides that:

1. Each Party recognises that the protection of personal data and privacy is a fundamental right and that high standards in this regard contribute to trust in the digital economy and to the development of trade.
2. Each Party may adopt and maintain the safeguards it deems appropriate to ensure the protection of personal data and privacy, including through the adoption and application of rules for the cross-border transfer of personal data. Nothing in this agreement shall affect the protection of personal data and privacy afforded by the Parties' respective safeguards.[91]

The EU's practice corresponds with the Commission's Trade Strategy, according to which the Commission will seek to use free trade agreements 'to set rules for e-commerce and cross border data flows and tackle new forms of digital protectionism, in full compliance with and without prejudice to the EU's data protection and data privacy rules'.[92] The refusal of the EU to lower its standard of data protection in the context of international trade negotiations and in the

---

[88] Article 8.81.

[89] Strategic Partnership Agreement between the European Union and its Member States, of the one part, and Japan, of the other part [2018] OJ L 216/4 [hereinafter *SPA*], Article 1(1)(d).

[90] Article 39 SPA. The protection of personal data is also addressed in the context of counter-terrorism and passenger name records, articles 8(3), 37 SPA.

[91] European Commission, 'Texts proposed by the EU for the Trade deal with Indonesia: Cross-Border Data Flows and Protection of Personal Data and Privacy', available at https://trade.ec.europa.eu/doclib/docs/2018/july/tradoc_157130.pdf accessed 06/09/2021, Article 2(1), (2).

[92] *Trade Strategy* (n 47) 12.

context of the adoption of adequacy decisions addressed to third states, makes the transfer of data to a third state conditional on the state's acceptance of the EU's understanding of data protection as a fundamental right. Thereby the GDPR which has to be read in light of EU fundamental rights, and which sets out the conditions for the lawful transfer of data, is used as a specific vehicle not only to uphold the essence of the EU's fundamental rights linked to the protection of personal data to the benefit of individuals in the EU but also to promote them to the outside world for the benefit of the populations of third states. The latter in particular occurs when a third state incorporates the EU's standard of data protection into its domestic legal system. The GDPR's requirements relating to adequacy decisions addressed to third states and the increasing connection between international trade and data encourages this so-called '*de jure* Brussels effect'.[93]

VI. THE EU AND THE PROMOTION OF VALUES: THE UNIQUE CASE OF DATA PROTECTION

In general, the EU is required by Article 3(5) TEU, to 'uphold and promote its values and interests' in its relations with the wider world and to 'contribute to the protection of its citizens'. The Union is also asked to contribute to free and fair trade, the protection of human rights, and 'the strict observance and the development of international law', amongst other things.[94] The missionary principle is also mirrored in Article 21 TFEU, which requires the Union's external action to 'be guided by the principles which have inspired its own creation, development, and enlargement, and which it seeks to advance in the wider world: democracy, the rule of law, the universality and indivisibility of human rights and fundamental freedoms [...]'.[95]

Is the manner in which the EU upholds and promotes the essence of its understanding of data protection as a fundamental right through the external reach of the GDPR and in particular in the context of the travel of data from the EU to a third state unique when compared with its traditional approach of promoting its values to the outside world? The answer partly depends on the interpretation of the missionary principle itself. The exact impact and signif-

[93] For a discussion of this so-called '*de jure* Brussels effect', see J Scott, 'The Global Reach of EU Law' in M Cremona and J Scott (eds), *EU Law Beyond EU Borders: The Extraterritorial Reach of EU Law* (2019 OUP) 21, 31–35.

[94] Article 3(5) TEU.

[95] Article 21(1) TEU. See also Article 21(2), (3) TEU. On the missionary principle, see M Broberg, 'What is the Direction for the EU's Development Cooperation after Lisbon? A Legal Examination' (2011) 16 *European Foreign Affairs Review* 539, 548–54.

icance of Article 3(5) TEU on its own or read in combination with Article 21 TEU has been debated, and in particular whether those provisions create an obligation and competence for the EU to respect human rights abroad and thus extra-territorially, and if so how far this obligation would extend, potentially going beyond the respect for fundamental rights, also including the protection of individuals from the conduct of other actors as well as the fulfilment of rights.[96] A literal interpretation of Article 3(5) TEU suggests several obligations for the EU. It has to uphold but also to promote its interests and values which include 'respect for human dignity, freedom, democracy, equality, the rule of law and respect for human rights' in its relations with the wider world.[97] In addition, it has to 'contribute to [...] the protection of human rights' which indicates an obligation to act in line with its existing human rights obligations when taking into account the CJEU's reasoning in the *Air Transport* case by analogy.[98]

Thereby Article 3(5) TEU seems to merely reaffirm the EU's existing legal obligations.[99] According to settled case law, the respect for fundamental rights constitutes a condition for the lawfulness of EU acts.[100] The EU Charter which codified much of the EU's *fundamental rights acquis* is addressed to the EU's institutions, bodies, offices and agencies.[101] Thus, whenever the EU acts based on the competences conferred to it and EU law applies, the EU Charter applies and as argued by Moreno-Lax and Costello, this is the case irrespective of where EU action takes place.[102] Although the EU Charter does not explicitly address its territorial scope, this understanding implies an extra-territorial element. The missionary principle requires the EU to pursue its values as well as the objectives and principles mentioned in Article 21 TEU through its external relations. The EU institutions have to take them into account when they are developing their external policy preferences and strategies and also when they

---

96 L Bartels, 'The EU's Human Rights Obligations in Relation to Policies with Extraterritorial Effects' (2014) 25 *European Journal of International Law* 1071, 1073–75; E Cannizzaro, 'The EU's Human Rights Obligations in Relation with Extraterritorial Effects: A Reply to Lorand Bartels' (2014) 25 *European Journal of International Law* 1093, 1099.

97 Article 2 TEU.

98 Case C-366/10, *Air Transport Association of America and Others v Secretary of State for Energy and Climate Change*, ECLI:EU:C:2011:864 para 101.

99 Cannizzaro (n 96) 1095–99.

100 Joined cases C-402/05 P and C-415/05 P *Kadi and Al Barakaat International Foundation v Council and Commission*, ECLI:EU:C:2008:461, para 285.

101 Article 51(1) EU Charter.

102 V Moreno-Lax and C Costello, 'Extraterritorial Application of the EU Charter of Fundamental Rights: From Territoriality to Facticity, the Effectiveness Model' in Peers et al (n 34), para 59.62.

are implementing specific external policy fields, such as the common commercial policy which provides the legal framework for the EU's international trade relations.[103]

The content of the EU's obligation to respect fundamental rights in the context of its trade relationships has been elaborated on by the General Court in *Front Polisario*.[104] In the field of external economic relations, including the decision of whether or not to conclude an international agreement with a third state, the EU institutions in general enjoy broad discretion.[105] The General Court found that the Council is under the obligation, before adopting a Council Decision on the conclusion of an international trade agreement, to examine the agreement's potential impact on the population of the concerned territory and in particular to ensure that the agreement will neither be to the detriment of the affected population nor that it will entail infringements of fundamental rights.[106] The Council's discretion will be violated in case of a manifest error of assessment.[107] The Court's judgment has since been set aside on appeal,[108] but the need for a human rights impact assessment as a procedural human rights obligation has not been explicitly rejected.[109]

With the GDPR's requirements for the lawful transfer of data to a third state, the EU complies with the obligations created by the missionary principle, as far as its value and fundamental right of the protection of personal data is concerned. The essence of the EU's understanding of data protection as found in the EU Charter has been put into concrete form through the GDPR, a piece of secondary legislation. By implementing the GDPR correctly and by making the lawful transfer of data to a third state conditional on an essentially equivalent standard of data protection, the EU continues to protect the rights of individuals, based on the notion that the protection of data will need to travel with data. Through the global reach of the GDPR, which raises interesting questions under international law and in particular with regards to the topic of jurisdic-

[103] Article 21(3) TEU in conjunction with Articles 205, 207(1) TFEU. M Krajewski, 'The Reform of the Common Commercial Policy' in A Biondi (ed), *EU Law after Lisbon* (OUP 2012) 292, 296, 297.

[104] Case T-512/12 *Front Polisario v Council*, ECLI:EU:T:2015:953 [hereinafter *Front Polisario*].

[105] Ibid., paras 164, 223.

[106] Ibid., para 228.

[107] Ibid., paras 223, 225.

[108] Case C-104/16 P *Council v Front Polisario*, ECLI:EU:C:2016:973.

[109] M Cremona, 'Extending the Reach of EU Law: The EU as an International Legal Actor' in M Cremona and J Scott (eds), *EU Law Beyond EU Borders: The Extraterritorial Reach of EU Law* (2019 OUP) 64, 77, 86. C Ryngaert, 'EU Trade Agreements and Human Rights: From Extraterritorial to Territorial Obligations' (2018) 20 *International Community Law Review* 374, 390.

tion, the EU works towards upholding its fundamental rights and promotes the protection of personal data to the outside world also to the benefit of natural persons living outside the territory of the EU. Nevertheless, the protection of populations in third states does not appear to be the EU's primary objective and rather seems to be a side effect of the protection of individuals in the EU. For example, the negotiations between Japan and the EU on trade, leading to the conclusion of the EPA as well as the negotiations on data took place at the same time. It was the legal reform of the Japanese Act on the Protection of Personal Information (APPI) in 2017 which brought the Japanese domestic legal framework for the protection of personal data closer to the EU's standard of data protection, and pathed the way for the Japan Adequacy Decision.[110] The GDPR's strict requirements meant that the EU-Japan EPA has to respect the 'EU *acquis* on data protection' and that data protection could not be traded off.[111]

The Commission's adequacy assessment, driven by the aim to discover whether a third state provides an essentially equivalent standard of data protection already entails a sort of inbuilt human rights impact assessment as a legal requirement. Unlike in *Polisario*, the primary focus is not put on the population of the third state, but rather on the impact the transfer of data to a third state would have on the rights of individuals in the EU. In the context of trade-related initiatives, the EU usually tends to address the impact of a potential trade agreement on the human rights of natural persons in both the EU and the potential partner state as part of its general impact assessment. This practice reflects a political commitment and not a legal requirement.[112] Thus, with its strict data protection conditionality and with its substantive as well

---

[110] Commission Implementing Decision (EU) 2019/419, preamble, recital 11; *Q&A Japan Adequacy Decision* (n 11) 1; R Walters et al, 'Japan' in R Walters et al, *Data Protection Law: A Comparative Analysis of Asia-Pacific and European Approaches* (Springer 2019) 239, 261. On Japan's approach to data privacy and a discussion of the APPI, see F Wang, 'Cooperative Data Privacy: The Japanese Model of Data Privacy and the EU-Japan GDPR Adequacy Agreement' (2020) 33 *Harvard Journal of Law & Technology* 661, 668–91.

[111] European Parliament, EU-Japan Economic Partnership Agreement (Resolution), European Parliament non-legislative resolution of 12 December 2018 on the draft Council decision on the conclusion of the Agreement between the European Union and Japan for an Economic Partnership (07964/2018 – C8-0382/2018 – 2018/0091M(NLE)), P8_TA(2018)0505, para 22.

[112] European Commission, 'Guidelines on the Analysis of Human Rights Impacts in Impact Assessments for Trade-Related Policy Initiatives', available at https://trade.ec.europa.eu/doclib/docs/2015/july/tradoc_153591.pdf accessed 06/09/2021, 2; Cremona (n 109) 72–73. See also European Commission, Commission Staff Working Document, 'Impact Assessment Report on EU-Japan Trade Relations, Accompanying the Document: Recommendation for a Council Decision Authorising the Opening of

as procedural requirements as far as adequacy decisions are concerned, the GDPR system appears well-equipped to contribute to the effective promotion of data protection as one of the EU's values.

VII. ADVANTAGES OF THE GDPR SYSTEM FOR THE EFFECTIVE PROMOTION OF THE PROTECTION OF PERSONAL DATA

Making the transfer of data to a third state conditional on an essentially equivalent standard of protection in the context of adequacy decisions and keeping the GDPR requirements separate from the content of international trade agreements helps to ensure a high level of data protection and seems advantageous when compared to the EU's traditional approach of including a general human rights conditionality in its trade agreements.[113] Since the 1990s the EU has started to make preferential access to its market conditional on the respect for human rights and democracy through the inclusion of reciprocal human rights clauses in its trade agreements.[114] These clauses make the respect for human rights and democratic principles an essential element of the agreement. If the clause has been breached by one party, and in case no specific provisions have been included to determine the consequences of the breach, the other party may terminate the agreement or suspend its operation in whole or in part according to Article 60 Vienna Convention on the Law of Treaties. More recent trade agreements will often not contain a human rights clause themselves but will be linked to a political framework agreement which makes the respect of certain values an essential element of the framework agreement and which will provide a non-execution clause, allowing for the adoption of appropriate measures.[115]

Negotiations on a Free Trade Agreement between the European Union and Japan' SWD (2012) 209 final, 46–47.

[113] The EU Global Strategy expresses the EU's aim to 'use […] trade agreements to underpin sustainable development, human rights protection and rules-based governance', for example. See European Union, 'Shared Vision, Common Action: A Stronger Europe: A Global Strategy for the European Union's Foreign and Security Policy' (June 2016), available at https://eeas.europa.eu/sites/eeas/files/eugs_review_web_0.pdf accessed 06/09/2021, 26–27.

[114] L Bartels, 'Human Rights and Sustainable Development Obligations in EU Free Trade Agreements' (2013) 40 *Legal Issues of Economic Integration* 297, 300.

[115] L Bartels, 'The European Parliament's Role in Relation to Human Rights in Trade and Investment Agreements' (Study requested jointly by the European Parliament's Subcommittee on Human Rights and by the Committee on International Trade) (February 2014) EXPO/B/DROI/2012-09, 12–14.

However, not all potential trading partners to the EU will accept a human rights conditionality that allows for the suspension of the trade agreement if breached. During the negotiations for the SPA, Japan and the EU disagreed on the inclusion of an essential elements clause.[116] According to Article 2(1) of the SPA with Japan,

> [t]he Parties shall continue to uphold the shared values and principles of democracy, the rule of law, human rights and fundamental freedoms which underpin the domestic and international policies of the Parties. In this regard, the Parties reaffirm the respect for the Universal Declaration of Human Rights and the relevant international human rights treaties to which they are parties.

Nevertheless, the EPA does not contain an explicit linkage clause to the SPA and Article 43 SPA only allows for the suspension of the SPA itself, in case of a 'particularly serious and substantial violation of the obligations described in [Article 2(1) …], which respectively constitutes an essential element of the basis of the cooperation under this Agreement, with its gravity and nature being of an exceptional sort that threatens peace and security and has international repercussion'.[117] '[O]ther appropriate measures outside the framework of this Agreement' may be taken to enforce this rather weak human rights clause but this does not seem to include the suspension of the EPA, as Article 43(8) SPA provides that the SPA 'shall not affect or prejudice the interpretation or application of other agreements between the Parties'.[118]

Other advantages of the GDPR system besides its strict conditionality is the requirement of a periodic review of the adequacy decision at least every four years,[119] the monitoring of developments in the third state on an ongoing

---

[116] E D'Ambrogio, 'The EU-Japan Strategic Partnership Agreement (SPA): A Framework to Promote Shared Values' (January 2019) European Parliamentary Research Service PE 630.323, 4.

[117] Article 43(4), (6) SPA.

[118] See also Y Nakanishi, 'Significance of the Strategic Partnership Agreement between the European Union and Japan in International Order' (April 2020) 3, available at https://blogdroiteuropeen.com/2020/05/07/the-significance-of-the-strategic-partnership-agreement-between-the-eu-and-japan-in-international-order-yumiko-nakanishi/ accessed 06/09/2021. The SPA between the EU and Canada on the other hand explicitly allows for the termination of CETA (EU-Canada Comprehensive Economic and Trade Agreement). Strategic Partnership Agreement between the European Union and its Member States, of the one part, and Canada, of the other part [2016] OJ L 329/45, Article 28(6), (7). Canada, too, had struggled to accept the human rights clause. See K Meisner and L McKenzie, 'The Paradox of Human Rights Conditionality in EU Trade Policy: When Strategic Interests Drive Policy Outcomes' (2019) 26 *Journal of European Public Policy* 1273, 1282. On the general reach of non-execution clauses, see Bartels (n 114) 303.

[119] Article 45(3) GDPR.

basis,[120] and a uniform framework of enforcement which all help to ensure that an adequate level of data protection is upheld by the third state.[121] Unlike the EU's human rights clauses which differ in their conditions and strength, the GDPR requires the Commission to repeal, amend or suspend the adequacy decision in case the third state no longer ensures an adequate level of protection. As discussed above, the discretion of the Commission is limited and the interpretation and validity of adequacy decisions can be challenged in the context of a preliminary reference procedure in front of the CJEU.[122] Free trade agreements that include a human rights clause on the other hand tend not to set up specific organs tasked with the monitoring of their implementation, although arising issues can be discussed by some of the organs that have been set up by the respective agreement.[123] As discussed by Lorand Bartels, the extent to which the interpretation and application of human rights clauses are subject to dispute settlement under the respective trade agreement may differ greatly.[124] In practice, the rather selective enforcement of the EU's human rights clauses, a form of sanctioning of the trading partner, has generated wide-spread criticism.[125]

The GDPR approach also differs from the EU's general approach of promoting human rights through its trade agreements as far as the question of which values are being promoted is concerned. Although individual human rights clauses might differ, the standard essential elements clause in bilateral trade agreements tends to refer to the standard laid down in the Universal Declaration of Human Rights',[126] and thus to international standards of human rights that are widely accepted as rules of customary international law and which are also binding on the EU.[127] With the GDPR, the EU on the other hand

---

[120] Article 45(4) GDPR.

[121] Articles 45(5), 93(2) GDPR.

[122] Article 267 TFEU. *Schrems II* (n 35) paras 118–120. Article 77 GDPR provides the right for data subjects to lodge a complaint with a supervisory authority.

[123] Bartels (n 114) 301.

[124] Ibid., 304.

[125] L Beke et al, 'The Integration of Human Rights in EU Development and Trade Policies' (2014) Fostering Human Rights among European Policies (FRAME), available at http://www.fp7-frame.eu/reports/ accessed 06/09/2021, 68–9.

[126] Bartels (n 115) 8; see also Annex 2 for a comparison of different human rights clauses. Article 12 of the Universal Declaration of Human Rights addresses the right to privacy.

[127] In the context of the EU's Generalised System of Preferences, GSP+ states have to ratify and implement the core international human rights treaties, for example. Regulation (EU) No 978/2012 of the European Parliament and of the Council applying a scheme of generalised tariff preferences and repealing Council Regulation (EC) No 732/2008 [2012] OJ L303/1, Article 9, 15 and Annex VIII, Part A on Core human and labour rights UN/ILO Conventions.

promotes its unique understanding and standard of the protection of personal data as a fundamental right.[128] Thereby the EU signals its confidence and ambition with the GDPR to be a global standard setter as far as the protection of personal data is concerned.

In its goal to promote a high standard of data protection, and to shape the debate, the EU cooperates with others and engages in a dialogue with its international partners, including the UN, regional organisations such as APEC, and the G20 forum.[129] The EU's international cooperation for the protection of personal data is not merely a political objective but underpinned by Article 50 GDPR which requires the EU to take appropriate steps in this regard. Recently, the EU Commission participated in the negotiations for the modernised Council of Europe Convention 108 + in order to avoid inconsistencies with the EU's legal data protection regime.[130] Overall, the GDPR provides a solid legal framework for the promotion of the EU's standard of the protection of personal data, reflecting the significance the EU has attributed to the protection of data as a fundamental right.

VIII. CONCLUSION

In its relation with third states, the EU aims to ensure that the level of data protection individuals enjoy in the EU is not undermined when data moves outside of the Union. Adequacy decisions that attest that a third state provides a comparable standard of data protection and which in consequence enables the lawful transfer of data from the EU to the third state without the need for specific authorisation, are a vehicle for the EU to promote its own approach to data protection. The dialogue between the EU and a potential trading partner on data can be pursued alongside the EU's trade negotiations and the EU-Japan relationship leading to the conclusion of the EU-Japan EPA and the first reciprocal finding of an adequate standard of data protection between both parties is a key example in this regard. Nevertheless, the legal framework provided by the GDPR ensures that the protection of data cannot be traded off during the

---

[128] International human rights instruments, including the Universal Declaration of Human Rights influenced the development of the EU's fundamental rights and the EU Charter. See A Rosas, 'The Charter and Universal Human Rights Instruments' in S Peers et al (n 34), paras 60.01–60.20, 60.39–60.41, 60.46, 60.51–60.54; Kranenbourg (n 34) paras 08.57–08.61.

[129] *Exchanging and Protecting Personal Data in a Globalised World* (n 44).

[130] Council Decision (EU) 2019/682 authorising Member States to ratify, in the interest of the European Union, the Protocol amending the Council of Europe Convention for the Protection of Individuals with regard to Automatic Processing of Personal Data [2019] OJ L 115/7, preamble, recital 1. Kranenborg (n 34) para 08.64.

trade negotiations themselves, creating a strict conditionality requirement as far as the protection of personal data is concerned. This might create an obstacle for the conclusion of future trade agreements with specific third states that are not prepared to adapt to the essence of the EU's protection of personal data but it visualises the importance the EU has attributed to the protection of personal data as one of its fundamental values. With the global reach of the GDPR and in particular with its provisions on the transfer of data to third states, the EU complies with the requirements of the missionary principle. In contrast to the EU's approach of promoting its values and interests in its external trade relationships through the inclusion of general human rights clauses in its free trade agreements which tend to refer to international human rights instruments or by linking trade agreements to political framework agreements that contain such human rights clauses, the EU directly promotes its internal approach to data protection as a European fundamental right and thus its *data protection acquis*. With the GDPR, the EU fulfilled its aim of establishing 'a new global standard' of data protection for the benefit of individuals, based on European values and which can serve as a cornerstone for creating trust in AI.[131]

[131] *Coordinated Plan on AI* (n 40) 6.

13. The digital transformation of the global green bonds market: New-fashioned international standards for a new generation of financial instruments

Georgios Pavlidis

I. INTRODUCTION

Over the last ten years, there has been a clear trend in financial markets favouring environmental, social, and governance (ESG) investing. The trend was first manifest in equity markets but soon spread to other asset classes, especially fixed income instruments.[1] International bond markets have a market capitalisation of USD 128.3tn,[2] consisting of corporate bonds (USD 40.9tn) and SSA bonds, namely, supranational, sovereign, sub-sovereign, and agency bonds (USD 87.5tn). Bond markets currently attract more investments than equity securities listed on stock exchanges, especially from institutional investors. As the COVID-19 pandemic hit the global economy, ESG considerations were side-lined, at least in the initial stages of the crisis. The objectives of sustainable development, protection of the environment, and climate change mitigation are usually the first to be put on hold in times of crisis.[3] Nevertheless, the global market for sustainable debt has made an impressive comeback reaching

---

[1] Georg Inderst and Fiona Stewart, *Incorporating Environmental, Social and Governance (ESG) Factors into Fixed Income Investment* (World Bank 2018).

[2] According to the estimates of the International Capital Markets Association (ICMA), based on Bloomberg Data, this consists of $87.5 trillion in SSA bonds (Sovereigns, Supranational and Agencies) and $40.9 trillion in corporate bonds. See: https://www.icmagroup.org/Regulatory-Policy-and-Market-Practice/Secondary-Markets/bond-market-size/ accessed 16 July 2021.

[3] Charlotte Burns, Peter Eckersley and Paul Tobin, 'EU environmental policy in times of crisis' (2020) 27(1) Journal of European Public Policy 1. See also: Yves Steinebach and Christoph Knill, 'Still an entrepreneur? the changing role of the

a record USD 732bn in 2020. This was due to the design of post-pandemic economic recovery plans, all of which favour sustainable growth and resort to the issuance of sustainable bonds.[4] The European Union (EU), with its ambitious Recovery Plan for Europe and the EU Green Deal,[5] is a prime example of this process, which can reshape the European economic and financial landscape. In this context, the issuance of green bonds, namely, fixed-income debt instruments earmarked to finance green projects, is expected to increase exponentially in the following years. The challenge will be to build a credible, efficient, and transparent green bond market to drive the global green transition.

Standardisation and digitalisation can increase the credibility, efficiency, and transparency in the green bond markets, from issuance and initial distribution of bonds to reporting. Regarding the latter, the credibility of sustainable and green finance is greatly dependent on the quality of data, not only financial but mainly extra-financial, such as data on the 'sustainable performance' and 'green performance' of a project. International and regional standards stress the need for such meaningful and material data;[6] nevertheless, the variety of green initiatives is steadily increasing and now includes projects in renewable energy, energy efficiency, climate adaptation, payments for ecosystem services, and biodiversity offsetting, which will bring a corresponding increase in the volume and complexity of data to be reported.

To deal with this new complexity, sound rules and standards must be developed to ensure transparency and a level playing field.[7] Moreover, digitalisation

---

European Commission in EU environmental policymaking' (2017) 24(3) *Journal of European Public Policy* 246.

[4] Bloomberg, 'Social bonds propel ESG issuance to record $732 Billion in 2020' (*Bloomberg Green*, 11 January 2021) https://www.bloomberg.com/news/articles/2021-01-11/social-bonds-propel-esg-issuance-to-record-732-billion-in-2020 accessed 16 July 2021; *Financial Times*, 'Green bonds will be war bonds for the post-Covid generation' (FT Adviser, 17 March 2021) https://www.ftadviser.com/opinion/2021/03/17/green-bonds-will-be-war-bonds-for-the-post-covid-generation/ accessed 16 July 2021.

[5] In summer 2020, the European Council adopted the EU recovery plan and multiannual financial framework (MFF) for 2021-2027, with the objective to 'ensure that the next MFF as a whole contributes to the implementation of the Paris Agreement'; see Conclusions of the Special meeting of the European Council (17–21 July 2020) 14. The EU intends to borrow €750 bn under NextGenerationEU, 30 per cent of which will be raised through green bonds.

[6] UNEP Finance /United Nations Global Compact, 'Driving meaningful data: financial materiality, sustainability performance and sustainability outcomes' (September 2020) 3.

[7] Alan Morrison and Lucy White, 'Level playing fields in international financial regulation' (2009) 64(3) *The Journal of Finance* 1099; Fernando Restoy, 'Fintech regulation: How to achieve a level playing field' (Bank for International Settlements, Financial Stability Institute 2021) 9.

needs to be mobilised to further increase transparency and efficiency. For example, in the field of extra-financial reporting for green bonds, digitalisation can facilitate and accelerate the compilation, analysis, and reporting of 'green performance' data from multiple green projects. Data collected through sensors and the internet of things (IoT) could thus be analysed by artificial intelligence (AI) algorithms, recorded on the blockchain, and ultimately delivered to the markets promptly, accurately, and with minimum cost. Thus, we argue that the issuers and the investors can reap similar benefits from digital innovation in the entire lifecycle of a green bond, a potential that will sway the markets into embracing such innovation and implement it at scale.

II. THE MARKET FOR GREEN BONDS

Green bonds are increasingly popular debt instruments, which may be issued by financial or non-financial private entities, alongside public entities (supranational, sovereign, sub-sovereign, and agency issuers).[8] The feature that distinguishes green bonds from other fixed-income instruments is the 'green' character, namely, that they are asset-linked and earmarked to finance environmentally friendly projects.[9] Green bonds are used to finance an increasingly wider range of sustainable and transition investments, whilst new types of instruments have emerged that deviate from the use-of-proceeds model. For example, KPI-linked bonds (key performance indicators) or SDG-linked bonds (Sustainable Development Goals) do not finance a specific green project, but their financial characteristics depend on the issuer's progress towards sustainability targets that are monitored and externally verified.[10]

Issuance in green bond markets was growing steadily in the years preceding the COVID-19 crisis, as part of a general trend favouring ESG investing. In 2019, 500 private and public issuers opted for the issuance of green bonds

---

[8] Heike Reichelt and Colleen Keenan, 'The Green Bond Market: 10 years later and looking ahead' in World Bank, *Green Bonds* (World Bank 2017) 1; World Bank, *What are Green Bonds?* (World Bank, Public-Private Infrastructure Advisory Facility 2015) 7.

[9] Annica Cochu and others, 'Study on the potential of green bond finance for resource-efficient investments' (Study prepared for the European Commission 2016) 22. For a different security design, see: Dion Bongaerts and Dirk Schoenmaker, 'Green certificates: a better version of green bonds' (Bruegel Policy Contribution 2020)

[10] International Capital Markets Association, 'Sustainability-Linked Bond Principles: Voluntary Process Guidelines' (ICMA 2020); PIMCO, 'Best Practice Guidance for Sustainable Bond Issuance' (PIMCO 2020); Dhara Ranasinghe, 'Sustainability-linked bond market to swell up to $150 billion', *Reuters* (22 March 2021).

globally, launching 1800 financial deals totalling USD 259bn.[11] The trend was manifest both in developed and emerging markets, with the latter entering the game and attracting USD 52bn in new issuances, which represented a substantial increase of 21 per cent compared to 2018.[12] As a result, optimism was prevalent, ESG investing was projected to rise further, and most analysts were expecting 2020 to be a record year for green bonds.

The COVID-19 crisis, which erupted in early 2020, has been a breaking point. It negatively affected market conditions, dampened investment prospects in the short-term whilst creating long-term uncertainty.[13] Unsurprisingly, this has affected the issuance of green bonds globally, which has dropped to half of the previous year's levels. However, the initial shock did not have a universal affect; developed markets were hit less hard than emerging markets, and SSA issuers were better off than private issuers.[14] As the crisis unfolded and sluggishly became more manageable, markets began turning their interest to the post-COVID economic recovery. In this context, green bonds are expected to be a preferred option for long-term investing by responsible investors.[15] For their part, corporate and SSA issuers are expected to resort to green bond issuance to finance sustainable projects, foster their ESG resilience, and position themselves better for the global transition towards a greener economy. Supported by these factors and as the world economy kick-starts, the issuance of green bonds has already started to recuperate.[16]

---

[11] Climate Bonds Initiative, 'Green Bonds Global State of the Market 2019' (CBI 2019).

[12] International Finance Corporation, 'Emerging Market Green Bonds Report 2019: Momentum builds as nascent markets grow' (World Bank/IFC 2020) 5.

[13] Organization for Economic Co-operation and Development, 'Global financial markets policy responses to COVID-19' (OECD 2020) 4; International Capital Markets Association, 'COVID-19: The Impact on Capital Markets and the Response' (ICMA Quarterly Report No 57 2020) 4.

[14] Climate Bonds Initiative, 'Global State of the Market for 2020, Interim Report' (CBI 2020) 4.

[15] There is no clear consensus on the green bond pricing and existence of green bond premiums; Stefen MacAskill and others, 'Is there a green premium in the green bond market? Systematic literature review revealing premium determinants' (2021) 280 *Journal of Cleaner Production*; see also the 2016–20 report on 'Green Bond Pricing in Primary Market' by the Climate Bonds Initiative.

[16] Ben Caldecott, 'Defining transition finance and embedding it in the post-Covid-19 recovery' (2021) *Journal of Sustainable Finance & Investment* [Latest Articles] DOI: 10.1080/20430795.2020.1813478; Lukasz Krebel and others, 'Building a green stimulus for Covid-19: A recovery plan for a greener, fairer future' (New Economics Foundation 2020) 25; Genevieve Pons and others, 'Greener after: A green recovery for a post-COVID-19 world' (2020) 40(1) *SAIS Review of International Affairs* 69.

Digitalisation and standardisation have the potential to accelerate this process in the post-COVID era, as they significantly enhance transparency and verifiability in the green bond markets. Sustainable development,[17] as embodied in the UN SDGs and the UN Agenda 2030,[18] presupposes transparency and verifiability of information. ESG responsible businesses already employ sustainability indicators and integrate them into their business processes and extra-financial reporting cycles;[19] they do so not only to comply with climate change regulations but also to attract responsible investors who increasingly favour sustainable projects and invest their funds accordingly. Digitalisation can increase the reliability of sustainability reporting. Nevertheless, we argue that digitalisation alone cannot deal with factors such as the multicity, complexity, and lack of comparability of ESG standards and objectives, which can only be addressed through the standardisation of the ESG indicators and the methodology for impact reporting.[20] The combination of digitalisation and standardisation can enhance the credibility, transparency, and efficiency of ESG investing, particularly the issuance of green bonds.[21]

---

[17] Aarti Gupta, Ingrid Boas and Peter Oosterveer, 'Transparency in global sustainability governance: to what effect?' (2020) 22:1 *Journal of Environmental Policy & Planning* 84; Aarti Gupta and Michael Mason (eds.), *Transparency in global environmental governance: Critical perspectives* (MIT Press 2014); Michael Mason, 'Transparency for whom? Information disclosure and power in global environmental governance' (2008) 8(2) *Global Environmental Politics* 8, etc.

[18] See United Nations, 'Transforming our World: The 2030 Agenda for Sustainable Development' (UN 2015); United Nations Development Programme, 'Sustainable Development Goals' (UNDP Booklet 2015). See also European Commission, 'EU Delivering on the UN 2030 Agenda' (EU Factsheet 2019).

[19] Global Reporting Initiative, UN Global Compact, 'Business Reporting on the Sustainable Development Goals: An Analysis of the Goals and Targets' (February 2019); Carol Adams and others, 'Sustainable Development Goal Disclosure Recommendations' (ACCA, Chartered Accountants ANZ, ICAS, IFAC, IIRC and WBA 2020) 6.

[20] KPMG, 'The Time Has Come: KPMG Survey of Sustainability Reporting 2020' (KPMG 2020) 56 https://home.kpmg/lu/en/home/insights/2020/11/the-time-has-come-survey-of-sustainability-reporting.html accessed 16 July 2021; Ian Mackintosh, 'Why Corporate reporting standards are starting to converge' (EY Reporting 2019) https://www.ey.com/en_gl/assurance/why-corporate-reporting-standards-are-starting-to-converge accessed 16 July 2021.

[21] International Financial Reporting Standards Foundation, 'IFRS Consultation Paper on Sustainability Reporting' (IFRS 2020); Patrick de Cambourg, 'Ensuring the relevance and reliability of non-financial corporate information: an ambition and a competitive advantage for a sustainable Europe' (Report submitted to the French Minister for the Economy and Finance, May 2019).

III. STANDARDISATION AS A PREREQUISITE FOR DIGITALISATION OF GREEN BONDS

In 2007–08, two major supranational issuers, the European Investment Bank (EIB) and the World Bank, paved the path for developing a flourishing new market with their flagship issuances of labelled green bonds.[22] The growth of the green bond market went hand in hand with standardisation initiatives. First introduced in 2014 and updated in 2018, ICMA's Green Bond Principles have been the text of reference in this domain.[23] More recently, the EU has developed its own Green Bond Standard,[24] which goes further than the ICMA Principles, further harmonises standards, and employs the EU classification system for sustainable activities (EU taxonomy).[25]

To illustrate the interplay between digitalisation and standardisation, we examine one of the key components of green bond issuances, extra-financial reporting.[26] In the form of impact reports, extra-financial reporting is not something new in sustainable finance, and it is safe to say that issuers and investors

---

22 World Bank, 'Green Bond Impact Report: 10 Years of Green Bonds' (World Bank 2018); European Investment Bank, 'Achievement of the First Green Bond: An Innovative Milestone in Financial Markets' (EIB Climate Awareness Bonds Newsletter 2017) https://www.eib.org/en/investor_relations/documents/eib-cab-10-years-newsletter.htm accessed 16 July 2021.

23 International Capital Markets Association, 'Green Bond Principles: Voluntary Process Guidelines for Issuing Green Bonds' (ICMA 2018); Georgios Pavlidis, 'International standardisation and digitalisation of green bonds: The case of extra-financial reporting' (2021) *Revue internationale des services financiers / International Journal for Financial Services* (forthcoming).

24 EU Technical Expert Group on Sustainable Finance, 'TEG report on EU green bond standard' (June 2019); Georgios Pavlidis, 'Une nouvelle norme européenne sur les obligations vertes : l'importance de garder l'élan' [2020] 4 Revue Internationale des Services Financiers 11.

25 Regulation (EU) 2020/852 of the European Parliament and of the Council of 18 June 2020 on the establishment of a framework to facilitate sustainable investment, and amending Regulation (EU) 2019/2088 [2020] OJ L 198/13. See also the SDG Finance Taxonomy that was adopted by the United Nations Development Programme (UNDP) in 2020; UNDP China, 'Technical Report on SDG Finance Taxonomy' (UNDP 2020); Christoph Nedopil Wang and others, 'Addressing the missing linkage in sustainable finance: the SDG Finance Taxonomy' (2021) *Journal of Sustainable Finance & Investment* [Latest Articles] https://doi.org/10.1080/20430795.2020.1796101

26 KPMG International, 'Sustainable Insight: Gearing Up for Green Bonds' (KPMG Global Center of Excellence for Climate Change and Sustainability 2015); Aaron Maltais and Bjorn Nykvist, 'Understanding the role of green bonds in advancing sustainability' (2020) *Journal of Sustainable Finance & Investment* DOI: 10.1080/20430795.2020.1724864.

are familiar with the concept.[27] However, as the market for green bonds grows, stakeholders demand high-quality green reporting and, more generally, sustainability reporting. In turn, enhancing the quality, transparency, and comparability in reporting strengthens the credibility of the green bond markets, ostracises deceiving issuers, and ultimately attracts more ESG responsible investors. This is particularly true with large institutional investors, which have been integrating ESG factors into their investment portfolios and rely on verifiable disclosures of ESG risks for making informed decisions.[28] Indeed, the commitment of the issuers to mitigating ESG risks and offering quality reporting to investors may be dictated not only by the prospect of future benefits, such as efficiency gains, green tax credits, image, and reputation gains but also by pure regulatory pressure.[29]

In this equation, the quality of extra-financial reporting will be a determinant factor for the credibility of the green bonds market. Nevertheless, before exploring digitalisation in extra-financial reporting, one has first to define the concept of materiality.[30] Indeed, before digitising green performance data, one must determine which will be the objectives of the reporting, which data

---

[27] See International Finance Corporation, 'Green Bond Impact Report Financial Year 2020' (IFC/ World Bank 2020), which was published on the 10th anniversary of IFC's Green Bonds Program; Ans Kolk, 'A decade of sustainability reporting: developments and significance' (2004) 3(1) *International Journal of Environment and Sustainable Development* 51; Christiano Busco and Elena Sofra, 'The evolution of sustainability reporting: Integrated reporting and sustainable development challenges' in Paolo Taticchi and Melissa Demartini (eds.), *Corporate Sustainability in Practice* (Springer 2021) 191.

[28] For example, the top 50 asset managers in the world, managing over USD 60tn in assets, have signed onto the UN voluntary sustainability code (United Nations Principles for Responsible Investment) and taken steps to implement it though ESG reporting; see Alicia McElhaney, 'How the world's largest asset managers are finally taking ESG seriously' *Institutional Investor* (1 March 2021).

[29] Daniel Kinderman, 'Time for a reality check: Is business willing to support a smart mix of complementary regulation in private governance' (2016) 35 *Policy and Society* 29; Emanuele Campiglio and others, 'Climate change challenges for central banks and financial regulators' (2018) 8(6) *Nature Climate Change* 462.

[30] On materiality in sustainability reporting, see: Daniel Reimsbach and others, 'In the eyes of the beholder: Experimental evidence on the contested nature of materiality in sustainability reporting' (2020) 33(4) *Organization and Environment* 624; Robert Eccles, Michael Krzus and Sydney Ribot, *The Integrated Reporting Movement: Meaning, Momentum, Motives, and Materiality* (Wiley 2014) 135; Riccardo Torelli and others, 'The materiality assessment and stakeholder engagement: A content analysis of sustainability reports' (2020) 27:2 *Corporate Social Responsibility and Environmental Management* 470; Felix Beske and others, 'Materiality analysis in sustainability and integrated reports' (2020) 11:1 *Sustainability Accounting, Management and Policy Journal* 162.

are necessary to achieve such objectives, and who the prime audience and stakeholders will be. The 'impact' of a green project cannot be measured without first deciding on the appropriate metrics, such as for carbon emissions/footprints or water use. A 'one size fits all' approach simply would not do,[31] therefore, digitalisation presupposes the development and broad use of standardised metrics for every sector of economic activity. Several organisations, such as the Global Impact Investing Network (GIIN),[32] have proposed their ESG metrics.[33] Nevertheless, we are currently faced with a proliferation of metrics and reporting standards, which often overlap. Moreover, there are 'differences in the way the organisations approach materiality, with several organisations focusing on the impact of risks on a company and other organisations focusing on a company's impact on the environment'.[34] Manifestly, the success of future digitalisation initiatives greatly depends on the development of a commonly agreed definition of materiality, accompanied by standardised impact metrics.

Furthermore, digitalisation of extra-financial reporting in green bonds cannot work without a reliable independent verification system by a third party. Responsible investors cannot rely only on the issuer's affirmations or reputation, but their investment decisions must rely on reliable third-party verifications. This is crucial for reducing information asymmetries in the markets and discarding 'green-washing' practices, namely, issuers attempting to mislead investors by misrepresenting a project as environmentally sound.[35] Two major standardisation initiatives, ICMA's Green Bond Principles and the EU's Green Bond Standard, recognise the key role of independent external verification. In practical terms, the issuer must commission an independent third party to review the issuance of the green bond, including the green

---

[31] Charles Vörösmarty and others, 'Scientifically assess impacts of sustainable investments' (2018) 359:6375 *Science* 523; Chiara Mio, Marco Fasan and Antonio Costantini, 'Materiality in integrated and sustainability reporting: A paradigm shift?' (2020) 29:1 *Business Strategy and the Environment* 306.

[32] Global Impact Investing Network, 'Understanding Impact Performance' (GIIN 2020).

[33] Georg Inderst and Fiona Stewart, *Incorporating Environmental, Social and Governance (ESG) Factors into Fixed Income Investment* (World Bank 2018) 7.

[34] IFRS (n 21) 6; Armando Calabrese and others, 'Materiality analysis in sustainability reporting: A method for making it work in practice' (2017) 6(3) *European Journal of Sustainable Development* 439.

[35] Maria Jua Bachelet and others, 'The green bonds premium puzzle: The role of issuer characteristics and third-party verification' (2019) 11(4) *Sustainability* 1; Addisu Lashitew, 'Corporate uptake of the sustainable development goals: Mere greenwashing or an advent of institutional change?' (2021) *Journal of International Business Policy* 184.

project's ESG impact. The aim of the review in the pre-issuance phase is to assure alignment of the issuance with a given set of standards, such as the ICMA's Principles, which can lead to a rating or certification.[36] The aim of the review in the post-issuance phase is to assure allocation of proceeds to eligible projects (reports on the use of proceeds) and to report the actual impact of the green project (impact reports), which also may lead to the verification of a certification.[37]

Standardisation, combined with digitalisation, can also help address another challenge, the labour intensiveness of extra-financial reporting.[38] It has already been mentioned that such reporting in green bonds requires the collection and analysis of voluminous and complex data on environmental impacts. Moreover, reporting is not one-off or sporadic under current market practices, but it takes place periodically throughout the life cycle of the green project, usually annually.[39] The workload and costs of reporting are also increased by national regulations imposing enhanced reporting requirements. This may, in turn, reduce the appeal of green bonds for issuers unless new approaches, such as digitalisation, kick in and manage to alleviate these constraints.

To conclude, there is a need to harmonise the rules and standards on green bonds, especially regarding materiality and disclosure requirements. This step is essential before moving forth with digitalisation and scaling up fully digitalised green bonds. The EU has recognised this need and made significant progress in putting together its taxonomy for sustainable activities,[40] an EU Green Bonds Standard, alongside other legislative initiatives.[41] Other international

---

[36] Among several ratings and certifications, we can mention the Moody's Green Bond Rating, the S&P's Green Evaluation, and the Climate Bonds Certification.

[37] Reports on the use of proceeds are more widely used than reports on environmental impact. In 2019, one in two green bond issuers provided both types of reports, which was particularly true in the context of larger deals ($500 million or more); Climate Bonds Initiative, 'Post-Issuance Reporting in the Green Bond Market' (CBI 2019) 2.

[38] EU Technical Expert Group on Sustainable Finance, 'TEG report on EU green bond standard' (June 2019) 22.

[39] Deloitte, 'Thinking Allowed: The future of corporate reporting' (Deloitte 2016) 8 https://www2.deloitte.com/content/dam/Deloitte/ch/Documents/audit/ch-en-audit-thinking-allowed-future-corporate-reporting.pdf accessed 16 July 2021.

[40] Regulation (EU) 2020/852 of the European Parliament and of the Council of 18 June 2020 on the establishment of a framework to facilitate sustainable investment, and amending Regulation (EU) 2019/2088 [2020] OJ L 198/13.

[41] See e.g., the revision of the Non-Financial Reporting Directive and the enhancement of non-financial reporting standards; European Financial Reporting Advisory Group, 'Progress report published for project on preparatory work for the elaboration of possible EU non-financial reporting standards' (EFRAG 2020); see also: John Quinn and Barry Connolly, 'The Non-Financial Information Directive: An assessment of its impact on corporate social responsibility' (2017) 14 *European Company Law* 15;

initiatives, such as the International Platform on Sustainable Finance, have attempted to coordinate and align national and regional standards, including those on extra-financial reporting. Nevertheless, cooperation amongst regional standard-setting bodies is important, but the 'bottom-up' approach has its limitations and, compared to a 'top-down' harmonisation initiative, will have more difficulties in ensuring global consistency of standards.[42]

IV. DIGITALISATION KICKS IN: THE GENESIS OF BLOCKCHAIN BONDS

Over the last decade, blockchain, IoT, and AI, which form the so-called 'BIA Trinity', have allowed for the development and commercialisation of numerous new applications. This trend is here to stay in all areas of social and economic life, including the sustainable finance ecosystem.[43]

Blockchain bonds are one of the innovations that promise to revolutionise international finance, with issuers and investors already exploring the issuance, initial distribution, and trading of such instruments in the bond markets. As their name indicates, blockchain bonds are issued directly onto the blockchain as security tokens. They continue to exist on the blockchain for operations. From a technical point of view, blockchain bonds rely on open source blockchain technologies, several of which are very advanced and have gained the confidence of market participants. Several examples can better illustrate the design and particularities of blockchain bonds:

First, the World Bank and the Commonwealth Bank of Australia issued a flagship blockchain bond, called Bond-i,[44] issued in 2018. The issuance relied on blockchain technology for the issuance of bonds and their transfer through the instrument's life cycle. More specifically, blockchain was used for the primary issuance of bonds, the bond auction, the bid capture, the book-build, and allocation of bonds and subsequent secondary market operations. Another advantage of the project is that it allows for enhanced and real-time visibility of transactions, at least to authorised participants.

David Monciardini, 'The 'Coalition of the Unlikely' driving the EU Regulatory process of Non-Financial Reporting' (2016) 36 *Social and Environmental Accountability Journal* 76; Daniel Szabo and Karsten Sorensen, 'New EU Directive on the Disclosure of Non-Financial Information' (2015) 12 *European Company and Financial Law* Review 307.

42 IFRS (n 21) 6.

43 Darius Nassiry, 'The role of Fintech in unlocking green finance: Policy insights for developing countries' (Asian Development Bank Institute, Working Paper No 883, 2018) 10; Eero Tolo, 'Will digitalisation transform the financial sector too?' (Bank of Finland Bulletin 2016).

44 Bond-I stands for 'blockchain-operated new debt instrument'.

Second, an end-to-end blockchain bond was issued in 2019 (USD 20 million, one-year maturity) by the Spanish bank, Banco Santander. The issuance relied on the public open-source Ethereum blockchain;[45] the bonds were securely tokenised in a permissioned manner, and they remained on the blockchain until the end of their maturity. Because of the digitalisation and automation of bond issuance, the number of intermediaries involved in the process has been significantly reduced.

Third, the EIB issued its first digital bond in April 2021 (€100 million, two-year maturity), employing the Ethereum blockchain platform for registration and settlement.[46] The most interesting feature of this issuance is the partnership between the EIB and the Banque de France in the context of the latter's Central Bank Digital Currency (CBDC) experimentation. Indeed, the joint lead managers of the bond issuance will settle the underwriting and pay the issue monies to the EIB using a representation of CBDC on the blockchain, although fiat currency will be used to repay the principal at maturity. The idea to use CBDC in the context of bond issuances had also been tested by Société Générale, which issued €40 million in covered bonds in May 2020, registering them as security tokens on the blockchain.[47] Additionally, in that case, the issuer was paid in CDBC issued by Banque de France. These two projects have demonstrated that CBDC can be employed for the interbank settlement of financial securities, automating, and simplifying the function of payment systems and market infrastructures.

Furthermore, all these examples illustrate that blockchain technology can be used with success in the phases of bond issuance, initial distribution, transfer of ownership, payment, and settlement.[48] In any case, a designated entity (tokenisation agent) is needed to register the bonds on the blockchain and act as the custodian of the cryptographic keys. Investing in such instruments takes place following the model of on-chain delivery-versus-payment. The bonds, the coupons, and the cash used to complete the investment can be represented digitally as tokens. Both in the initial issuance and the aftermarket, blockchain technology ensures (i) an auditable and immutable transaction record; (ii)

---

[45] For the press release, see https://www.santander.com/en/press-room/press-releases/santander-launches-the-first-end-to-end-blockchain-bond accessed 16 July 2021.

[46] For the press release, see https://www.eib.org/en/press/all/2021-141-european-investment-bank-eib-issues-its-first-ever-digital-bond-on-a-public-blockchain# accessed 16 July 2021.

[47] For the press release, see https://www.societegenerale.com/sites/default/files/200023_pr_societe_generale_performs_the_first_financial_transaction_settled_with_a_central_bank_digital_currency.pdf accessed 16 July 2021.

[48] Richard Cohen and others, 'Automation and blockchain in securities issuances' (2018) *Butterworths Journal of International Banking and Financial Law* 144.

real-time reporting and instant communication between investors and issuers;[49] (iii) direct holding of assets, which remains secure even in the absence of custodians; (iv) consistency of data across bond market actors, without the need of data reconciliation. Financial transactions can take place on the blockchain more efficiently, because they are recorded and validated in a distributed and immutable database without the need for a trusted custodians and intermediaries, thus reducing associated transaction costs.

In the same way, the disclosure of green data in non-financial reporting increases transparency, reduces information asymmetry and prevents 'green-washing', namely, the practice of misrepresenting a project as environmentally sound. In the absence of credible non-financial reporting, it is difficult for stakeholders other than the issuer to obtain factual information on the performance of the green project and the proper use of green bond proceeds. Issuers of green bonds already resort to the services of external reviewers and certification bodies in order to mitigate information asymmetries and protect responsible investors and ultimately the market itself against 'green-washing'. Non-financial reporting is a significant data service that the issuer needs to provide to investors and to the financial market authorities, with external reviewers ensuring data accuracy. As will be discussed, IoT, AI and blockchain can further improve the data accuracy and the efficiency of non-financial reporting in green bonds; they can reduce costs, automate data harvesting and analysis and bring credible green performance data to investors in real-time.

V. A NEW BREED OF FULLY DIGITALISED GREEN BONDS?

Could the model of blockchain bonds be transposed into the specific field of green finance? A first attempt took place in February 2019 with a bond issuance (€35 million, six-year term) by the BBVA Group.[50] The green bond was a structured instrument, the return of which was linked to the evolution of the swap rate for euros. The transaction was a private placement, the investor being a global insurance company, whilst the proceeds were earmarked to finance eligible green projects. In this regard, the issuance obtained a green

---

49 HSBC, 'Sustainable Digital Finance Alliance, Blockchain: Gateway for Sustainability-linked Bonds' (HSBC Centre of Sustainable Finance 2019) 9 https://www.sustainablefinance.hsbc.com/mobilising-finance/blockchain-gateway-for-sustainability-linked-bonds accessed 16 July 2021.

50 BBVA Group, 'BBVA issues the first blockchain-supported structured green bond for MAPFRE' (BBVA Press Release, 19 February 2019) https://www.bbva.com/en/sustainability/bbva-issues-the-first-blockchain-supported-structured-green-bond-for-mapfre/ accessed 16 July 2021.

certification by an independent third party. Blockchain technology and, more specifically, the blockchain platform that BBVA internally developed, was used to negotiate the conditions of the issuance (structure and prices). The issuance was surely innovative in this regard, but one must consider that this was simply a private placement, whilst blockchain was not used in other phases of the bond's life cycle, consistent with the World Bank's Bond-i issuance.

The next big challenge will be creating a new breed of fully digitalised green bonds, using blockchain from its issuance until the reporting phase,[51] which in the case of green bonds covers both the use of proceeds and the proof of impact. The World Bank's Bond-i has already used blockchain in most phases of the bond's life cycle (primary issuance, bond auction, bond allocation, payment and settlement, transfers in secondary market), but digitalisation has not been applied in the reporting phase (tokenised proof of impact), which appears at first like a daunting task. Nevertheless, there have been successful uses of digitalisation for green data reporting, which could be implemented and scaled up in the green bond markets. For example, a successful initiative of UNDP in Lebanon aimed to reforest depleted forests (CedarCoin initiative).[52]

Scaling up digital green reporting would implicate collecting, uploading on the blockchain, and ultimately delivering green data to the digital wallets of investors in real-time.[53] Data that are relevant to a given sustainable project would need to be collected using sensors. Given the huge volume of datasets and the lack of well-structured data formats, AI analytics will have to be employed to be used to organise such data volumes, make sense out of them, and compile impact reports. For example, the Global Mangrove Trust supports the planting of mangrove trees in the Bay of Bengal and uses blockchain, satellite telemetry, and AI to allow sponsors to verify that the trees they have

---

[51] Organization for Economic Co-operation and Development, 'The Tokenisation of Assets and Potential Implications for Financial Markets' [2020] OECD Blockchain Policy Series 24 https://www.oecd.org/finance/The-Tokenisation-of-Assets-and-Potential-Implications-for-Financial-Markets.htm accessed 16 July 2021.

[52] CedarCoins are digital tokens that allow the owner to finance the planting of cedars in Lebanon. The transaction includes a 'proof of planting', which is also in use in other reforestation initiatives worldwide; United Nations Development Programme, 'Adopting a cedar tree brings diaspora money home' (UNDP Lebanon 2019) https://www.undp.org/blogs/adopting-cedar-tree-brings-diaspora-money-home accessed 16 July 2021.

[53] Wanli Chen and Qianxia Wang, 'The role of blockchain for the European bond market' (Frankfurt School Blockchain Center 2020) 11; see also Stockholm Environment Institute, 'The Green Assets Wallet: First Blockchain for Green Bond Impact Data' (SEI 2019) https://www.sei.org/about-sei/press-room/first-blockchain-for-green-bonds/ accessed 16 July 2021.

sponsored have indeed been planted and how the forest is growing year after year.[54]

In this paradigm shift towards automated reporting, digitalisation will allow us 'to harvest recognised metrics, codified as data tokens that communicate in real-time to investors and build a shared asset history on the ledger [...] accessible to multiple stakeholders'.[55] Not only will this model enhance the reliability and the traceability of the green data, but it will also slash the average cost of reporting. It has been estimated that the cost of IoT devices, data gathering, aggregation, and reporting can be thus reduced by up to ten times in the lifecycle of a green project.[56] Fortuitously, the major economic sectors that employ IoT and already harvest data automatically (transport, energy, and water)[57] are the ones where the issuance of green bonds and climate-aligned bonds is on the rise. This would render more feasible the transition towards fully digitalised green bonds, which also cover extra-financial reporting.

Two questions are raised in this context. The first question is who will own Big green Data and who will have access to it. Even if IoT sensors are used to harvest data and AI is employed to analyse data and correct eventual errors, the ultimate responsible for data accuracy is the entity that issues the green bond. Under international standards, such as the ICMA Principles, reporting green data to investors is a key task of the issuer, who has to ensure that the relevant technology (sensors, AI), ESG metrics and ESG reporting procedures are reliable and do not mislead investors. The second question is whether environmental data can be transferred easily due to national law such as data localisation, security law and other barriers, if human activities are involved. Indeed, national legislation may impose to the issuer of the green bond the obligation to keep data within the jurisdiction it originated from, thus preventing the transfer and processing of data in another jurisdiction. In some sectors, such as healthcare, banking and payment systems, there may be stricter requirements for processing data abroad, discouraging companies from doing so. In the case of green investments, the disclosure of data related to the asset ownership and the performance of the asset entails risks, such as privacy breaches and harm of

---

[54] See https://globalmangrove.org/news. A similar innovative application is TreeCoin, a blockchain-based digital currency used for reforestation and timber cultivation.

[55] HSBC (n 49) 6.

[56] Ibid., 17.

[57] Sandro Nizetic and others, 'Internet of Things (IoT): Opportunities, issues and challenges towards a smart and sustainable future' (2020) 274 *Journal of Cleaner Production* 122877; Kyoochun Lee, 'The Internet of Things (IoT): Applications, investments, and challenges for enterprises' (2015) 58(4) *Business Horizons* 431; Jayavardhana Gubbi and others, 'Internet of Things: a vision, architectural elements, and future directions' (2013) 29(7) *Future Generation Computer Systems* 1645.

national security. Green performance data, such as the performance of strategically important renewable energy projects, may fall within the scope of data localisation laws, which will definitely hinder international issuances of green bonds in an increasing number of jurisdictions.

Moreover, the success of a transition towards digitalised green bonds depends greatly on the definition of the exact metrics that will be used for automated reporting. It must be clear to all stakeholders which specific data will be collected, analysed, and reported. This is a prerequisite for ultimately generating impact indexes for a green project or several green projects. The impact indexes will have to combine several indicators (energy generated, energy saved, air quality, CO_2 emissions, etc.) collected from multiple monitoring points over specified times. Furthermore, there are proposals in favour of the so-called 'pull' reporting systems, where performance data is delivered to the 'digital wallet' of investors, regulators, or other stakeholders with permissions, from which the user can choose the data to pull out,[58] provided that the aforementioned national data localisation laws do not require otherwise.

VI. CONCLUDING REMARKS

The use of blockchain, IoT, and AI can revolutionise green finance, alleviate unnecessary costs and burdens, and enhance transparency and credibility in the green bond market. Digitalisation can benefit the issuance, initial distribution, trading, and reporting of green bonds. It can also pave the way for follow-on innovations, facilitating fragmented ownership of green assets, alongside the aggregation of several green projects and assets into one bond.[59] Businesses and regulators already explore interesting new ideas, such as the development of blockchain-based bond exchanges, which allow for fractional ownership of bonds. This is the case of the BondbloX Bond Exchange (BBX), which obtained authorisation from the Monetary Authority of Singapore in August 2020, and the Joinvest platform, which was approved by the Financial Supervisory Commission of Taiwan to function in the regulatory sandbox for one year. In the same logic, the Philippines Bureau of the Treasury has developed and launched a mobile application to allow small retail investors to purchase treasury bonds, replacing banks in financial intermediation. Even more

[58] Eloy Barrantes and Henning Zülch, 'Digitaler Geschäftsbericht als Hidden Champion – Vom Pull- zum Push-Reporting' (2019) 19 Zeitschrift für internationale und kapitalmarktorientierte Rechnungslegung 156; HSBC (n 49) 20.

[59] Climate Bonds Initiative, 'Scaling up Green Bond Markets for Sustainable Development' (CBI Consultation Paper 2015) 17 https://www.climatebonds.net/resources/publications/scaling-green-bond-markets-sustainable-development accessed 16 July 2021; HSBC (n 49) 5.

cross-cutting innovations are underway, such as the project of the Singapore Exchange to build the regions first 'end-to-end digital infrastructure in the fixed income space' and to 'streamline the listing, straight-through processing and settlement of bonds and activities in bond lifecycle management'.[60]

In this rapidly evolving digital ecosystem, it is difficult to ensure regulatory clarity on the use of blockchain in securities issuances. For this reason, standardisation initiatives, such as the ICMA Principles and the EU Green Bond Standards, need to address digitalisation specifically to facilitate its adoption in green bonds markets. This should include developing common standards for the digitalisation of extra-financial reporting (use of proceeds reports and impact reports). Indeed, new-fashioned international standards are needed for a new generation of financial instruments, such as blockchain green bonds. Furthermore, combining digitalisation with international standardisation will further allow the scaling of green bond markets to meet the growing demand. Although green bonds represent 2 per cent of the global bonds market, the demand and offer in sustainable bonds and blockchain-enabled instruments are expected to grow exponentially in the aftermath of the COVID-19 crisis, supported by government policies, international and regional initiatives, particularly at the EU level (Green Deal, Green Bond Standard, and Digital Finance Package). Therefore, the circumstances are auspicious for experimenting with the development of fully digitalised green bonds and sustainable digital finance in general, which can increase transparency, accelerate clearing and settlement, simplify securities trading, and facilitate reporting to investors, and for supervisory purposes.

---

[60] For the press release, see https://www.sgx.com/media-centre/20210129-sgx-and-temasek-jv-ties-covalent-build-end-end-digital-infrastructure accessed 16 July 2021.

14. Conclusion to *Data Governance in AI, FinTech and LegalTech: Law and Regulation in the Financial Sector*

Aline Darbellay

I. DATA GOVERNANCE AND RELATED RESEARCH ASPECTS

In a nutshell, the chapters in this book have surveyed the current law and regulation relating to data governance. They have tackled issues relating to the digital transformation of the financial sector in the broad sense. Accordingly, the authors have developed original insights about financial technologies (FinTech), legal technologies (LegalTech) and insurance technologies (InsurTech).

As an initial step, attention has been paid to the concept of data governance. As pointed out in the book, data governance encompasses the process of managing the availability, quality, accuracy, usability and security of data. In particular, AI and machine learning rely on data quality. Furthermore, data governance mechanisms should ensure data security, along with other internal cybersecurity measures. According to *Lieder* and *Pordzik*, data governance means a cross-functional framework for managing data as a strategic enterprise asset. This endeavour relates to the firm's decision-making about its data. As such, data governance forms part of corporate data governance. Data management is the day-to-day realisation of data governance. The firms should plan how to use data, especially in a context where data becomes interconnected. A core question consists of how to choose the best data governance model for a firm. This results from the growing importance of data as an asset of firms in every sector.

Whilst data governance is a cross-functional topic, the book has covered it from the perspective of the banking and financial sector. It is nevertheless worthwhile noting that various activities fall within this broad scope, including the insurance sector. In this regard, *Chen* has highlighted the fact that data is necessary for insurers to better assess insurance risk and manage the assets.

Insurers acquire data from various sources. In fact, the growing field of InsurTech makes data governance even more important.

With respect to the technologies, the contributions have laid emphasis on the use of blockchain, Internet of Things (IoT), Big Data technologies, Machine Learning (ML) and other forms of Artificial Intelligence (AI). Various actors are involved, including the incumbent financial intermediaries – banks and stock exchanges – as well as disrupting FinTech actors. The chapters in this book have identified both opportunities and risks relating to the digitalisation of the financial sector. The authors analysed consequences and suggested responses to open questions.

This conclusion brings together the arguments made by the various range of authors. Several chapters have explored the economics of data, from the phase of data production to data analytics. *Geranio* has explored how information is incorporated into prices. She has described four categories of data, including three traditional categories, i.e., macroeconomic data, corporate data, and trading or market data, as well as a new category, i.e., alternative data. In this realm, the demand for data is key. It is crucial to consider who produces data and who pays for it. Alternative data produced amongst others by Fintech actors has gained prominence since it is increasingly used thanks to AI. This involves for instance social media and sentiment data. In addition, several chapters have identified the market failure caused by monopoly or market powers. Accordingly, many BigTech companies and digital platforms dominate their markets. This fact is particularly relevant owing to network effects. Further, economic theories help explain why the consent regime fails to work in the realm of data protection. According to *Yang*, behavioural limitations may explain why the majority of data subjects tend to accept unfavourable data clauses.

The book is an important contribution to the literature on digitalisation and financial law by addressing legal and regulatory challenges posed by the digital transformation of the financial sector. The chapters in this book have examined the existing legal and regulatory regimes in several jurisdictions, including the European Union, Japan, Singapore, the United Kingdom and the United States. Due to the diversity of competent jurisdictions and their sovereignty, with respect to data flows, silos may be formed based on the locations of the users. *Lee* has discussed data fortress as a potential outcome. Promoting the international debate is needed with a view to preventing states from creating barriers to the free flow of data across borders. Accordingly, the book has also addressed the topic from an international and transnational perspective. In this vein, *Schmidt* has addressed the extraterritorial effects of the EU General Data Protection Regulation (GDPR) as well as the EU's ambition to be the global regulator of AI. Indeed, the EU is determined to shape the international framework for the deployment of AI based on a European approach. Its objective consists of influencing the international debate.

Several chapters have identified to what extent FinTech and Big Data technologies pose challenges to the existing data protection laws. Indeed, most pressing data challenges centre around privacy rights. The widespread use of data-intensive business models gives rise to problems relating to violations of privacy rights. This gives rise to concerns about the question of property rights over data and who owns the data. According to *Lee*, questions arise as to whether the data should be shared and as to how to control and process data. Related questions stem from data portability and the right to erasure. *Geranio* has contributed to the debate as to the question of the ownership of trading and market data more specifically. She has also addressed pricing policies in the sense of charging fees for sharing data.

With respect to data protection, several chapters have identified the issues related to the consent-based regime. They found that the informed consent regime is inefficient as Big Data companies essentially seek to obtain blanket consent from data subjects. Data subjects end up giving blind consent, thereby accepting unfavourable data clauses. They have proposed alternative models to supplement the informed consent regime.

In terms of the normative frameworks, the topics related to digitalisation and finance contribute to the debate of regulation *versus* self-regulation. For instance, *Chen* has explained the regulatory and self-regulatory framework prevailing for insurers in Singapore. In this vein, the Personal Data Protection Act (PDPA) established the fundamental principles and regulations. Moreover, the Monetary Authority of Singapore (MAS) issued guidelines. In addition, this system is complemented by self-regulation regarding personal data protection and privacy policies of insurers, including for instance a consent provision for personal data to be collected and used.

From the perspective of the timing of regulation, several chapters have addressed the debate of ex-ante regulation versus ex-post adjudication, for instance *Yang*'s chapter on data protection in the Big Data era. Also, according to *Polčák*, the EU Directive on the security of network and information systems (NIS Directive) and the EU GDPR have not primarily used ex-post liability as a desired method but rather ex-ante compliance. This chapter on cybersecurity has argued for performance-based rules that are not too specific but generally define the desired effects of regulation whilst leaving it for regulated entities to develop their own internal rules. Nevertheless, the problem stems from combining the need for a clear compliance-oriented corporate solution and the general nature of performance-based rules. In terms of the regulatory approach, *Pavlidis* has compared the bottom-up approach *versus* the top-down initiative. He has suggested that the bottom-up approach has its limitation due to the fact that it will have more difficulties in ensuring global consistency of standards.

With respect to regulation and innovation, there is a need to recognise not only the link between both aspects but also the trade-off that may be involved. According to *Donald*, in tightly regulated industries, developments propelled by technological advances can be strongly channelled by law and regulation. He has illustrated this aspect with the examples of legal technologies (LegalTech) as well as the indirect holding system for securities. In the same vein, *Darbellay* has explained both the technological and regulatory incentives leading to the shift from investor-pays to issuer-pays business models in the credit rating industry as well as the more recent evolution consisting of driving the financial sector towards open banking. Also, *Pavlidis* has shown that the growth of the green bond market is supported by government policies, international and regional initiatives, particularly at the EU level, thereby creating incentives towards the development of sustainable digital finance. Furthermore, according to *Polčák*, in the case of cybersecurity, the legal and technical agendas interact so that there is a need to distinguish between the technical and the regulatory dimensions of cybersecurity.

Last but not least, new business models may contribute to democratising governance. This trend appeared as a response to dissatisfaction with the current global financial system. In this regard, some of the technological advances may pave the path towards decentralisation. This entails both advantages and disadvantages. Further, the decentralisation may fail to work when new types of intermediaries are created in the process. In any case, the relationships between governments, data-driven companies and data subjects have evolved owing to the digital transformation that is taking place. In sum, discussion through these various lenses is valuable in order to assess the arguments made in the book.

II. TECHNOLOGICAL, LEGAL AND ECONOMIC RESPONSES TO DATA GOVERNANCE CHALLENGES

In this section, the research findings are presented. The legal issues raised by digitalisation and finance can be addressed from several viewpoints as reflected in the various chapters of this book. In the chapter on cryptocurrencies, *Lee* has assessed the effectiveness of data protection and privacy laws against three policy goals: personal autonomy; development of the digital economy; and crime prevention. His research has contributed to the emerging academic literature on cryptocurrencies. He has drawn conclusions from the economics of cryptocurrency. From the legal perspective, *Lee* has measured the effectiveness of data protection law and privacy rights under different types of cryptocurrencies: unstable coins, stable coins, and state-backed cryptocurrencies. Moreover, he has discussed the politics of information in cryptocurrency. He has expressed his views on the nature of information as a public good. As a result of his study, he has found that current data protection and privacy laws can only address part of the issues at stake so that the legal and regulatory frameworks need to be overhauled.

In the chapter on legal technologies (LegalTech), *Donald* has explored the data management problem. He has assessed the legal profession as a data management industry. Since lawyers are subject to stringent regulation but LegalTech companies are not, concerns have been raised about the fact that they may end up surpassing law firms in the provision of many legal services. *Donald* proceeds from the assumption that they will eventually perform basic legal tasks more effectively than lawyers do. In doing so, they benefit from data that lawyers feed into them since they aggregate data from individual firm clients for general use. This trend gives rise to questions related to the use of client data to grow legal technologies. There is a possible conflict between the lawyers' duties to safeguard the data of individual clients and their incentives to pool information of all clients for better analytical exploitation. Whilst many law firms feed their client data into LegalTech companies, problems may arise if a new industry is built that law firms may no longer control. This gives rise to the issue as to what access and use of client data are permitted. *Donald* has questioned whether a lawyer should obtain express approval from clients for extracting the value of work products and client data to develop or improve LegalTech applications. Fiduciaries may not take advantage of their relationships with the beneficiaries beyond the properly disclosed fees earned. For the sake of comparison, *Donald* has examined the creation of the indirect holding system for securities, whereby the change of technology led to the transfer of data and ownership from the issuers of securities and their investors to the financial industry. He referred to the transition that took place in the corporate world in the late 1960s regarding the transfer of shares. Owing to increasing volumes, new technologies triggered a major disruption in securities trading. The choice made by leading banks and endorsed by regulators consisted of omitting the transfer of shares and using a central securities depository (CSD). In the process, data about shareholders was taken away from issuers. Ever since data has then been kept in the hands of the financial industry. To this day, nearly all shareholder data is controlled by CSDs. *Donald* concluded that control over data is key. Nevertheless, he added that the logic of network effects supports the growth of external LegalTech firms.

In the chapter on data protection in the Big Data era, *Yang* has suggested that the informed choice model is broken. He has described economic theories stemming from both neoclassical economics and behavioural economics that explain the failure of the informed consent regime in the realm of data protection. He has proposed an alternative public-private-partnership model that includes two aspects. First, his public template proposal suggests that responsible authorities establish mandatory and non-mandatory data clauses with a view to protecting the fundamental rights of data subjects. Second, his enhanced internal control proposal suggests that Big Data companies establish independent data committees with a view to approving data processing and substituting for the informed consent by data subjects. This alternative model involves a shift of focus from *ex-ante* consent to *ex-post* gatekeeping. Indeed, *Yang* has suggested that ex-post internal control of data processing would be more efficient than *ex-ante* consent since data subjects typically give blind consent to unfavourable data clauses.

In the chapter on information gatekeepers, *Darbellay* has examined the issue of conflicts of interest in the digital platform markets. She has explored to what extent digital platforms perform a function as information gatekeepers. She has analysed the role of law and regulation in addressing the new types of issues relating to the use of algorithm-driven intermediaries to process financial information. The question has arisen as to how to mitigate the new forms of conflicts of interest that have emerged owing to shifting business models. She has assessed the need to focus on platform governance. In addition, the author has discussed whether digital platforms owe fiduciary duties to the users of their services. Finally, limitations to the regulation of information must be taken into account with a view to striking a balance between the various interests at stake.

In the chapter on crypto-assets, *Lee* and *Van de Looverbosch* have explored the confused relationship between property and data. Their contribution has shown the link between crypto-assets taken as property, and data governance. This has involved the analysis of different types of crypto-assets, in particular payment tokens and asset tokens. The authors have analysed four court cases involving cryptocurrencies in four different jurisdictions. In particular, these court cases have shed light on the property law characterisation of cryptocurrencies such as Bitcoin. These cases have reflected how legal precedents can lead to the recognition of crypto-assets as transferable intangible property. *Lee* and *Van de Looverbosch* have proposed an approach in which a distinction is made between property that consists of data, and data itself. This chapter allows for a better understanding of how digital property and data governance are intertwined. This results in facilitating the design of an effective governance framework. Accordingly, it helps crypto-asset providers to design internal data governance to protect both clients' property and their data. It is also of interest to policy makers with a view to proposing data governance to be adopted by crypto-asset providers who protect and manage the proprietary data for their clients.

In the chapter on consumer protection, *Karaiskos* has addressed data governance and consumer protection. His contribution has focused on the regulation of financial instrument transactions in Japan. In particular, he has assessed the challenges posed by the increased use of AI in the financial sector. Owing to the recent developments in the era of digitalisation, he has analysed the main benefits and drawbacks of the application of the existing rules as compared with the necessity for new regulation. He has highlighted the importance of striking the right balance by ensuring adequate consumer protection in the field of financial instruments. In addition, *Karaiskos* has extensively focused on the suitability requirements under Japanese law. In this regard, he has provided an analysis of major case law relating to the principle of suitability. He has also assessed the relationship between regulatory and self-regulatory frameworks.

In the chapter on insurance technologies (InsurTech), *Chen* has laid emphasis on the importance of data for insurance companies. According to him, the InsurTech sector entails both opportunities and risks. On the one hand, the intensive use of data contributes to creating opportunities to generate profits. On the other hand, the growing use of customer data gives rise to risks in terms of consumer protection. As a consequence, there is an increasing need to establish data governance frameworks for insurers. The author has illustrated his reflection by referring to life insurance policies. He has addressed the aspect of outsourcing risks of customer data to third-party service providers. He has concluded that Singapore's regulatory approach is based on personal data protection law and voluntary guidelines. He has also tackled the related enforcement issues.

In the chapter on board duties, *Lieder* and *Pordzik* have addressed data governance issues relating to directors' duties. They have examined the duties of the board of directors whilst outlining the board responsibilities and identifying liability risks. Their contribution covers German law, thereby taking into account the dual board structure prevailing in Germany. In particular, they have analysed the duty of care of the members of the management board, i.e., the duty to act in the best interests of the company. They have discussed the duties of the board in the area of data governance, for instance with respect to ensuring data quality and data security. This issue is especially relevant given the lack of normative contours in this specific realm. The authors have argued that there is a need to focus on the data handled and stored in the company and on how data is used at any level of the corporation. The board may not escape from responsibility by delegating certain decisions to AI. If AI is used, the board has a responsibility to ensure data quality because AI-driven decisions are then taken based on available data. Nevertheless, according to the business judgment rule, board members are protected if they act on the basis of adequate information. Therefore, this chapter has underlined the importance of information in corporate reality.

In the chapter on financial market infrastructures, *Geranio* has discussed data production by stock exchanges and other trading platforms. She has shed light on how data is produced and distributed, thereby addressing the economics of data production. Accordingly, the core issue relates to the incorporation of information into prices. This relates to the pricing of data fees. According to the author, different types of fees include access fees, usage fees, non-display fees and redistribution licence fees. Pre-trade data is one of the main sources of revenue for stock exchanges. Data flows are for instance essential to the fulfilment of regulatory requirements, including the EU best execution rules. In this vein, regulation stirs up the demand for data. Exchanges maximise profit. For instance, they may charge higher fees to provide information more quickly and smaller fees for delayed information. According to *Geranio*, they face a trade-off in the sense that selling price data may generate revenue but worsen market efficiency and liquidity. Since stock exchanges have the technological infrastructure needed to collect, manage and disseminate information, they have dominated the market. On the one hand, regarding the data selling business, the question has arisen as to whether stock exchanges abuse their dominant position and impede competition. On the other hand, new data providers have entered the market for alternative data, including social media and sentiment data, so that this growing market has hitherto been competitive. Indeed, there is some level of competition between incumbent data providers and new data providers such as Fintech actors. According to the author, alternative data provides original and valuable investment insights.

In the chapter on cybersecurity certification, *Polčák* has discussed the EU Directive on the security of network and information systems (NIS Directive) as the regulatory tool in cybersecurity at the EU level. He has also laid emphasis on the EU Cybersecurity Act. In particular, he has analysed the features of the newly introduced EU cybersecurity certification mechanism. In this realm, the EU has followed a performance-based regulatory model according to which the law lays down general rules and principles whilst requiring that regulated entities develop and implement their own rules. *Polčák* has criticised this model because of the legal uncertainties. He has addressed the question as to whether uncertainties may be mitigated thanks to the certification mechanism. Concerns have been raised about the issue of virtualisation. Even though the EU scheme has focused on cybersecurity in general, it is worthwhile noting that various fields of critical infrastructures need to develop and implement cybersecurity measures. The author has argued that the financial sector has been at the forefront of securing its IT infrastructures, thereby being more advanced than other essential services in terms of cybersecurity measures. The author has concluded that the inclusion of the financial sector into the EU cybersecurity framework is therefore considered problematic. Further, he has distinguished between the technical and regulatory dimensions of cybersecurity. Technical and legal agendas interact. What is challenging in terms of organisation is how various branches of financial institutions – IT, security, compliance – have to tackle the issue. With respect to the ex-ante compliance regime for cybersecurity at the EU level, it was brought by the Cybersecurity Act by establishing a framework for certification of IT products, services and processes. There are two key processes, i.e., the adoption of a certification scheme at the level of the Member States and then the certification itself. According to the author, implementation in the EU will be challenging. As the EU cybersecurity framework is general, its success will depend on the quality of the certification schemes.

In the chapter on the promotion of fundamental values, *Schmidt* has analysed the aspects of the EU data protection framework relating to the promotion of its values and interests. The EU has expressed its willingness to influence the international debate owing to the fact that the deployment of AI poses risks for the protection of personal data and the right to privacy. *Schmidt* has assessed the role of data protection in the EU's external relations. In this respect, digitalisation poses new challenges for the protection of fundamental rights. The EU's approach to AI highlights the EU's ambition to establish itself as a competitive international actor. The author has addressed the global reach of the GDPR and the question of the lawful transfer of data to third states. She has elaborated on the case of adequacy decisions authorising the transfer of personal data to third states, which may be made by the Commission to the extent that third states provide an adequate level of protection. In fact, the adequacy assessment is made by taking into account the fundamental values the EU is founded on, in particular human rights. Therefore, the respect for fundamental rights is a condition for the lawfulness of data transfers to third states. As such, *Schmidt* considers that adequacy decisions are vehicles for the EU to promote its own approach to data protection.

In the chapter on digital green bonds, *Pavlidis* has discussed the challenge of building a credible, efficient and transparent green bond market to drive the global green transition. This topic is at the crossroads of digitalisation and sustainable finance. Reporting is explored as a key aspect of sustainable finance, which is based on a wide range of data. According to the author, digitalisation and standardisation can increase the efficiency of the green bond markets, from the issuance of green bonds to the phase of reporting. What is crucial is the comparability of environmental, social, and governance (ESG) standards. In the case of extra-financial reporting for green bonds, digitalisation may facilitate the analysis of green performance. Data collected through the internet of things (IoT) could be analysed by AI algorithms. The idea is to attract ESG responsible investors, including large institutional investors. *Pavlidis* has addressed the challenge of the labour-intensive reporting, i.e., owing to the collection and analysis of voluminous data on environmental impacts. He has discussed the need to harmonise the rules and standards on green bonds, especially regarding materiality and disclosure requirements. He has viewed blockchain bonds as an innovation that may revolutionise international finance. Accordingly, the model of blockchain bonds may be used in the field of green finance. The next challenge stems from creating fully digitalised green bonds whilst using the blockchain during various phases of the bonds' life cycle. According to the author, digitalisation has already applied for instance in the phase of trading in the secondary markets but not yet in the reporting phase. Therefore, his chapter is forward-looking.

III. OUTLOOK

The discussion in this chapter has highlighted the fact that there are a variety of responses to data governance challenges. The authors have attempted to define the legal contours of data governance whilst taking into account the influence of shifting business models. The chapters have surveyed the issues relating to the FinTech, LegalTech and InsurTech sectors. The chapters in this book make a significant contribution to this important debate, which will continue to rage as digital finance is evolving at a fast pace. The topic deserves special attention as competitive and diverging interests are at stake.

The authors have identified both opportunities and risks arising out of the digital transformation of financial markets. They have proposed solutions to challenges, ranging from market-based responses to legal and regulatory responses. They have explored the growing field of data governance under key jurisdictions. Nevertheless, they have laid emphasis on the need for an international and transnational debate. Several authors have suggested that legislation at the international level is the way to achieve harmonisation, whilst recognising that jurisdictions that have extraterritorial reach tend to export their values over their borders. At any rate, the legal architecture should be overhauled with a view to balancing the interests of the incumbent as well as the disruptive actors of the digital marketplace. It is unlikely that the policy makers and regulators will be able to solve all the problems and issues discussed in this book. Therefore, data governance relating to the use of new technologies will continue to gain prominence on the legal and regulatory agendas in the years to come.

Index